Created and Directed by Hans Höfer

INSIGHT GUIDES
SOUTH INDIA

Edited by Manjulika Dubey and Bikram Grewal

APA PUBLICATIONS

SOUTH INDIA

ABOUT THIS BOOK

India, always an incredible travel experience, holds an irresistible attraction for APA Publications in its series of *Insight* and *Short Stay* guides originated by **Hans Höfer**, a West German designer trained in the Bauhaus tradition. The recent years have seen the success of *India*, *Rajasthan*, and the first in the Great Adventure series, *Indian Wildlife*. *South India* is one of the new titles; others on this perennially fascinating country are in various stages of production.

The Indian team of APA has undergone some changes. APA's executive editor, **Bikram Grewal**, found himself feeling singularly serendipitous when he bumped into his old friend **Manjulika Dubey** at a cocktail party. Manjulika, with several years of book publishing behind her, was immediately deemed to be a fit replacement for APA's former editor, **Samuel Israel**, who had moved to Bombay after having completed the spadework on the *South India* guide. After some weeks of coaxing, Manjulika joined the APA family and took over the reins of the current guide. She has proved to be a great addition.

Among our regular authors is **Dr Kamala Seshan**, geographer and lecturer at the NCERT (National Council for Educational Research and Training). To this volume she contributes an article on the geography of peninsular India.

Dr D.B. Chattopadhyaya provides APA readers with a panoramic view of South Indian down the ages. The author of several authoritative papers and books, Dr Chattopadhyaya is a leading historian currently teaching at the Jawaharlal Nehru University.

With a degree in the Social Sciences, and as one of the editors of a leading business magazine, **Sushila Ravindranath** has written an analysis of South India as it has changed politically and economically over the last few decades.

Dr M.N. Srinivas is currently Chairman of the Institute for Social and Economic Change. An internationally acclaimed anthropologist and the author of a number of books, Dr Srinivas chose to write on an eminently suitable theme — Society and Culture in South India.

Dr N. Pattabhiraman, who has written a piece on the performing arts in this part of India, has had an active interest in the field for years. He is the founder and managing trustee of the Sruti Foundation, which promotes excellence in classical dance, and also edits the monthly *Sruti*.

Dr Shobita Punja, who works in the field of culture with the Ministry of Education, has authored two pictorial books, *Indian Museums* and *Khajuraho*. Having studied Art History at Stanford University, Dr Punja has been able to deliver a comprehensive account of painting, sculpture and architecture in South India.

Jaya Jaitly had previously contributed an essay on India's crafts to the *India* guide and is currently writing a book on textiles. She brings her wide and invaluable experience of work in the field of the handicrafts industry and textiles to her essay on South India's crafts tradition.

V. Abdulla's work experience includes

Grewal

Ravindranath

Srinivas

Pattabhiraman

V Abdulla

making two feature films in his native language, Malayalam, and running the publishing firm of Orient Longman in Madras. He is engaged in translating Malayalam classics into English. For the *South India* guide, Mr Abdullah commissioned much of the writing on Tamil Nadu and Kerala and has contributed some of the articles as well.

His wife, **Ummi Abdullah**, is an expert cook who learnt the art mainly on the job. Apart from authoring two popular cookery books and holding diplomas from the All India Catering Institute, she operates a cottage industry, making masala powders and pickles.

Nirmal Ghosh works in the advertising department of one of India's leading daily newspapers but is a keen amateur photographer and wildlife enthusiast who has contributed photographic features to several leading magazines.

Uzra Bilgrami, born in Hyderabad, is a practising metalsmith. She writes on her native state of Andhra Pradesh, where she has travelled extensively in the course of her work for Dastkar, a craft development agency.

Prasad Bidapa and **John Abraham**, who have contributed most of the section on Karnataka, are a creative design team who have made their mark in Bangalore. Bidapa is a native of Coorg and his inspiration very much derives from the ethos of his home state. Having travelled widely in Karnataka during the course of the many projects he has worked on, his empathy for his subject is immediately evident. Abraham is a copywriter and freelance journalist who has covered Bangalore and Mysore, Bijapur, Badami and their surrounding areas for this book. He lives in Bangalore and enjoys writing about it. Childhood journeys acquainted him with the other places and subjects his articles cover, a familiarity extended by the background research he came to do on them in the course of his career.

S. Muthiah has for many years been involved in travel writing and has seen much of South India. An authority on Madras, he has written several works on the city as well as two major cartographical publications. Here, he collaborates on the Kerala and Tamil Nadu sections of the guide. **S. Krishnan**, who joins Muthiah in writing the section on Tamil Nadu, is based in Madras. He is a freelance writer who contributes to several national and international journals.

K.S. Padmanabhan, the Managing Director of one of the leading book distribution companies in India, has been involved in book publishing since 1962. He writes the article on Lakshadweep, the coral archipelago off the Indian coast.

Rajam Krishnan, who has contributed the articles on Chidambaram and Madurai, has been a college teacher of English literature in her home town, Madras, a radio broadcaster and a writer. She has travelled extensively in Tamil Nadu and lived in several of the places she describes.

Special thanks are due to **Naomi Meadows** and **Ashok Ranganathan** for their help. **Toby Sinclair** was as always ready with his expertise in the area of maps and visuals, apart from assistance and advice at every stage of the layouts.

U Abdulla

Bilgrami

Muthiah

S Krishnan

Padmanabhan

CONTENTS

TRAVEL TIPS

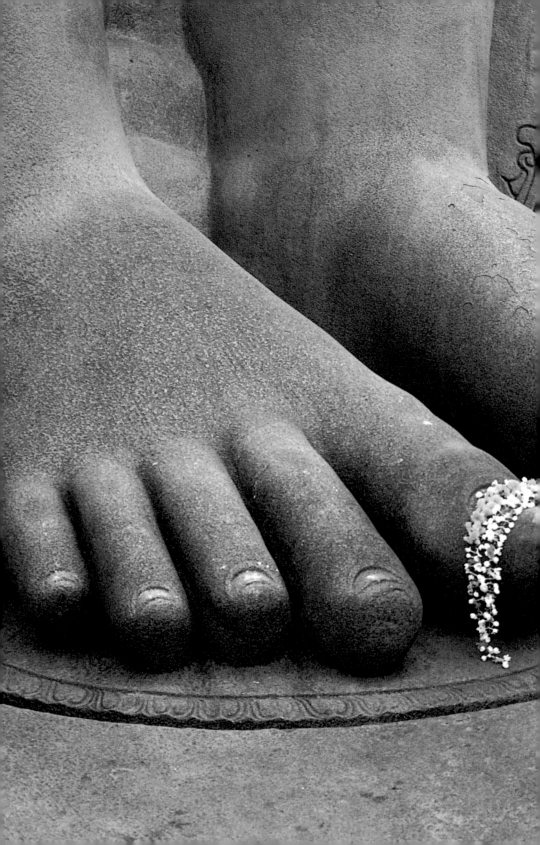

INTRODUCTION

The Vindhya and Satpura mountain ranges form the geographical divide between northern and southern India. Politically, South India had earlier been thought of as the former Madras Presidency and the adjoining princely states of Hyderabad, Mysore, Travancore and Cochin. With the integration of the princely states and the redrawing of the map of India on a linguistic basis in 1956, this area was carved, with some additions and subtractions, into the modern states of Andhra Pradesh, Karnataka, Kerala and Tamil Nadu.

The real divide between these states and the Indo-Gangetic plain is two-fold: firstly, the languages spoken in them have little connection with the dominant languages of the north, though all of them have in varying degrees a linkage with Sanskrit; secondly, the south, though exposed through the ages to international maritime and trade contacts, remained relatively isolated from the successive invasions that periodically convulsed most of India. Even at the zenith of the Islamic empire, large parts of South India remained out of their orbit (though Andhra Pradesh and Karnataka had enclaves of Muslim domination for centuries). It is one of history's ironies that the most extensive conquest, the British subjugation of India, should have started in the mid-18th century in Tamil Nadu.

This relative isolation led to distinct styles of architecture and different forms of music, dance and drama than found elsewhere in the country. Even among the four southern states there are physical and cultural diversities. Most of Karnataka and large parts of Andhra Pradesh, including the capital cities of Bangalore and Hyderabad, lie in the region of the Deccan plateau. Tamil Nadu and Kerala consist mainly of tropical coastal plains, though both of them share the Western Ghats, the fractured and uplifted rim of the plateau. Kerala, which bears the brunt of the southwest monsoon, has verdant tropical vegetation and the only surviving rain forest in India. Andhra Pradesh, Karnataka and Tamil Nadu are largely dependent on man-made irrigation, particularly on the series of barrages, anicuts and dams built on the Krishna, Godavari and Kaveri rivers.

Scenically, the southern states have all that a visitor could look for: dramatic coastlines both on the Arabian Sea and on the Bay of Bengal, meeting at Cape Comorin on the Indian Ocean; many isolated beaches, dense forests and game reserves with a bewildering array of flora and fauna; swift flowing streams and large rivers meandering lazily to the sea; and the beautiful Nilgiri and Annamalai ranges.

Preceding pages: *gopurams* of the Madurai temple; elephants decked for Pooram festival in Trichur; worshipper at Sravanabelagola; Kalaripayattu gymnasium, Kerala. **Left**, Thaiyyam participant, Kerala.

The Deccan peninsula, lying between 8° and 15°N, and 75° and 86°E, is the remnant of a once large and stable plateau. Parallel to the west coast and close to it lie the Western Ghats, a series of step-like terraces and weather-worn hills stretching from the Tapti river valley in the north to Kanniya-kumari on India's southern tip. They form the high western edge of the Deccan plateau, which slopes gently eastwards to the Eastern Ghats on the other coast of peninsular India. The Western and Eastern Ghats unite in the Nilgiri Hills in the extreme south, like a grand knot in a necklace around the Indian peninsula.

The landscape of South India is varied. Along the west coast, from North Kanara district in Karnataka to the tip of the peninsula lie some of India's oldest ports and harbours, many of them now in disuse. One that survives is Karwar, at the head of a narrow inland area, now a shipbuilding harbour and fishing port. Small, swift-flowing rivulets cross this region.

Abundant flora and fauna: The coastal strip broadens out southwards, providing some of the finest beaches in the country along this coast. Inland, up into the Western Ghats in Kerala and Karnataka, extensive rain forests are still found, protected from human depredation by the inaccessible scarp and dissected landscape of the hills. There is an abundance of flora and fauna, particularly exotic butterflies and the wild elephant, and it is the only home of some species, like the lion-tailed macaque. The plant life in some of these forests has yet to be properly catalogued and studied. This is also a region rich in plantation crops such as cardamom, tea and coffee.

The coast of Malabar on the southwestern tip has numerous and extensive mud-banks. Laterite soil forms the foothills of the plateau, and behind these areas are highlands of glistening greisic rock. The alluvial lowlands are cut across all the way inland by interconnected creeks from the sea. Life in these areas – from transportation and soaking coconut husk to stringing out the day's catch of fish and prawns – revolves around these picturesque backwaters.

Inland of this section of the coastal strip lie Vembanad Lake and the Annamalai Hills. Cutting across this mountainous rib is the Periyar river which empties its headwaters across the Palghat Gap. These low gaps of the Palghat and Shencottah are the inroads from the Coimbatore plateau to the west coast.

The hills to the north of these gaps, the cloud-covered Nilgiris, reaching 6,000 to 8,000 ft (1,800 to 2,440 m), are the highest in the peninsula. The dense forests in the tropi-

cal region have a variety of ferns and wild berries, along with the aromatic Nilgiri lily. These hills, situated in the path of the southwest monsoon, are the catchment areas for the Vaigai and Periyar rivers.

Plateaux and gorges: The interior of the peninsula has several distinct plateau regions which belong to the Deccan lava region and the older Archaen greises. The Telengana plateau to the north is a dry, dessicated terrain with only the Godavari flowing across it. To its south, between the Bhima and the Godavari, lie broad, much-eroded valleys heaped with rocks "as if giants had amused themselves with childish games"

(*Hyderabad Gazette*, 1909). The vegetation here is mostly savannah-type with thorny scrub, while in the more moist areas date palms are found. Southwestwards is the "trap dyke land" along the tributaries of the Pennar, which drains into the sea near Nellore through laterite plains characterised by fertile land dotted with large tanks, which are man-made reservoirs.

The gorges of the rain-fed Krishna and Pennar rivers and their tributaries form long valleys, like silver threads on a broad spread of rock, with white sand and shingle beds. It is along these long valleys that the big tanks are found – mostly on the Madras-Bombay rail route – and the great pilgrimage centres

of Renigunta and Tirupati. The landscape is grey and the plains are dotted with mango groves.

Lakes, deltas and valleys: The upper part of the eastern coast is dominated by the vast deltas of the Krishna and Godavari, which irrigate some of the most productive lands in the region. Mangrove coasts with sand dunes are to be found where the rivers meet the sea.

Preceding pages, Hogenakkal Falls in all its splendour, Tamil Nadu. Left and right, the varied terrain of peninsular India includes the lush Nilgiri ranges and the intricate backwaters of Kerala.

The Colair Lake lies between the two deltas and is ideal for fish cultivation. It is in this section that the legendary ports of Machilipatnam and Kakinada are situated. Once they exported India's famous printed cloths; today they are used mainly for the export of bauxite. Andhra's rich coastal land is lashed frequently by cyclones and is often flooded during the monsoons.

Overlooking Renigunta along the Tirupati escarpment is the Nellore plain, which marks the beginning of the Coromandel coast extending south into Tamil Nadu. It is well-known for its rich paddy fields and the high-yielding Nellore cow with its distinct swept-back horns. The saltwater lagoon at Pulicat just north of Madras is an interesting feature of this region.

The coast of Tamil Nadu, the land of the Cholas, is a lowland dipping into the sea. From narrow streams in the large open valleys of the Adyar, Cooum and Korteliyar rivers, the coastal plain runs along a narrow path of marine and river sand deposits, backed by casuarina, lime quarries and salt pans.

Westwards lies the Coimbatore plateau, bound by the Bhavani, Amravati and Annamalai tributaries of the Kaveri. From the Krishnarajayar reservoir the Kaveri flows over several rapids to enter the plains at Sivasamudram. The Thanjavur plain is a gift of the Kaveri, where the Chola kings constructed a grand anicut to control its waters. The huge Kaveri delta is approximately 4,000 sq miles (10,350 sq km) and fans out between Porto Novo and Point Calimere. It is, in essence, the ricebowl of Tamil Nadu, and its prosperity is reflected in the majestic temple towers of Thanjavur.

Southeastwards from the delta is the cotton belt of Madurai, Ramanathapuram and Tirunelveli districts, almost entirely supported by tank irrigation. In the northwest are the Palani Hills from where the Vaigai starts in the Varshugrad valley.

The entire peninsula is a rain-dependent area. Separated from the northern plains by the Satpura and Vindhya ranges, the peninsula has a variety of land forms – plains, plateaus and hills – and rivers that may not be as wide as the northern rivers but are almost as long. It is a geographical area with distinct characteristics, home to a rich and varied culture and civilisation.

Any reference to South India, even to one only casually familiar with the country, is likely to evoke a series of images: the rugged Deccan plateau contrasting with the paddy-green valleys of rivers meandering towards the Bay of Bengal; the haunting music; the dance styles believed to be derived from principles laid down by the legendary sage Bharata; the majestic temple *gopurams* (gateways) towering above the coconut groves; the sculptures in bronze and stone, exquisite in both conception and technique of execution, and many more. These images in fact relate to many facets of a tradition which took centuries to evolve, and point to various stages of an unbroken history in which many cultural currents converged and gave shape to many regional variations.

Archaeological perspectives: As elsewhere in the country, the cultural beginnings of South India have to be traced back to the phase for which no written records are available. The earliest culture patterns are manifest in the varieties of archaeological material which specialists have resurrected, sometimes as chance discoveries and sometimes in the course of planned excavations. In 1863 Robert Bruce Foote chanced to pick up a paleolith from a laterite pit at Pallavaram near Madras; since then, Early Stone Age tools have been found in various parts of the South. The important discovery of hand axes and other stone tools from Attirampakkam near Madras points to the existence of a similar cultural pattern in the extreme South in prehistoric times. Here, primitive hunting-gathering cultures went through stages of evolution, from Early through Middle and Late Stone Ages, to the stage when the beginnings of agriculture and domestication of animals resulted in profound changes in early man's living conditions and social relations. This transformation began in what archaeologists call the Neolithic or New Stone Age and progressed steadily through different stages of use of metal technology, initially of copper or bronze and then of iron. It is possible to reconstruct the stages of this change from excavations which archaeologists have carried out in Karnataka, Andhra and Tamil Nadu. At the initial stage of this culture change, tools were still made of stone but with a different kind of technique. Man, moreover, was no longer merely a hunter; he had learnt the domestication of such animals as cattle, goat and sheep; had started producing handmade coarse pottery and terracotta figurines, and had come to construct settlements on granite hills, on levelled terraces or on plateaus.

If the beginnings of this kind of culture change can be traced back from the end of the third millennium to the beginning of the second millennium BC, further progress was slow, despite the introduction of metal around the middle of the second millennium BC. Nevertheless, new cultural elements made their appearances: circular huts, very much similar to those still made by local tribals, were built; varieties of gram and millet were cultivated; the horse was probably added to the list of domesticated animals; and metal tools came into use.

Beginnings of history: In the north, particularly in the Ganges basin and certain outlying areas, *janapadas* and *mahajanapadas* had already emerged with their villages, market-places and urban centres. There had developed an extensive network of routes connecting different regions and providing Magadha, a *mahajanapada* of south Bihar, enough stimulus to build an almost pan-Indian empire by the 4th-3rd century BC. The megalithic South was not totally outside the orbit of these changes; the *mahajanapada* of Asmaka in the central Godavari valley is believed to have been in existence in the 6th century BC. However, interaction with regions to the north was slow, and the Magadhan empire's interest in the South may have been motivated by the desire to acquire resources. Kautilya, the famed author of the political treatise *Arthasastra*, parts of which date back to this period, highlighted the advantages of *dakshinapatha*, the term denoting the southern route as well as the region. The Magadhan emperor Asoka Maurya wrote edicts for the Deccan which was part of his empire and for a major centre Suvarnagiri (Hill of Gold). Beyond the Deccan, Asoka mentioned the Cholas, the

Pandyas, the Cheras and the Satyaputras; the references were not to established states but to dominant communities, and one can see in the distinction between the Deccan and the southern region of the Cholas, Pandyas, Cheras and Satyaputras some essential differences in the manner in which the early history of the two regions developed.

The inclusion of the Deccan in the Magadhan empire was not merely a political phenomenon; it also resulted in movements of people and ideas, and thus new cultural elements were incorporated in the already changing structure of South Indian society. For the Deccan, two significant developments derived from the idea of a state headed

by a monarch and from ideas associated with Buddhist and Brahmanical social and religious ideology. Initially, in several localities of the Deccan, there emerged local ruling elites known from their coins which were fashioned after coins originating in the north. They called themselves *rajas, maharathis* or by other designations, and the centres of their power also became urban centres in which commercial exchange took place and religious monuments, particularly Buddhist *stupas* and *viharas,* were constructed. Since

Above, rock sculpture of Buddha at Sankaran in Visakhapatnam district.

the end of the 1st century BC these small centres of power came to be integrated into the empire of the Satavahanas. At the height of their power the Satavahanas, whose main base was in Maharashtra, called themselves *Dakshinapathesvaras* (Lords of *Dakshinapatha*). They had, by the 2nd century AD, expanded throughout the entire stretch of the Deccan to coastal Andhra in the east and Vidarbha in the north. The Satavahanas performed Vedic sacrifices, conformed to Brahmanical norms, defended the *varnadharma* (the principle of the division of society into four *varnas*) and, at the same time, patronised Buddhist *bhikshus* (monks) by constructing rock-cut *viharas* or monasteries for them and giving them land. The Satavahana officials were present in different parts of their empire and performed similar acts of religious patronage. It was the different strata of ruling elites, merchants and lay devotees of this period who, by their acts of patronage, created magnificent *stupa* sites such as Amravati in coastal Andhra and the rock-cut caves located near the passes connecting the western coast with the Deccan plateau. In both Karnataka and Andhra, there also emerged urban centres such as the famous early historical site of Nagarjunakonda of coastal Andhra, which were centres of commerce and religion.

Dravidadesa (Tamil country) lay outside the orbit of both the Magadhan empire of the north and the Satavahana empire of the Deccan, but the early anthologies of Tamil poems, *Sangam*, speak of the crowned kings of the Cholas, the Pandyas and the Cheras in addition to tribal chiefs in Tamilaham or Tamil country which would comprise the modern states of Tamil Nadu and Kerala. The state apparatus was yet to develop, but the authority of the crowned kings, who were more like chieftains, was recognised in their respective regions. The Cholas ruled in Cholamandalam, the Coromandel region, which included the Kaveri basin; the Pandya domain comprised the Madurai, Tirunelveli and Ramanathapuram region, drained by the Vaigai and the Tamraparni; and the Chera domain was in Kerala. The *Sangam* poems present to us the picture of a society in transition; there were Brahmanic elements present, and the virtue of making gifts to bards and Brahmins was lauded. Some short inscriptions, written in what is called the

Tamil-Brahmi script and dated to this period, refer to donations to Jainas who formed an influential ideological group in Tamil Nadu during the early Christian era.

The picture is very much different in the Tamil epic *Silappadikaram* and its sequel *Manimekalai* which refer to Madurai in the Pandya country and the port city of Kaverippattinam or Puhar in the region of the Cholas. These texts reveal a society very prosperous through trade. The wide network of trade which had developed both in the Deccan and the far south in the first few centuries of the Christian era was both in land and littoral. Magadhan expansion drew traders and other social groups from the north in their quest for local resources. From the end of the 1st century BC, a new thrust came when knowledge of the southwestern monsoon winds for purposes of navigation brought in merchants from the Roman world to the Indian coasts for spices. Local literature mentions the phenomenon of Indo-Roman trade; Tamil texts refer to the settlements of Yavana merchants in the port city of Puhar and to Yavanas at Musiripattinam in Kerala. But by far the most important records on this trade come from the writings of Western authors and from evidence provided by archaeology. An unknown Greek sailor who must have sailed along the western coast left a logbook, *The Periplus of the Erythraen Sea*, which not only lists the important emporia on both coasts and the items of merchandise but also refers to the transport of goods across the Deccan to the ports of the west coast. Ptolemy's *Geography*, written about a century later in the middle of the 2nd century AD, supplements this evidence and suggests that by his time the emporia on the east coast had become both much more numerous and important than before. Archaeological evidence on Indo-Roman trade is provided not only by many Roman coin hoards, the majority of which have been found in peninsular India, but also by other objects of Roman association such as pottery and art objects which turn up regularly at excavations at the early historic sites of peninsular India. Excavations conducted at Arikamedu, near Pondicherry, have shown it to be an Indo-Roman trading station. The period also witnessed the beginnings of commercial and cultural relations with Southeast Asia, as trade with the west dwindled gradually.

The Pallavas and the Chalukyas: The peninsular cities and the kingdoms of which they were important foci faced decline after the 3rd-4th centuries AD, as did urban centres in other parts of India, but this does not mean that peninsular society reverted to a primitive stage. From about the 6th century, but with modest beginnings earlier, there emerged two major regional kingdoms with large agrarian bases: that of the Pallavas in Tamil Nadu and of the Chalukyas in Karnataka. The Pallavas were first known from their Prakrit inscriptions of south Andhra and Tamil Nadu, but at the height of their power they used both Sanskrit and Tamil in their documents. The nuclear area of the kingdom was Tondaimandalam in the Palar basin with its centre at Kanchipuram. The growth of Kanchi as a major political and religious centre, with its temple-building activities through centuries, is closely linked with the rise of Pallava power. So was the case with Mamallapuram, or Mahabalipuram, a great centre of Pallava period art, which was a littoral centre of Pallava power. Beginning with the reign of Simhavishnu in the 6th century and through the reigns of his successors Mahendravarman I, Narasimhavaraman I and Paramesvaravarman, Pallava power rose to great heights in the 7th and 8th centuries and brought them into repeated conflicts with the Pandyas of south Tamil Nadu and the Chalukyas of Badami in Karnataka. The Chalukyas, who were the builders of the rock-cut caves at Badami and of the temple complexes at Pattadakal and Aihole in Karnataka, by the middle of the 7th century had consolidated their power to the extent that the Chalukyan ruler Pulakesi II (610-642) could claim to have defeated Harshavardhana, undoubtedly the most powerful ruler of North India at that time.

Notwithstanding the constant conflicts between the kingdoms and depletion of resources, the period of Pallava-Chalukya ascendancy saw some significant developments in peninsular India. In the political sphere, the monarch was the head of the state but had to function with subordinate rulers or feudatories. Both the Pallavas and the Chalukyas had feudatories who wielded autonomous power in their own localities, and in the conflicts between kingdoms such feudatory families as the Gangas and Kadambas in Karnataka or the Banas in Andhra and Tamil

Nadu played key roles. Secondly, this period witnessed donations of land to Brahmins (*brahmadeya*) and to temples (*devadana*) as a regular pattern. They assumed a much grander scale and significance in later periods of South Indian history. The emergence of *agrahara* settlements, where Brahmins were the dominant community, and of large estates owned by South Indian temples can thus be traced back to this period. It resulted in the expansion of Brahmanical ideas and institutions on a significant scale. This advance can also be seen in juxtaposition with the general decline of Buddhism and Jainism, and although there were sporadic cases of patronage extended to them even in later

Deccan too, in the temple structures or the rock-cut caves built by the Chalukya rulers, it is the Shaivite or Vaishnavite deities which predominate. Secondly, in Tamil Nadu, this period coincided with the emergence of the Bhakti movement which underlined total devotion to a personal god. The Nayannars (Shaivite saints) and Alvars (Vaishnavite saints) were composing devotional hymns in praise of their respective gods and making the temple centres their bases. Tradition has it that Pallava Mahendravarman, who is credited with the composition of the Sanskrit farce *Mattavilasaprahasana*, originally professed Jainism but discarded it in favour of Shaivism under the influence of the Shaivite

periods, at least Buddhism suffered an overall decline. Jainism survived in Karnataka, though not without opposition from other religious sects, and contributed substantially to the development of Kanarese literature.

In Tamil Nadu, the decline of Buddhism and Jainism is directly associated with two factors. One was the growing importance of Puranic Hinduism, with its accent on worship of deities with sectarian affiliations such as Shaivism (worship of Shiva) or Vaishnavism (worship of Vishnu). In the

Above, tortoise-shaped ritual bath at the early Buddhist site of Nagarjunakonda.

saint Appar. The hymns of the Shaivite and Vaishnavite saints became popular because they were composed in Tamil, and even in official documents, as in land grants, the beginnings of the use of Tamil and Kanarese, along with Sanskrit, go back to this period.

The Cholas and their contemporaries: Dynastic changes in South India were rapid; so were alignments between local powers entrenched in their respective regions for centuries. In this respect, South Indian history represents a trend which is typical of Indian history in general. There was rapid succession in Karnataka and western Deccan from the Badami Chalukyas to the Rashtrakutas to the Chalukyas of Kalyana and so on. But there also arose large state structures which provided political cohesion to the macroregions for centuries and shaped their cultural pattern. In the period following the Pallava-Chalukya ascendency, there arose several such state structures, among whom the most prominent were those of the Cholas in Tamil Nadu, of the Hoysalas in south Karnataka and of the Kakatiyas in Andhra.

The Cholas, originally feudatories of the Pallavas, started by gaining control of the Kaveri basin by the middle of the 9th century and then by expanding into other regions. Thus Parantaka I in the first half of the 10th century conquered the land of the Pandyas in

further ascendency under Kulottunga I (1070-1122) who united the Chola family with the Vengi Chalukya family of coastal Andhra, and by the 12th century the Chola state was unquestionably the strongest state structure in South India.

One remarkable feature of Chola expansion was the recognition by rulers like Rajaraja and Rajendra of the need for a strong navy. Overseas trade had by then revived, and the demand for textiles, spices and precious stones had resulted in the establishment of a number of Arab mercantile settlements along the coast of India. Overseas trade also extended to south China through Southeast Asia; Chola interest in this trade is

south Tamil Nadu and called himself *Maduraikonda* (the conqueror of Madurai). Further expansion took place under Rajaraja I (AD 985-1016) and Rajendra I (AD 1012-44), best known of the Chola rulers. Rajaraja not only brought the whole of Tamil Nadu under his control but also undertook expeditions to Andhra, Kerala, Sri Lanka and the Maldive Islands. Rajendra despatched an expedition to North India which reached the interior of Bengal; this was not designed to achieve permanent territorial expansion, but more as a symbolic act which would give the Chola monarch the status of a *Chakravarti* (universal monarch). Chola power gained

suggested both by the number of emissaries sent to China and by Chola naval expeditions to Southeast Asia. In fact, the emergence of a wide network of trade not only in the Chola kingdom but also in the Deccan and in Kerala, is suggested by numerous inscriptional documents of merchant groups across the peninsula and beyond, from as distant an area as Sumatra. Chola naval expeditions were also sometimes in the nature of plundering raids bringing in immense booty, and inscriptions record in detail the treasures gifted by the Chola rulers and other members of the royal family to temples built by them. The Brihadisvara temple at Tanjore built by

Rajaraja and the Gangaikondacholapuram temple built by Rajendra received substantial donations of land, cash, gold ornaments and other precious items.

Although it is argued by some that the Chola state was a segmentary state, with the king exercising only ritual sovereignty in the empire, the 4 centuries of Chola rule gave a new political and cultural cohesion to the far South. Many of the patterns of administration and cultural life which were crystallised in the Chola empire had parallels in other parts of the peninsula as well. The Chola empire, despite the growing commercial network, rested on a solid agrarian foundation. The smallest agrarian units of admini-

Gangas from south Karnataka, and from the period of Vishnuvardhana I (1110-52) to the period of Ballala III (1291-1342) were a major political power in South India, centered in the Hassan district. Despite repeated conflicts with other contemporary powers like the Cholas and the Chalukyas, the Hoysala region experienced agrarian expansion. Like the Cholas, the Hoysalas were great builders. At their capital at Dorasamudra, also known as Halebidu (old settlement) or Halebid, they build temples in addition to a majestic Shaiva temple. The Vaishnava temples were at Belur and Somanathapura, and they too received large donations from the royalty and subordinate rulers.

stration, comprising several villages, were the *nadus*. The Cholas integrated the *nadus* with bigger administrative units like the *valanadus* and the *mandalams* and through the hierarchical administrative structure ensured a flow of resources to the State.

The Hoysalas of south Karnataka came up from a tribal base in the hills of southwestern Karnataka. Initially feudatories of the Chalukyas of north Karnataka, they rose to prominence by displacing the Western

Far left, carved lintel at Madhukeswara temple. **Left**, temple caves at Badami. **Above**, gold objects excavated at Hampi.

The Kakatiyas, also originally feudatories of the later Chalukyas of Karnataka, made the comparatively barren tract of Warangal to the northeast of Hyderabad the base of their independent power from about the beginning of the 12th century. Under some able rulers the Kakatiyas became a major power in Andhra from the 12th to the early 14th century, not only through a sustained policy of agrarian expansion and support provided to overseas trade, but also through repeated administrative reorganisations.

In addition to these major powers, there were a number of other ruling families in different localities who either aligned themselves with the major powers or, like the Pandyas of southern Tamil Nadu and the Kulasekharas of Kerala, fought them to retain their autonomy. However, these repeated political struggles should not obscure the fact that, as in the period of Pallava-Chalukya ascendency, between the 9th and the 13th centuries, many of the key institutions that characterised South Indian society attained considerable maturity. Regular grants of various kinds show temples and Brahmin settlements to have been major integrating factors in society. Construction of irrigation tanks on a large scale, not necessarily undertaken by the royalty alone, also drew different segments of society together. Such old

gence of such protests as Virashaivism or the sect of the Lingayats, originally in Karnataka but gradually spreading to other parts of South India. Many of the tensions which characterise South Indian society in later times had their origin in this period.

Islamic expansion: By the close of the 13th century, the large state structures were beginning to collapse. This was not a direct result of invasions by the Islamic powers of the North; however, many of the major powers of the South did face invasions and suffer defeats. The establishment of Turkish rule in Delhi by the close of the 12th century had created a new type of political regime and in the beginning of the 14th century,

tanks still dot the landscape of South India and some are of such dimensions as to be called *samudram* (ocean).

The processes of social integration notwithstanding, there were conflicts at various levels. Within the Brahmanical ideological framework, the period witnessed intense philosophical debates as reflected in the works of such proponents of different schools as Sankaracharya, Ramanuja and Madhavacharya. Conflicts and cases of persecution arising out of religious sectarianism were not infrequent. The overall domination of Brahmins in society and the over-arching presence of the caste system led to the emer-

during the reign of Alauddin Khilji, the first inroads were made into the Kakatiya kingdom, the Hoysala kingdom and the Pandya kingdom of Mabar (south Tamil Nadu). Undertaken by Malik Kafur between 1303 and 1311, these forays yielded a huge amount of plundered wealth and promises of tribute to the Delhi Sultanate. Such raids continued, but Islamic influences started becoming an integral part of the Deccanese culture only with the establishment of the Bahmani kingdom. Created in 1347 by Hasan Gangu, a rebel official of Muhammad-bin-Tuglaq, and lasting till early 16th century, the kingdom included the whole of the northern Deccan down to the river Krishna. One well-known Bahmani ruler was Firuz Shah Bahmani who was acquainted not only with Islamic literature and Turkish, Arabic and Persian languages but with various branches of science as well, and who was conversant with local languages like Marathi, Telugu and Kanarase. By inducing learned scholars from Iran and Iraq to settle in his kingdom, he transformed it into a major cultural region of the Deccan.

Another major phase of Bahmani history is represented by the close of the 15th century when Mahmud Gawan, an Iranian merchant, became the prime minister. Besides enhancing the political status of the state, he of their rule, the Bahmanis have left a rich cultural heritage in the form of surviving religious, military and civil architecture in which many elements were synthesised.

To the south of the Krishna was the empire of Vijayanagara – the arch rival of the Bahmanis – with its centre at Hampi (near Hospet in Karnataka), a sprawling and magnificent capital built on the bank of the Tungabhadra in a granite rock area traditionally identified with Kishkindha of the early Sanskrit epic *Ramayana*. Tradition again traces the foundation of the empire to two brothers, Harihara and Bukka, originally feudatories of the Kakatiyas. They aligned themselves with the Muslim power in the Deccan and

reorganised its administrative structure.

The Bahmani kingdom was indeed a cultural bridge of that time between the North and the South, but internal weaknesses ultimately broke it up into five kingdoms: Bijapur, Golconda, Ahmadnagar, Bidar and Berar. With the annexation of Berar by Ahmadnagar and of Bidar by Bijapur, the remnants of Bahmani rule were ultimately represented by Bijapur, Ahmadnagar and Golconda. Because of the eclectic character

Left, Hebrew leather scroll from the Cochin synagogue. **Above**, 19th-century view of Bijapur by a British naval officer.

even were converted but finally, as proteges of the sage Vidyaranya, founded Vijayanagara in 1336 and became upholders of Hindu interests in the Deccan. The empire of Vijayanagara which lasted through four dynasties, i.e. Sangam, Saluva, Tuluva and Aravidu, was of a multi-ethnic composition, and despite the growing importance of Bahmanis in its administration, it employed both Muslims and Europeans in various services. The Vijayanagara capital attracted visitors like Abdur Razzak, Nuniz and Paes who came from distant countries. In fact, much of what is known about the pattern of life in the capital is derived from their accounts.

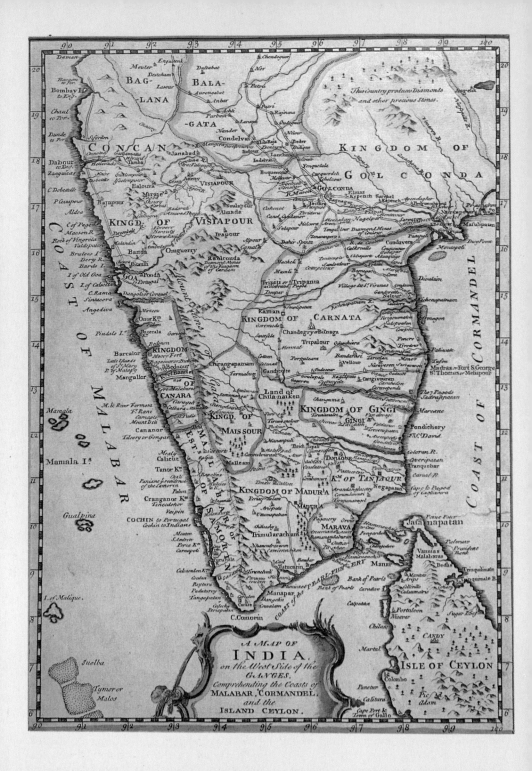

A MAP OF INDIA, on the West Side of the GANGES, Comprehending the Coasts of MALABAR, CORMANDEL, and the ISLAND CEYLON.

The greatest monarch of Vijayanagara was Krishnadevaraya (1509-29), who not only achieved military victories against the Bahmanis, against Orissa and other powers but also was an able administrator and realised, like other contemporary powers, the importance of trade, both internal and overseas, for enhancing the wealth of the country. The multi-ethnic population of Vijayanagara included Jews and Parsis. Judging from the accounts of 16th-century travellers like Varthema, Barbosa, Ralph Fitch and others regarding the extent of commercial activities in Kerala, Golconda, the Andhra coast and the Vijayanagara and Bahmani kingdoms, Mughal expansion from the North and European commercial expansion into South India was inevitable.

The Mughals: The consolidation of Mughal power in the north began to affect the political regions of South India only from the period of Akbar (1556-1605), the greatest of the Mughal rulers, who conquered parts of Ahmadnagar, though it was fully annexed only during the reign of Shah Jahan. Bijapur and Golconda too submitted to the authority of the Mughals, and Aurangzeb, Shah Jahan's son, was appointed governor of the Deccan. However, it was never fully integrated into the Mughal empire, and the growing strength of the Marathas in the west aggravated the problems of the Mughals in the Deccan. When Aurangzeb became emperor, he had to send a large army to the Deccan to curb the activities of the Maratha chief Shivaji, whose father was originally a feudatory of the Bijapur sultan. For the Deccan, as for many other parts of India, Maratha plundering raids were a constant menace and the imposition of *Chauth* and *Sardeshmukhi*, taxes which people living outside the Maratha region had to pay, further worsened the condition of the people of the Deccan. However, one important consequence of Mughal expansion in the Deccan was the creation by Nizam-ul-Mulk, a powerful noble at the Mughal court and erstwhile *Wazir* of the Mughal emperor, of the independent state of Hyderabad in 1724, which lasted till the middle of the 20th century.

A major development was the penetration of European commercial interests into India,

which had started towards the end of the 15th century. Attempts to establish direct trade relations with India were necessary for new European powers in the 15th-16th centuries; they had to break the Arab and Venetian monopolies in India trade, and to bypass the Ottoman empire of the Turks. Alternative routes were being desperately sought, and the arrival of the Portuguese Vasco da Gama at the port of Calicut in Kerala in 1498 heralded a new era, not only in the history of South India but in the entire East.

Although the Portuguese had the virtual monopoly of eastern trade for about a century, the English, the Dutch, the French and others finally followed them. Initially their trade was carried on from "factories" at certain centres, with small settlements around them, and was independent on concessions obtained from local rulers and from the Mughals. Gradually, however, there arose fierce competition among the European trading companies which began contending for territorial control. Portuguese power soon came to be restricted to several centres on the west coast. Similarly the Dutch East India Company, which had extensive interests in Southeast Asia and trade depots at Cochin, Nagapatnam in Madras and Masulipatam on the Andhra coast, as well as in other places, could not survive competition from the English East India Company and shifted its major interests to Indonesia.

The fiercest competition was between the French and the English, and from their bases in the Deccan and the South, particularly Fort St George in Madras (established around the middle of the 17th century), the English kept harrying French interests. Despite the brilliant manoeuvres of Dupleix, the French Governor-General of Pondicherry, French power after mid-18th century was virtually confined to Pondicherry.

The British attempts at territorial expansion were initially not very successful, but with the occupation of Bengal in 1757 and with secure bases in Madras and Bombay, they advanced rapidly, particularly as the Mughal empire was crumbling away. In the Deccan and the South, protracted struggles against Hyder Ali and Tippu Sultan of Mysore and against the Marathas ended in victory for the British. The fall of Seringapatam, the capital of Tippu Sultan, in 1797 of course brought back the original family of

Left, 18th century political map of peninsular India.

Rajas to Mysore, but like other rulers of "native" states they too were completely subservient to the British. By the middle of the 19th century the British, starting as merchant adventurers, had become masters of India, and despite the continued existence of many local *Rajas* brought South India too under their complete hegemony.

Imperialism and after: In trying to understand the impact of British imperialism from an all-India perspective, one needs to keep a few general points in mind. First, the British economic exploitation of India changed in nature over time. Since the end of the 18th century, the British gradually converted India into a market for their own products,

what became pan-Indian nationalism. Examples of popular movements are varied in space and time; one can refer to the series of formidable tribal rebellions in the forest and hilly areas of Andhra Pradesh from late 19th century to early 20th century; to the peasant uprisings of the Moplahs of Malabar in Kerala from the first half of the 19th century to the beginnings of the present century; and to the massive Telengana uprising in Andhra from 1946 to 1951, involving at least 3,000 villages spread over 16,000 sq miles (25,600 sq km) and drew the ideological support and participation of the communists.

The nature of South India's participation of the mainstream national movement is

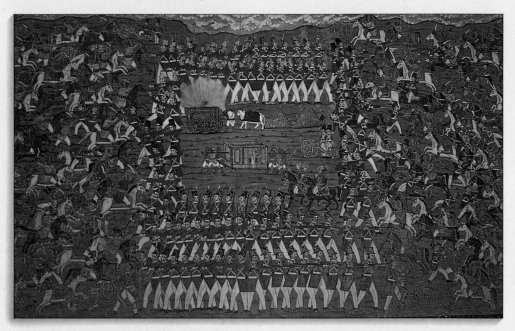

while using the country as a quarry for raw materials. This spelt doom for traditional indigenous industries. Second, after the great revolt of 1857, India ceased to be ruled by the East India Company and passed on to the British crown, enabling the British to rule their most prized colony directly. Third, imperialism did not mean economic exploitation alone but also ideological domination.

The growing resentment against the stranglehold of the structure created by the British found expression at two levels, not always directed against the British themselves: spontaneous popular rebellions and movements, and middle class participation in

related to the emergence of an English-educated middle class. After the great revolt of 1857, British enthusiasm for introducing social reforms in India ebbed considerably, but the universities of Madras, Calcutta and Bombay had already been established. The British education policy of creating a subservient literate social class produced surprising results. The Indians' response to Western education and ideas began to foster national consciousness, a critical concern at the evils of their own society and an effort to rediscover their own cultural heritage.

Initially, the articulation of this consciousness took the form of various regional associations and regular publications, in both English and regional languages. For example, the Madras Native Association, already established in the middle of the 19th century, was followed in 1881 by the Madras Mahajan Sabha. In 1886 the headquarters of the Theosophical Society was located in Madras and under the leadership of Mrs Annie Besant the Society wielded considerable influence, as did her Home Rule League at a later stage. The publication of such journals as the *Hindu*, the *Swadeshmitran*, *Andhra Patrika* and *Kerala Patrika* did much to disseminate nationalistic ideas, as did the writings of such stalwarts as Subrahmanya Bharati. Active efforts at social re-

sponse from the South; prominent personalities like Subrahmanya Aiyar and Ananda Charlu participated in its early sessions. The various stages of the freedom struggle – the Non-cooperation movement, the Civil Disobedience movement and the Quit India movement, despite uneven intensity of participation, were indeed mass movements as elsewhere during the Gandhian era of the national struggle, bringing to prominence leaders like Pattabhi Sitaramayya, Sarojini Naidu and Chakravarti Rajagopalachari.

It would, however, be wrong to consider the national movement as a unilineal or unified movement even in its South Indian context. Its regional ramifications took di-

forms were widespread. In Andhra Pradesh, Virasalingam's Rajahmundri Social Reform Association (established in 1878), Natarajan's publication, *Indian Social Reformer*, and the Hindu Social Reform Association, started in Madras in 1892, testify to concerted efforts to deal with what were considered evils in contemporary society.

The formation of the Indian National Congress in 1885 drew enthusiastic re-

Left, fresco from Srirangapatnam, Tippu Sultan's palace. **Above**, British Governor-General of the Madras Presidency with guests and local dignitaries, late 19th century.

verse shapes, for example in the anti-Brahmin movements spearheaded by the Justice Party in the 1920s and 1930s in Tamil Nadu, or in the demand for a separate state for Telugu-speaking people put forward by the Andhra Mahasabha. Independence came in August 1947, and the integration of independent princely states like the Nizam's Dominions or the State of Travancore in Kerala with the Union of India was also achieved; but the new leaders of India still had to find solutions to the problems which the long-drawn history of British imperialism and the many-hued struggles against it had generated.

On 15 August 1947, the political map of South India was very different from what it is today. It consisted of the huge Madras Presidency, the princely states of Cochin, Travancore, Mysore and Hyderabad, and a number of smaller principalities. While the rulers of all these states accepted the reality of India and acceded to the Indian Union, the Nizam of Hyderabad resisted.

The Nizams, descendants of a governor appointed by the Mughal emperor Aurangzeb, ruled over nine dominions with Hyderabad as their capital. In 1947, the then Nizam, a colourful character known to be one of the richest men in the world and also the most miserly, held out for almost a year. In 1948, following popular resistance to the Nizam's rule, the troops of the Government of India occupied his dominions and Hyderabad became a part of the Indian Union.

The post-Independence period saw a resurgence in regional pride in the South. There were some cultural differences among the people of the South and, besides, they did not speak the same language. Tamil, Telugu, Malayalam and Kannada were the major languages of the region. The demand for reorganising the country on the basis of language gained momentum, especially in the South. The process was hastened in 1953 when Potti Sriramulu, a Telugu patriot, died on an indefinite fast demanding a separate state for the Telugu-speaking people. In the same year, Andhra Pradesh came into being with Telugu as its language, the first state in India which was formed on a purely linguistic basis. The former state of Hyderabad, where the majority spoke Telugu, was incorporated into Andhra Pradesh.

In 1956, the States' Reorganisation Act was passed and the Indian states were reorganised on the basis of language. The South was divided into four states. The Telugu-speaking districts formed Andhra Pradesh, the Kannada-speaking parts became the

Preceding pages, guests in traditional finery at a Syrian Christian wedding in Kottayam, Kerala. **Left** and **above right**, never a dull moment on Indian streets with the various modes of transport available.

Mysore state (later called Karnataka), those areas where Malayalam was the principal language became Kerala, and the Madras Presidency reduced in area with Tamil as its predominant language. The name of Madras state was later changed to Tamil Nadu.

Jawaharlal Nehru, the visionary first Prime Minister of India, disapproved of linguistic states because he felt that this would lead to factionalism and fragmentation of the country. His fears have been justified to a large extent; however, it is doubtful whether

in the long run it would have been possible to prevent this reorganisation. At the time when the four southern states were formed, the Congress was firmly in the saddle in all of them except Kerala.

Like the rest of the country, with the exception of Bombay and Calcutta, the South was not industrialised. However, the region which is now known as Tamil Nadu did have some industries like cotton textiles, cement, sugar and leather which had sprung up using the available local infrastructure. Madras also had a fairly well developed port. Many British trading houses like Parry's, Best & Co., Spencers and Gordon Woodroffe had their headquarters in Madras. Mysore state, too, thanks to its enlightened *Dewans* like Sir M. Vishveshwaraiya, had a small industrial base. The Krishnaraja Sagar dam was built on the Kaveri with a power plant at Sivasamudram. An iron and steel plant was set up at Bhadravati. But Andhra Pradesh and Kerala at the time of Independence had virtually no industrial base.

The industrial scene in the country began to change in the 1950s, when the government of India took a conscious decision to develop indigenous industry and impose import restrictions. To accelerate industrialisation, the government set up plants to provide basic inputs like iron and steel required by the new

Limited, a unit of BHEL (Bharat Heavy Electricals, a public sector conglomerate set up to manufacture power plant equipment), and Madras Fertilisers Limited, are some of the big public sector projects which came up in Tamil Nadu during this phase. The first nuclear reactors in the South have also been commissioned near Madras.

The local entrepreneurs of Tamil Nadu also came into prominence during this period. Heavy investments were made primarily in the automotive industries and in the heavy engineering industry which makes sugar, textile and cement machinery. In fact the growth of the automobile and auto component sector was so rapid that Madras came

industries.

Tamil Nadu: In the early days of post-Independence industrialisation, Tamil Nadu came into its own. What is particularly striking about the state's progress is that Tamil Nadu as a manufacturing location has very little to recommend itself. It has no raw material or mineral base, and the markets for its products are spread far and wide. However, thanks to an enlightened state government which had the full support of the central government, both the public sector and the private sector flourished for almost two decades. The Neyveli Lignite Corporation, Integral Coach Factory, Madras Refineries

to be known as the Detroit of India. Tamil Nadu has also in recent years become an important centre for leather exports. Leather exporters have moved away from crude untanned leather to high value-added items like shoes and fashion accessories. Another area where the state has shown remarkable growth is in granite exports. A local manufacturer has exported granite mausoleums to the West. The state is also the major centre for the handloom trade and exports.

Although industrialisation was given a tremendous boost in the state, the agricultural sector was not neglected. Even today, agriculture is the mainstay of the state's economy. Rice cultivation has reached new heights, and the yield per hectare for rice amounts to 2.5 tonnes, among the highest in India. Tamil Nadu's sugarcane yield of 100 tonnes per hectare is a world record. The state is now successfully experimenting with soya cultivation.

Tamil Nadu progressed on many fronts such as rural electrification and primary education. Its leaders during two decades after Independence were legendary figures like K. Kamaraj, R. Venkataraman (the present President of India) and C. Subramaniam. However, all was not wholly idyllic. The Dravida Kazhagam (DK), founded by the social reformer "EVR", E. V. Ramaswamy

Naickar, fought among other things for the uplift of the lower castes. After Independence EVR was not in favour of entering electoral politics. Some of his followers felt otherwise and broke away from the DK to form the Dravida Munnetra Kazhagam (DMK) in 1949.

One of the founder-leaders of the DMK was D. N. Annadurai, a prolific writer of

A strong nexus prevails in South India between politics, religion and the cinema. Left, Mrs Gandhi has an audience with a naked Jain ascetic. Above, "NTR", hero of hundreds of Telugu mythological films and a leading politician.

great repute. He was one of the first politicians to use the powerful media of state and, later, cinema to build up his party. The DMK took up the cause of the Tamils. The fact that New Delhi was far away and the greater part of the country was controlled by the Hindi-speaking people created a sense of insecurity among the Tamils. The feeling that the Congress rulers of the state were not quite sensitive to the susceptibilities of their people grew rapidly. The DMK was able to exploit these fears to encourage Tamil chauvinism. In the 1967 elections the Congress was trounced in the state. The DMK romped home with a vast majority and Annadurai became the Chief Minister.

Andhra Pradesh: Andhra Pradesh also set up a few public sector projects after it was formed, to hasten the process of industrialisation. The public sector giant BHEL started a unit in Hyderabad, the Electronics Corporation of India (ECIL) was established, the Singareni coal mines were developed, a steel plant was put up in Vizag and harbour facilities improved at Vizag port.

However, till the late 1970s there were no major private entrepreneurs in Andhra. It remained, and still is, principally an agricultural state. It has a widely diversified farming base with a rich variety of cash crops. It has an agricultural surplus and is rightly known as the Granary of the South. The crops which are extensively cultivated apart from paddy are tobacco, chillies, cotton, groundnut and sugarcane. Andhra Pradesh is also the major producer of tobacco in the country with a virtual monopoly on Virginia tobacco, a major item of export.

Till the early 1980s, the Congress remained in power in Andhra. By and large the Telugu-speaking people were devoted to the Nehru family, particularly to Indira Gandhi. However, the state was constantly rocked by rumblings of discontent. This is mainly because Andhra consists of three distinct regions– the coastal region, made up of eight districts generally called Andhra, the interior region consisting of four districts collectively known as Rayalaseema, and the Telengana region comprising the capital Hyderabad and nine districts surrounding it – each with its own loyalties. Between 1969 and 1972 there were riots in Telengana and Andhra over the issue of a further division in the state.

The central government was not in favour of a bifurcation. Finally, the Prime Minister Mrs Gandhi worked out a compromise formula which was accepted by the people, and peace was restored. Although two rivers, the Krishna and the Godavari, flow through Andhra and during the south west monsoon brings much rain to it, the Rayalaseema region is drought-prone. The people of this region have always felt that they have not been treated fairly by the successive state governments. Andhra has also been a hotbed of Naxalite activity, an extreme leftist movement which gained ground in the late 1960s and the early 1970s.

Karnataka: If any southern state received in the country. Among food crops, Karnataka produces 49 percent of the country's *ragi* crop and is the major coffee producer in the country. Karnataka's Coorg district is full of small coffee holdings. The largest coffee plantation company in the country is also based in this state.

Politically, Karnataka was very much a pro-Congress state till the 1980s, but in recent years opposition parties have come into power.

Kerala: Although the smallest among the southern states, Kerala has the highest density of population and also the highest level of literacy. It has the distinction of having elected the first Communist government in

the bounty of the central government, it was Karnataka. After Independence, Bangalore grew into a city dominated by public sector units. Because of its temperate climate, major electronics units like Bharat Electronics Limited and the Indian Telephone Industries were set up in Bangalore. Over the years Karnataka has built up a strong industrial base, especially in the machine tools and electronics industry. Its base in electronics was to make Bangalore a boom town when the electronics explosion occurred in industry in the 1980s.

Apart from its industrial base, Karnataka accounts for 85 percent of the silk produced

the world way back in 1957. Ever since, Kerala's electoral politics has resembled a roller coaster. The Communist ministry headed by EMS Namboodiripad, one of the veteran Marxist leaders of India, was dismissed by the central government in 1959. During its term in office, it introduced land reforms and Kerala ceased to have large landlords. About 32 political parties operate in Kerala, and the state has been alternately ruled by the Congress, the Marxists and various alliances. Kerala with its high population has its own problems in the areas of food, employment and housing. Industrially it is probably the least advanced of the southern states. It does have Cochin port, a fertiliser complex, a state-promoted Electronics Corporation, a private sector aluminum unit and the Vikram Sarabhai Space Research Centre. Unfortunately, Kerala has also earned a reputation for militancy of labour, which acts as a disincentive to potential investors. Coupled with this, the unprecedented drought situation has made this once power-rich state into a chronically power-hungry one because of its dependency on hydro-electric power sources.

For historical and climatic reasons, the state has developed into a major producer of cash crops rather than food crops. Kerala produces among other things, 92 percent of

DMK government in Tamil Nadu took a strong anti-centre and anti-Hindi stand. There is a general view that investment from the central government declined in the state after the DMK came to power. The DMK also, in its early days, did not favour industry and looked upon it with total mistrust. But this attitude changed in a few years. M. Karunanidhi, who succeeded Annadurai (the latter died within 2 years of coming to power), is another successful scriptwriter-turned-politician, and who is an eminent and practical man. During his regime several steps were taken to set up promotional agencies to help industry grow in the state.

However, trouble started brewing in the

India's rubber, 70 percent of its cardamom, 70 percent of its coconut, 70 percent of its pepper and 80 percent of its tapioca. However, the state produces only about 50 percent of its food needs.

The Last Two Decades: When the DMK came to power in Tamil Nadu in 1967, it was still not apparent that within the next two decades the entire South would be ruled by the regional parties which were seen as representatives of the people's aspirations. The

Rapid industrial growth in South India (left) has led to the opening of several container ports such as the one in Cochin (above).

DMK itself. Karunanidhi fell out with M. G. Ramachandran, the popular movie actor who owed a great deal of his enormous success to the scripts of Karunanidhi. In 1976, "MGR" (as he was popularly known) broke away from the DMK and founded the All Indian Anna Dravida Munnetra Kazhagam (AIADMK). In the 1977 state elections he proved his popularity by defeating the DMK, and became the first ever film-star-turned-politician to rule a state.

MGR was a phenomenon. His carefully built-up image of a do-gooder in films became his real image. People worshipped him; he could do no wrong. Even in his later years when illness affected his power of speech, his popularity did not fade. Till his death in 1988 he was unshakable. When he died his party split and lost power to the DMK. M. Karunanidhi made a triumphant comeback, after more than a decade in the wilderness, but in the last general election has lost further ground.

Under MGR that state economy did not fare well. MGR did not have a feel for industry; he was more interested in initiating welfare schemes. His noon meal scheme introduced for the primary school children became a model for several other states.

While Tamil Nadu was lagging behind in the 1970s, many developments took place in Andhra Pradesh. During this phase, power was readily available in Andhra, which led to the establishment of several big cement plants. The landlord class too began to make the transition from agriculture to trading and manufacture. Oil and natural gas was found in the Godavari basin, which opened up the prospects of several gas-based industries in the region.

Politically, the 1980s proved to be a turbulent period for Andhra Pradesh. Although the state continued to be loyal to the Congress, the Congress high command proved to be insensitive to the feelings of the people. Between 1980-82, the Chief Minister was changed four times, and about 362 ministers were appointed, all because the high command willed it. The local Congress leaders could not stand up to the centre. Rebellion was brewing.

Leadership came from N.T. Rama Rao, another filmstar-turned-politician. He was also immensely popular as an actor and was well known for the godly roles he had played. In 1982 he founded the Telugu Desam (TD) party "to pay back the insults heaped upon the Telugu people". In the 1983 elections, the TD practically wiped out the Congress. Since then Rama Rao has become a national figure as one of the leading lights of the opposition coalition which is fighting the Congress at the centre.

The 1980s also proved to be a period of political change for Karnataka. The state turned against the Congress in 1982 and elected the Janata party to power. Its leader Ramakrishna Hegde became the Chief Minister of the state. Hegde, considered to be one of the most sophisticated and shrewd politi-cians in the country, remained the Chief Minister for 6 years. His ministry survived several scandals, and Hegde had to curb the infighting in his party. He finally resigned in 1988, and the Janata Ministry was dismissed a few months later. The state is now back under Congress rule.

Although most of the industry in Karnataka was in the public sector, the situation began to change dramatically in the 1980s. Many of the big commercial establishments which had their headquarters in Calcutta, uncomfortable with the Marxist government of West Bengal, decided to move to Bangalore's green and temperate environs. Some of the big names which have moved to Bangalore are Brooke Bond and Lipton, the tea companies. Some of the Bombay companies like Britannia (the biscuit makers) have also shifted because Bombay has become too expensive and congested. Karnataka has a number of projects in collaboration, particularly with U.S. corporations such as Texas Instruments, Hewlett Packard, Digital Electronics Corporation, General Foods and Gould. Several industrial estates have sprung up in recent times. The headquarters of the national space research is also located in Karnataka.

Kerala was one of the major beneficiaries of the Gulf boom of the mid-1970s. Kerala's labour force went in hundreds of thousands to the Middle East which was in the midst of the oil boom. The non-resident Indians sent back millions of petro-dollars, which have transformed the green countryside. Though construction is flourishing, the hard-earned money has not really been put to much productive use.

In spite of repeated droughts and a grim power situation, much progress has been made in the four southern states after Independence. Oil has also been found in Tamil Nadu. A petrochemicals complex is being planned in the state which will usher in another industrial upsurge. Additional nuclear power plants are being planned in Tamil Nadu and Karnataka, and rocket launching centres are in existence – or soon will be – in the four states.

Right, bus decorated for the Hindu festival of Navaratri. Modernisation has not loosened the hold of custom and religion on the South Indian way of life.

SOCIETY AND CULTURE

South India and North India share similarities as well as differences. The institutions of caste and the joint family, and beliefs regarding the relative purity and impurity of persons, places, things, diets and occupations, are found all over India, but they assume different forms in different regions. This phenomenon finds expression in a political cliché, India's "unity-in-diversity". The cliché, however, fails to take note of the linked phenomenon that instances of apparent "unity" often conceal differences.

Thus, in the traditional caste system of India, both the barber and washerman occupy a low rank, but in parts of North India the barber is also the matchmaker for the high castes and hence has a relatively higher status, while the washerman is assigned a low rank because of his washing of the highly "polluting" menstrual, puerperal and funeral clothes.

South India is a plateau fringed by plains in the east and west. The mountains of the Western Ghats skirt the plateau in the west while the lower, more broken Eastern Ghats are dotted about different parts of South India. The Nilgiris, which form the highest range in the south, are the meeting point of the two mountain ranges. The Nilgiris were a frontier region, as it were, until a century ago, peopled by tribal groups such as the Badaga, Toda, Kota and Kurumba. The area is now a holiday resort and a supplier of tea and potatoes to other parts of India.

In the South, the landscape is generally undulating, except in the coastal plains and the deltaic areas of the principal rivers, the Godavari, Krishna and Kaveri. Some parts of South India are endowed with tanks or artificial lakes which serve both as reservoirs and as sources of irrigation. Generally, each tank forms part of a system whose waste waters flow into a stream.

One of the pleasures of travelling in the South is the frequent occurrence of these tanks in whose ambience are grown not only

Preceding pages, Lambadi tribal women dance to celebrate the coming of Spring. **Left**, Kerala farmer's rice straw hat offers protection against the elements.

millets, paddy and sugarcane but also mango, coconut and other fruit-bearing trees. Often, the traveller is startled by the sight of a majestic temple tower rising sheer from an expanse of green paddy fields.

Ever since the reorganisation of Indian states on the basis of linguistic homogeneity (November 1956), South India has four states: Andhra Pradesh (population 53.5 million, area 106,000 sq miles/275.600 sq km), Karnataka (population 37.1 million, area 78,000 sq miles/202,800 sq km), Tamil Nadu (population 48.4 million, area 50,000 sq miles/130,000 sq km), and Kerala (population, 25.4 million, area 15,000 sq miles/39,000 sq km), and a Union Territory, Pondicherry (population 600,000 million, area 2,000 sq miles/5,200 sq km), of which each is a separate political entity with its own Chief Minister. Pondicherry was a part of France till November 1954, when it became a political unit of India under a Lieutenant Governor.

All the Dravidian languages – Tamil, Telugu, Kannada and Malayalam – are cultivated languages, but they have been influenced by Sanskrit, the classical and sacred language of the Hindus. In the case of Tamil, the oldest and most individualistic of the Dravidian languages, the influence of Sanskrit goes back to the age of Sangam literature (2nd-4th century AD). Moreover, all Indian languages, including Tamil and Malayalam, have derived their alphabet from the Brahmi script. In addition to the cultivated languages, there are many regional dialects.

Each of the Dravidian languages has a rich literature, Tamil perhaps being the richest, and in proverbial literature perhaps even superior to Sanskrit. The epics, *Ramayana* and *Mahabharata*, and a few of the more popular *Puranas* (mythological literature celebrating a god or goddess or a centre of pilgrimage) have been translated into these languages. The epics are also rich in poetry. Each language also has a body of folk songs and tales which are now being written down as part of a process of increased awareness of group, regional and linguistic identity. All these languages have also experienced "purity" movements under which they have tried to expunge "foreign" words – which has meant the discarding of Sanskrit, Persian and, of course, English words and phrases.

Traditionally, Sanskrit has been the language of philosophy and religion, and of prayer and ritual. However, under the influence of the powerful Bhakti movement, which started in the 7th-8th centuries in Tamil Nadu and spread to other parts of South India before moving north, there was a determined effort to use the spoken language of the people for communicating religious and ethical ideas. Caste, untouchability, over-developed ritualism were all attacked and, on the positive side, members of the so-called "lower" castes, including

ethos of Islam and the Middle East as a source of sustenance. Urdu was used extensively in the North by both Muslims and Hindus, but in recent decades it has become identified increasingly with Muslims.

Significant changes have occurred in each of these languages during the last 70 years or more. The need to mobilise a mostly illiterate people for the national struggle for independence from the British led to the development of a style of speaking and writing which was intelligible to one and all. The development of journalism in the regional languages also facilitated the evolution of a clear prose style. Modern literary forms, the short story and the novel, plays and essays, and literary

women, were encouraged to join the movement. The importance of performing manual work was stressed, which was something quite new if not revolutionary, considering the low status which it had in the caste system. Thanks to the Bhakti movement, the Dravidian languages have a body of protest literature as part of their heritage.

Urdu, which is popularly associated with Muslims and North India, actually originated in the Deccan. It started as the language of Mughal armies in the Deccan, and was even called "Dakhni". As the language spread, a literature was created in it with Arabic as its script, and the language and

and social criticism, became popular in the regional languages. The post-Independence years witnessed a sharp increase in the number of magazines and novels catering to increasing numbers of people who wanted information and entertainment in their own mother-tongue.

Rural society: Traditionally, the village community has been the fundamental unit of economic, political and social organisation. There were two major types of villages in South India, the nucleated and dispersed. The nucleated type prevailed everywhere except on the west coast. In the latter area, a collection of discrete farms were grouped together for administrative purposes and called a village. In the nucleated village, on the other hand, the houses and huts lay huddled together in a small area surrounded by fields cultivated by the villagers. But however tiny the settlement area, the village was internally differentiated, each caste occupying a street or segment. In the fertile Tanjore delta in Tamil Nadu, the street occupied by Brahmins was called *agraharam* while the street occupied by the ex-untouchables was called *cheri*, and each caste avoided the other's street.

The most frequent form of land revenue obtained in South India was the Ryotwari system, in which the landowner paid rent on

his land directly to the government. This did not mean, however, that the landowner cultivated the land himself. He may have had a tenant, share-cropper or bonded labourer, or all three. In another system, a group of landowners, generally related by paternal kinship, owned all the arable land in the village, and the head of the lineage paid the rent on behalf of all the shareholders in the estate. This system obtained in parts of Andhra Pradesh and Tamil Nadu was perhaps more

Left and above, Lambadi women enjoy wearing colourful clothes and elaborate jewellery. The Todas are inhabitants of the Nilgiri hills.

widespread in the past. Land was occasionally given at a concessional rent to those who had rendered distinguished service to the state, or to learned and pious Brahmins to earn religious merit for the donor. All concessional and hereditary tenures were abolished in the land reforms following Independence.

Payment in land occurred at all levels: it was customary to endow a temple with a few acres of land so that the crop could maintain the priest and also make possible daily offerings of food to the deity.

Traditionally, each large village had a headman and an accountant. The headman looked after law and order while the accountant kept the land records, and the two were responsible for collecting the land tax and remitting it to the government treasury. Each was paid a share of the total amount collected as tax. These offices, mostly hereditary, were abolished in the post-Independence years, and nowadays the task of collecting revenue is entrusted to an official appointed by the government.

Arable land was generally owned by the higher castes excepting in areas where hereditary village servants, drawn from the untouchable castes, were paid in perpetuity with grants of small quantities of land. However, the bulk of the land was generally owned by the members of the peasant castes, referred to as "dominant castes" in the literature on Indian villages. The smaller landowners worked on their land while the bigger landowners had tenants, share-croppers and hereditary servants doing the manual work for them. The owners only supervised the work.

Producing a crop necessitated cooperation with members of other castes. The blacksmith, who also did carpentry work, made and repaired ploughs and other agricultural implements, the potter, the oilman, the barber, and the washerman were all paid by the landowner with quantities of grain at harvest. Besides these, some grain was given to the village temples, and to the many mendicants and poor who generally gathered round the threshing-yard.

Ritual and religion: All over South India, every village has a shrine to a goddess (commonly referred to as Mari but also called by other names such as Kali, Bhagavati, Chamundi and Ellamma), associated with functions such as protecting the village from epidemics of plague, cholera and smallpox and often also with the protection of infants. With the disappearance of epidemics, the deities have lost their *raison d'être*, but their worship continues.

The Nandi bull, the vehicle of the great god Shiva, is worshipped in parts of South India and is supposed to look after the rain, fodder and agriculture. The great gods of Hinduism and their various manifestations are worshipped generally by the higher castes, especially Brahmins. They are supposed to look after the general welfare of the people, and do not have specific duties like the village deities.

and their manifestations, who are propitiated with offerings of fruit, flowers and vegetarian food.

Weekly markets, a feature of rural South India, were far more important economically and socially before the rapid development of roads and transport following Independence. Peasants were also partial to pilgrimages. The annual festivals of deities in the post-harvest season provided them with reasons for travel and relaxation. Cattle fairs were also frequently held at these festivals. In recent years, the religious field of the South Indian peasantry has widened enormously to include pilgrimages to the great temples at Tirupati, Madurai, Sri-

Sometimes shrines are erected to the deity of a caste or a cluster of paternally linked lineages. The ex-untouchables traditionally worshipped a form of Mari, and at her periodical festival fowl, sheep and even male buffaloes were sacrificed. Animal sacrifices were commonly made by non-vegetarian castes but, since Independence, state governments have discouraged them. Also, the spread of education, increased urbanisation and better living conditions have all favoured the emulation of the culture and religion of the highest castes, Brahmins, Lingayats and some trading groups. This has increased the popularity of Shiva and Vishnu

rangam, Rameshwaram, and even Benares, Allahabad and Hardwar in the North.

The village panchayat comprising several elders maintained law and order in the village: physical assault, theft, encroachment, failure to return a loan, all went to the panchayat for settlement. But there were offences against caste, custom, diet and morality which sometimes went to the elders of the concerned caste or castes, or directly to the elders of the dominant caste. In this connection, it is essential to mention that the burden of maintaining the social and cultural order devolved on the dominant castes. The latter are ubiquitous in rural India, and generally account for a sizable percentage of the village population. The other group usually represented in some strength are ex-untouchables who perform manual labour on the land.

Members of minority religions such as Muslims and Christians accepted the power and authority of the dominant castes, and the latter in turn felt bound to protect minority culture and religious practices. In some Karnataka villages Hindus have animals slaughtered in the *halal* way in order for their Muslim guests to partake of the festival (or wedding) dinner. Similarly, Muslims occasionally make votive offerings at Hindu temples. Hindu-Muslim conflict is largely an urban affair, and in any case it is muted in South India.

Radical changes have occurred in rural India since Independence with the introduction of land reforms, with making the practice of untouchability in any form a cognizable offence, with the introduction of adult franchise, with the strengthening of local self-government agencies, and with the spread of education to groups and sections which did not have access to it before. Rapid population growth has resulted in land becoming scarce, forcing an increasing number of men to become landless labourers or migrants to urban areas in search of jobs. The growing penetration of money into rural areas, particularly the more prosperous ones, is leading to the erosion of the multi-stranded relationships between landowning patrons and clients, in favour of cash-based particular transactions. This has been compounded by the tremendous development of roads and transport which are diminishing the difference between urban and rural areas. Finally, the popularity of television and the transistor radio has reduced the isolation of villages and brought them within the ambit of the wider, encompassing society, polity and culture.

South Indian kinship practices are not only different from the North Indian but may be described as opposed to them: South Indians prefer to marry close relatives, such as the mother's brother's daughter, father's sister's daughter and, excepting in Kerala, even an elder sister's daughter. These practices are more or less common to all the castes, with the result that member of a local caste group are usually related to one another in many ways. Until World War II, the marriage network of an endogamous caste in the rural areas rarely exceeded a radius of 20 miles (32 km). It is only the rich, educated and Westernised members of the upper castes in rural areas who ventured beyond and married into a different endogamous group (but part of the same caste category). This kind of change has happened especially with the dominant peasant castes whose sub-groups were spread over a wide area and divided from each other on differences in some detail

of ritual or custom. Thanks to this process of "horizontal stretch", the marriage field has in recent decades expanded significantly for many castes.

All sections of the population have a rich religious life: daily life is marked by prayer to the domestic deities and, among the higher castes, bathing and eating are also at least partly ritual acts. The year is marked by festivals, among which the more important are the birthday of Krishna, the festival of the elephant-headed Ganesha, Navaratri (nine nights), Dussera, the Deepavali (festival of lights), Sankranti (harvest festival), Shivaratri (worship of Shiva) and finally, the new

Traditional educational institutions like the Muslim *madrasa* (left) and the Hindu *math* (right) co-exist with modern secular schools.

year. Karnataka and Andhra Pradesh follow the lunar calendar, while Tamil Nadu and Kerala follow the solar. The solar new year falls usually a month after the lunar new year. The harvest festival of Kerala, Onam, precedes the harvest festivals of other regions by over 3 months: Onam has now assumed the character of a "national" festival of Kerala, marked by magnificent boat races.

Hindu astrology is mixed up with Hindu religious beliefs, but is popular with all the other religious groups as well. There is a minority of Western-educated rationalists who denounce astrology and many of the other beliefs and practices of the Hindus, but are not themselves above consulting an as-

what is even more important, a cushion against failure.

Religious minorities are represented in strength in South India with the Muslims at the top (16,627,025) followed by the Christians (10,288,654) and Jains (356,596). Traditionally, the minorities lived like distinct castes. One of the positive features of a caste society is its capacity to accommodate diverse groups within the local community.

In each linguistic area, Muslims were divided into distinct groups, though marriage and commensality cut across these barriers. By and large, Muslims did not have a close nexus with land except perhaps in areas of the former rulers like the old

trologer during a crisis!

The Hindu-Buddhist ideas of *samsara* (rebirth), *karma* (fruit of action), *dharma* (moral and religious order) and *moksha* (salvation – differently conceived in different sects) are popular and do continue to influence behaviour; but in post-Independence India the sudden access of large numbers to education and employment, and the increase in purchasing power, has resulted in a sharp rise in consumerism and materialist values. The urge of mobility, personal, familial and caste, drives people in all directions. Religion, astrology and godmen all provide invaluable support for mobility and,

Hyderabad state and Mysore. The bulk of the Muslims were traders and artisans while the educated members entered the professions, the bureaucracy and the army, police and forestry service, at different levels.

But with the progress of the freedom struggle, a large number of Muslims gradually saw that their interests were different from those of the Hindus. In independent India they are an articulate minority, determined to assert their right to have access to

Above, **Kerala church wedding: some Hindu practices have been assimilated into Syrian Christian rituals.**

education and government jobs, on the one hand, and to lead their own cultural and religious life, on the other. In cities like Bangalore, Madras and Hyderabad, many of them have become wealthy through trade and commerce.

Most of those who converted to Christianity hailed from the lower castes, except on the west coast of India where many converts have been high-caste, almost from the first century after Christ. They are again divided by language, sect and caste, and caste differences have proved particularly resistant among them. In fact, in many South Indian churches different castes occupy distinct pews. Marriages usually occur within the caste, except among the educated and Westernized. While conversion to Christianity has improved the living conditions of the converts and provided them with access to education, health and employment, it has failed to dissolve the stigma of untouchability. In fact, there is now a move among converts from untouchables to demand that they be treated as on par with Hindu and Sikh Scheduled Castes so that they may get the benefits of job reservation.

Mention must also be made of the Syrian Christians of Kerala who are divided into several sects, and have their own churches in Kerala. Syrian Christians claim to have been converted to Christianity by the Apostle St. Thomas during his visit to India in the 1st century AD. They are an integral part of Kerala society like the patrilineal Nambudri Brahmins and the matrilineal Nayars and Izhavans. Many Syrian Christians retain a tradition of being descended from Brahmins (like some converts to Catholicism during Portuguese rule on the west coast). Syrian Christians constitute a powerful minority in Kerala, and educated members of the community are prominent in the professions and government service all over India. The community has contributed nurses to hospitals everywhere in India and outside.

The Jains may not be a numerically significant minority but they are culturally important. Jain kings ruled parts of Karnataka till the 12th century AD and Jain writers were pioneers in Kannada literature. The Jains are also known by the great statue they erected for one of their *tirthankaras* (great sages), Bahubali, on top of a hill in Sravanabelagola in Hassan district of Karnataka. At Karkala, in south Kanara district, huge stone statues continue to be carved for export to different parts of the country.

Traditionally, it was not uncommon for the members of one religion to worship the deities and sacred objects of another faith. Thus, Hindus visit the graves of Muslim *pirs* or saints particularly at their *urs* (festival). Hindus also visit, for instance, the Church of Mother Mary at Velanganni ("Our Lady of Velanganni") in Tamil Nadu, and many converts to Christianity continue to worship Hindu gods. Perhaps Hindus are more prone to syncretism than the others but the latter are not totally free from it. Thus the modern Hindu godman, Sri Satya Saibaba, has devotees from all religions and from every part of the country.

Food: No account of the culture of South India should miss the richness, variety and sophistication of the cuisine in different parts of the region.

Rice is grown in the irrigated areas of South India, and also in the heavy rainfall areas on the west coast (but without irrigation). Millets such as *ragi* (*Eleusine coracona*) and *jowar* (sorghum) are grown in the dry areas and form the staple diet of the poor, along with a gruel made of rice, *ragi* or *jowar*. Rice is the staple of the landed classes. In Kerala parboiled rice is used by all though the very poor often eke it out with cooked tapioca floor. Along the west coast, the various products of the banana, coconut and jackfruit (*Artocarpus integrifolia*) are used in a variety of ways in cooking. For non-vegetarian groups, fish and other marine products are an indispensable part of diet.

The bulk of the population of South India, with the exception of Brahmins, is non-vegetarian, though the upper Hindu castes generally keep away from beef and pork. But even those who eat non-vegetarian food do so once a week or fortnight and only certain better-off groups in urban areas are able to afford meat daily.

However, food habits are beginning to change, particularly in the urban areas. Modern bakeries are popular, even among the poor. The preparation of pickles, *papads* and snacks is rapidly becoming a non-domestic activity employing wage labour. Tea and coffee shops serving beverages and snacks are popular in South India, and are rapidly spreading to the villages.

South Indians are by and large rice eaters, but the familiar image of a mound of rice and a couple of pungent curries to go with it is all wrong. The crisp *dosai* and the white fluffy *idli* are known all over the world and relished by many a discerning gourmet. It is not as if the four South Indian states serve the same type of food; each region has its ethnic variations, though a common bond is apparent.

Rice is common to all four, with a distinct preference for what is called raw rice in most regions, except in Kerala where parboiled rice is generally preferred. The Tamils and the Kannadigas of Karnataka prefer to have their rice with *sambhar*, made of *dal* (lentils) and vegetables, with plenty of tamarind for taste, *rasam*, a thin, peppery soup, assorted vegetables called *kootus* followed by a generous helping of curds (yoghurt) to be mixed with rice as the last course. This is usually the menu for both lunch and dinner. The meal is traditionally served on fresh banana leaves which are thrown away afterwards — a hygienically sound custom. The Telugus, the inhabitants of Andhra Pradesh, prefer more chillies with their curries, and as a first course they mix a powder made of ground lentils and chillies with rice, adding a generous helping of *ghee* (clarified butter). An unwary visitor who tries the savoury Andhra dishes might find his eyes watering for the rest of the evening. The Keralite rice meal includes, in addition to *sambhar*, many bland curries, such as *olan* (a thin gravy made of pumpkin and coconut) and *kalan* (made of yam with yoghurt and coconut). Among the more delectable vegetable *kootus* is a thick stew of assorted vegetables.

Bananas, both raw and ripe, are used in various types of curries and crisps in Keralite cuisine. The banana chips made in Calicut are a class apart, the wafer-thin round slices made according to recipes handed down generations. *Pappads*, big and small, made with various combinations of ground grain but without *masala* (spices), and fried in oil, are part of an authentic South Indian meal. The *pappad* is known as *pappadam* in Kerala

Preceding pages, South Indian cuisine enjoys a worldwide popularity.

and *appalam* in the other southern states. The two have distinct flavours because of their different ingredients.

Though the South Indian meal is basically curry and rice, *chapatis* and *poories* are available as tiffin. So are *dosais* (pancakes made of rice and lentils), *idlies* (steamed rice cakes), and *vadais* (fried doughnuts made of lentils), which make a good breakfast. Other items are *pongal* and *uppuma* (made of rice or semolina) and a variety of savoury snacks in various shapes and sizes, ranging from the concentric *murukkus* to *omapodis* and savoury *boondhis*. All these snacks are made of rice and gram flour, and fried in oil. *Bhajis* and *pakoras*, vegetable or onion fritters dipped in a batter of ground gram flour, are also very popular. Karnataka's *bisi bele bath* (rice seasoned with lentils, tamarind and spices) is a delicacy worth trying.

It is certainly not vegetables all the way in South India. The majority of South Indians are non-vegetarians and they cook meat, chicken and fish in a variety of ways. Although the basic combination of spices is the same, there are sharp ethnic variations which provide their regional flavour. Chillies dominate Andhra food while coconuts are essential in Keralite cuisine.

Hyderabad, the capital city of Andhra Pradesh, boasts a Muslim cuisine of its own, somewhat similar to the Mughlai dishes of North India. The Deccani or Hyderabadi biryani or pilauf, long-grained Basmati rice cooked with meat or chicken *masala* in its own stock, is a delight for any gourmet. So are the *kababs*, of barbecued meat, hot and succulent from the glowing charcoal burners at Char Minar, the centre of old Hyderabad. *Kababs* are of course served at most non-vegetarian restaurants.

The Tamils have their Chettinad style of cooking to offer, in which a variety of meat and fish dishes are cooked with chillies and ground coriander. Madras city has now rediscovered Chettinad cuisine, and a number of five-star hotels have Chettinad restaurants rigged out in authentic decor. There are also independent Chettinad restaurants which provide delicious fare. The Tamils make tasty, though pungent, curries with tender shark. The *sora puttu*, shark meat scrambled with masala, is a great delicacy. The smaller non-vegetarian restaurants that abound in Madras city go by the name of – hold your breath! – "military restaurants". An age-old distinction in Tamil Nadu cities is the one between non-vegetarian and "civil" food which is vegetarian. Madras city also has a number of Udupi restaurants which cater good vegetarian food cooked by experts from Udupi, way down in South Kanara.

In Kerala, non-vegetarian food is prepared in a *masala* in which coconut predominates. Sea food is aplenty in this small state with its long coastline. The typical meal of the Keralite consists of rice and fish curry. Fish is cooked in a variety of ways — fish *moillee*, fish curry, *meen varattiyathu* (fish in a thick *masala* sauce), *masala* fried fish, *meen mulagittathu* (fish in a thin sauce made of chillies and tamarind or raw mangoes) and *meen vattichathu* (fish in a thick coconut gravy with tamarind and a little chilli), to mention just a few.

The Christians of Central Travancore cook the delicious *meen pollichathu* (a special kind of baked fish curry). A local variety of tamarind called *kodampuli* or *meenpuli* has medical qualities and is popular in central Travancore. It gives the "Christian" style of fish-based dishes a unique taste. The duck preparations of central Travancore and the pork curry of Trichur are a delectable experience. The poor man's food of tapioca and fish, boiled together with tumeric and chillies, is both filling and nourishing. Steamed rice cakes, called *puttu*, is a popular breakfast item, eaten with boiled gram in *masala* or with fish. Muslims, especially in the northern Malabar area, cook a variety of delicious dishes. The Malabar Muslims or Moplahs make rice *chapatis* called *pathiri* and a number of special chicken and meat dishes. Stuffed chicken, stuffed fish, *meen pathiri* (a kind of steamed rice pie filled with fish *masala*) and water mussels stuffed in their shells, steamed and later fried, are a few of the items worth mentioning. Many of these may not be available in the restaurants attached to the better hotels in Kerala but they are available in smaller eating houses in Calicut, Tellicherry and Cannanore.

Two South Indian dishes, the *appam* (called *vellappam* in Kerala) and the *idiappam* merit special mention. They are available in Tamil Nadu and Kerala. *Appam* is made of ground rice and coconut with no oil base in the cooking. It is eaten with coconut milk or with any vegetarian or non-vegetarian curry. The steamed *idiappam* is made of rice flour and looks like vermicelli. It can also be accompanied with either vegetables or meat. The *appam* has an anglicised name in Sri Lanka where it is also called "hoppers"; *idiappam* is referred to as "string hoppers".

The South has a plethora of chutneys and pickles with local variations. Andhra boasts a large variety of pickles, mainly based on the mango. They are generally preserved in oil and are extremely sharp in flavour. The Andhra *avakka* pickle and *gongura* chutney are most appetising, but they cannot be recommended for those not used to chillies. The Tamilian and Kannadiga pickles are a little milder, even though they may seem sharp to Western palates. The Keralite *kadumanga* pickle, tender mangoes mixed with powdered chillies and mustard and preserved in brine, is tasty and mild.

The common sweet after a meal, particularly on special occasions, is the *payasam*, a liquid milk-based pudding with either rice or vermicelli, and a little aromatic spice for flavour. This is common to all the four states, though there are ethnic variations. Kerala has its *ada prathaman* which is also milk based, and the *chakka prathaman* made of ripe jackfruit and *gur* (jaggery). Boiled ripe banana or candied banana chips go with the meal. A Tamil specialty is the *chakkara pongal* made of rice, *gur* and spices. There is also the *athirasam*, made of rice flour and *gur*, and deep fried like a *poori*; this is common in some parts of Tamil Nadu. Karnataka has quite a number of desserts which would appeal to anyone's sweet tooth. Its *polis*, pancakes made of flour and rolled with different types of sweet fillings, are well known. So is the *Mysore pak*, a cube-shaped cake made of ground gram, sugar and *ghee*. Apart from these Southern specialties, the sweets commonly seen all over India are also eaten and relished in the South: the spherical *laddu*, made of gram flour and sugar; the *jilebi* and *jangri*, made of fermented flour or lentils, deep fried in circular patterns and soaked in sugar syrup; *gulab jamuns* made of dried milk and drenched in syrup; and a variety of *halwas*.

Several factors have influenced the development of South Indian architecture. Among them are the hot tropical climate, the dramatic monsoon rains, the availability of good tropical wood and a wide variety of stone for building, and frequent contact with foreign influences. All these combined to shape several different styles of architecture, sculpture and painting. Each style was linked with the other by the course of political and economic development and the movement of ideas and philosophies over the land and its people.

The study of architecture in South India is often restricted to religious architecture, which was built in materials such as stone and brick. Secular buildings in this region, being constructed from perishable materials such as bamboo, wood and mud, often escape historical mention. Yet it was from these structures that religious architecture drew inspiration and ideas.

Buddhist Architecture: As Buddhism travelled southward to Andhra Pradesh, Tamil Nadu, Karnataka and on to Sri Lanka, several religious structures were erected on the way. At Amravati and Nagarjunakonda in Andhra Pradesh, large *stupas* (burial mounds) were constructed around the 2nd century BC. Solid rubble hemispherical structures with a huge stone railing, ornamental carved gateways and pillars. These celebrated monuments are unfortunately in ruins. The few remaining sculptures from these locations are now housed in the Government Museum in Madras, the Site Museum at Amravati and the Island Museum at Nagarjunakonda.

The Amravati stupa, though similar in design to those constructed in Central and North India, seems to have evolved unique features which in turn influenced later trends in the region. Its limestone sculptured panels are good examples of the superior craftsmanship of the region during the early years of the Christian era. Human figures carved within the panel are crowded together, each shown in movement and exhibiting a variety of perspectives, costumes and headgear. A mood of joy and exuberance pervades these sculptures.

Similarly, the image of Buddha in Amravati is unique in style and form. The figures of Buddha found in the northwestern provinces of Gandhara have distinctive Greco-Roman features with sharp aquiline noses, thick wavy curls, moustaches and bushy eyebrows. In Amravati, the Buddha's figure is delicately proportioned, slim and youthful, and the oval shape face is smooth with half-closed meditative eyes and almost no eyebrows. These figures are among India's finest early Buddhist sculpture and their diminutive scale does not hint at the gigantic figures of Buddha that are to be found in later sculptures at Sri Lanka, Nepal, Burma, Thailand, China and Japan.

Jain Architecture: Jainism, like Buddhism, also travelled to the southern states leaving its architectural heritage in Orissa, Andhra Pradesh, Karnataka and Tamil Nadu. The prosperity of the mercantile Jain community and several rulers provided sustained patronage for artistic achievements for more than 2,000 years in this area. In Sittannavasal, near Pudukottai in Tamil Nadu are rock-cut Jain temples excavated from the hillside which date to the 8th century AD. These caves contain mural paintings similar in style to those at Ajanta in the Aurangabad district of Maharashtra.

In Karnataka, the Jain temple designs draw their inspiration from secular wooden architecture, with its sloping tile roofs and pillars, as in the case of the Mudabidri Jain temple in Udupi (AD 1000). Other Jain temples followed the plan of Hindu religious architecture with pillared halls or *mandapas,* flat roofs and pyramidal towers.

Shravanabelagola has a colossal monolithic image of Gomatesvara, the largest freestanding statue in India. This site was established around the 9th century AD and remains to this day an important one for the Jain community.

Hindu temple architecture: Village temples and shrines marking spots sacred to the

Hindus scatter the length and breadth of South India. Famous temples have grown around such sanctified locations such as Chidambaram, where Lord Shiva challenged his consort Parvati to a dance competition, and Madurai, where Shiva as Sundaresvaran married Meenakshi ('the goddess with fish-shaped eyes').

The reign of the Pallava kings (6th-9th century AD) ushered in an age of experimentation in art in South India. At Mahabalipuram, the Pallava sea port, about 22 miles (35 km) from present-day Madras, huge granite boulders and parts of the hillside were carved into temples with rooms, pillars and sculptured walls. It is here that one can study the

festivals. The chariots were made of wood with huge wheels, and were drawn by animals or by the devotees themselves. Many temples in India, therefore, have a border of elephants and horses near the base.

The architect-artist's next problem was designing the roof for the stone temple. At Mahabalipuram the Draupadi Ratha has a village hut roof, but the Arjuna Ratha has a roof carved in two distinct horizontal levels with miniature hut roof designs along the edge and topped by a many-sided cupola called the *shikhara*. The Dharmaraja Ratha has a roof of three levels with tiny roof motifs, while the Bhima Ratha also has a roof designed on the thatch principle, its sides

experimental designs for temple architecture. The *pancha rathas* (five chariots) at Mahabalipuram are five rock-cut temples, each one carved out of the living rock. The Draupadi Ratha is a simple temple consisting of a square room for the deity (the *garbha griha* or sanctum) and a roof fashioned out of the stone to resemble an ordinary village hut, a copy of wood and thatch construction. It rests on a platform supported by tiny carved elephants.

The concept of the temple as a chariot of the gods is derived from an ancient practice, still prevalent, of carrying the idol in procession through the streets of the city during

forming a curved gable-like arch over a rectangular room. This design was later used as the roof design for gateways or *gopurams* to the temples. This experiment seems to have pleased the South Indian artists; it became the accepted form of the Dravida temples, and was codified in the *Shastras* or canons.

Each temple was built on mathematical formulas of exacting precision. The square or rectangular sanctum containing the deity was the dark centre of the temple. Above it rose a roof made up of many receding horizontal levels, with miniature roof designs, ascending in a pyramidal shape to be an octagonal *shikhara* that would carry the *kalasa* (or sacred water-pot of plenty) and the emblem of the god enshrined within the temple.

While northern and eastern Indian temples evolved a curvilinear or conical *shikhara*, the South Indian temple roof is predominantly pyramidal. This ingenious temple design was used to construct the shore temple at Mahabalipuram, and the magnificent Kailashnath temple in the Pallava capital of Kanchipuram. The roof in the latter is larger and higher, and the *vimana* (outer walls) are decorated with elegant sculptured panels. As rituals and religious functions developed, there was need for more space in front of the sanctum, for the

assembly of devotees. *Mandapas* were erected beside the temple for special functions – the Kalyana Mandapa or marriage hall, Natya Mandapa or hall for recitals of devotional music and dance.

The Kailashnath temple at Kanchipuram is an important landmark in South Indian architecture, for it perfects the proportions of the building plan. Its massive pyramidal *shikhara* suggests Mount Kailash in the

Left, 16th century fresco from the Veerabhadra temple in Lepakshi. **Above**, painting from Brihadeswar temple, Visakhapatnam.

Himalayas where Lord Shiva is said to reside. The *vimana* walls are adorned with Pallava stone sculptures of gods and goddesses, each set in their appropriate cardinal positions. Pallava figures are rendered with great elegance – long, slim limbs, narrow waists and minimal jewellery. Shiva, to whom the temple is dedicated, is depicted in many manifestations – as Nataraj, the Lord of Dance, accompanied by musicians; as Dakshinamurti, the Sage of Learning, teaching his devotees, both human and animal, with his beautiful consort Durga, and as Gangadhara, who bore the might of the descending Ganges on his head, subduing the powerful river as she meandered through his matted locks to fall gently to earth.

Although the Chalukyan kings threatened Pallava power in several battles from their centres at Badami, Aihole and Pattadakal, the supremacy of Pallava art was never in doubt. The Kailashnath temple provided the inspiration for the Virupaksha temple, built in the 8th century in Pattadakal, Karnataka. The Chalukyan empire, because of its central geographical location in peninsular India, served as the meeting place for several formative styles of architecture. The major Chalukyan sites seem almost workshops or laboratories for experiments in temple architecture. On the magnificent cliffs of Badami, early rock-cut caves have been carved out with sculptured pillars, ceilings and walls similar to those at Ajanta and Ellora in Maharashtra. At Pattadakal, one can see within a comparatively small area, temples with plans and roofs that were later to be adopted in eastern and central India, along with temples in conformity with the Dravida or South Indian styles.

The quality of stone sculpture from these temples is also outstanding. There are carved narrative and decorative panels on pillars, walls and ceilings, figures of deities in their various manifestations and episodes from the *Ramayana*, bracket figures and architectural mouldings with floral motifs. Research in this area has suggested that artisan guilds worked together, the master craftsman providing the plan, while artisans cut and shaped each rock to be assembled at the temple site. The master craftsmen lent an overall perspective, maintaining unity of style in all parts of the building and the sculptures.

With the break-up of the Chalukyan empire, ideas from Badami, Aihole and Pattadakal spread to different area. The Rastrakutas took the design of the Kailashnath temple to Ellora in Maharashtra for their magnificent sculptured rock-cut Kailash temple. It was in this way that ideas spread across the length and breadth of India, suggesting an underlying unity amidst regional diversity in temple architecture.

Back in South India in the 9th and 10th centuries, the Chola dynasty was gaining a foothold. The wealth amassed from agricultural prosperity and trade with the Far East stimulated patronage of the arts. The Chola capital in Tanjore (Thanjavur) was the

In 1930 a series of paintings were uncovered along the internal circumbulatory passage of the Tanjore temple. The murals of Shiva and of the Chola patrons are exquisite, similar to the ones found at Kanchipuram in the Kailashnath temple. The colours, subdued by age, are muted earth mineral hues of rust, red, ochre and white. The Brihadesvara temple has a large collection of metal images gifted by various patrons. Bronze sculptured masterpieces of the Chola period are known for their superb quality and the mastery of the technique of casting. The best collections can be seen at the Tanjore Art Gallery, the Madras State Museum and some at the National Museum, New Delhi.

centre of activity. The great Brihadesvara temple took 15 years to build and was consecrated around 1009-10 AD. It follows the standard Indian temple plan with a *garbha griha* and a *mandapas*, set within a walled enclosure. The tower of the Brihadesvara is 210 ft (63 m) high, the largest and tallest in India, a big step upward from its humble origins at Mahabalipuram. The many-sided *shikhara* hewn out of a single granite block 77 ft (25.5 m) square is said to weigh 80 tonnes. It is said that a huge wooden ramp was built several miles long to roll the *shikhara* up to its position 200 ft (61 m) above the ground.

These bronzes were first modelled in wax with all details and the image was then coated in mud paste. When the mud mould dried, it was heated, and the melting wax was allowed to escape through a hole at the base. Into the hollow mud mould a hot molten mixture of five metals was poured in. When it cooled, the mould was broken and the bronze image was given some final touches and polished. This technique of cire-perdue or lost-wax process is still practised in Tanjore today in the city workshops.

Metal images were installed in minor shrines in temples, and since they were movable, they represented in main temple deity in processions on festival occasions. The bronze images were clad in silk, decked with sandal paste and floral garlands, and ceremonially taken out in procession in temple chariots or *rathas* for devotees to receive *darshan*.

A sculptured figure was conceived according to a set of basic principles set down in the Shastras. The form is divided into 9 to 13 parts, the stone block into 16 squares, with *apsaras* or divine sky nymphs in the corners, consorts beside the figure, and the *vahana* (animal mount) of the deity below, along with devotees. The figure was identified by iconographic details of form, composition, hand gestures, weapons, *vahanas*,

earth from the floods, Rama, the hero of the epic poem *Ramayana*, and Krishna, the child god, the cowherd and divine lover.

Shiva holds a trident, with a leaping deer in one hand; he is called Pashupati, the Lord of Creation and Protector of the animal world. Female deities, referred to as Devis, such as Durga, Kali or Parvati, the female principal of Shiva, are equally powerful. Each deity also has an animal symbol that manifests their qualitative aspects. Shiva, the upholder of Dharma, rides the bull Nandi, Vishnu the Garuda or regal bird of virtue, while Durga, the mighty destroyer of evil, rides on a tiger.

The Chola artists seemed to have taken these guidelines and interpreted them to their

costumes and others. In the vast Hindu pantheon, Brahma the Creator is represented as a sage with long flowing beard and five heads that enable him to observe the universe. Vishnu holds a conch signifying the sound of creation in one hand and the wheel of time in the other, for he is both Creator and Preserver. Vishnu has 10 incarnations that saved the world from destruction – the most popular being Varaha, the boar that saved the

Left, pillared hall, Simhachalam temple, Visa-khapatnam. **Above**, carved bracket, Meenakshi temple, Madurai.

advantage, elongating the figures to achieve longer limbs, slim waists and slender oval faces. Chola bronzes are recognisable by iconographic details and the sheer elegance of their presence.

The dancing Shiva or Nataraja carries in one hand a drum beating the rhythm of life, in the other a small flame symbolising destruction, which is a part of creation. His third hand is raised in the gesture of protection from ignorance and darkness, which is personified as a dwarf demon being trampled by him underfoot. The cosmic dance of Shiva is framed by a circle of flames, for in Hindu philosophy the metaphor is of wisdom and light dispelling darkness and ignorance.

Interestingly, the Tanjore Brihadesvara temple has many copper plates that record temple management, finance and donations. The temple in South India grew from its humble origins as the home of village deities into the centre of village or city life. The temple acquired produce from the land, cattle and donations for upkeep of the building, payment to Brahmins, and oil to feed the lamps. It was also the cultural centre for music, dance, literature, sculpture and painting. As in centres like Kanchipuram, to this day, the Brahmins associated with the temple ran *gurukuls* or schools where young

ways or *gopurams* were erected at cardinal points on these boundary walls that could lead the pilgrim's eye to the heart of the city. The temple cities of Chidambaram, Madurai, Srivilliputtur, Srirangam and many others grew with additions made by several ruling dynasties and patrons. The *gopurams* rose high into the sky, often more than 100 ft, towering edifices of stucco figures and sculptured embellishments, painted today in gaudy enamel colours, while the main *shikhara* of the temple diminished in size, often lost in the haphazard maze of additional buildings of the temple complex.

Today, as you wander through the city streets of Madurai, you will see rows of

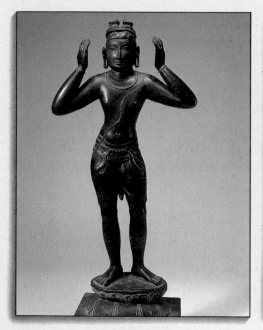

students were taught the holy scriptures, and where ancient manuscripts were copied and preserved. Around the temple grew markets where pilgrims from neighbouring villages could come not only to pray, but to collect supplies and sell their wares. The whole town came to be enclosed within the many consecutive walls of the temple, each one added to accommodate the expansion and growth of the town.

During the later Vijayanagara, Pandya and Nayaka periods (13th-17th century) temple expansion continued with the addition of *mandapas*, tanks for bathing, and walls to encompass the township. Several tall gate-

shops and florists near the main temple, residential houses for Brahmins, metalware shops, all in distinct areas, each marked by locations prescribed by caste rules laid down in the texts for town planning and temple architecture.

In Karnataka, the Hoysalas came into power around present-day Mysore and Hassan after the fall of the Chalukyas in the early 11th century. In the Hoysala temples the square *garbha griha* prescribed in the *Shilpashastra* has been rotated to form a star shape, and instead of a single sanctum two or three cellas have been added to form a complex star-shaped plan, which is carried through from the platform to the *shikhara*.

The temples of Belur, Halebid and Somnathpur are built on raised star-shaped platforms. The wall surface of the *vimana* in these temples is broken into horizontal bands of sculptural motifs, the lowest band consisting of elephants, horses and foliage, and above, at eye-level, narrative panels with depictions of the *Ramayana* and *Mahabharata* and stories of Krishna. Further above are rows of *yalis* (mythological creatures) and *hamsas* (legendary birds), surmounted by larger vertical panels of gods and goddesses in various poses. At Belur the overhanging eave of the temple roof is supported by single stone brackets superbly

In Kerala, the Dravida stone temple design coexisted with local forms of wood and tile construction. The temple plan was often circular instead of square or rectangular, and the walls were adorned with sculptured wooden pillars and brackets and with murals. The circular *garbha griha* was given a tiled conical roof, often extended to a two-tiered *shikhara*, forming a pagoda-like structure. The whole temple was enclosed in a courtyard with an elaborate gateway. In Kerala the earliest mural is dated to the 16th century to a temple at Ettumanoor in Kottayam district. Later murals are in Padmanabhapuram Palace, now in Tamil Nadu, and the Mattancheri Palace in Co-

carved with frames and lace-like foliage. These figures are all in movement and sport an abundance of heavy jewellery. The stone used in these temples differed from the hard granite of the Pallava temples and the sandstone of Badami and Aihole. Here a heavy textured black chlorite schist was used which could be carved in intricate detail and set free from the stone bases.

Chola bronzes: Bharata carrying Lord Rama's sandals on his head (far left) and Nataraja, Lord Shiva in the cosmic dance of creation (left). Above, detail from the descent of the Ganja, Mahabalipuram.

chin, Kerala.

In the Central Deccan region, around the Krishna river, the Vijayanagara empire was established with its capital at Hampi (now in Karnataka). Here lies an important example of a Hindu pre-modern capital city, and excavations are still in progress to reveal the buildings, temples and city plan. Hampi is set amidst lush river and plains, hills and huge granite boulders that provided natural protection as well as building material. Between the 13th and 14th century the Krishna, Virupaksha, Venkatesvara and the Hazara Rama temples were built. In front of the Hazara Rama temple is a remarkable small temple chariot complete with realistic turning stone wheels.

All Hindu architecture was based on the engineering principle of beams and pillars. Where stone was used, the space between pillars could not be very wide for fear that the stone roof beam would collapse. Hence, temple doors are narrow and halls or *mandapas* are crowded with pillars supporting the stone beam above. Nomenclature for *mandapas* refers to this phenomenon in such terms as "hall of 500 pillars", or "1,000-pillared hall". The pillar design changed with each dynasty in a manner similar to the "orders" of Greek and Roman columns. The Pallava royal emblem, the lion, is to be seen

architectural and engineering principle that transformed the history of building in India: the use of the arch in building, instead of pillars and narrow beams, and the construction of domes instead of diminishing *shikhara* tiers. There is archaeological evidence of trading contact with Greece and Rome in Arikamedu in Pondicherry, and Indians were familiar with Roman sculpture, pottery and coins. However, the principle of the arch was introduced to India only in the 11th century when the slave kings built the first mosque in India with wide arches at the Qutb complex in Delhi. Under an official of the Tughlaqs, the Bahmanis in the South established an independent kingdom, build-

at the base of many Pallava pillars, while the Vijayanagara and Nayak dynasties of later centuries employed the motif of the rampant horse and rider in their pillared halls at the Madurai and Vellore temples.

The Hoysala temple pillars within the *mandapa* are monoliths, fashioned with circular mouldings, presumed to have been produced on a lathe. How the huge stone pillars were rotated or abrasives applied to erode the stone is still not fully understood.

Islamic architecture*:* While the temples of South India were being built, a fresh influence entered northern India in the 9th, 10th and 11th centuries. With Islam came a new

ing forts and palaces at Gulbarga and Bidar in Karnataka in 1425 with several elements derived from their Islamic heritage. Under the Qutb Shahi dynasty, a huge fortress was built on the rocky hills of Golconda in 1512 and tombs with bulbous domes were constructed in many places. Bijapur became a stronghold of the Deccani Sultanate and here Islamic monuments were erected, such as the Juma Masjid and the Gol Gumbaz, the

Above, Krishna temple, Cochin. The fashioning of round copper roofs, unique to Kerala temples, is a lost art.

tomb of Sultan Mohammed Adil Shah who died in 1657.

The plan of a mosque consists of a large open courtyard, where the congregation assembled for prayer. The *Mihrab* or facade demarcating the direction of Mecca is framed with arches, calligraphic designs and often a dome. A minar or tower was placed on one, two or four sides of the courtyard, and was used by the priest to call the faithful to prayer five times a day.

The Indian artisans soon adapted to the new architectural challenges. The use of the arch enabled the architect to span wide areas without the obstruction of a "hundred pillars". Expansive doorways and windows offered an airy lightness to the building. The rooms thus created were bridged by squinches to convert square rooms into circular bases for the huge domes which were constructed. The Gol Gumbaz in Bijapur in Karnataka is the largest single-chambered building in India, with a dome measuring 144 ft in diameter. In decoration, too, where Hindu temples are peopled with figures of gods and goddesses, Islamic buildings are embellished with stone screens or *jalis*, verses of the Quran in calligraphy, geometric designs in inlaid stone work, and stucco and plaster painted decorations.

European Architecture: While many of the Deccani kingdoms were brought under Mughal rule, the 17th and 18th centuries saw the building of the first European structures on Indian soil. It must be remembered that Greeks, Romans and Arabs were well established on the west coast by the 2nd century AD, and Christian and Jewish settlers had made their home in Kerala, building modest churches and synagogues for their use.

Vasco da Gama landed on the site of the Roman settlement at Calicut in Kerala in 1498. By the mid-16th century there were three settlements of the Portuguese at Daman, Diu and Bassein. The first English factory was established at Surat in Gujarat in 1613. In 1639 a new station was established in Madras, and work began the following year towards building a new fort called Fort St George and factory and the "white" or Christian town with residential areas. St Mary's church at Fort St George was consecrated in 1680 and is the oldest Anglican Church in the East. The church is simple in plan, but contains an interesting record of the early East India Company in the gravestones of the cemetery. Other secular buildings of this period are the old Secretariat in Madras, the old Banqueting Hall, now Rajaji Hall, and the former Ice Factory on Marina Beach. These buildings are characterized by their classical style making full use of Indian masons, local *chunam* (whitewash) and building materials.

From the territory of Hyder Ali and Tippu Sultan of Mysore came the greatest resistance to British expansionist policies. The fort of Srirangapatnam, where Tippu Sultan fought his last battle and died in 1799, and the Summer Palace are a curious mixture of Islamic, Hindu and European ideals.

Apart from official and religious buildings, by the 1800s European residential houses too acquired a distinct style. The English "bungalow" originated in Bengal from the term *bangla* or "big house in the village" with a long rectangular plan and open verandahs suitable for the hot summer, set in gardens with organised flower beds. The homesick Englishman and family sent for many things from England to decorate their Indian homes, including seeds for roses, dandelions, honeysuckles, oak, fir, pear and chestnut. Bangalore with its soothing climate and the southern hill stations of Ooty (Ootacamund), Coonoor and Kodaikanal offered the British a "home away from home". Little cottages with English gardens called "Spring Haven", "Swiss Cottage", "Gorse House" and "Three Elms" were built as summer retreats and residential houses. In Ooty St Stephen's Church was consecrated in 1830, the building timber for the church being obtained from Tippu's Lal Bagh palace at Srirangapatnam. Residential houses in Bangalore were characterised by wooden trellis-work canopies or "monkey tops", tiled gabled roofs and wide-roofed porches.

Soon after 1857, the attitude of the British in India changed drastically, and all concentration was directed away from the South to building the cities of Calcutta, Bombay and finally the new capital city of Delhi.

Today, in any South Indian village or town, you will see how the past coexists with the present, the ancient with the new, buildings of different religions beside one other: a saga of history, continuity and change, affirming the contribution of the South Indian artists to the mosaic of Indian culture.

South India offers a variety of performing arts for the visitor to savour. It has a great tradition of classical music and dance and is home to a rich folk tradition as well.

The classical music of South India is known as Carnatic music, sometimes written as Karnataka music, which may give the wrong impression that it is the music of Karnataka. Carnatic music has grown from the same roots as the classical music of the North, known as Hindustani music, but has developed on distinctly different lines over the last several centuries.

Both systems are based on the same general concepts of *raga* and *tala* and both are melodic in character. Broadly, a *raga* is a melodic scheme with a definite scale or notes and an order of sequence of these notes. There are certain typical phrases which give each *raga* its distinct flavour. *Tala* means rhythm, but in the Indian context its essential feature is its cyclic or repetitive nature. In other words, a set of rhythmic units are juxtaposed in a cycle which repeats itself. In Indian classical music generally, and in Carnatic music particularly, rhythm has acquired a high degree of sophistication.

The feature that distinguishes Carnatic classical music is the importance it accords to the song as a vehicle for the elaboration of a *raga*. A song may be prefaced, as it often is, by a free rendering of the melody, but it is the composition – a combination of *sahitya* or lyrics, melody and rhythm – which provides the definitive framework.

This feature has found its finest exposition in the compositions of the three great composers – Syama Sastry, Tyagaraja and Muthuswamy Dikshitar – described as the trinity of Carnatic music, analogous to the three facets of the godhead. All three were born in Thanjavur district and were contemporaries; their lives spanned parts of the 18th and 19th centuries. Of the three, Tyagaraja was the most prolific and his compositions are the most popular.

Preceding pages, musical soiree in bright setting, Durbar Hall, Mysore palace. **Left**, classical stance in Bharata Natyam, also seen in many temple sculptures.

Many other composers, both pre- and post- "trinity", have contributed to the great song repertoire of Carnatic music, but it is the "trinity" that helped established the *kriti* – a form of composition with three parts – as the dominant element of Carnatic classical music. A Carnatic music concert typically consists of several such *kritis*, and a smaller selection of other types of composition. Incidentally, Carnatic music concert does not have a score written separately for performance on instruments. What instrumentalists do is to perform as though the music were being sung.

The typical concert ensemble consists of the main performer and a set of accompanists. The main performer could be a vocalist, or an instrumentalist playing the *veena*, the flute, the *gottuvadyam*, the *nadaswaram* or other such traditional Indian instruments, or an instrument of Western origin like the violin, the guitar, the mandolin, the saxophone or the clarinet.

Most performers, vocal and instrumental, with the exception of violin soloists, have a violinist among their accompanists. The set of accompanists also generally includes a person who strums the *tambura* or drone which signals the pitch, and a player of the two-headed drum known as *mridangam*. Usually, the rhythm section also includes musicians playing the *ghatam*, an up-ended earthen pot, the *kanjeera*, a tambourine-like percussion instrument, and occasionally the jew's harp, known locally as *morsing*.

The rhythm section usually performs only when the key musician is rendering the song; it remains silent when the musician is presenting the *raga* in its free form prior to the start of the song.

The content of a South Indian classical music recital is not determined in advance, except in the case of radio and television broadcasts. Moreover, the musicians do not rehearse in advance. In a sense, therefore, the performers create music on the spot, making use of the scope for improvisation which exists within the formal structure of each composition.

The improvisational element is dominant during *alapana*, which is the elaboration of the *raga*'s melodic line prior to the start of the song proper; the *niraval* which consists of musical variations linked to the lyric; the *swara prastara*, which is the use of combinations of notes or solfa syllables used especially to highlight the character of the song and the *raga*; and *tala vinyasa* or the segment of the concert handed over to the rhythm section.

The atmosphere that prevails in a Carnatic music concert is often informal. Members of the audience are apt to walk in and out at any time, to converse, and to applaud and otherwise voice their reactions while the musicians are still performing. To those used to the disciplined decorum of the Western clas-

rendered in a Carnatic music concert need not present any difficulty to a listener from an alien land. A song could be in Telugu, Tamil, Kannada, Malayalam, Hindi or Sanskrit, and it is the exceptional Indian who can follow the lyrics in all these languages.

The language of the music itself is more important than the language of the lyrics. This observation is fully borne out by the pleasure experienced in listening to Carnatic songs rendered by instrumentalists alone.

A visitor to South India should not miss the opportunity of taking in a classical music concert, if only to understand that Indian classical music has another face than that presented by North Indian artists of global

sical music concert, this could be disconcerting. Enjoyment of the Carnatic concert therefore requires some adjustment on the part of a visitor from abroad. It is best to enter into the unique atmosphere and listen to the music in a relaxed manner, without any preconceived notions.

One aspect of the concert which might offend a sensitive listener is the degree of sound amplification. The volume is apt to be turned up, contributing to the discomfort of all except those who have become accustomed to the high-decibel performances of rock and similar kinds of music of the West.

The language of the lyrics of the songs

reputation, like the sitar maestro Pandit Ravi Shankar. Performances available on a given day can be ascertained from the local English-language newspapers.

Allied to classical music are programmes of light classical music, devotional music, popular music and film music. All of these are presented on the stage, as well as broadcast by radio and television.

Congregational singing devoted to the praise of the deity is an old tradition. The Sanskrit term for it is *nama sankeertanam*. Swami Haridhos Giri, a modern-day guru, leads a *nama sankeertanam* programme in Madras on the second Sunday of every month. Similar programmes are often held in several other cities.

Film music in different languages of the country fills the air everywhere. A flick of the radio switch or the television knob will bring it to the visitor. It should be possible to look up and attend live concerts as well.

Programmes of classical and other types of music are held throughout the year in Madras, Bangalore, Trivandrum and some other cities, but during certain months music pours like heavy monsoon rain. April is one such month, when the birth anniversary of Rama, the divine hero of the *Ramayana*, is celebrated with several parallel festivals of music in Madras, Bangalore, Hyderabad and

excitement. Music lovers from other parts of India as well as from abroad throng the events, which include morning sessions devoted to lecture-demonstrations. Inaugural evenings at the major centres resemble first nights at the opera in the cities of the West, attracting the social elite dressed in their finery.

There is more variety in the dances performed in the South. Bharata Natyam, an efflorescent art form of Tamil culture, predominates, but other forms have in recent decades achieved classical status and a degree of popularity: Kuchipudi, Kathakali and Mohini Attam.

Bharata Natyam can be traced to ancient

Coimbatore especially. After the summer lull, the music season picks up again in August in Madras and October in Bangalore and Trivandrum. But it is doubtful if there is anything quite like the Madras December festival season. Within a span of 2½ weeks, more than 400 music concerts are offered in the city, not to mention dance performances. There are several concerts a day at several places and the atmosphere is charged with

Left, dancer and accompanists: fresco from Tippu's palace, Srirangapatnam. **Above**, part and parcel of the classical dances – intricate finger movements.

times. In its present form, it largely follows a format developed by four brothers, masters of the arts of music and dance, known collectively as the Thanjavur quartet. Like the music trinity, they were natives of the Thanjavur district in the delta of the river Kaveri which offered a fertile soil for a bountiful crop of artists.

Until the early 1930s, this dance form was known as Sadir or Dasiattam and was virtually the preserve of a caste or community of musicians and dancers in the service of temples. The men were musicians or dance masters. The women, or the chosen among them, known as *devadasis*, were dedicated to the temple; they performed ritual dances and fulfilled other obligatory tasks connected with worship. They were called upon, too, to present dance recitals for the enjoyment of the king and the nobility.

Today, the dance is no longer an intrinsic part of temple ritual. It has become a secular art, presented on the stage for the benefit of spectators, performed by anyone who chooses to learn it. The whole world has become the stage for Bharata Natyam; it is performed virtually in all the inhabited continents. If the Indian diaspora has taken South Indian artists from their native habitat to distant parts of the world where they now live and flaunt their artistic achievements,

above all, *bhakti* or devotion to god. In a speech, she once said:

"The *sringara* we experience in Bharata Natyam is never carnal – never, never. For those who have yielded themselves to its discipline with total dedication, dance like music is the practice of the Presence; it cannot merely be the body's rapture...

"Bharata Natyam is an art which consecrates the body which is considered to be in itself of no value. The yogi by controlling his breath and by modifying his body acquired the halo of sanctity. Even so, the dancer who dissolves her identity in rhythm and music makes her body an instrument, at least for the duration of the dance, for the experience and

young women – and some men too – from North India, Europe, Great Britain, North America, Australia and the Far East have mastered this dance enough to become performing artists. Once a provincial specialty, Bharata Natyam has now acquired a universal face.

The dancer who first helped Bharata Natyam to acquire international stature and conferred pride on the community of traditional dancers was the late T. Balasaraswati, known widely and simply as Bala. Bala conveyed *sringara* or romantic love as the quintessential mood of the dance, yet never let anyone forget that Bharata Natyam is,

expression of spirit."

Bala's remarks explain why Indians revere Bharata Natyam as a divine art. This is not esoterica or Hindu mysticism, but an aesthetic philosophy that guides great artists everywhere.

A traditional recital begins with an invocation or a floral offering to a divine being, usually the elephant-headed Ganapati, the god who removes all obstacles. The sequence that follows consists of *alarippu, jatiswaram, sabdam, varnam, padams* and *javalis, tillana* and *sloka.* This is the sequence considered appropriate for revealing the spiritual through the corporeal, though the pattern is held as a great one from a purely aesthetic viewpoint also.

Alarippu, based on rhythm alone, is pure dance. The concentration on rhythm helps to free the dancer from distractions and prepare her for the presentation ahead.

In *jatiswaram*, melody is added to rhythm, but without word or syllable. In this item, melody and movement coalesce.

Sabdam, with lyrics added to the melody and rhythm, represents the next stage in the evolution. The dancer now seeks to interpret the words and their meanings as well.

The *varnam* is the *pièce de résistance* of the recital. Describing the sequence of the recital as a progressive journey into a temple,

tions which follow the *varnam*, the emphasis lies on the interpretation of mood through *abhinaya* or mime. In the *tillana*, the dancer reverts to pure rhythm, prior to concluding the programme on a note of prayer. However, not all Bharata Natyam artists today follow this sequence, although the majority still do.

Kuchipudi, which had its origin in Andhra Pradesh, has only recently achieved recognition as a fine art. Historically it was – and to some degree continues to be – a vehicle for presenting to unsophisticated spectators scenes from Hindu epics and mythological tales through dance-dramas combining music, dance and acting. Over the years,

Bala envisions that in the *varnam*, the dancer enters the holy presence of the deity, the sanctum sanctorum. "This is the place," according to her, "which gives the dancer scope to revel in the rhythm, moods and music of the dance. The *varnam* is the continuum which gives ever-expanding room to the dancer to delight in her self-fulfilment, by providing the fullest scope to her own creativity as well as to the tradition of the art."

In *padams* and *javalis* and other composi-

Left and above, Yakshagana players dressed in elaborate costumes, Karnataka.

great teachers and choreographers – among them Guru Vempati Chinna Satyam – have refined the presentations a great deal. Kuchipudi dance dramas and recitals, consisting of a series of solo dances, are today appreciated by sophisticated urban audiences as well, not only in India but also abroad.

The lyrics used in Kuchipudi are usually in Telugu, though Sanskrit verses are also not uncommon. While Kuchipudi, like Bharata Natyam, comprises pure dance, mime and histrionics, it is the use of speech as well that distinguishes its presentation as dance-drama. Also, while the basic technique of

Kuchipudi is similar to that of Bharata Natyam, even an uninitiated spectator would be able to see that it has a distinct identity. According to one expert observer, Bharata Natyam is "restrained and perhaps geometric", while Kuchipudi is "freer, more flexible and essentially a histrionic form".

Kuchipudi dance-dramas each present a particular episode or a series of episodes. A solo recital, on the other hand, typically consists of such items as the *sabdam, bhama kalapam* which is the main item, *padams* and *tarangams*. In *bhama kalapam*, the dancer has enormous scope for the dramatisation of characters. The main character is Satyabhama, a beautiful but arrogant queen who

the lyrics are at a discount and the words of the songs are virtually drowned by the rat-a-tat of the drums.

An interesting feature of Yakshagana is that the characters are permitted speech, unlike in Kathakali, giving veteran performers an opportunity to improvise and develop the dialogue. The dance element is less prominent. What is likely to capture the attention of a visitor is the costumes and makeup, which reflect the essential traits of the characters.

The Yakashagana repertoire consists of the new as well as the old and there are more than 300 plays in existence, written from the 16th century onwards. The best plays of

goes through the process of discovering the path of true love and devotion. In the *tarangam*, the dancer frequently performs a balancing feat, her feet poised on the edge of a brass plate as she moves around.

Like Kuchipudi, the Yakshagana of Karnataka also fulfilled a social purpose. A musical play in form, it has traditionally served – and to some extent still does – as a popular vehicle for tales of fantasy drawn from myths and legends and presenting a moral, generally the victory of good over evil. With songs and verses employed for the narration of the themes, it is operatic in nature. Yet, in contemporary presentations,

Yakashagana are offered by a few temple troupes.

Kathakali is to Kerala what Bharata Natyam is to Tamil Nadu. It has been described as a true representation of the artistic traditions of India and "one of the most magnificent theatres of the imagination". While linked directly to ancient Sanskrit drama, it has in its evolution absorbed elements of ritual, cult practices, martial arts and other aspects of life in the land of its birth.

Kathakali is a highly stylised dance-drama which serves to present story themes derived from the *Ramayana*, the *Mahabarata* and other Hindu epics, myths and legends. The dance aspect consists of pure dance as well as mime.

What is most striking about Kathakali is the emphasis given to *aharya-abhinaya*, the use of costumes, ornaments and facial makeup. This, according to one observer, helps to transform the dancer into a type rather than a character. According to the qualities that they represent, the characters fall into five main types, and the makeup illumines these types.

Kathakali makes strenuous demands on its exponents, notes dance critic Sunil Kothari, because "it is the only dance form in which the entire body, both skeleton and muscles,

belongs to the genre of drama. A temple art performed traditionally by a specific community, Kudiyattam embraces elements of music and dance as well. The performers use makeup similar to Kathakali but are permitted speech, albeit in a stylised manner. Because it is theatre committed to deep interpretation, it is often several days or even weeks before a Kudiyattam drama cycle is completed.

Mohini Attam is also called the Dance of the Enchantress, because it emphasises the seductive and graceful aspects of woman. Resurrected in the 1930s from virtual oblivion, Mohini Attam has since gained national recognition, even if it is still a lesser known

down to even the smallest facial muscle, are used to portray emotion."

The same commentator observes: "The actor in Kathakali never speaks except with his hands. The text of the drama is sung for him and is the baseline for his interpretation. It is in histrionics or interpretive dancing that the Kathakali artist excels, the spectator's experience enhanced by the thrilling drum beats."

Allied to Kathakali is Kudiyattam which

Left, above and above right, Kathakali requires elaborate preparation and distinctive makeup for each character.

dance form. It is a solo female dance in which the striking feature is the rhythmical swaying of the dancer from side to side and the smooth and unbroken flow of body movement. The dance is focussed essentially on feminine moods and emotions. Leading performers today include those who are not natives of Kerala.

The classical dances of southern origin are, of course, complemented by a variety of folk dances. As in most other countries and cultures, many of these dances are linked to the passage of the seasons and the celebrations of key events in community life such as harvests and religious festivals.

The deep-rooted tradition of India intricately knits together its religious and social system with its vast and widespread community of artisans and weavers. Within this all-encompassing umbrella there are immense variations and differences which create the diversity of its cultural heritage. This is most vividly displayed in the crafts and textiles of South India where, in Andhra Pradesh, Karnataka, Tamil Nadu and Kerala, towns, villages and hamlets have been known for hundreds of years for their special and distinct craftsmanship.

Crafts are known by the name of the village where their producers first concentrated, such as "Bidri" from Bidar. A specialised form of miniature black pottery is found in Hoskote, a small town in the southern part of Bangalore in Karnataka. A "Kanchipuram" is all that need be said to refer to a silk handloom *sari* of a particular style woven in Kanchipuram. Irkal, Dharwar, Pochampalli, are magical names in the directory of weaves of South India. This characteristic of a place becoming synonymous with a certain craft is true of many parts of India, but particularly of South India.

The hierarchy in the caste structure set out centuries ago placed the craftsman within an ordained pattern of existence. Potters, cobblers, blacksmiths, weavers and basket-makers lived as professional groups within the rural community, passing on their skills to their children and working according to the needs of a well defined market. Generations of experience and a deep relationship with religion dictated both the form and the norms of work. Creativity was the prerogative of the individual, but craftsmanship was guided by certain canons set out in the *Shilpashastras*, Sanskrit treatises on the various art forms.

Crafts and textiles were largely related to

temple festivals and religious occasions. Brass lamps and icons, stone figures and "temple *saris*" are the most popular and identifiable South Indian crafts, but even in jewellery, mat-weaving and other crafts the distinctness of the South establishes itself.

Andhra Pradesh is predominantly a textile producing state where a variety of silk and cotton fabrics are woven by more than 600,000 weavers. The number has dwindled considerably for economic reasons, but the handloom weaves are still vibrant and plen-

tiful. Three decorative processes connected with textiles are very much a part of the Andhra tradition. The first is the patterning done by resist-dyeing or tie-dyeing the yarn prior to weaving. The pre-conceived pattern emerges as the yarn is woven, and the edges of the motifs and figures have a "spread" or "flame" effect. Chirala and Pochampalli are the best known areas for these *ikat saris*. Bold geometric designs of birds, animals and flowers set in squares with borders and end pieces are woven in both cotton and silk. The *rumal,* square like a scarf, in red, black and white, is a well known loom product of Andhra Pradesh. There is an old tradition of

Preceding pages, intricate designs are ceremonially rendered on the Kathakali stage and swept away before each performance. **Left**, Kalamkari depicting Lord Krishna's triumphal dance on the head of the serpent Kaliya. **Above right**, Lakshmi, Hindu goddess of wealth, awaits installation on temple verandah in Mercara, Coorg.

pre-soaking the yarn in oil and alkaline earth for some days which lends to the scarf a singular aroma and gives it the local name of *telia,* or oily, *rumal.*

The second and most common form of ornamenting textiles is to create a pattern by changing the colour of the yarn during weaving, and by elaborate forms of placement of the warp and weft to create motifs and varied textures. Siddipet, Dharmavaram, Narayanpet and Gadwal *saris* are among the rich and vivid textiles embellished with gold thread at the borders and end panels. In a variety of counts from thick to superfine, in checks, stripes and solid colour, these *saris* emerge from the small huts and worksheds

then painted in with a "pen" made of a bamboo stick padded at one end with cotton cloth. Kalamkari is produced in Machilipatnam and Kalahasti; the latter is well known for its temple hangings depicting scenes from religious epics and legends. Here, too, the outlines are hand-painted with pigments obtained from local plants and flowers. The traditional colours of ochre, soft pink, indigo, madder red and iron black are the characteristic tints of Kalamkari fabric. The traditional temple cloths are more ornate and exquisite and serve as decorative or collector's items, while the repeat-design fabric captures a wider market for furnishings and garments.

dotted across the countryside. Men sit at the loom for over 8 hours a day, while their wives and children assist in pre- and post-loom tasks such as stretching or dyeing the yarn, or washing and finishing the yards of fabric. The click and clatter of the loom, the brilliant hanks of yarn hanging about them, and the age-old confidence in the skill at their fingertips are the more beautiful moments of the otherwise harsh existence that shrouds the handloom weaver.

Kalamkari is a hand-painted fabric which derives its name from the word *kalam* for pen and *kari* for work. Outlines of birds, trees, creepers and flowers are block-printed and

Nirmal is the name of both the location and the craft practised in a part of Adilabad district. Using dyes made of local ingredients to create memorable scenes from the *Mahabharata* and *Ramayana*, ornate table tops, boxes and trays are produced with an eye on the contemporary rather than the traditional. A deep and attractive coloured wood found in the Tirupati area is red sanderswood, locally known as *raktachandan*, from which dolls and household articles like bowls and dishes are now made, as well as religious figures. Venkateswara, the deity of the nearby Tirupati temple (a famous centre of pilgrimage) and Lord Krishna in his most popular and recognisable attributes are some of the figures carved in this tough but elastic wood. Special chisels such as the *valu uli* and *gubba uli* are used to carve the different features of the body. The man-woman pair of dolls with distinct cloths and ornaments are among the more whimsical toys made of this wood.

Kondapalli, a little village in Vijayawada district, produces a fascinating range of toys realistically depicting the lives of the people. The essence of village life is captured in scenes of a variety of fruit and vegetables, a woman cooking or pounding grain, a washerman at work, a man climbing a palm tree and an incredible range of weavers carrying

enough heat to melt the lac and make the colour stick.

Art and craft forms in the folk idiom usually developed as adjuncts to different modes of worship of local temple deities, as in shadow theatre using ornamental painted leather puppets, locally called *tholu bomalatta*. Made of translucent skin (goat, cow or deer), coloured with bright dyes in red, pink, brown, green and black and ornamentally perforated, the two-dimensional puppets take the shape of mythological characters from the *Ramayana* and *Mahabharata*. They are manipulated on bamboo sticks against a cloth screen behind which flickering oil lamps create a vibrant backdrop. Drum-

out 13 different weaving processes. This mini-panorama of daily life is a perfect example of how the traditional crafts of India are rooted to the soil and of the meticulous effort that goes into their making.

Ettikopakka in Visakhapatnam district creates bright lacquer toys made on hand- or machine-operated lathes. The lac stick is pressed against the wooden toy as it turns on the lathe; the friction created produces

Traditional skills continue to thrive against the odds brought by modernisation. Left to right: Kalamkari painting; Bidri inlay; Tanjore metalwork; and brass overlay on wood carving.

beats and narration complete the setting for traditional folk theatre. While the actual theatre puppets can be as tall as 5 ft, miniaturised versions are now made for the souvenir hunter.

The Rambadi tribe of gypsies in their appearance and attire make a striking contrast to the Telugu rural folk in the areas surrounding Bijapur. Their bright red, black and yellow skirts, blouses and head cloths, richly decorated with Banjara embroidery and flashing mirror pieces, resemble the style of the nomadic tribes of Rajasthan and Gujarat. Strips of coloured fabric are joined together in a patchwork manner with white thread, and embellished with glass beads and shells. Banjara embroidery is now being adapted to bags, cushion covers, belts and quilts for the urban market.

Carpet-weaving has come to be generally associated with Kashmir and other parts of northern India; but the South has its own tradition in the famed Deccan rugs of Eluru and Warangal, established in the 17th century when artisans moved south with the Mughal army. They are a type of flat-weave durry with geometric designs or Persian origin known by the old Mughal name of *shatrangi*, with other names of local origin used for central and border designs. Some are named after Telugu patrons of the carpet

Karimnagar's silversmiths have devised an interesting method. The late Kamaladevi Chattopadhyay, the most prominent leader of the crafts revival movement in India, has described how little strips are cut "from a sheet of alloy of silver and copper known as *tankam*, that are spread to make up the entire design, then placed on a furnace. Then well heated dry paddy husk is sprinkled on it and it bursts into flame and melts the *tankam* pieces. The molten *tankam* evidently penetrates into crevices and ensures the firm binding together of the little bits that form the components. The block is then cooled in cold water." The most well-known item of Karimnagar filigree work is its perfume

industry such as Ramchandra Khani and Gopalrao Khani. This comes from the old Persian practice in which designs were given poetic names like "Shah Nawaz" and "Gulbanthi". The colours are light, with a later introduction of delicate floral patterns on a cream-coloured ground. Carpet-making thrives in this area as it has a twin tradition of weaving and cotton growing to support it.

Karimnagar is known for its fine silver filigree work, in which silver is pressed or moulded into trellis, creeper and leaf patterns to produce jewellery with a typical lacy effect. It needs deft fingers to twist and set the tiny components together, for which

containers.

Pembarthi in northern Andhra Pradesh has long been the home of a special kind of repoussé brasswork from the Kakatiya dynasty. The styles and forms are similar to the work seen in the temples of Lepakshi and Ramappa. Large vases, pots and wall panels are the more distinctive of its products.

Hyderabad, the capital city of Andhra Pradesh, combines Islamic and Western influences in its craftware. Wandering down narrow lanes in the Charminar area of town, a traveller can come across discarded artifacts and textiles of a bygone age. It was the West that fascinated the fabulously wealthy nobles of Hyderabad. Their palaces were replicas of those in Europe and were designed and decorated by Italian engineers. The men dressed in the Western fashion and their wardrobes extended down corridors of specially built closet space. The pearl market flourishes to this day in Hyderabad and some of the effete requirements of the nobility still linger on with the production of chandeliers, statues and ornate bric-à-bracs (which are nevertheless no match for the indigenous forms of craftsmanship).

Bidriware is a high-profile craft of the Deccan and consists of artifacts made of an alloy of zinc, copper, lead and tin with an inlay of fine silver wire on its blackened surface. This exquisite technique dates back to the Bahmani dynasty and was patronised by the Mughal rulers whose Persian heritage accounts for the floral and geometric patterns. The forms were devoted to the needs of the nobility. Painstaking decoration and skilled techniques combine to put Hyderabad and Bidar, the original home of Bidri work in Karnataka, on the craft map of the South.

Karnataka is rich in the quality of the craft it offers – no flimsy, ephemeral stuff, but textiles, stone, sandalwood carving and pottery in the soundest of artistic treatment. The Belur and Halebid temples are exquisite examples of the tradition of stone-carving developed during the Hoysala period. The quiet atmosphere of these old temples accentuates the images prolifically carved on their walls. There is symphony of movement and music, as gods, goddesses, musicians, dancers, chariots and charioteers swarm across the walls of dark grey stone which glistens almost black, after a light drizzle of rain. Present-day stone workers have neither kingdoms nor patrons to work for, so they turn to carving facsimiles of old statues. Charming oil lamps for prayer rooms, spice containers and miniature kitchen utensils as toys for children are still made. But unfortunately the old glory has gone, since stone friezes have a limited market in the modern context, and modern day improvements are at an early stage.

Among artisans, wood and stone carvers

are considered of the same status and caste. The *Shilpashastras* prescribe the kind of wood required for a particular image, the auspicious time and season for felling a tree and for propitiating the resident spirit. Religious significance is imbued in those crafts which require a high degree of skill.

Karnataka wood carvers of the Vishwakarma community use ebony, rosewood and sandalwood for precise and elaborate work. Once the observer learns to look past the ubiquitous trail of wooden elephants that invariably emerges as the most typical example of Karnataka's crafts, it will absorb the versatility of woodcraft in the trays, boxes, statues, fans and a host of other ob-

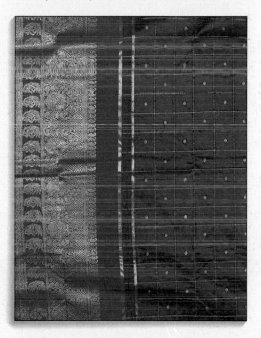

jects that are created here. The charm of sandalwood is in its aroma, golden colouring and velvety feel. It is possible to be duped by counterfeit pieces – ordinary wood dipped for a while in sandal perfume – but the real thing is well worth the high price tag. Sandalwood artisans, called *gudigars*, obtain their wood from the forests of Karnataka. Rosewood is dark brown, with a deep red glow. This is inlaid with pieces of lighter coloured wood to form geometric or pictorial decoration. Dwindling forests put up raw materials costs, posing a problem for many woodcrafts-people, who turn to lower quality substitutes and plastic inlay. The past glory

Left, it takes a weaver several weeks to complete a 6-yard sari; Kanchipuram in Tamil Nadu. **Above right**, the finished product.

of the wood-carver can be seen on the doorways and wall panels of old temples and in coastal Karnataka, where wooden cult figures were worshipped by folk communities.

The silks of Karnataka are lustrous and vivid, emerging, as everywhere else, from the tiny huts where handloom weavers repeat patterns embedded in their aesthetic memory. During the Vijayanagara Empire the prosperity of weavers reached its zenith. The community known as Saliya weavers have a lullaby which describes the child's forefather as creating his weaves on a loom that had a silver plank and a rope made of a costly bronze alloy. The range of silks, both in *saris* and in fabric length, attracts many

sari is an earthy cousin in cotton with distinct contrasting borders, sometimes in silk. The borders have the *rudraksha* pattern imitating the pitted dark red seed used to make necklaces of auspicious significance. Tiny spokes or spires representing temples are also frequently used to define the edge in border designs.

A special embroidery called *kasuti* is done on deep blue, green and brown Dharwar saris in the Hubli area. A fine and distinctive stitch used to create peacocks, elephants, temples, the tulsi plant (basil) and even cradles, *kasuti* consists of cross and zigzag running stitches using only single or double threads. The motifs spread them-

trousseau shoppers from the country.

The famed Coromandel coast, known for its trade in exotic spices, was the doorway for the import and export of silks. Shimoga, Arasikere and Halebid were the great silk producing areas, in those halycon times. Silk yarn produced here is supplied to weavers who have their own specific range of colours, border design and motifs according to the district and area of work.

Saris in silk with gold thread are a specialty of Bellary. The *irkal sari* and blouse pieces in bright coloured handlooms are produced in the villages of Irkal and Galedgudda in Bijapur district. The Dharwar

selves sparsely on the main body of the *sari* and collect in a close cluster nearer the *pallav* or end border.

Thick cottons with broad borders in brilliant reds, ochres, greens, blues and browns reflect the heritage of the peasant *sari* which, for convenience in the fields, must be of a colour and width that does not soil easily. These are the styles most popular among those who belong to the movement for the revival of handlooms. Apart from the fine fabrics, flat-woven floor rugs in brilliant primary colours and geometric designs are produced in Navalgund.

Toy making is an important part of Indian

handicrafts as it absorbs its sustenance from the ageless curiosity and creativity of the child. Festival toys, educational toys, religious toys and toys of pure whimsy are all part of the widespread and varied toy tradition. On the way to Mysore from Bangalore is the small township of Chennapatna, a flourishing centre for lac-painted wooden toys. It was the capital of the region in the 16th century and the Chitragar artisan community excelled in the manufacture of delightful sets of miniature cooking vessels complete with mortar, pestle and rolling pin. The innovativeness of the craftsman who keeps abreast with change shows in the folk-style aeroplanes and telephones he makes for today's

metal workers, weavers and goldsmiths who were wholly dedicated to serving the temple and the surrounding community, besides the thousands of pilgrims who would throng the holy centres. Each temple complex became a beehive of religious, commercial and artisanal activity with flower markets, temple processions, music and dance alongside.

Kanchipuram was famed as the capital of the Cholas and Pallavas between the 7th and 13th centuries. Over 150 temples with all their gods and goddesses created a tremendous demand for the artifacts and accessories that go with festivals dedicated to the various deities. Weavers were required to provide skirts, sarongs, and *angavastrams* or

child. Balls, rattles and other non-ethnic toys make for a growing export market.

In **Tamil Nadu** the intermingling of religion and craft is the most pronounced. Most of the metalwork, handloom and jewellery making traditions drew their patronage and sustenance from the many famous temples in the state. Stone and metal images and vessels for religious use had to be cast and the idols then required to be draped and ornamented. This created a concentration of

Left, coir factory in Alleppey, Kerala. **Above**, lacquer work is a cottage industry; Ettikopakka, Andhra Pradesh.

shawls to cover the upper portion of the torso. Curtains, veils and turbans with special ornamentation all formed part of the fabric needs of each temple.

The creation of any metal figure or vessel had since early times been imbued with spiritual significance as the substance was solid and permanent. The *cire perdue* or lost wax method of moulding meant that when the molten metal was poured into the earthen or waxen mould in order to take its shape, there were some crucial moments when it seemed that it was a divine presence rather than the artisan's hand that controlled the creation of the artifact. The metal was also presumed to absorb the energy of the cosmic body it represented, so that when an icon was installed in the inner sanctum of a shrine, the energy was believed to be lodged there. If the image was carried out during festivals and processions, the shrine was considered empty of power and energy. Various acts of propitiation were thus necessary to render the entire process both auspicious and successful, necessitating the physical and aesthetic purification of the craftsman.

The main centre where solid casting of metal is done is Swamimalai in Thanjavur, which fashions exquisite icons in bronze, as well as ornamental plates in copper, brass and silver. Madurai, Salem, Chingelpet and

Crafts are caste-related activities, and Tamil Nadu has a number of craftspeople from the sublime metalsmiths to the lower castes like those involved in basket and mat-weaving. The high quality of skill in both the higher and the everyday crafts testifies to the state's position as one of the richest in its traditions. The simple basket is made in palm or palmyra leaf, dyed or given raised textures to produce a variety of shapes and sizes of boxes, trays, mats, bags and screens. The baskets and boxes are so light and attractive that one is tempted to acquire a large number of them and then decide for what purpose they should be used. Tirunelveli, Raman-thapuram and Kanniyakumari are the main

Tiruchirapalli are other metal work centres producing an incredible variety of temple lamps, from tiny single-wick pieces to elaborately ornamental 5 ft-high creations which can hold enough oil to light up a stage performance all through the night.

Metalsmiths claim descent from Vishva-karma, the architect of the gods, who governs the hands and tools of all artisans, and each metal is said to have its own alchemic and healing properties. Specific prayers are normally recited before work begins, for indeed the gods must come to dwell in the artisan's fingertips and mind as well as in his creation.

basketry centres.

Tamil Nadu excels in handlooms, too, both silk and cotton. The weavers who congregated around temples made Kanchipuram a household word for the traditional silk *sari* in bold colours with broad contrasting borders and *pallavs* and gold threads forming lines, checks and motifs. Kanchipuram weavers also produce the most brilliant cottons in India. A typical Kanchipuram, whether in silk or cotton, is recognisable by its border design of the *gopuram* or temple spire pattern, broad contrast borders and distinct elegance. A special feature of some of the *saris* is the difference in colours of the upper and lower border, termed Ganga-Jamuna, signifying the two most famous rivers of India whose confluence marks the holy centre of Prayag or Allahabad.

The city of Madras abounds in goldsmiths, many of whom live and work around the Mylapore temple, an imposing structure with its typically ornate *gopuram* surrounded by a water tank.

Jewellery making began as a household industry where the goldsmith would sit at a low table, blowing through a long thin pipe to direct the tongue of flame towards the part of the metal to be melted or welded into shape. Today they sit at the doorways of their tiny shops making gold plated "dance jewel-

silks, special jewellery, and dances to musical instruments made by hand, illuminated by an ornamental lamp made by metalsmiths before a carved wooden or metal statue of Lord Ganesh, the elephant god. The most typical items of jewellery are the *thalaisaman* (headpiece), with the *rakodi*, worn just above the flowers in the hair, and the *chandrasuryan* (moon and sun) on either side, as the head symbolises the firmament. The ear ornaments consist of three pieces, the *maatal* (chain), *jhimki* (hanging earring) and the *thodu* which fits on to the lobe. For the neck there is the *adigai* which consists of a choker and pendant, and a longer chain with a broad *padakkam* or pendant designed in red, green

lery". Silver jewellery is dipped in gold and a bright pink paper is laid in pre-moulded grooves before placing a pale pink stone in it. The end result is "ruby"-studded "gold" pieces in the traditional patterns required for classical dance.

The interrelation of the arts and crafts with religion is best seen in the costume of the classical Bharata Natyam dancer who performs as a devotee, wearing handloom

Left, stone carver of Tanjore. **Above**, polychromatic stucco figures from Hindu mythology swarm over temple *gopurams* in Mylapore, Madras.

and pearly stones with peacock or floral designs set in a half-moon-like frame. An undulating bangle, *vanki,* for the upper arm, gold bangles for the wrist, an *odyanan* or broad ornamented belt, and occasionally a hair ornament called *sarpam* or snake to decorate the long plait, completes the ensemble. Most Bharata Natyam dancers from all over the country order their jewellery from this fascinating centre at Mylapore and at Nagercoil which has the largest number of skilled goldsmiths.

Kerala is a lush land rich in an ancient heritage of martial arts, folk theatre, classical dance, temple-related crafts, unique wooden architecture and a beautiful coastline which lays it open to a variety of influences from other parts of the world. The skills of the craftspeople of Kerala, as in most of South India, are directed towards highly sophisticated religious requirements as well as simple utilitarian needs.

The bell-metal vessels made by the Moosaris of Kerala are a very special set of solid forms. Huge vessels almost 6 feet in diameter in an alloy of copper and tin are cast in the *cire perdue* technique after invocatory rituals are performed. Some of the more classic pieces are the *urli, charakku* and *varpu* usually used for cooking food on a mass scale. It is fascinating to see rice being

from whom the Moosaris of the Kammala caste (makers of eye-pleasing objects) claim descent. These attractive long-handled mirrors are expensive, but since they are created from a rare technique and art form they are valued as collectors' items.

The jewellery of Kerala is very special too. Designs of necklaces in gold are distinctive and have never been copied by artisans in other parts of the country. Very fine and highly skilled work is required to create the delicate *poothali* and the green-stoned *pachhakalluthali*. The goldsmiths of Trichur are well known and the best shops for both gold ornaments and bell-metal vessels are around the Vadakkumnath temple in the

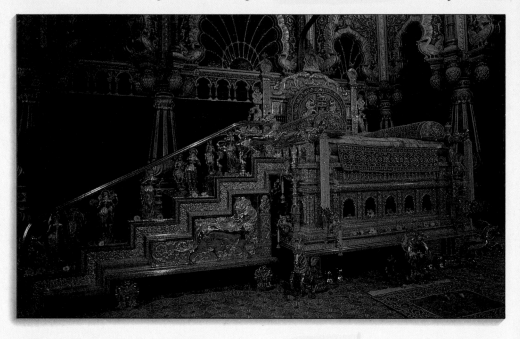

cooked in these to feed the elephants at the Guruvayur temple. Oil cans, jugs, drinking glasses, ladles, jewel boxes are the smaller items made for household use. Hanging lamps, *changalavelakku* and *kuthuvelakku,* spouted water jugs, rounded gourd-shaped water containers and smaller temple lamps in the soft yellow tones typical of bell-metal are seen all over Kerala.

In the town of Aranmala live two brothers who possess the skill of making metal mirrors, mixing secret herbs with molten metal to produce a highly reflective surface. According to legend the technique was revealed to a woman of the Vishva-karma community

heart of the town.

Wood carving, particularly in the old traditional homes of Kerala and on the ceilings of temples scattered all over south Malabar, demonstrates rich techniques and a variety of subjects. Deities, elephants and floral and geometric patterns cover large panels and pillars. Dark ebony, rosewood or teak are used for carving in Kerala. The present-day Kathakali masks, elephants, jewel boxes and other such tourist-oriented products give only a hint of the grandeur of old traditions. Trivandrum and Cochin are the wood carving centres that make contemporary pieces, while the grand old architectural woodwork can be seen at the Padmanabhapuram palace and Sri Padmanabha temple.

As one drives out of Cochin past the outlandish, multi-coloured manifestations of "Gulf-returned" architecture (from the migrant workers who brought in money from the Middle East) and crosses the deep green Alwaye river, the palm clusters become dense and tiny palm-leaf thatched or tiled huts, dotting the coastal belt, dominate the landscape. Kodungallur, the historic port town of Malabar, is famous for its Sri Kudumba temple. The making of palmyra and screwpine mats is a widespread village craft here. These, along with articles made out of coconut shell, keep the women ac-

Kerala handlooms are typical of the life-style of its people – restrained, dignified and austere. Men and women wear the white *mundu* or *sarong*-like cloth with a narrow coloured border. A touch of gold thread with a *chutti*, an arrow-like design at the upper and lower corners, is the most traditional style. For marriages and special occasions the *kasavumundu* in unbleached cotton is worn. Here the border is a 3-4 inches (8-11 cm) broad strip of pure *zari* or gold thread which sets off the fine 100 x 120 count cream-coloured handloom cotton body of the fabric. The upper garment or *angavas-tram* is another cloth of the same kind, which when worn together looks like a *sari* without

tively involved in cottage industry. It is a secondary income-generating activity, with the menfolk being occupied in traditional work like fishing and toddy-tapping. Screwpine mats are woven by hand on the ground into sleeping mats or as wrappings for fish or for light machinery. The more refined and sophisticated quality is seen in table mats, handbags, sun hats and other such "modern" objects for commercial markets.

Left, golden throne of the Wadiyars, rulers of Mysore. <u>Above</u>, carved wooden panel: Vishnu, the Hindu god of creation, sleeps on the coils of the celestial serpent Anantha.

the frontal pleats. Weaving areas are Palghat and Trivandrum.

In Kerala, the genuine crafts are in the temples, and in homes, villages and by-lanes so far untouched by new religious sentiments or modernity in the form of nylon and plastic. Development and revival work has reactivated artisans but is now geared more for the urban consumer who looks at handicrafts as *objets d'art*. The dichotomy of progress versus preservation of traditions is therefore most piquant in South India, but the strength and vitality of its heritage still supports the creation of some of the richest crafts in the country.

Indian cinema has completed 75 years of existence and celebrated the event with star-spangled éclat. The South Indian cinema, younger by 15 years, comprises the Tamil, Telugu, Kannada and Malayalam cinema.

For a long time Madras city was the centre of film production in South India, and films in all four South Indian languages as well as some in Hindi were produced here. Madras is next only to Bombay in film production; in some ways, Madras city has a lot more to offer producers by way of technical facilities such as well equipped studios and organised production schedules. But today, most Telugu films are produced in Hyderabad, Kannada films in Banglore and Mysore, and a large number of Malayalam films in Trivandrum which boasts the country's only state-owned film studio for feature films, the Chitranjali Studios.

The South Indian cinema has one major distinction, though opinions may differ on its effectiveness or utility. This is the fact that Tamil and Telugu cinema have been the breeding ground of politicians. Against one Ronald Reagan who made a name in Hollywood as an actor and then became President, South India has produced a whole crop. M. G. Ramachandran, popularly known as "MGR", who acted in a large number of films as a swashbuckling conquering hero, the embodiment of righteousness, later became the Chief Minister of Tamil Nadu and remained so for more than a decade. In fact the Tamil cinema grew with the Dravidian movement, which became a powerful political force that swept away the Indian National Congress from the state. The first Dravidian Party (then called DMK) Chief Minister, the late C. N. Annadurai, as well as his immediate successor, M. Karunanidhi, were script-writers with large followings.

That the Madras experience was no lone phenomenon has been proved by Andhra Pradesh, where N.T. Rama Rao was Chief Minister for 10 years. His film roles – usually Hindu gods in devotional films called "mythologicals" – are extremely popular

with Telugu audiences. The position is not the same in Karnataka and Kerala, where the superstars have their following, but have not succeeded in attaining political power.

India leads the world in the production of feature films: as many as 912 were produced in 1984, and 773 films were made in 1988. The proportion of South India films to the all-India figure was as high as 82 percent in 1984 but came down to 60 percent in 1988. The statistics of South Indian feature films made in 1988 are impressive nonetheless – Tamil, 152; Telugu, 162; Kannada, 67; and Malayalam, 83. They show a decline from 1985 when the figures were 190, 198, 69 and 137 respectively.

The old-time Tamil movies were basically entertainment with a capital "E". Stalwarts such as S. S. Vasan, who produced block-busters like *Chandraleka* (the highest grosser of its time); Nagi Reddi, who owned the largest film production complex in Asia with as many as 14 studio floors; and A.V. Meiyappan, with his own studios, are names to remember. Their blockbusters became big box office hits, and many of them were re-made in other languages, including Hindi. Technical values have also improved, though the story content is still thin and cliché-ridden. Tamil directors of the present day include K. Balachander, Bhagyaraj and Bharathi Raja. A few younger directors with the courage to go off the beaten track are also making their presence felt, but there is still a long way to go.

Among the superstars of yesterday, the most important was the late M. G. Ramachandran. His arch screen rival, Sivaji Ganesan, is a better actor and he too dabbled in politics, though he did not go far. He has practically retired from the screen now, though his son Prabhu holds the banner aloft in filmdom.

Among the outstanding actors today are the award-winning Hasan family – Charuhasan, his daughter Suhasini and his brother Kamalhasan. Kamalhasan is a successful producer himself; among his achievements are *Pesum Padam* (Talking Picture), a film with no dialogue, and *Nayakan*, a story of a local Godfather à la Marlon

Brando. Another superstar in Tamil cinema is Rajanikant who has the distinction of having played a role in a Hollywood stunt and suspense movie.

Among the present-day actresses of note are Suhasini, Radhika, Sarita, Amala and Archana. All these represent the modern educated young woman, and they interpret their screen characters with finesse. Unfortunately the films themselves are still far from satisfactory by modern artistic standards. Song and dance and irrelevant comedy, stunt fighting and violence, with as much sex as the censor permits, are still the order of the day in Tamil films.

The picture is not very different on the Telugu screen, which is perhaps still more backward from many points of view. Mythologicals and what is called folklore-full of gods and demons and trick shots-formed the mainstay of Telugu films for a long time, followed by social and romantic themes. The great artistes of the Telugu screen were Akkineni Nageswara and N. T. Rama Rao. The Telugu screen has produced character actors like the late Nagiah and Ranga Rao who were equally popular in Tamil cinema. An artiste who made an outstanding contribution is Sharada, who won the all-India best actress award three times over, twice in Malayalam and once in Telugu. A Telugu film which won the coveted Gold Medal as the best feature film of 1979 was *Sankarabharanam*, a musical popular all over India. New trends are emerging, with new directors and new artistes trying to make the grade. What hampers their making meaningful and artistically worthwhile films is that escapist entertainment is much more in demand.

Kannada films had a comparatively sluggish growth till 1965, when the state government began giving incentives by way of subsidies and tax reliefs to encourage Kannada cinema. The switch from Madras as centre of production to Banglore took time to materialize. Though melodrama and what is called the "love triangle" persisted, a few courageous pioneers were able to achieve a breakthrough. *Samskara* (Ritual), based on a well known novel by U.R. Ananthamurthy, with a brilliant screenplay by Girish Karnad (who also acted in the film), won the National Award in 1970. This was followed by three more feature films which won national awards in 1975, 1977 and 1986. This brilliant record, and the work of directors like Karanth and Kasaravalli, promise a superior brand of Kannada films in the near future.

Malayalam films stand out for their artistic and esthetic excellence, and can be rated second in an all-India perspective, next in line to the Bengali cinema. Run-of-the-mill films are also produced in Malayalam, but again there are also many outstanding ones. Perhaps this can be partly explained by Kerala's literacy rate – the highest in India – and the number of talented Malayalam novelists and short story writers who enjoy a wide readership.

The very first Malayalam movie, a historical called *Marthanda Varma*, completed in 1928, was based on a well known novel. Significant landmarks in the history of Malayalam cinema include the film *Neelakukil*, based on a story by the outstanding novelist Uroob. The film, by P. Bhaskaran and Ramu Kariyat, brought to a wider audience for the first time the beautiful countryside of Kerala. It won the President's silver medal for the second-best film of 1956. This honour won by the state was followed by the President's gold medal for *Chemeen* (Red Fish) as the best film of 1965, directed by Ramu Kariat, and based on a well-known novel.

M.T.Vasudevan Nair, one of Kerala's leading contemporary writers, has shown his mastery of the cinematic medium by his brilliant screenplays. He has also directed films, and his very first film *Nirmalayam* won both the President's gold medal for the best film of 1973 and the best actor award for its hero, the late P.J. Antony.

The Malayalam cinema has brought into prominence great directors who have won national and international fame. Aravindan made his debut with *Utharayanam* which won the special jury award for the best film on the Indian freedom struggle. Since then, Aravindan's films, with their subtle interplay of human emotions, have won a number of Indian and foreign awards.

Chidambaram (The Abode of Siva) won the President's gold medal for 1985 and also the best actress award for its heroine, the late Smita Patil.

Another great director in Malayalam cinema is Adoor Gopalakrishnan who came to the limelight with his very first film,

Swayamvaram, which won the President's gold medal in 1973 and the best actress award for its heroine, Sharada. Gopala-krishnan's later productions, *Elipathayam* (The Rat Trap) and *Mukhamukam* (Face to Face) have been significant contributions to the cinema, and any film that carries his name is worth seeing. Another director, Shaji, began as a cameraman, but won the President's gold medal (1988) for his first film, *Piravi* (Birth), and the best actor award for its 80-year old hero Premji. The film has gone on to win international awards.

There are other directors who have shown their mastery over the medium in producing brilliant off-beat films. Among these are

lead in more than 700 films. The present ruling superstars in Malayalam movies are Mammootty and Mohan Lal. But apart from these, there are those artistes who carry the success of the films on their shoulders by sheer talent. Among these must be mentioned Gopi and Balan K. Nair, who have won acclaim as winners of all-India best national awards, and Tilakan, who is destined to go far as the best character actor on the Malayalam screen.

It is a peculiar feature of Malayalam movies of today that no heroine has made her mark. Actresses flit from one region to another irrespective of language, according to the prevalent fads and the director's choice.

John Abraham who died under tragic circumstances, George, Pavithran, Padmarajan, who is a well known writer himself, and Mohan. Among the directors more in tune with the requirements of the box office are I.V. Shashi, Hariharan, Bharathan, Joshi and Satyan Anthikkad, but they too are competent film makers.

Among the actors, Malayalam film actor Prem Nazir found his way into the Guinness Book of Records for having played the male

Above, typical sequence from a tear-jerker: long-suffering heroine imploring the deity's intercession.

Indian cinema depends entirely on the playback system. Songs by well known singers are sung in the recording studios and are played back for the heroines on the screen to make the appropriate lip movements to synchronise voice and action. This has taken a step further now, and most dialogue is dubbed after the filming is over. The main male lead characters dub their own dialogue but very often the female characters, especially the heroines, make appropriate lip movements to dialogues spoken in languages not their own. Visitors who are movie-goers should keep this in mind when viewing Indian films.

South India is a land of rolling hills and lush plains, dry scrub-forested plateaus, deep valleys of moist evergreen forest and a coastline which is one of the most beautiful and most extensive in the world. Much of the peninsula is lashed by two monsoons, the southwest monsoon from late May to August and the far gentler northeast monsoon in the winter months. The amount of rainfall varies regionally, with much of the peninsula's interior receiving substantially less than the coasts and the hills which flank it, acting as watersheds.

The plant life is mainly dry tropical forest with patches of moist evergreen and rainforest such as the Silent Valley and the *sholas* of the Western Ghats. Lush and diverse montane subtropical forest also exist at high altitudes, ranging from 3,300 ft to 5,500 ft (1,000 m to 1,700 m), in the Western Ghats. The flora and fauna of peninsular India form part of the Indian bio-geographic subregion (within the Oriental Region), with remnants of the vegetation of East Africa harking back to the ancient connection with Gondwanaland.

The Eastern and Western Ghats also support many unusual faunal forms which show a close affinity to those found in India's northeastern hill tracts. The small populations in the Ghats are relicts of forms that must have once been distributed across the country. The humid upland forests of the Ghats act as faunal refuges for these forms that have been severely affected by ecological impoverishment in all except the least disturbed and accessible habitats of their former ranges.

The states of Karnataka and Tamil Nadu boast some of the largest intact jungle tracts south of the Vindhyas. In the early years, these extensive jungles were the private hunting preserves of former rulers, notably of Mysore. It is only because of the protection extended by the princes that the jungle has survived; much of these areas are offi-cially protected today, and form a contiguous chain of national parks, reserves and sanctuaries.

Two large herbivores characterise the forests of South India, the majestic Asian elephant and the formidable gaur (*Bos gaurus*), a large wild ox. The contiguous jungles of Nagarahole National Park, Bandipur Tiger Reserve, Mudumalai National Park and Wynaad Wildlife Sanctuary, together with the beautiful Periyar Tiger Reserve further south in Kerala on the Kerala-Tamil Nadu border, support the largest population of elephants outside India's northeast. Easily accessible from Mysore, these reserves provide accommodation for visitors. However, one of the most comfortable stays would be those provided by Kabini Lodge at Karapur in Nagarahole National Park.

Nevertheless, the reserves are definitely the best areas for observing elephants as they drink, bathe and gambol with their young in lakes and waterholes. Ivory poaching has taken a great toll on bulls, but some large tuskers can still be seen, single or dominating their herds. It is in these forests that the elephant-capturing method known as *Khedda* was practised until 1971.

Khedda involved the building of a large, strong stockade in a strategic location in the jungle. Several domestic elephants and "beaters" over days or even weeks would herd wild elephants towards the stockade and entrap them. Thereafter two of the strongest domestic elephants with experienced *mahouts* would enter the stockade, subdue the wild elephants individually and frog-march them out. They would be shackled to trees and trained to accept human company and finally to obey commands. *Khedda* was a frequent practice in areas which required large domestic elephant stables for logging.

The gaur is the largest plains-dwelling bovid in India. Young bulls are coffee-brown in colour and older ones jet black, with characteristic white stockings. Mature bulls are compact, up to 6 ft (1.82 m) tall at the shoulder and up to a tonne in weight. They are not averse to hilly terrain and are largely forest-dwellers, but emerge into

Preceding pages, herd of wild elephants sporting in Bandipur, Karnataka. **Left**, the forests of the South harbour a growing population of big cats.

open meadows to graze. Their highest concentrations are found in South India.

Tamil Nadu: The Nilgiris are the region's most attractive feature, forming the southern limit of the main Western Ghats system. The Palghat Gap, an area of dry lowlands, separates them from the Anamalai ranges further south.

The western slopes of the main plateau of the Nilgiris rise abruptly from levels of 330 to 1,000 ft (100 to 300 m) through a steep escarpment to about 6,000 ft (1,800 m). A similar steep rise on the southern slopes makes the Nilgiris a sharply defined geological feature. The plateau is undulating, with valleys at 5,000 ft (1,600 m) or so and peaks rising to more than 8,000 ft (2,500 m). Temperature variations during the year are modest, but there are significant differences according to altitude. Habitat types include rain forest, wet evergreen, mixed deciduous, and thorn forest where rainfall is less than 39 inches (1,000 mm). This last type is not dissimilar to parts of the East African savanna and even supports typically African tree species like acacia. The blackbuck (*Antilope cervicapra*), India's most elegant antelope, is found here.

The montane zone is characterised by *sholas* or sheltered, very dense evergreen forests, and open grasslands, home of the Nilgiri tahr which the eminent American wildlife biologist George Schaller describes as an "evolutionary link between primitive goat-antelopes and true goats". Once extensively hunted, the tahr is now making a comeback after strict protection, and can be best observed south of Coimbatore in the Eravikulam National Park in Kerala, which has a population of about 550. Temperatures rarely drop below freezing point in the higher reaches of the tahr's typical habitat, but the atmosphere is often misty, rainswept and cold.

Mudumalai Reserve, established in 1940 in the Nilgiris, is the oldest sanctuary in the state of Tamil Nadu. It is contiguous with Karnataka's Bandipur Tiger Reserve (a Project Tiger Reserve) and the Wynaad sanctuary of Kerala. Mudumalai's habitat is moist and dry deciduous forest, with teak (*Tectona grandis*) dominating. The teak forests of this and adjoining areas are both natural as well as of plantation origin. Elephants and gaurs are of course very visible.

Predators include the tiger (*Panthera tigris tigris*), leopard (*Panthera pardus*) and the wild dog or *dhole* (*Cuon alpinus*).

Dholes are the most visible of the predators. Once remorselessly hunted as vermin and driven to near-extinction in large parts of their range, they have made a comeback in Bandipur and Mudumalai. Moving around in packs, their hunting method is to run down a deer to the point of exhaustion, then close in for the kill. They keep in touch with each other by making peculiar whistling sounds, especially when the pack is trying to reassemble after a hunt. A rust or sand colour, *dholes* weigh about 33 lb (15 kg) and are generally 15 inches (38 cm) high at the

shoulder. The females are slighter than the males, and both have bushy tails.

The largest wildlife refuge in Tamil Nadu is the Anamalai Wildlife Sanctuary, with a sizable population of Nilgiri tahr and the lion-tailed macaque, a handsome black, maned monkey which also inhabits the Kalakadu Mundanthurai sanctuary in Tamil Nadu and the Silent Valley National Park in Kerala. The former constitutes one of the few tropical rain forests left quite undisturbed by human development. Apart from great floral diversity, its striking faunal diversity is apparent from the fact that it holds five species of primate: the nocturnal slender loris, the bonnet macaque, the Hanuman or common langur, the Nilgiri langur and the lion-tailed macaque.

A sanctuary of particular note is Point Calimere, projecting into the Bay of Bengal on the south-eastern coastline just north of Sri Lanka. Blackbucks and chitals (*Axis axis*) inhabit the coastal forest and plains, and after the northeast monsoon the shoreline comes alive with shorebirds, ducks and waders, mostly migratory. Dolphins are occasionally seen in the lagoon.

There are several small waterbird sanctuaries in the state, with large populations of cormorants, grey herons, open-bill storks, spoonbills and others. One of India's few

coastal plains rise steeply to the ridges of the Western Ghats at about 5,000 ft (1,500 m); eastwards the Ghats slope gently onto the Deccan plateau. Habitats range from montane *sholas* to wet evergreen, semi-evergreen, moist deciduous, dry deciduous, dry evergreen, thorn scrub and wetlands, including mangroves. Again, as in Tamil Nadu, four species of primate are found occurring together in the Brahmagiri hills.

Tigers are concentrated in the sanctuaries of Bandipur, Nagarahole and Bhadra. Leopards are fairly visible, especially in Nagarahole, and have increased in population.

Elephants and gaur are the most prominent herbivores. Sambar (*Cervus unicolor*),

patches of mangrove swamps outside the Sunderbans of West Bengal can be found at Pichavaram: it is rich in marine life and waders.

Karnataka: Neighbouring Karnataka state with a coastline on the Arabian Sea is endowed with striking climatic – and hence habitat – variations. An annual rainfall of about 230 inches (600 cm) at its western edge declines to less than 32 inches (80 cm) within 90 miles (150 km) further east. The

chital, barking deer (*Muntiacus muntjak*) and the nocturnal, rarely-seen mousedeer (*Tragulus memmina*) are present. The forests of the state also support chinkara (*Gazella gazella*) and blackbuck on the northern plateau. There are about 2,000-blackbucks roaming the grounds of the Ranebennur sanctuary. The four-horned antelope (*Tetra-cerus quadricornis*) can be seen in the drier parts of Nagarahole, Bandipur and Biligirirangans.

Wolves are normally seen in scattered small packs on the northern and southern plateaux, in scrub and plantation habitat interspersed with fields. The most prominent predator is again the *dhole,* found mainly in protected forests.

The sloth bear (*Melursus ursinus*) is found almost throughout Karnataka's wild habitat range and in fact is widely distributed throughout South Indian forests in general. The mugger or marsh crocodile (*Crocodylus palustris*) is found in the Kaveri river, which is also famous for that sporting fish par excellence, the redoubtable mahseer. The Government is active in the conservation of sea turtles, mainly Olive Ridleys (*Lepidochelys olivacea*); several hatching areas are found on the coast.

Birdlife is extensive, and includes the great Indian bustard at Ranebennur. Ranga-

A 10 sq mile (26 sq km) lake near Thekkady formed in 1895 by a masonry dam is the fulcrum of an ecosystem that supports the elephant, gaur, sambar, wild boar, tiger, leopard, *dhole,* Nilgiri langur, lion-tailed macaque and the Malabar giant squirrel. The dead trees raising their ghostly branches skywards from the lake's surface make it an unworldly sight.

Two species of squirrel are found in Periyar and throughout much of South India. The Malabar giant squirrel (*Ratufa indica*) is found in deciduous to evergreen forest, feeding on a large variety of fruit, bark, leaves and seeds, especially the seeds of teak which is prominent in most South Indian lowland

nathittu and Kokkare Bellur are well-known waterbird and wader sanctuaries and breeding areas.

Kerala: The southwestern state of Kerala is a lush green land, dotted with plantations of pepper, rubber, tea and cardamom. The most characteristic tree apart from the ubiquitous coconut palm is the jackfruit (*Artocarpus heterophyllus*). The most well-known of Kerala's sanctuaries is Periyar Tiger Reserve, located on the crest line of the Western Ghats. The forest consists of grasslands, deciduous and evergreen habitats, and, in fact, was once the private hunting preserve of the erstwhile princely state of Travancore.

jungles. The smaller flying squirrel (*Petinomys fuscocapillus*) is more nocturnal and can be seen at dusk.

The Silent Valley National Park is a 35-sq mile (90-sq km) pocket of rain forest of primeval beauty. Its name was written in conservation history when a nationwide campaign in the early 1980s prevented it from being inundated by a proposed reservoir. It is a virtual genetic storehouse of rare plants and herbs, and apart from the elephant, lion-tailed macaque and tiger it is also the typical habitat of the spectacular king cobra or hamadryad (*Ophiophagus hannah*). These two reserves, along with Eravikulam and Wynaad, ensure that representative forest areas of Kerala are well protected.

Andhra Pradesh: Further north, Andhra Pradesh has India's largest Project Tiger Reserve, Nagarjunasagar Sri Sailam. The state is endowed with diverse habitats such as the wetlands of Kolleru and Pulicat – rich in birdlife – the mangroves of Coringa, lush coastal lands, dry grassland and scrub of the Deccan plateau, humid moist deciduous forest of the northern Eastern Ghats and the dry deciduous forest of the Nallamalais. There is a corresponding diversity of flora and fauna. Climatically, the coastal belt is humid, while the Deccan plateau is semi-arid to arid.

Birdlife includes the great Indian bustard and the lesser florican. Jerdon's or double-banded courser (*Cursorius bitorquatus*), believed extinct since 1900, was rediscovered by the Bombay Natural History Society in Cuddapah district in 1986, to the jubilation of naturalists.

The elusive slender loris takes refuge up on the treetops with the birds, deep in the forests of Chittoor district. The wolf (*Canis lupus*) is the main predator of the desert. Wait-

Left, the three parks of Nagarahole, Bandipur and Mudumalai contain the richest herds of gaur. <u>Above</u>, the rare lion-tailed macaque.

ing and watching from the Deccan plateau, it pounces on its victim without the help of its fellow mates, although it lives in pairs or in scattered packs and occasionally organises cooperative hunting. More common is the *dhole*, as the wild dog is known in India, particularly in the Eastern Ghats. Dholes communicate with each other by whistling and are effective in catching their prey as a pack of ambushers. Gaur are found in forested tracts, and chinkara, four-horned antelope, blackbuck and nilgai (*Boselaphus tragocamelus*) in drier habitats. Until the 1960s the wild buffalo roamed parts of Visakhapatnam district, but these have now retreated to Bastar in Madhya Pradesh. A small herd of elephants has appeared, having migrated from the jungles further south. The mugger is widely present, and the estuarine or salt-water crocodile (*Crocodylus porosus*) is present in the Coringa sanctuary, in the delta region of the Godavari river. The saltwater crocodile has apparently earned a special reputation, mainly because it consumes cows, goats or even human beings to vary its diet. The stocky medium-sized fishing cat (*Felis viverrina*) and a sub-species of the common otter (*Lutra lutra*) can also be easily spotted at Coringa.

Nagarjunasagar Sri Sailam consists of tropical dry deciduous forest, with an average elevation of 2,000 ft (600 m), the highest point being 3,000 ft (917 m). It is dissected by the Krishna river and two large dams, Nagarjunasagar and Sri Sailam. Parts of this region are inaccessible, while other parts have been constantly, and still are, overrun by tourists, vehicles and cattle. This enclosure is, in many respects, India's most unwieldy Tiger Reserve because of its size (1,300 sq miles or 3,568 sq km) and these pressures. The tiger population, though, is reported to be over 60 and the leopard population almost 60.

In general, South India supports the highest populations of wild dog and gaur in India, and perhaps of elephants as well. It is also endowed with larger virgin jungle tracts than those found anywhere else in India, with the exception of the northeastern tracts, western Uttar Pradesh and parts of Madhya Pradesh. The diversity of forest types is unique to the region, as is its climatic diversity, so that it supports a wide range of plant and animal life, often in settings of pristine beauty.

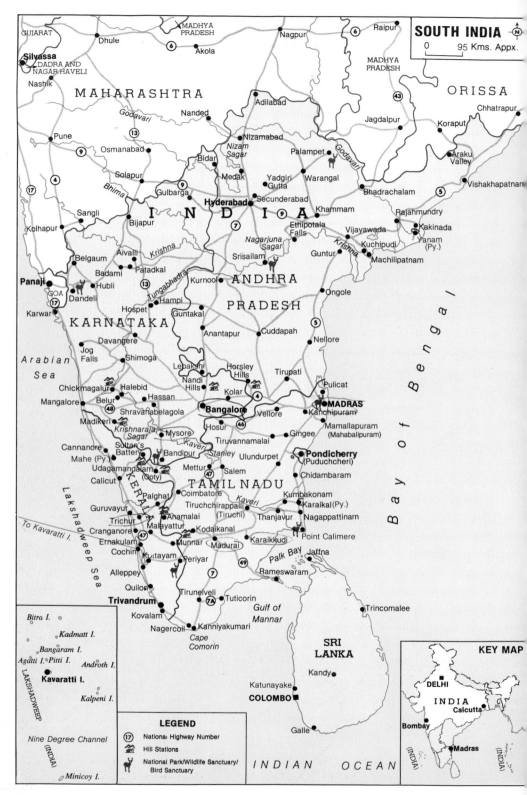

0   95 Kms. Appx.

GUJARAT

MADHYA PRADESH

Dhule

Akola

Nagpur

Raipur

ORISSA

Silvassa

DADRA AND NAGAR HAVELI

Nashik

MAHARASHTRA

Godavari

Nanded

Adilabad

MADHYA PRADESH

Jagdalpur

Koraput

Chhatrapur

Pune

Osmanabad

Nizamabad

Nizam Sagar

Palampet

Godavari

Araku Valley

Vishakhapatnam

Solapur

Bhima

Bidar

Medak

Yadgiri Gutta

Warangal

Bhadrachalam

Rajahmundry

Sangli

Gulbarga

Secunderabad

Hyderabad

Khammam

Kakinada

Kolhapur

Bijapur

INDIA

Ethipotala Falls

Vijayawada

Kuchipudi

Yanam (Py.)

Belgaum

Krishna

Nagarjuna Sagar

Srisailam

Guntur

Krishna

Machilipatnam

Panaji

Aivalli

Badami

Patadkal

Kurnool

ANDHRA

Hubli

GOA

Dandeli

Tungabhadra

Hampi

PRADESH

Ongole

Karwar

KARNATAKA

Hospet

Guntakal

Davangere

Anantapur

Cuddapah

Nellore

Arabian Sea

Jog Falls

Shimoga

Lepakshi

Horsley Hills

Tirupati

Pulicat

Chickmagalur

Halebid

Nandi Hills

Kolar

Belur

Hassan

Mangalore

Bangalore

Vellore

MADRAS

Kanchipuram

Madikeri

Shravanabelagola

Hosur

Mamallapuram (Mahabalipuram)

Cannanore

Sultan's Battery

Mysore

Krishnaraja Sagar

Kaveri

Tiruvannamalai

Gingee

Mahe (Py.)

Bandipur

Stanley

Ulundurpet

Bay of Bengal

Udagamandalam (Ooty)

Mettur

Salem

Chidambaram

Calicut

KERALA

Palghat

Coimbatore

TAMIL NADU

Kumbakonam

Karaikal (Py.)

Guruvayur

Anamalai

Kaveri

Thanjavur

Nagappattinam

Trichur

Tiruchchirappalli (Tiruchi)

Cranganore

Malayattur

Kodaikanal

Karaikkudi

Point Calimere

Ernakulam

Munnar

Madurai

Cochin

Kottayam

Periyar

Palk Bay

Jaffna

Alleppey

Rameswaram

Quilon

Tirunelveli

Trivandrum

Tuticorin

Gulf of Mannar

Trincomalee

Kovalam

Nagercoil

Kanniyakumari

Cape Comorin

SRI LANKA

Kandy

To Kavaratti I.

Lakshadweep Sea

Bitra I.

Kadmatt I.

Bangaram I.

Agatti I. Pitti I.

Androth I.

Kavaratti I.

Kalpeni I.

LAKSHADWEEP

Nine Degree Channel

(INDIA)

Minicoy I.

Katunayake

COLOMBO

Galle

INDIAN OCEAN

LEGEND

(17)   National Highway Number

Hill Stations

National Park/Wildlife Sanctuary/ Bird Sanctuary

KEY MAP

DELHI

INDIA

Calcutta

Bombay

Madras

(INDIA)

(INDIA)

ANDHRA PRADESH

The northernmost state of South India, Andhra Pradesh is the largest of the four states with an area of 275,068 sq km and a population of 58 million. The official language is Telugu, though Urdu is widely spoken in the capital, Hyderabad, and in the neighbouring Telengana district. Andhra Pradesh was formed by amalgamating the princely state of Hyderabad with the Telugu-speaking parts of the Madras Presidency.

Geographically it consists of the semi-arid Deccan plateau and fertile coastal plains irrigated by the Krishna and Godavari rivers. Andhra Pradesh has considerable topographical variations, with dense forests in the northeast, flat paddy lands in the coastal plains, several noteworthy beaches along the Bay of Bengal (particularly Bimliptatanam near Waltair) and the stark boulder-strewn region around Hyderabad relieved only by several man-made lakes. The main crops of the state are paddy, millets, sugarcane and tobacco.

Andhra Pradesh has absorbed all the vital elements of India's past. It is historically linked with India's neighbours: from its ports Indian culture spread to Sri Lanka, Indonesia, Cambodia and Thailand. Buddhism, brought here by the Mauryan emperor Ashoka's missionaries, took root under the Sathavahanas at the turn of the millennium and inspired some of its finest artistic expression. Under them, and later the Pallavas, the Chalukyas and the Kakatiyas, Andhra made important contributions to the classical Indian repertory of sculpture, architecture, Hindu law, music and dance. The era of the Bahmanis and the Qutb Shahi Sultans brought about a flowering of Indo-Islamic architecture, miniature painting and the Urdu language.

Traces of this rich heritage remain, at the Buddhist sites of Amravati and Nagarjunakonda, in the early Chalukyan temples at Alampur, at the Kalinga capital of Mukhalingam, and in the temples of the Vengi Chalukyans at Draksharama and Bikkavolu. These and the Kakatiya edifices in the north of the state, the Vijayanagara in the south, and the Qutb Shahi architecture around Hyderabad, all flourished in the varied terrain of Andhra.

Preceding pages: the Bhutanatha temple, Badami; the church of Velankanni, Tamil Nadu; monsoon breaking on the seashore; clear line to Visakhapatnam.

HYDERABAD

Hyderabad, the capital of Andhra Pradesh, is the creation of the Qutb Shahis. In 1512 Sultan Quli, powerful feudatory of a weak king, followed the example of his neighbours and made himself master of the territory he governed. It is a well documented age, both in local chronicles and in travellers' accounts, among which those of the Frenchmen Tavernier, de Thevenot and Bernier are the best known. The Qutb Shahis were patrons of art and literature, and fostered the culture and language known as Dakhni – the culture a synthesis of Indo-Persian and South Indian elements, the language a forerunner of Urdu. The Deccan again became the great trading centre it had been since Roman times, when Pliny complained that India was draining Rome of her gold. For the incomparable Kunasamudram steel, the diamonds, the beautiful painted cloths, glimmering gold brocades and fine muslins were exchanged gold, silver, horses, spices, silk and wine.

The Qutb Shahis were of Turkoman origin. There were seven rulers of the line. Their greatest feats, military as well as artistic, were achieved during the reigns of the fourth and fifth rulers, Ibrahim Quli and Mohammad Quli, but after them a decline set in. In 1687 they were conquered by Aurangzeb and the last of the Qutb Shahis, Abul Hasan Tana Shah, died in Aurangzeb's prison. The rule of the Asaf Jahis which followed saw the gradual increase of British influence. In return for his help in their wars with Tippu Sultan the British conferred the title "Our Faithful Ally" on the Nizam of Hyderabad. In the 19th century a determined effort was made to curb this influence, and Hyderabad managed to remain in control of its own affairs until it became part of independent India in 1947.

In the reorganisation of the states, part of the Nizam's dominions were merged with neighbouring states and part, with the addition of some coastal districts and Rayalseema, became what is now Andhra Pradesh.

The architecture of the Qutb Shahis is a form of the Deccan style, which is derived from the Pathan with Persian and Hindu influences. Early Deccan architecture can be seen at Gulbarga, and later developments with regional variations throughout the Deccan Sultanates. The characteristics of this distinctive regional style are lofty proportions, bulbous domes of relatively smaller volume not covering the whole roof, prominent minarets and pointed arches. It is based on sound building principles and a high level of technical skill and often faced with cut plaster decoration and brilliant encaustic tiles, a style in which provincial charm wins over classical severity.

In 1589 Mohammad Quli laid out a new city 6 miles from Golconda, on the east bank of the river Musi. Crossing the river had been made easier by the construction, 11 years before, of the **Purana Pul**, which in 1645 the French traveller Tavernier compared to the contemporary Pont Neuf in Paris. The **Charminar** is the hub of Mohammad Quli's city and the masterpiece of Qutb Shahi architecture. It is a pity that traffic around it is so heavy that there is hardly any place to stand and look at it.

The monument is built of stone with stucco plastering and decoration, square in plan, each side measuring a 100 ft. Each face is pierced with a large pointed arch with a string course, a lotus bud above the point, and decorative medallions on each side. Between this and the minarets at the corners is a row of vertical arches, and above it a prominent cornice supported on brackets and carried around the minarets above a lotus-petal capital.

The upper storey of the main square consists of a row of arches and capitals matching in height the first double-storey gallery of the minarets. Above this is a prominent decorated band, also supported on brackets, and again extended round the minarets. Then comes a screen with smaller arched openings, and another screen which stylistically seems to be of a later date.

The minarets rise to a height of 180 ft from the ground. There are two more single-storey galleries after the first. The two lower sections are polygonal, the next plain and the last arched, each section smaller in diameter than the one before. They are topped with domed finials rising out of lotus petal bases. Inside the central part, there are shallow arched alcoves in the thickness of the large arches, a balcony at first floor level, and representations of Shia *alams* (battle standards) in cut plaster.

The whole is of graceful proportion and fine workmanship. It was built in 1591, two years after the foundation of the city. De Thevenot, who visited Hyderabad 65 years after it was built, says, "Nothing in this town seems so lovely as the outside of that building, and nevertheless it is surrounded with ugly shops made of wood, and covered with straw, where they sell fruit, which spoils the aspect of it."

Part of the upper floor housed a school, and part a beautiful mosque. Unfortunately, access to the upper floor is not allowed. There are various legends about the Charminar's origin and purpose: that it was built to celebrate deliverance of the city from plague, that it was meant to be in the form of a religious symbol, but these are guesses with no historical basis.

About 75 yds (67.5 m) north of the Charminar are the four huge arches, the

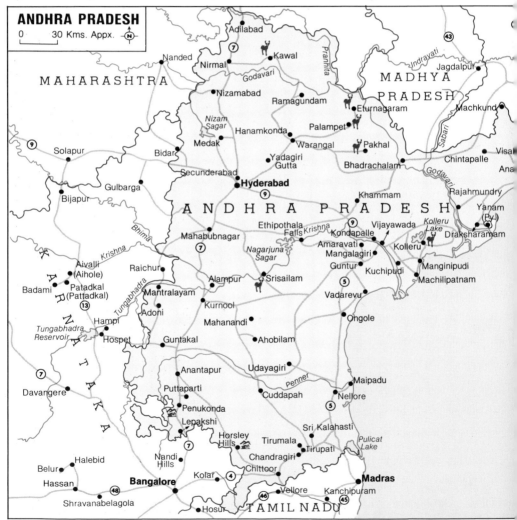

Char Kamaan, between which the royal guards used to be stationed in the times of the Qutb Shahis. If you go through the western arch, known as Mitti-ka-Sher – a corruption of Sihir-i-Batil (Land of Dreams) – you find shops selling old saris and brocades. This whole area up to the river is where the Qutb Shahi palaces used to be, and inside the Sihir-i-Batil was another gateway with doors of ebony and sandalwood studded with gold.

The streets in this area are lined with shops selling gold and silver jewellery, pearls, paper kites in season, rough glasses and cheap chinaware. Near the little wayside shrine guarded by a plaster tiger is the entrance to a square of silversmiths and jewellers where you can buy old silver jewellery.

Larh Bazar, a narrow street, is the traditional centre for bridal accessories and bangles, and leads to the **Chauk**, traditional hunting ground for antiques.

The **Jami Masjid**, close to the Charminar, is the oldest mosque in Hyderabad. It was built in 1597 and is pleasingly free from decoration. There is a fine chronogram over the entrance, and the prayer hall has an interesting facade.

The **Makka Masjid** close by is the largest mosque in South India. It is built of stone with two domes. Fifteen arches in three bays support the roof, and the prayer niche is carved out of a single slab of granite. It was completed by Aurangzeb, and Hyderabadis like to say that it is because of his parsimony that the minars are so short. The Asaf Jahis are buried here. Musa Khan, supervisor during Abdullah Qutb Shah's reign of the long-drawn-out building of the Makka Masjid, levied a *damri* for every rupee spent, and with this built the beautiful **Toli Masjid** on the Karwan, the old high road between Purana Pul and Golconda.

Of the other Qutb Shahi buildings near the Charminar, the **Badshahi Ashurkhana** and the **Darul Shifa** are the most interesting. The first, which houses the religious symbols of the Shias, still has its original encaustic tile decoration in the earlier parts of the building, the central niche and the western wall. These tiles with their beautiful calligraphy and geometric designs remind one of what the facades of other Qutb Shahi buildings must have looked like in their original state.

The Darul Shifa, built in 1595, is one of the most important buildings left standing, and it is a pity that it is in such poor condition. It was a hospital and medical school. High doors lead to an imposing courtyard surrounded on three sides by a double-storey building with large rooms on both floors. Unani (Greek) medicine was taught and practised here, and all expenses were met by the state. The baths have disappeared, but on the outside along the road can be

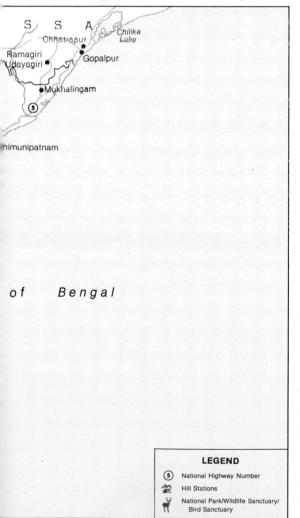

S S A
Okhatrapur · Chilika Luhu
Ramagiri
Udayagiri · Gopalpur
Mukhalingam
⑤
himunipatnam

o f   B e n g a l

LEGEND

⑤ National Highway Number
Hill Stations
National Park/Wildlife Sanctuary/ Bird Sanctuary

seen the remains of the caravanserai, where the relatives of the sick could stay. The mosque nearby is contemporary with it and has some fine tiled medallions.

Dusty and badly displayed though it is, the large Mughal jade collection in the **Salar Jung Museum** is outstanding. There are several beautifully carved and inlaid pieces, including gem-studded boxes, animal-headed daggers and knives and delicate translucent leaf-shaped drinking bowls. The museum has exceptional collections of manuscripts, miniature paintings and Indian jades, arms and armour, Chinese porcelain, Indian textiles and *pichwais*, ivory, Indo-Persian glass and Bidriware are very fine.

The Western collections are curious rather than beautiful: Salar Jung's taste, impeccable in Eastern art, runs to the florid where Western art is concerned. The development and different styles of Indian miniature painting can be followed from the comprehensive collection shown here. It ranges from early

Jain Kalpasutras and vibrant 17th century Malwa Raga-Ragini paintings to the first impact of Persian artists, European influence and finally to superb examples of the Mughal, Deccan, Rajput and Pahari schools, *siyah qalam* (pen and ink) drawings and illustrated Deccan manuscripts.

The arms gallery has an interesting collection of different styles of swords and daggers, some made of Kunasamudram steel, said to have forged the chisels of the Egyptian pyramid-builders. There are historic Mughal weapons and a resplendent diamond-encrusted ceremonial sword of Salar Jung. The Arabic and Persian manuscripts include a 9th century Koran in Kufic script, an original Diwan of Hafiz, the great Persian poet, calligraphic masterpieces and royal autographs.

Golconda: Built on the site of an earlier Kakatiya fort, five miles from Hyderabad, Golconda rises 400 ft (122 m) from the plain. It was built by Quli Qutb Shah and during Qutb Shahi times gained an aura of riches and romance which has

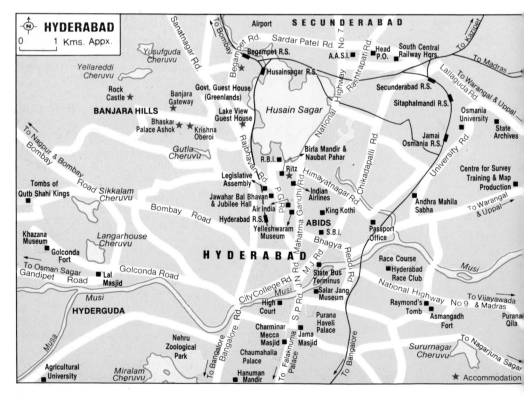

never quite been dispelled. It was the Qutb Shahi capital until the end of the 16th century.

The outer wall, 50-60 ft (15-18 m) high, encloses houses, shops, water reservoirs and fields. It is of massive thickness, built of huge blocks of local granite weighing more than a ton each. There are 87 semicircular bastions or *burj*, some still with their armament. Each bastion has a name. The Petla Burj commands stretches of country to the west. The Musa Burj, a three-storey bastion to the southeast, was built after the first Mughal invasion by Musa Khan, the builder of the Toli Masjid, and has an inscription with an account of a battle of the Mughal campaign in both Telugu and Persian.

There are eight gates, four of which are in use. The direct road from Hyderabad winds through the Fateh Darwaza, the gate through which Aurangzeb's conquering army entered, led by his son Prince Muazzam in 1687. That was the only time Golconda was ever captured, and even then it was by treachery and

not in fair fight. Invited to attack Golconda by Mir Jumla, a powerful Deccan noble out of favour with the king, Aurangzeb had to raise the siege in 1656 on orders from his father Shah Jahan. The second time he came, so he said, to put down heresy but he returned to Delhi laden with the fabled treasure of Golconda, including the Koh-i-noor diamond. Even so, the fort had held out for 8 months until he managed to bribe one of the defenders to open the gate. The name of Abdulla Khan Pani is remembered for his treachery, as is that of Abdul Razak Lari for his gallantry in the same siege.

Golconda at this time was the centre of the world trade in diamonds. There were mines in the south of the kingdom, and a large part of the royal revenues came from taxes levied on their working. Stones over a certain size were the prerogative of the rulers and there was a skilled cutting and polishing industry. Pearls were also imported and drilled here, as they still are.

The **Bala Hissar gate** is the only

Wine
and attar,
traditional
products of
Hyderabad for
the Nizam's
court and the
aristocracy.

entrance to the fort. It is a huge doorway protected by a curtain wall and teak-wood doors studded with metal spikes, and leads into a large inner porch. On the right are mortuary baths, straight ahead are the guards barracks and Nagina Bagh, and on the left is the three-storey armoury. Looking up, you can see the innermost wall of Golconda; it is an imposing sight, the huge blocks of cut stone butting onto natural outcrops of granite.

Turning left past the armoury, you come to **Taramati's mosque** on your right. It has a small platform in front supported on arches, pretty parapet and wall treatment and no dome or minarets. Taramati was Abdulla Qutb Shah's companion, and is buried in the royal tombs.

On the left, near the outer wall, are the camel stables and Hall of Justice, and straight ahead are the remains of the royal palaces. These are the most interesting ruins in the fort. From the huge pointed arches and massive walls with cut plaster decoration, rectangular and arched niches, and the traces of mother-of-pearl inlay and polychrome tiles, they appear to be of early Qutb Shahi origin. Some of the buildings are either two or three storeys high, and there once were gardens with fountains, Turkish baths and mirror-tiled dressing rooms. In their original carpeted, silk-hung and lamplit state they must have been a magnificent set of apartments.

Three stone stairways lead up to the **Baradari** at the top of the fort. As you go up, you can see the pipes for the water system along the side walls. A series of Persian wheels took the water from reservoirs to the top, from where it was piped into baths and flush cisterns. On the way up there are changing views of the ruined palaces below and the countryside around, with the tombs to the northwest. Halfway up the hill there is a well, baths, the remains of Abul Hasan Tana Shah's garden, a small jail, a grain store and a mosque. An inscription at the grain store reads that it was erected by Abdullah.

At the top is a temple and the double-

The bazaars around the Char Minar offer bargains for pearls, cloths and metalwork.

storey Baradari. The large hall on the first floor is finely proportioned, and may have been used as a durbar hall. Steps lead to a terrace and stone *takht* (throne). On the western side, the outer wall is protected by earthworks; the projecting bastion is the Petla Burj. At some distance can be seen the mosque of Pemamati and the pavilion of Taramati. On the northwest are the Qutb Shahi tombs with Banjara Hills rising all along the northern side. It was in these hills that Aurangzeb camped during his first campaign, and the local Banjaras who supplied his army. Far away can be seen Husain Sagar with Secunderabad beyond, and on the east is the city of Hydcrabad.

Mir Alam reservoir is nearby, with the hill of Falaknuma rising beyond it, and the army parade grounds are on the southeast. Coming down again towards Bala Hissar gate, near the guard lines is the double-storeyed building known as the office of Akanna and Madanna, the ministers of Abdullah Qutb Shah, though again this is pure speculation.

The Nagina Bagh, because of its typical Mughal layout, is presumed to be a late addition.

Outside the Bala Hissar gate are two massive arches known as Habshi Kamaan. The rooms above these housed the Naubat Khana (ceremonial musicians) and the Ethiopian guard. As you approach Banjara gate, towards the Tombs, the road winds between the walls of the fort, and carvings of mythical animals can be seen. On the right is the Katora Hauz, built by Ibrahim Quli and used by Abul Hasan Tana Shah for bathing. In the royal necropolis are buried all but the last of the Qutb Shahis, with their wives, concubines, children, doctors and ministers.

The Qutb Shahi tombs: These tombs are remarkable for the unity of their design: from the earliest to the last they conform to the Qutb Shahi canon. Unlike the mosques, they all have a central dome, more or less onion shaped, rising from a lotus-petal calyx, and small domed minarets. Stucco decoration is one of their hallmarks. Most of the graves are of black basalt with good calligraphic inscriptions. At the centre of the enclosure is the **Hamaam**, the mortuary baths built by Sultan Quli. The simple interior space is impressive, with a beautiful inlaid platform and arrangements for hot and cold water.

To the west is the earliest tomb, **Sultan Quli**'s, contemporary with the Hamaam. The early style shows its Bahmani derivation in its simple outline and limited surface decoration. The outer walls of the tomb chamber are divided into three arched panels on each face, and the interior is octagonal. The tomb has inscriptions in Naskh and Tauqi style.

Facing the Hamaam is the tomb of **Mohammad Quli**, the most impressive of all. It stands on a double terrace and the facade, differing from the others, is in pillar and lintel style, the slim octagonal columns rising 22 ft (6.6 m) high. The end bays on each face are closed with arched recesses. The octagonal columns at the corners become small domed minarets above a broad decorative band; in between the columns is an

Golconda Fort is 20 minutes away from the city

arched and crenellated parapet. In Qutb Shahi days these tombs were carpeted, curtained and lit. Tavernier reports, "At the tombs of the Kings about four in the afternoon there is a dole of bread and pilau to all the poor that come. If you would see anything that is fayre you must go to view these tombs upon a festival day for then from morning till night they are hung with rich tapestry." Aurangzeb's army camped here in 1687, and much of the polychrome decoration was destroyed at that time.

Beyond Mohammad Quli's tomb is **Ibrahim Qutb Shah's**, on a high plinth with black basalt doorways and a double row of arched recesses. Some of the tilework still remains. In a smaller dome on this terrace lies the tomb of his son Mohammad Amin, and both tombs evidently have fine calligraphic inscriptions; Mohammad Amin's has the only Kufic inscription in Golconda or Hyderabad.

Jamshed Quli was second in the Qutb Shahi line, and his seven-year stewardship was a sort of interregnum between the great reigns of his father and brother. He is supposed to have been responsible for the murder of his 93-year-old father in the Jami Masjid. The tomb said to be his (though there is no inscription) is perhaps the most architecturally satisfying, a double-storey facade of octagonal plan, with arched recesses at both levels, a decorated balcony supported on brackets, a matching crenellated cornice with small minarets at each angle and an almost hemispherical dome.

Just inside the gate to the right is the tomb of **Hayat Baksh Begum**. This remarkable woman was the only child of Mohammad Quli, the founder of Hyderabad, and was educated to rule by her father. She shared the duties of kingship with her husband Sultan Mohammad, whose tomb is nearby, and was the regent and virtual ruler of the kingdom during her son's long minority. The tiny mosque in front of her tomb is known as Aurangzeb's mosque; he is said to have build it here out of regard for Hayat Baksh. The mosque behind and to the

The outer walls of Golconda extend for 8 miles around the citadel.

left of this tomb has been newly restored and cleaned, and is one of the finest in Hyderabad.

Outside the enclosure is the tomb of **Abdullah Qutb Shah**, the sixth in the line, set on a large terrace. The five-arched upper storey is set well back from the seven-arched lower part, a technique also deployed on the tombs of his parents Sultan Mohammad and Hayat Baksh. The stucco decorations of this tomb are particularly fine and some traces of the glazed tilework remain.

The Asaf Jahi era began in 1724 when Nizam-ul-Mulk, the Mughal governor of the Deccan, declared his independence of the declining Mughal dynasty. His successors had to contend with the struggle for supremacy between the Marathas, the French, and the East India Company, and allied themselves now and then with one or another of these forces. A colourful figure recorded in the annals of Hyderabad was Monsieur Raymond, a French adventurer who arrived in Pondicherry in 1775 at the age of 20 and rose to command the Nizam's troops and later to direct his ordinance factories.

Raymond is reckoned to have been a brilliant general. He caught the fancy of the ordinary people, and Malleson says, "No European of mark in India ever succeeded in gaining to such an extent the love, the esteem and the admiration of the natives of the country." He was devoted to his country and to the cause of his employer, and became embittered at the increase of British influence over the Nizam. In 1798 he committed suicide after shooting his pets. The **tomb of Monsieur Raymond** on a little hill in Sarurnagar is marked by a simple obelisk of black granite with the initials, "J.R." At the anniversary of his death an Urs or festival used to be held, as for the local holy men, for Musa Ram or Musa Rahim, as he was known.

The Residency: An addition to Hyderabad during the days of the East India Company is this Regency mansion built in 1803 by James Kirkpatrick, resident at the court of the second Nizam, to replace the much smaller villa

Golconda fortifications overlooking the elegant tombs of the Qubt Shah rulers.

used by the previous incumbents. It was built on land donated by the Nizam and its construction was also paid for by him: "Nizzy will pay!" declared the Resident, and the Nizam did, including inflated prices for some discards from the Brighton Pavilion.

Designed by an officer of the Royal Engineers, the Residency is full of architectural solecisms which the visitor may find either charming or irritating. The main facade has a six-columned portico in the Corinthian style, the pediment still bearing the arms of the East India Company. A pair of lions flank the granite steps, replacing the original sphinxes. The Durbar Hall is well proportioned with a gallery, Ionic columns, a beautiful painted ceiling and chandeliers and mirrors acquired from the Prince Regent.

Kirkpatrick, a great favourite of the Nizam, was an unusual man who spoke fluent Urdu and Persian. He caused a scandal by sheltering and later marrying a girl from a good Hyderabadi family, a relative of the Prime Minister, who is said to have taken refuge in his house from an enforced marriage. To prove his love, he built for her the suite of rooms in Indian style known as the **Rang Mahal**. Also of interest in the Residency grounds is the architect's model of the building and the cemetery, last resting place of some of the English worthies of the time. The Residency now houses the Women's College, and there are plans for its renovation.

There is nothing of architectural interest in the modern public buildings of the city, none that have the character of the earlier styles. The buildings of the early 20th century, **Osmania University** at Tarnaka, the **High Court** and **Osmania Hospital** facing each other across the river Musi, with the State Library nearby, are built in a style of Islamic pastiche; but they have an undeniable grace and convey the flavour of the last glorious fling of the old order in Hyderabad, the high Edwardian period between the two World Wars, which the great photographer Raja Deen Dayal has so faithfully recorded.

Set amid tranquil gardens, the Qutb Shahi tombs are inspired by Persian architectural models.

In the **Bagh-e-Aam** or Public Garden is the **Legislative Assembly** building, also dating from the same period, some charming pavilions still being used for public receptions, and the **State Archaeological Museum**. Sadly, the space this building affords is grievously cramped and as a result priceless treasures from Andhra's past can be seen scattered about the gardens of the Archaeological Department.

The museum collection has a superb Chalukyan Mahavir of the 12th century in polished black basalt. The Buddhist gallery has a 4th century standing Buddha from Oppokondur, and some pieces from Amravati. There are also some Kakatiya sculptured columns and roof slabs in the garden of the museum, reassembled as a little pavilion, some Islamic inscriptions in black basalt, and a good collection of ancient weapons on display.

Opposite the Bagh-e-Aam is **Naubat Pahar**, an imposing 300-ft high natural feature from where the Mughal *firmans* or edicts were broadcast in the 17th century. The **Birla Observatory** and **Planatorium** is located here.

Hyderabad Zoo or the **Nehru Zoological Park**, to give it its full name, is situated on the banks of a reservoir named after Mir Alam, the prime minister of the second Nizam. It is a delightful sprawling area, much of which has been left wild. Some of the animals inhabit large moated spaces rather than cages. There is a nocturnal animals pavilion, a crocodile hatchery and a large cage of aquatic birds.

Husain Sagar, a large 17th century reservoir, separates Secunderabad from the older city of Hyderabad. The "bund" or retaining wall dates back to the reign of Ibrahim Qutb Shah and was built by his brother-in-law Husain Shah Wali, after whom it is named. The statues on the bund date back to 1986.

Secunderabad originated as a British cantonment under British law in 1806. Its military past and present day commercial activity make it somewhat more orderly, if less colourful, than chaotic Hyderabad.

he **Vidhan Sabha**, he state legislature of Hyderabad.

THE LAND OF
THE "ANDRAE"

The original site of Nagarjunakonda, (104 miles/166km south of Hyderabad), the Hill of Nagarjuna, is now under the reservoir of Nagarjunasagar. Before it was submerged, evidence was found of early settlements from the Stone Age up to medieval times, but its most brilliant period was the century of Ikshvaku rule, beginning in the second quarter of the 3rd century AD. At this time the valley was known as Vijayapuri – there is no known connection with Nagarjuna, the Buddhist philosopher of the 2nd century.

A valley on the banks of the Krishna river, Nagarjunakonda was protected on the other three sides by natural fortifications. Satyavahana culture had been established in the Godavari-Krishna basin since 200 BC, and thrived in the immediate post-Christian era.

According to the Roman historian Pliny, the country of the "Andrae" had thirty well fortified towns. The economy that produced this wealth was based on crafts and trade more than on agriculture, and the civilisation was urban rather than rural. Trade flourished, especially with Rome but also with Southeast Asia, the most important product being the local muslin. More than a thousand years before the European "factories", the Romans had their trade emporia in coastal Andhra.

Buddhism was the religion of the people. At Nagarjunakonda the Ikshvaku rulers were Brahmanic, but their princesses inclined towards Buddhism, and were responsible for the building of many of the *chaityas* and monasteries. Chamtasri, sister of Chamtamula, the first of the Ikshvaku line, built the earliest of the Buddhist monuments found at the site, the Mahachaitya complex. Donors' tablets show that though there was royal patronage, the artisans and craftsmen, both individually and in guilds, were the backbone of the Sangha. Obviously wealth was not concentrated in a few hands but distributed through society.

The Ikshvaku rulers were native to Andhra, and were inheritors of Satyavahana culture, though less refined. Under their rule the centre moved from Amravati to Nagarjunakonda (22 miles/35 km northwest of Vijayawada Guntur), perhaps the artists and sculptors too. The Nagarjunakonda reliefs have the same style and idiom, the same technique, but there is a certain naivete in facial types, and a simplicity in the attitudes of the figures when compared with those of Amravati. Nature, both animal and plant, plays a larger part. The stone used for carving by the Buddhists in Andhra is always the same, white limestone with a grey-green tinge. Like Greek sculpture, it was originally painted.

Nine important monuments from the Ikshvaku period have been rebuilt inside the medieval hill fort which is now an island lying on the eastern bank of the reservoir. The Brahmanic temples are the earliest found in South India. By far the larger number of monuments is Buddhist, and contained most of the sculpture now in the museum.

From the ruins of secular buildings a fascinating picture emerges of a planned city with wide roads, drainage and sewerage, public baths, assembly rooms and inns for travellers. Sculptured reliefs depict games and entertainments such as wrestling, dancing and drinking, and there are stones engraved for dice games.

The only amphitheatre in ancient India was found here, with superb accoustics, suggesting a high regard for music and a connection with contemporary Rome. An impressive giant statue of the Buddha dominates the museum. Like the other Buddha statues of Andhra, this follows the conventions of Mathura (between Delhi and Agra). But in the carving of the panels and roundels the Nagarjunakonda and Amravati sculptors not only carry on the tradition of Sanchi and Barhut in Madhya Pradesh and Mathura – the deep relief and varied planes to catch the light – but also echo from Gandhara the animation of the figures and the rhythmic lines of the composition.

The memorial columns are rare examples of secular art, commemorating the achievements of soldiers and artisans. The terracotta heads are witness to Hellenistic contacts, borne out by the numbers of Roman coins found here. The jewellery, ritual vessels and reliquaries are in precious metals, but it is the sculpted drum slabs, beams, cornices and pillars that are the treasures of Nagarjunakonda.

Vijayawada: The Krishna, one of India's great rivers, dominates the bustling commercial town of **Vijayawada**. All is calm and peaceful on its banks, while the town itself, impressive in extent, is a nightmare of unmarked, unplanned and crowded streets with no trees, parks or green spaces.

Bandar Road is the only exception, and here the **Victoria Jubilee Museum** is an example of a small local museum, set in a shady garden of old trees. In its open verandahs it has a small but good collection of sculpture, among them an important white stone early Shiva, two-armed and seated with a Nandi, one of

the earliest Pallava sculptures from the Krishna valley. Inside are prehistoric finds, local crafts and coins. The Buddhist gallery, though small, has some rare pieces from nearby sites.

Though the town is modern, it has ancient roots. The **Mogalrajapuram cave temple** has an early but badly disfigured representation of Shiva Nataraja. The **Akanna-Madanna temple** is cut into two levels of the hillside, and in the grounds have been re-assembled some capitals and beams from a 9th century Vengi Chalukyan temple from Jammidoddi, with delightful smiling dwarfs holding up the ceiling. They seem to bridge a gap of 3 centuries, faint reflections of an earlier tradition.

The **Ondavalli caves** are at a pleasant riverbank site on the other side of the river from the town. These cave temples, dating from the 6th and 7th centuries, with the remains of sculpted columns and wall niches for sculpture, foreshadow the free-standing temples of the 8th century.

Fifteen miles (25 km) north of Vija-

Fishing boats, Visakhapatnam.

yawada is **Kondapally**, a village famous for its painted wooden figures. Its rural charm has been eroded by the thermal power station nearby, but Kondapally fort is worth the short, stiff climb. It was built by the Reddi kings of Kondaviddu in the 13th century and has later additions by the Qutb Shahis.

Machilipatnam, from "Maisolipatnam", is the centre of Kalamkari, the painted cloths of antiquity that have been exported from here for over a thousand years. It was to collect and export these that the first English and Dutch factories were established in the 17th century. The Kalamkari process involves 14-15 stages after the preparation of the dye, including fixing the colour by the use of mordants.

Amravati: At Amravati (22 miles/35 km north of Guntur), in the 2nd century AD, the art of the Krishna valley achieved its highest point. Andhra, through the influence of Buddhism and trade with Rome, was already emerging from its simple tribal seclusion, when in the 1st century AD it came under Satyavahana rule. They had already been great patrons of art in western Deccan, and they brought with them a tolerant, liberal and cosmopolitan culture that fostered art and learning.

Buddhism at this time was in a state of flux, reflected in the art of the time: Buddha is now shown in human form for the first time, whereas before he was represented only by symbols. In these iconic figures the influences of Mathura and Gandhara are evident.

In the sculpted medallions and panels of Amravati, all these influences come together: the physical characteristics of the local people and their worldly and unmystical approach to life, the ideals of Buddhism, the sophistication of Satyavahana civilisation, the derivations from Mathura, Gandhara and West Asia, all put down with a sureness of touch attained by the Amravati sculptor after 300 years of practice. Coomaraswamy describes the Amravati style as "the most voluptuous and the most delicate flower of Indian art".

Today only a low mound remains,

Rickshaw depicting mythological characters.

with a paved path around it. A few of the slabs from the stupa find themselves in the **Amareswara temple** nearby. The temple itself, though of respectable antiquity and originally Eastern Chalukyan in style, has been restored and renovated. But most of the damage was done at the end of the 18th century, when a local landowner systematically raided the site for building materials for a new town.

The **Museum** at the site houses some important pieces from the various phases of Amravati's development and from other nearby Buddhist sites. An early stele carved in low relief from the 2nd century BC shows scenes of contemporary life at Dhanyakataka. A *yakshi* from the 2nd or 1st century BC wearing heavy jewellery is very much in the style of Sanchi and Barhut. From the mature phase, the presentation of Rahula to the Buddha and the story of the serpent king, both on parts of the railing, are outstanding. The life-size image of Buddha in the first gallery was found here, and the small bronzes,

among the earliest in South India. The Padampani figures in Gallery 2 are very fine. Some reliquaries and a gold necklace from Gummadidurru are in the reserve collection.

Northeastern Andhra: The coastline along the Visakhapatnam-Bimlipatnam road is a picture – blue sea, curving white sandy beaches, palm trees and feathery araucaria plantations. On the other side are the foothills of the Eastern Ghats. The sea is deceptively calm, but like the rest of the eastern coast the currents here are treacherous, and swimming is dangerous.

Visakhapatnam, in spite of its large dockyard, oil refinery, steel plant and other industries is a pleasant town, perhaps the most so in Andhra today. It has a natural harbour and a large naval base.

The Vaishnavite temple at **Simhachalam**, 12 miles (20 km) away, once belonged, with the villages around, to the Raja of Vizianagram. It is situated in a commanding position about 770 ft (240 m) above the plain, with wide views of the surrounding countryside. **Ondapalle caves.**

The temple dates from the 11th century, and is built in the Orissan style. Though it has suffered from later additions and renovations, the original reliefs on the walls are very fine, including several variations of the Krishna and *gopis* theme. In the courtyard is a large stone chariot with horses.

About 15 miles (25 km) towards Bimlipatnam the remains of a Buddhist monastery were recently discovered from the air by the Indian Air Force. This is the hill-top site of **Bavikonda**. Very little now remains except the water reservoirs cut into the red laterite and a few sculpted pillars in the same stone, but the site itself is enjoyable for its calm and natural beauty.

Near Anakapalle, at **Sankaran**, there is a remarkable complex of Buddhist *stupas* and *viharas* cut into the rocks.

The Eastern Ghats rise inland from Visakhapatnam. The road winds through thickly wooded hills with streams and waterfalls, the highest and scenically the most picturesque part of the state. There is a profusion of bird life and some wild animals, including panthers and a few tigers. There are coffee estates around Ananthagiri and Chintapalli, and the limestone **Borra caves** with stalagmites, stalacites and an underground stream nearby. The forests here and at Araku valley are the home of tribal people, the original inhabitants of the state. A wild-fowl sanctuary has been erected at **Pedda Cheruvu** near Vizianagram, while at **Kondakarla Ava** about 35 miles (50 km) from Vizag, migratory birds make their home during October and November.

There is a group of three small but beautiful temples at **Mukhalingam**, just 30 miles (48 km) north of Srikakulam on the Vamsadhara river. Mukhalingam was for a time the capital of the great Kalinga empire, which at its peak ruled all the country between the Ganges to the north and the Godavari to the south. The Eastern Ganga dynasty ruled here for over a thousand years, from the 5th to the 15th century. Their empire had links with neighbours to the south and west, the Vengis, Cholas and

Raja Mahal, Chandragiri.

Kadambas, and was visited by Buddhist pilgrims. One of them, the Chinese traveller Hieun Tsang, left a description of the city as he saw it in the 7th century. He saw a peaceful and prosperous land and comments on the abundance of flowers and fruit, on the vast jungles and the many impressive Buddhist *stupas*, most already falling into disrepair with the decline of the faith.

The three temples, the **Someswara**, **Madhukeswara** and **Bhimeswara**, were built in that order between the 6th and 12th centuries AD. The style is Orissan with local variations. They were probably built when the Saivite Eastern Ganga empire was well-established and show a confidence and maturity of style as in the contemporary temples at Bhubaneshwar, foreshadowing the great temple at Puri.

The Someswara, the smallest of the three, is of simple design. The horizontal bands of stone are broken by niches on each side and by the doorway on the west. Above the lintel the banding continues in the *deul* and is crowned by the *phalaka*, *gala*, and *amlaka shikhara* resting on four seated Nandi bulls at the corners. The whole effect is of graceful proportion and fine detail. The sculpture of the doorway and the niches on the walls deserves detailed study. In the central niche on the north wall is a poetic Kartikeya with a peacock at his feet. The whole is interspersed with exuberantly curling leafy vines in bands and panels.

The largest of the three is the Madhukeswara. Built on a rectangular plan, it has a courtyard, a central doorway facing east, and one central and four corner shrines.

The sculptured figures of Mukhalingam, though of somewhat exaggerated proportions, are characterised by a serene detachment of expression which is their great attraction. Warriors, kings and sages adorn the walls of the Madhukeswara. The south wall is a masterpiece, a series of beautiful units: the panels of elegant scrollwork, the niches with sculpted figures, the architectural details of the corner shrines, the

Below left, Raja Mahal interior. Below, Tirupati temple, the richest in India.

southern doorway and seven miniature *vimanas* making up a magnificent whole. The figures of Kumara, Durga Bhuvaraha, Bhikshatana, Shiva and Narasimha are outstanding, while "the door facing east may well claim to be the loveliest entrance to a temple in the whole of India."

The Godavari Delta: The area around **Rajamundry** and **Kakinada** is strewn with remains of Eastern Chalukyan architecture. This was the kingdom of the Vengi Chalukyans who ruled coastal Andhra for 400 years from AD 625. Their capital may have been **Eluru**, which today is a pleasant small town. The once thriving carpet industry here which in the 17th and 18th centuries produced among the finest carpets in India, is in the doldrums, though attempts are being made to revive it.

The reign of the Vengi Chalukyans was a time of wars, upheavals and chaos, but two powerful rulers, Gunaga Vijayaditya and Chalukya Bhim in the late 9th century were great temple builders and their works can be seen at **Bikkavolu**, **Draksharama**, **Chebrolu** and **Bhimavaram**.

Most of the temples are in use and have suffered from later renovations, additions and much whitewashing. Probably the one that has suffered least is the Bhimeswara at Chebrolu, untouched except for the *vimana*. The doorways are sculpted with figures of *dwarapalas*, dancers and musicians, and the Buddhist *purnaghata*, the vase symbol denoting the birth of the Buddha, reappears as a decorative motif. The glossy black stone torso of Kumara already shows Kakatiya influence.

During this period the architectural importance of sculpture was established; it began to dominate rather than decorate the temple wall. This tendency grew even further during Kakatiya times, and became quite overwhelming during the Vijayanagara period. In Vengi sculpture, an element of folk art combines with the earlier tradition of vigorous naturalism. To this idiom belong the delightful musicians and dancers of the panels from Jammidoddi, now

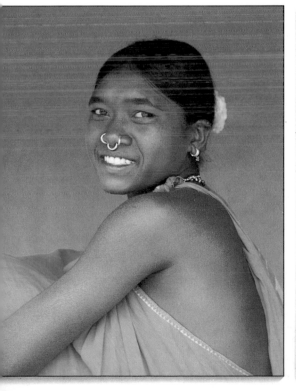

in the grounds of the Akanna-Madanna temple at Vijayawada, and the Mahisamardini from the same source, unique in the South for its detail.

Further south along the coast is **Chirala**, one of the great centres of handloom weaving in Andhra, and of the *telia rumal*, a fabric woven from oil-treated and tie-dyed thread, recognisable by its distinctive design and the oily smell of the new cloth. It has been exported to Arab countries for centuries and was the traditional head-cloth of the Arabs, the oil treatment being said to keep off the sun's rays.

The towns of Kalahasti and Tirupati are full of crafts fostered by the patronage of temples and pilgrims. At **Kalahasti temple**, hangings depicting religious and mythological themes are painted in vegetable colours using an elaborate technique involving 14 stages spread over 3 weeks. Icons are cast in bronze and carved in wood and stone, and bells and gongs are cast and lathe-turned in bell-metal.

Tirupati: Tirupati is a phenomenon. It attracts vast numbers of pilgrims all year round, and offerings of money and jewellery pour in every day. Easily approached by road or rail from Madras 106 miles (170 km) to the southeast, it is billed as the richest and busiest pilgrimage centre in the world, overtaking Mecca and Rome.

Perhaps a truer spiritual atmosphere is to be found at **Srisailam**, the Holy Hill, which has been venerated as the abode of the gods since pre-history. It lies in the Nallamalai range, once thickly wooded and full of wildlife and rare plants, now alas fast being denuded. The western approach to Srisailam for the pilgrim is from **Alampur**, the heart of "Chalukya Visaya", the country of the Badami Chalukyas from the 6th century until they were supplanted by the Rastrakutas in the middle of the 8th century. Badami Chalukyan art in Andhra began in the 7th century, and the style first seen at Aihole developed simultaneously at Pattadakal and Alampur, with its mature phase at Badami.

Within the walls of a moated fort on

Tirupati pilgrim, head shaven in fulfilment of a vow.

the south bank of the Tungabhadra river just before it joins the Krishna are eight temples and a museum. The architecture of the temples with their curved and tapering *vimanas* crowned with *amlaka shikharas*, and the delineated sculpture niches on the temple walls marks an important stage in the evolution of temple design. Unfortunately, much of the sculpture is missing or broken, but the museum houses a good collection.

The genius of the Alampur sculptor lies in expressing abstract concepts in the curves and tensions of the human body. Half-closed eyes and serene smiles convey mystical ectasy, divine power is channelled through the taut dance pose of Shiva Nataraja, and the Kumara and Devi and *mithuna* couples express the duality and interdependence of male and female.

The pillars at Alampur often have *purnaghatas* at the base and lion masks at the top, while the sculpture niches are elaborately defined with columns, domed *chaityas* above and small sculpted panels below. The diagonal

Florists do a brisk business at places of pilgrimage.

lines of the Shiva figures of Svargabrahma, the Nataraja on the north wall and the Tripuratankamurti on the south convey dynamic and powerful movement, while the figure of Parvati in the museum embodies serenity. There is a celestial airiness over the lintel of the *antarala* doorway of the Garuda Brahma. The largest temple of the group, the Balabrahma, has several notable icons, while the door panels of the Taraka Brahma are noteworthy.

Southwest Andhra: This area had been ruled by a branch of the Pallavas between the 8th and 10th centuries, and their capital **Hemavati**, now a small village near Hindupur, has evidence of their highly developed artistic sense. The **Mallikarjuna** and **Doddeswara** temples, incorporating the best traditions of the Karnataka and Andhra styles, are full of sculptural delights. In the Vijayanagara period this region was an important part of the empire; temples, forts and palaces in the Vijayanagara style can be found at **Tadpatri**, **Lepakshi**, **Chandragiri**, **Gandikotta**

and **Penukonda** and more Vijay-anagara temple art at **Markapur** and **Pushpagiri**.

The **Ramalingeswara temple** at Tadpatri was built in the 15th century and the **Venkataramana** in the early 16th. They are in the Chalukyan mode with Chola elements and the Vijay-anagara stamp: a lavish use of monumental sculpture. The northern *gopuram* of the Ramalingeswara, though unfinished, is considered by many, including Fergusson, to be the greatest achievement of Vijayanagara art:

"The wonders of the place are two gopurams… One of these was apparently quite finished, the other… never carried higher than the perpendicular part. In almost all the gopurams of India this part is comparatively plain, all the figure sculpture and ornament being reserved for the upper or pyramidal part. In this instance however the whole of the perpendicular part is covered with the most elaborate sculpture, cut with exquisite sharpness and precision… and produces an effect richer and on the whole perhaps in better taste than anything else in this style."

The characteristic blending of figurative, architectural and decorative elements begins at the lowest level, and an excellent Mahisamardini and a mysterious bowman feature on the outer side. The southern *gopuram*, though damaged, is comparable to the other. On the inner face a figure with folded hands in Vijayanagara head-gear is assumed to be Ramalinga Nayudu, the benefactor of the temple.

In the **Venkataramana** the artistic emphasis is on the walls and pillars of the *mandapam*. On the walls of the *ardhamandapa* are some beautiful Puranic reliefs. The 40 columns of the *mukhamandapa* support *surasundari* figures, the inner composite pillars bear riders on huge rearing, mythical, *yalis*. The mouldings are decorated with creepers, swams and elephants.

Lepakshi: Eight miles (13 km) east of Hindupur (85 miles/136 km north of Bangalore) on a little hill is the **Virabhadra temple**, built in 1530 by a

Village house.

Vijayanagara governor, Virupanna. It was said that he misused state funds to build it and forestalled royal punishment by blinding himself. A monumental Nandi, the biggest in India, proudly raises its head several furlongs away. The temple is in a walled enclosure, and on either side of the inner entrance are carved figures of the river goddesses Ganga and Yamuna with a background of foliage. Near the shrine is a huge Nagalinga carved out of a boulder.

The pillars of the *mandapas* have Vijayanagara capitals and carry figures of gods and goddesses, musicians or dancers. Some have single or double *yali* brackets. Sadly, these and the panels in relief on the walls of the *ardhamandapa* have been disfigured by layers of whitewash.

The glory of Lepakshi is its beautiful frescoed ceilings. Painting on cloth must always have played a part in temple ritual, though being fragile they have mostly perished. Frescoes no longer had a place when temple forms evolved from the cave to the free-standing, until the flat stuccoed granite ceilings of the Vijayanagara style again provided a suitable background. Certainly, 9 centuries later there is an echo in Lepakshi of the Ajanta frescos – in the colour palette, the differing skin tones of a group of devotees, their long tapering fingers and the drooping moustaches of some of the men. A more direct influence is the palm-leaf Kalpasutras of the Jains, painted in the 14th and 15th centuries: groups of people are always ranged in rows, and they have the sharp noses and "farther eye" of the Jain style. Here, too, the figures are flat and the poses stylised. But the Lepakshi painter makes his own contribution in the lively line, the invention that makes the patterns of the clothes so rich and various, the realism that introduces unorthodox elements into conventional scenes and the feeling that breaks through the stylised forms.

The ceilings of the *mandapam* and *antaralas* and some of the shrines are painted. Each bay is separately treated. Vegetable and mineral colours, red and

Grandfather and grandson wearing the sacred thread of the upper castes.

yellow ochre, black, blue and green were mixed with lime water and infused with the lime-mortar base. The background to most of the pictures is red, another Jain tradition. Gods, goddesses, groups of worshippers and donors are portrayed, as well as Puranic scenes. The Avatars of Vishnu are gracefully rendered. Bhairava is an expression of the painter's idea of the young Shiva, and the painter himself stands humbly nearby with folded hands.

The hunting scenes are full of lively incidents, the wounded cheetah biting the hunter and a rushing wild boar terrorising man and beast. Worshippers and attendants are signified by the *kaivaara* gesture of humility, one hand upraised. The temple donor Virupanna is shown with his brother, both in Vijayanagara caps, and groups of women, each in a distinctive sari, wear jewellery and flowers in their hair.

At **Chandragiri**, 7 miles (11 km) from Tirupati, are the Raja Mahal and Rani Mahal, late Vijayanagara structures of the 17th century. The three-storey Raja Mahal is the larger, with a brick tower at the centre and small towers at each corner. The beauty of the structure lies in the repetition on each floor of the row of Indo-Persian arches, and the prominent brackets supporting each level. The first floor has fine stucco decorations on walls and ceiling. The Rani Mahal is a similar structure, also with good stucco decoration.

The barren landscape of **Penukonda** with its black gneiss rocks 32 miles (50 km) north of Hindupur was the home of the defeated Vijayanagara king after his final battle. The fort here comprises a massive encircling wall and a pavilion on the hill-top. Nearby is the Gagan Mahal, still in good repair.

Northern Andhra: The virtues of the Kakatiyas, their patronage of art and letters, their bravery in battle and, above all, their happy knack of finding able and faithful servitors, shine even at a remove of 10 centuries. The dynasty became independent of its Chalukyan overlords about 1050, and ruled Telengana (northern Andhra) till 1323. Their

Temple carved out of rock at Lepakshi.

name derives from their family deity, the goddess Kakati, possibly a local version of Durga.

The first Kakatiya capital was Anumakonda, modern Hanamkonda; later they moved to **Warangal**, originally known as Orugallu or Ekasila, from the massive rock-hill near Warangal fort. Here they fought off attacks by the Yadavs of Deogiri, the Tughlaqs from Delhi, predatory neighbours and disaffected vassals. While Ganapatideva was a captive of the Yadavs, Rudra held the kingdom for his master. Rewarded by a large fief, the loyal general built the reservoir of Palampet and the temple that stands on the bund. Ganapatideva's daughter Rudramma led her army in battle and perhaps was killed in the field at the age of 80.

During Rudramma's reign, Marco Polo, the Venetian traveller, landed at the port of Motupalli, and commented on the fine cotton fabrics of Andhra: "In the Kingdom are made the best and most delicate and those of the highest price, in sooth they look like a tissue of spider's web." Literature, music and dance played an important role. The poetry of Tikkana vanquished the Jain religion, and Jain icons were broken and temples rededicated. Even the generals of the Kakatiya army were writers, notably Jaya Senapati whose *Nritta Ratnavali* is a classic work on dance.

Rudradeva, the first sovereign ruler of the line, built the Thousand-Pillar temple at **Hanamakonda** in 1162 in thanksgiving for victory in battle. The temple is in a walled enclosure, in two parts. The triple shrine or *trikuta* is connected to a *mandapa*, now roofless, by a platform on which there sits a beautiful monolithic Nandi in highly polished black stone. Like other Kakatiya temples, this is Chalukyan in style but with innovations. The *mandapa* has 300 pillars, while the "pillars" of the *trikuta* are vertical slabs with carved ends, arranged in a dentate pattern to look like pilasters. Two-foot-wide projecting stone slabs make up the cornice, their heavy unsculpted ends balancing the overhang. The doorways are carved

Ancient Buddhist site of Nagarjunakonda.

with figures and decorated with looped chain motifs in stone.

Warangal fort lies 88 miles (141 km) northeast of Hyderabad. Within its outer mud walls, the inner fortifications are of large stones fitted together. The fort was begun by Rudradeva when the capital was moved here, added to by his nephew Ganapatideva and finished by Rudramma, who ruled for 30 years. In 1323 it fell to Ulugh Khan, who later ruled Delhi as Mohammad Tughlak. Prataparudra, the last Kakatiya ruler, killed himself on the road to captivity. After this the fort changed hands several times until it was absorbed into the Qutb Shahi empire in the 15th century.

Inside the fort are four massive *toranas*, the gateways of the **Sahasralinga temple**, destroyed at the time of Ibrahim Qutb Shah. The scattered fragments are clearly from the high period of Kakatiya art, the reign of Ganapatideva, the same period as the temples at Palampet and Ghanapur. A large *linga* has figures carved on four sides with the stoic Kakatiya faces. The triangular panel of Lakshmi and her attendants illustrates the curious contrast between the lively body movements and set, mask-like faces of Kakatiya sculpture.

The repetition of decorative motifs to form a pattern is brought to perfection in the perforated screen of the doorway, and in the friezes of elephants, lions and swans interspersed with foliage. The *toranas* themselves, standing at the cardinal points, are striking for their size and beauty. The columns, brackets and architraves are carved with the Kakatiya genius in a harmonious blend of animals, plants and jewellery motifs.

The **Ramappa temple** at **Palampet**, 32 miles (50 km) north of Warangal, stands on the retaining wall of the Palampet dam. The reservoir is 8 miles (12.5 km) across, and is one of several irrigation works undertaken by the Kakatiyas. As Dr Yazdani said, "The titanic dykes and sluice-gates of Pakhal, Lakhnaram and Ramappa are object lessons even to the modern engineer." The temple was consecrated in AD 1213 and is of pink sandstone with hard

Nandi, Lord Shiva's mount, Ramappa temple.

black basalt for the sculpted elements. It is cruciform in plan with porches to each side of the central *mandapam*. The horizontal banding along the outer face of the basement level and the parapet wall of the *mukhamandapam* is made up of plain and ornamented bands, of projections and recesses, of figures in movement contrasted with floral motifs. There is a frieze of elephants marching round the temple, full of playful tricks. Above this is a row of gods and goddesses, musicians and dancers, Jain Tirthankaras and soldiers – a glorious medley expressing joy of life and release from convention.

Under the eaves of three of the porches, stretching from column to cornice, are 12 bracket figures of *madanikas*, women in graceful but strange dance poses. They are almost life-size, with long slender limbs carved in high relief. The simple modelling and restrained ornamentation are typical of the elegance of Kakatiya art. The Nagini figure is remarkable for its stylised simplicity. *Yalis* standing on elephants

rear up on other brackets. The Kakatiyas scattered these mythical beasts throughout their temples and what are fanciful creatures in their hands, when translated into the Vijayanagara idiom, grow to threatening size and fearsome aspect. The southern and western outer faces of the beams of the *mandapam* celebrate the marriage of Shiva, the lower faces his great feats. Triangular panels in the ceiling depict Agni, Yama and Varuna with their attendant animals and consorts. Another temple, at the eastern end of the same "bund", has sculptures of dancers on columns and on door jambs. At **Ghanapur**, 4 miles (6 km) east of Palampet, there are some ruined temples. The main shrine has delightful female *dwarapalas* (door keepers) and *madanikas*.

The local interest in goldsmithing and metal work which is evident in the sculptural motifs continues to this day. Karimnagar is a centre for silver filigree work, and throughout Warangal district, notably around Pembarthi, are clusters of metal workers.

Below right and below, bracket figures in Ganapeshvaralayam, Mulugu, Warangal.

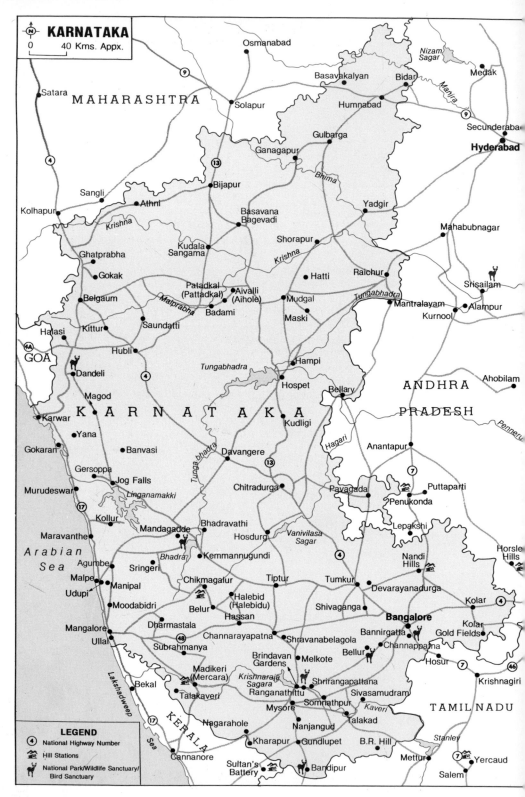

KARNATAKA

0   40 Kms. Appx.

LEGEND
- National Highway Number
- Hill Stations
- National Park/Wildlife Sanctuary/ Bird Sanctuary

MAHARASHTRA

GOA

KARNATAKA

ANDHRA PRADESH

Arabian Sea

KERALA

TAMIL NADU

Osmanabad
Satara
Sangli
Kolhapur
Athni
Solapur
Basavakalyan
Bidar
Medak
Humnabad
Secunderaba
Hyderabad
Gulbarga
Ganagapur
Bijapur
Mahabubnagar
Yadgir
Basavana Bagevadi
Shorapur
Kudala Sangama
Krishna
Ghatprabha
Gokak
Hatti
Raichur
Srisailam
Patadkal (Pattadkal)
Aivalli (Aihole)
Mudgal
Mantralayam
Alampur
Belgaum
Badami
Maski
Kurnool
Halasi
Kittur
Saundatti
Hubli
Dandeli
Hampi
Ahobilam
Magod
Tungabhadra
Hospet
Bellary
Karwar
Kudligi
Yana
Gokaran
Banvasi
Davangere
Hagari
Anantapur
Gersoppa
Jog Falls
Chitradurga
Pavagada
Puttaparti
Murudeswar
Linganamakki
Penukonda
Kollur
Bhadravathi
Hosdurg
Lepakshi
Maravanthe
Mandagadde
Kemmannugundi
Vanivilasa Sagar
Horsle Hills
Agumbe
Bhadra
Nandi Hills
Sringeri
Chikmagalur
Tiptur
Tumkur
Devarayanadurga
Malpe
Manipal
Belur
Halebid (Halebidu)
Shivaganga
Kolar
Udupi
Moodabidri
Hassan
Bangalore
Kolar Gold Fields
Mangalore
Dharmastala
Channarayapatna
Shravanabelagola
Bannirgatta
Bellur
Channappatna
Ullal
Subrahmanya
Melkote
Hosur
Brindavan Gardens
Krishnaraja
Krishnagiri
Madikeri (Mercara)
Sagara
Shrirangapattana
Sivasamudram
Talakaveri
Ranganathittu
Somnathpur
Bekal
Mysore
Kaveri
Talakad
TAMIL NADU
Nagarahole
Nanjangud
B.R. Hill
Stanley
Kharapur
Gundlupet
Mettur
Yercaud
Cannanore
Sultan's Battery
Bandipur
Salem

152

KARNATAKA

The state of Karnataka, 74,210 sq miles (192,204 sq km) in area, has a population of 38 million. It was formed by amalgamating the princely state of Mysore with the Kannada-speaking communities of Madras Presidency.

Karnataka has a long coastline stretching from Goa in the north to the Kerala border. It has many beaches, though not as well known as those of its neighbours. Inland are the Western Ghats which rise to a subdued 1,600 ft (488 m) in this state. Both flanks of the Ghats are forested and have large plantations of teak, sandalwood and bamboo. Most of Karnataka lies on the ancient Deccan plateau. Though the state has rivers, waterfalls (the best known being the Jog Falls), game sanctuaries (Bandipur) and a pleasant climate for most of the year, it is its historical legacies – Jain, Hindu and Muslim – that are of particular interest.

Sixty-odd miles (about 96 km) north of Mysore city on top of the Hillock of Sravanabelagola is the colossal monolithic statue of Gomatcswara, built by the Ganga kings in AD 983. Around the city of Mysore are the great Hoysala temples of Somnathpur, Halebid and Belur built in the 12th and 13th centuries. In north-west Karnataka at Hampi stand the magnificent ruins of the once great Hindu Vijayanagara kingdom – 14th to 16th century destroyed by the Deccan Sultanates after a titanic battle in 1565.

The Muslim Sultans also made a major contribution to the heritage of Karnataka. The Adil Shahi Sultans have left behind in the walled medieval town of Bijapur many beautiful mosques, tombs and palaces built in the Turkish style with simple lines and restrained embellishments. Srirangapatnam, Tippu Sultan's fortress, built on a beautiful island in the Kaveri, bears marks of his struggle and final capitulation to the British at the end of the 18th century. In Bangalore Tippu's father Haider Ali laid out the beautiful Lal Bagh gardens, to this day the city's finest park.

The Hindu Maharajas of Mysore, restored to grace after Tippu's fall, built several palaces in both Mysore and Bangalore and the temple on the hill outside Mysore called the Chamundeswari.

BANGALORE

Bangalore is India's most congenial city. Its citizens are contentedly inured to the litany, chanted by all those who come here, which lists the agreeable climate they enjoy, the greenery, the cleanliness, the sense of order, the post-card-pretty streets and the comparatively unhurried pace of life that still manages to co-exist with the accelerating tempo of industrialisation. While those residents who are trying to hold out against the onslaughts of rapid growth might not agree completely, they are secure in the knowledge that chaos is nowhere near as imminent as it might be in other Indian metropolises.

According to a World Bank report, Bangalore is among the fastest growing cities in the world, which might explain why the Bangalorean would rather talk about the present than the past. Under the overlay of Westernisation, however, is a core of tradition not immediately apparent to the outsider or the newcomer who hears English spoken as much as Kannada. The Kannadiga ethos prevails in easy equilibrium with a fluid cultural mix of other religions, languages, manners of dress, customs and lifestyles. The city presents a palette of external influences — from the relics of the once-dominant Raj to the hand-knitted sweaters sold by Tibetan refugees that cheerfully colour the pavements on Kempe Gowda Road. Through the cosmopolitan hubbub flows the traditional way of life of the native Bangalorean, who still listens to the *veena* recitals of Doraswamy Iyengar, whose wife still cooks her sweet *kesari bhath* as her grandmother did, and whose daughter still wears the customary chaplet of *kanakambara* flowers on her hair.

The capital of Karnataka, Bangalore is located in the southeast of the state on the Deccan plateau, at a height of about 3,000 ft (1,000 metres). The vegetation is deciduous and the entire terrain is sprinkled with lakes and ponds, rarely empty even during the peak of summer. The weather is its most alluring feature, with temperatures that range comfortably between 30 °C and 16 °C. The average annual rainfall, brought by the southwest monsoon from June to August, and the northeast monsoon from October to December, is about 40 inches (90 cm) and the area is productive of an extravagant variety of fruit and vegetables.

Phrases like "Gateway to the South" are bandied about by travel agents, in allusion to Bangalore's proximity to the tourist landmarks of the South. The city has always garnered its fair share of these labels: Garden City, Pensioner's Paradise, India's Cheltenham. Current references to it as India's Silicon Valley, in response to all that is happening here in the field of artificial intelligence, echo Jawaharlal Nehru's description of Bangalore two decades ago as "a picture of the India of the future".

Since the township proper is only about 450 years old, the fact that the area's history predates the colonial presence by several centuries is sometimes overlooked. Its military heritage, for instance, goes back much further than the time when swords, muskets and rockets were manufactured in Tharamandalpet for Hyder Ali, the legendary 18th century warlord. Battles were fought here in the 9th century – reference to one in the village of Bangaluru is inscribed on a *viragal* (literally, a "hero stone"), found in a temple in Begur village east of the city. Going by the Roman coins found at Yeshwantpur to the north, there was trade too with the West as early as the 1st century AD, probably in spices and textiles.

"The Town of Boiled Beans": Of the three derivations of Bangalore's name, one has it that a 10th century ruler, Veera Ballala, lost his way hunting in a forest. Night fell as he wandered around looking for his retinue, going deeper into the woods until, to his relief, he came upon a cottage in which lived an old woman. She offered him shelter and shared with him her modest dinner of *benda kalu*, or boiled beans.

Veera Ballala stayed the night, and before he left he told her (as kings do in such stories) that she could ask him for

Left,
Lal Bagh,
one of
Bagalore's
famous
gardens.

anything she wanted. All she asked for, however, was a supply of food enough for herself and for any other traveller who might seek refuge. Her request was granted, and this incident became so much a part of local folklore that when a village was set up there, it was called Benda Kaluru (Town of Boiled Beans), eventually commuted to Bangaluru.

Other stories, not as popular, concern the Vijayanagara chieftain Kempe Gowda I, who founded Bangalore. He ruled the township of Yelahanka, on what is now the city's northern outskirts. In 1537, he was looking to expand his overlord Achuta Raya's domain and found this uninhabited tract ideal, with its abundant water and bracing climate. On a day fixed by his astrologer, four carts were harnessed and sent off in four directions, as far as their bullocks could pull them. Kempe Gowda decreed that the points where they stopped would be the outer limits of his new city, and at each of these points he built a watchtower which still stands: in the north on the Bellary Road

(in Yelahanka), in the south at Lal Bagh, in the east at Ulsoor Lake and in the west near the Gavi Gangadhareshwara temple. (Of course, Bangalore has long since sprawled well beyond these four towers.) Kempe Gowda built a mud fort, first firing the dense forest growth to clear the necessary space. That gave the name its other provenance – Benda Kaduru, the Town of the Burnt Forest.

A third theory is that he named the town after the god Venkata, hence Venkata-uru, which was gradually honed down to Vengaluru and then to its present form.

From Hindu rule to Muslim: Within the walls of Kempe Gowda's fort, various trades and businesses flourished, each defined in its own *pettah*, some of which still have their original names – Chickpet, or little town, Hallipet, the cotton market, and Tharagpet, where grain was bought and sold.

The new town's profile was also defined by its founder's religious convictions: a devout Hindu, he built temples, hostelries for travellers and

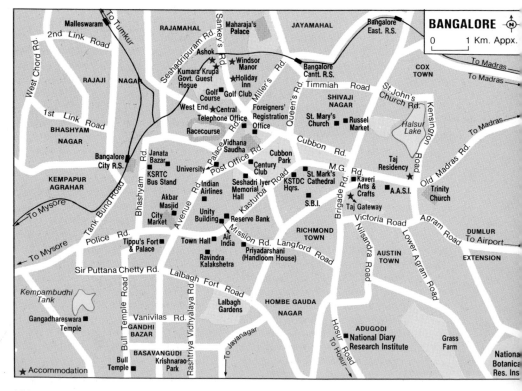

tanks for drinking water, and awarded land to scholars in acknowledgement of their learning.

After Kempe Gowda, Bangalore was seized by the Sultanate of Bijapur in 1638, from whom it was wrested by the Mughals 50 years later. They leased it to King Chikka Devaraya of the Wadiyar dynasty of Mysore, who managed to convince Kasim Khan, the Moghul general, to sell the city to him. This the general did without apparent qualm or foresight, for Rs 500,000.

The 17th century was a period of turmoil, with the British and the French fighting to claim as much of the Carnatic as they could for themselves. The regional rulers too, the Marathas, the Nizam of Hyderabad and the Wadiyars who now owned Bangalore, were all embroiled in strife. This the Wadiyar king could least afford, considering his kingdom was already plagued by internal power struggles and his exchequer depleted. Thus, the time was ripe for an ambitious man like Hyder Ali, a chieftain serving in the Mysore army, to seize

Shopping at Commercial Street.

power for himself. Hyder Ali deposed the ineffectual Chikka Krishnaraja and made Bangalore his personal fief. From then on, he and his son Tippu Sultan, both accomplished warrior-statesmen, dominated the Carnatic till the end of the 18th century.

With their well-trained armies, Hyder Ali and Tippu Sultan fended off their aggressive neighbours with such ease that even the British found their plans of dominion severely thwarted. Both father and son had to fight the British four times, in the Mysore Wars. But in the last Mysore War in 1799, Tippu was killed at Srirangapatnam and finally the Carnatic came under the British. They cannily put the Wadiyar heir back on the throne; as a placatory gesture to his subjects it was well-considered, and politically safe enough since the heir was only a 5-year-old boy.

British influence on Bangalore's development becomes evident only from about 1809 onward. This was when the Cantonment began to be constructed and the first batch of troops

moved in from Srirangapatnam to their new barracks at Agram, where the Air Force Hospital is today.

Bangalore under the British: The British adored Bangalore, its scenery and its weather. Even Winston Churchill, stationed here as a young officer, was moved to effusiveness in his descriptions of an ambience that, to all these homesick empire-builders, seemed "a bit of England in an alien land".

The layout of Bangalore's **Cantonment** began in 1809, and it rapidly became much more extensive than a mere encampment for "Lashkars", its original function. It was located to the north of the fort and the old town where the City Market is today. Both were separated by an open stretch of land 1½ miles (2.4 km) wide, the usual strategic practice that included the installation of toll-gates to control access to the Cantonment. The Cantonment's centre was the Parade Ground, originally a 2-mile (3.2 km) east-west strip. The Mall that ran along its southern periphery, the South Parade, is now Mahatma Gandhi Road. To the north of the Parade Ground were the sepoys' houses and Infantry Road, while the artillery and cavalry were stationed to the east. The Commissioner's bungalow, to the west, is now the Raj Bhavan, the Governor's residence. Road names were determined either according to troop location and movement (Calvary Road, Brigade Road), or the establishment of retail enterprise (Commercial Street).

Army families settled in, and the civilians followed. Merchants and moneylenders set up shop. Colonial gregariousness established polo and other horsy pursuits, the event of giddiest social import being the annual Bangalore Hunt.

In 1831 the British seized administrative control of Mysore after an apparent attempt at revolt by the Maharaja. Deciding not to take their hard-won territory for granted, the British not only increased the number of troops at Bangalore, but also established a Commission, making the city their administrative headquarters.

Vishvesh-varaya Tower dwarfs the General Post Office.

During the remaining half of the century, the series of Commissioners who then came to office were responsible for structures such as the Attara Katcheri that housed the Secretariat, the Central College and the Central Jail. The railway from Madras that ended at Jalarpet was extended to the city at the instance of Commissioner Bowring.

Many residential areas sprang up called "towns" – Cleveland Town, Fraser Town, Benson Town, painstakingly laid out on the northern and southern sides of the Cantonment, along wide tree-lined avenues. Their thoroughfares have names like Wood Street and Hayes Road, both found in what was a nostalgically named Richmond Town. Still visible are many of the bungalows that were built then, between 1880 and 1930, rambling single-storey structures placed neatly in their gardens at the end of driveways, some only symbolic in length, but no less essential for that. Many now sit in the looming shadows of blocks of flats and offices, the inexorable concomitant of city life.

Life in the *pettahs* of the city proper, during the British occupation, was in bustling dissimilarity to the detachment of the Cantonment. It was the archetypical Hindu town where life spilled out of the doorways, strung overhead with their rows of mango leaves, and into the streets.

In 1881 Bangalore was restored to the Maharaja, and thereafter his chief administrative officer, called the Dewan, supervised the state. To one such Dewan, Sir Visveswaraya, goes much of the credit for the process of industrialising the state.

When Mysore joined the Indian Union after Independence, the Maharaja became its Governor and in 1956 Bangalore became the state capital. In 1973, the state's name was changed to Karnataka, a name which (like that of its capital) has different origins, depending on who you ask. It came from either "Karu Nadu", the land of black soil, or "Karnadu", the high country, neither of which appears particularly apt. Nor is the third, though it is certainly a pretty

Bangaloreans enjoying the sunset.

THE ANGLO-INDIANS

Article 366(2) of the Government of India Act 1935 defines an Anglo-Indian as "a native of India whose father is or was of European descent". Of all the European colonizers, the British formed the majority and their dominion the largest, so it is their descendants who are commonly referred to as Anglo-Indians.

The character of the Anglo-Indian community is being redefined, as cultural and ethnic parameters change and numbers dwindle in the institutions once exclusively theirs, such as Bangalore's Bishop Cotton, Baldwin's and Cathedral. Young Anglo-Indian women now wear the *sari* and the *salwar* as often as they do Western dress. Anglo-Indian teenagers speak in the contemporary idiom of urban Indian youth, while intermarriage adds pace to a process of assimilation.

There is also the question of numbers: the Anglo-Indians have always been a numerical minority. In Karnataka, they number around 10,000; in the country, the community is about 100,000. Always a visible community in Bangalore, they have long been emblematic of what is perceived as the most colonial of Indian cities.

Gregarious as Anglo-Indians are, they flock to their clubs, the Bowring Institute or the Catholic Club in town, or the Recreation Club in Whitefield. There they pack the floor at the dances on New Year's Eve, Christmas or Easter (the band usually comprised local performers). Other communities like the Goan Catholics and the South Kanara Christians are just as Westernised, and many urban Indians are addicted to the convivialities of "club life", but it is the Anglo-Indians who traditionally seemed to typify it.

For a scattered, fragmented society, the bonds are Christianity (80 percent are Catholic) and the English language. Like most Indians, many are bi- and tri-lingual, though nearly all speak a fluent variety of the local vernacular. Dishes from both parent cuisines are relished with gusto, and some are ethnic. Since Anglo-Indians eat beef and mutton, their Indianised recipes tend to have evolved from Muslim ones.

Historically, a sense of displacement has always been the psychological burden of colonization's offspring. When the British established their East India Company in the 16th century, they found a community of Portuguese-Goan descent. As the company's commercial beachhead was extended, the English set about fortifying their outposts and bringing in soldiers to defend them. Englishmen lonely for sympathetic distaff companionship married Indian and Eurasian women; their children were the first Anglo-Indians.

It was inevitable that they identified with the British, who employed them in their armies and in the civil services. In late 19th century, with the advent of the telegraph and the railways, they staffed these departments. Alienation was just as inevitable, since they were never wholly accepted by the British or the Indians, for similar reasons.

After Independence, many of them emigrated to the U.K., Canada and Australia, their latent uncertainty surfacing with the British departure. Most settled happily, though not all of them integrated and a few even came back, perhaps with the realisation that alienation was not territorially limited. Immigration continues, but more in search of perceived economic betterment. Some of the older generation remain ambivalent, but isolation is something that concerns today's Anglo-Indians less and less.

conceit – "Karna-ata", an onomato-poeic amalgam of the sounds of bees, butterflies and birds.

`No other state capital has a structure comparable to the **Vidhana Soudha**, the Karnataka Secretariat, built in 1956, India's largest legislative-official structure. On the north side of Cubbon Park, its imposing neo-Dravidian lines distinguish it in a city known for its primarily colonial flavour – a flavour faithfully sustained, as in the Windsor Manor Hotel, whose guests are invariably astounded to learn that it dates only from 1982.

The traditional Indian inspiration was deliberate: before the building was designed, the then Chief Minister of the State was taking a Russian delegation around the city, whose members could only ask, "Why are all your buildings European? Have you no architecture of your own?"

The building, made mostly of local granite and porphyry, is primarily Dravidian, with a leavening of other ethnic influences, such as the Rajasthani *jha-*

rokas or balconies. Details are conscientious – the pillars with their elaborate bases, the domed ceiling ascending in many concentric circles, and the carvings with ornately wrought floral motifs as in the temples of Karnataka and Tamil Nadu.

Across from it, housing the High Court, is the elegant, two-storey **Attara Katcheri** or "18 courts", with its fluted Corinthian columns. The fact that it still stands is a tribute to the *esprit de corps* of Bangalore's citizens, who once responded to its proposed demolition with such vigour that the idea was expeditiously dropped.

The Attara Katcheri was built in 1864 and the 300 acres (135 hectares) of **Cubbon Park** were cultivated behind it later. And what delectation it is to come across, not just one such lush expanse right in the heart of a large city but two: further to the south of Cubbon Park is another, the **Lal Bagh**, started by Hyder Ali in 1740. This landscaped park, sprawled over 240 acres (97.2 hectares), is stocked with a profusion of

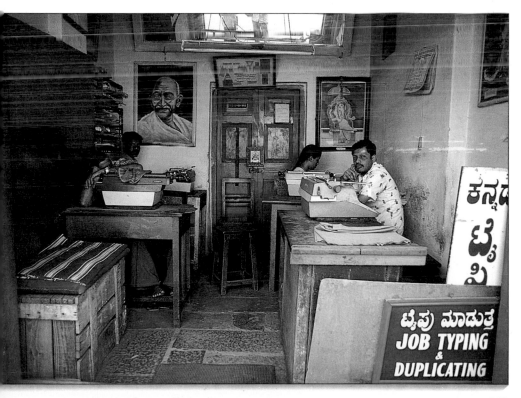

tropical and sub-tropical plants, some of them imported by Tippu Sultan.

The Bangalore Palace: Indian maharajas were as much prey to the imperatives of one-upmanship as anyone else, as this building confirms. It was built by the Wadiyar king in 1887, in stiff competition with his peers, who were busy reproducing French chateaux, among other genres. The local result was what is apparently a Tudor castle.

Tippu's Fort and Palace: Mud walls may have sufficed when Kempe Gowda built his fort in 1537, but Hyder Ali, with rapacious neighbours and colonial powers to worry about, rebuilt it in stone and enclosed it in a moat. The walls were embellished with arches in fine Islamic style. Hyder Ali acknowledged other religions (Tippu Sultan's mother was Hindu), which is why you will find a little temple dedicated to Lord Ganesh still standing within the fort walls, drawing people to prayer.

An excellent example of the esthetics and dynamics of 18th century military architecture, the fort has not been well maintained: walls have been knocked down to make way for roads, and parts of the moat were filled in when the Victoria Hospital was built. The eight gates that Kempe Gowda contructed, each named for the different locality it opened to, are no longer usable, except for the one rebuilt in granite by Hyder Ali, called the Delhi Gate. Still, it is a reminder of the other important militaristic influences on the city, apart from the British.

Of the few buildings of historical importance built during the last 5 centuries, Tippu's palace is one. It is Bangalore's foremost example of the Islamic mode, though only serving as an annex to the main palace that no longer exists. Built mostly out of wood, it has much fastidious carving on the pillars, arches and balconies. It served as another of Tippu's summer retreats, one he was very fond of: he called it Rashk-e-Jannat, "the Envy of Heaven". Much later on, when Bangalore was administered by the British Commission, the palace was used as its office.

Jacaranda branches frame a colonial church.

Now not used for anything at all, it is open to the public who can see little but the gradual ravages of neglect: the murals on the walls and ceilings that portrayed the exploits of father and son are barely discernible, though the garden, laid out in basic Islamic form, is reasonably well maintained.

Religious Architecture: Next to it is the **Venkataramanaswamy temple**, built by the Wadiyars in the Dravidian style. It is around 300 years old, and has been well looked after, with some recent additions being made to its structure, such as the two *gopurams* that were built in the last few years. During the Third Mysore War in 1790, it sustained considerable damage, much of which was restored by the Wadiyars, though some of the lavish stone pillars with the robustly carved lion-brackets remain gouged and pitted from cannon fire.

Bangalore has many temples of varying antiquity. The newer ones built during the last 50 years are also faithful to the Dravidian style, though the older ones with their legends and the wealth of associations that attach to them, have a deeper appeal – like the **Bull temple**, built by Kempe Gowda near one of his original watchtowers in Basavangudi, the suburb to the south of the city. It contains a massive, 15 ft (4.6 m) high monolith of Nandi, the bull entrusted with the sacred duty of carrying the god Shiva. Carved from a single boulder, the statue resembles the one on Chamundi Hill in Mysore.

Apparently, the temple was built to placate a rampaging bull that systematically devoured the entire peanut crop in the nearby fields. The original plan was to construct just the monolith, but when it was finished, it suddenly began to grow of its own accord, and ceased only when the temple was hastily erected over it. Whether this unnerved its flesh-and-blood counterpart is not clear, but the bull retired from the neighbourhood. Ever since, the local farmers have held a Kadalekaye Parishe, a sort of peanut fair outside the temple every year in thanksgiving.

Close by, near the Kempambudhi

Tank, is the **Gavi Gangadheswara** shrine, also built by Kempe Gowda. Dedicated to Shiva and his consort Parvati, this cave temple contains 33 idols, including one of Agni, the god of fire. It incorporates a clever architectural device: Kempe Gowda's architect so planned it that on the festival of Makara Sankranti in the middle of January, the last rays of the evening sun pass through an archway and a window, and between the horns of a Nandi bull, to alight on the image of Shiva. Large numbers of the faithful come year after year in homage, drawn by this exquisite sense of the eternal order.

There is a tragic tale about the one other shrine Kempe Gowda built in Koramangala, to the south of where the airport is now. As his fort was being built, its structure kept collapsing, over and over again, despite everything he could do to prevent it. A human sacrifice was proposed as a propitiatory gesture, and though the outraged Kempe Gowda rejected the idea, his daughter-in-law Lakshmidevi decided to offer her own life, and did so. The fort was completed, and in the selfless girl's memory this pretty shrine was named.

Every Cantonment layout had at least one church, as integral to the social fabric as the local club. Most of Bangalore's churches were built by the British, in either the Gothic or the European-classic style, with few, if any, of the colonially inspired features that exemplify the architecture of the Raj.

As has been noted, cemeteries in typical Cantonments were not laid out adjacent to the churches, but usually at some distance away. This practice probably had something to do with containing contagion during the many epidemics that beseiged the colonial community.

Some of the churches built after Independence are in the older styles, while those whose design references are contemporary do not really make any definitive statement.

Mosques in the city date back to long before Hyder Ali's reign – the oldest being the Sangeen Jamia Masjid off

An example of an early but well-preserved colonial house.

Avenue Road in the city, built by a Mughal officer. The black marble pillars in the Jumma Masjid, the oldest mosque in the Cantonment area, located just off Commercial Street, were salvaged from Tippu's palace in Srirangapatnam. The newest mosque in Bangalore is also its largest, a confection in white marble near the City Market which can hold a congregation of over 5,000 people.

The tomb of the Sufi saint, Tawakkal Mastan, again in the proximity of the City Market, attracts many pilgrims of all faiths, including the members of the annual Karaga procession which stops here in obedience to the saint's wishes. Such compliant secularity might seem unusual anywhere else, but Bangaloreans are comfortable with one another's religions. A healthy percentage of the worshippers at the weekly novenas in St Patrick's, the Infant Jesus and other Catholic churches in the Cantonment are non Christians.

The Karaga festival is another dramatic local event. It takes place around March or April at the Dharmaraja temple, when the *karaga*, an earthen pot that embodies Shakti, the goddess of primal energy, is taken out in night-time procession by one community of the gardeners' caste called the Thegalas. The honour is not assumed lightly: the chosen one, staff in one hand and sword in the other, must balance the florally-bedecked *karaga* on his head for more than 12 miles (20 km), wearing a saffron sari and his wife's conjugal necklace. Drummers and chanting devotees brandishing swords accompany him, and he is under pain of death not to drop his burden. His wife waits at home, a widow for the nonce, till he returns after immersing the pot in the Sampangi Tank.

Years ago, as Tawakkal Mastan rushed out to catch a glimpse of the procession, he tripped and was knocked unconscious, and trampled upon by the crowds. The priests stopped and tended his cuts and bruises with dabs of the sacred red *kumkum* powder, which healed him at once. Awestruck, the saint expressed the wish that the procession

Coconuts for sale.

should always visit his tomb – which it does, every year.

Museums and culture: As visual footnotes to heritage, the artifacts at the Government Museum and the Chitrakala Parishat are worth some hours of perusal. At the former, on Kasturba Road, are finds from the Neolithic era and relics of the 5,000-year-old Mohenjo-Daro civilisation. The Chitrakala Parishat has fine antique paintings in the Mysorean gesso technique, still retaining the patina imparted by a finishing rub with jade. There are collections of shadow puppets made from goat and deerskin and brightly painted marionettes, both types still extant in folk theatre.

As a result of prevailing cultural cross-currents, dancers and musicians from all over the country perform in the city as frequently as do celebrated Carnatic singers, or the itinerant Yakshagana folk theatre troupe. Carnatic music, like the dance form Bharata Natyam, is a classical discipline of the South which has commanded a steadfast following of Bangaloreans. The colourfully vociferous retelling of age-old themes in dialogue, song and dance that is the Yakshagana *prasanga*, or performance, once staged outside temples, is nowadays usually confined to an auditorium stage. Theatres are few and increasing costs also affect the formal Kannada theatre that is otherwise a vital and assured art form in both classical and contemporary idioms.

Entertainment: Theatre performances are not regular, understandably, in the face of the competition from television and the local film industry. Portraits of heroes and heroines in huge billboards loom over movie house entrances on Kempe Gowda Road, and the city's 100-odd cinemas do brisk business, as much in Hindi and English films, Tamil and Malayalam as in Kannada.

Even though Bangalore after hours is perkiest on weekends, the visitor has the week-night alternatives of restaurant-hopping and pub-crawling, the latter an activity only this city can offer. High on any out-of-towner's list of things to do

Nose studs, earrings and necklaces are essential items of female adornment in the South.

is a visit to one of the many pubs on or around Brigade Road, cheerfully noisy places that purvey excellent draught beer in surroundings presumably evocative of Merrie England. The pub scene signifies the gentrification of social drinking; apart from executives and other office-workers you will often find couples and sometimes even groups of women, which would be unthinkable in any conventional bar (except perhaps for those in the five-star hotels).

New restaurants open all the time, adding fresh possibilities to existing culinary options that include everything from Northwest Frontier cuisine to Thai food. Many of them are located in the vicinity of the triangle formed by Mahatma Gandhi Road (M.G. Road as it is universally referred to), St Mark's Road and Residency Road, a few in the five-star hotels and most of the others within easy reach. (One happy fact: unlike in other metropolises, places in Bangalore are easily accessible, each a short auto-rickshaw or taxi ride from the other.)

Prices are moderate, particularly at those restaurants specialising in the local cuisine, where gourmandising is all the more delectable in view of the very modest bill that arrives at the end of it. A local legend is the **Mavalli Tiffin Rooms**, whose mere initials are enough to start the queues forming as they do outside its door, just down the road from Lalbagh, from 6 every morning.

Shopping: What does the visitor take back from Bangalore? In a climate where the artisan's skill is nurtured, the range of choice is extravagant, and objects crafted from silk, sandalwood, rosewood, cane, ivory, copper and gold make evocative souvenirs. Certain techniques are indigenous to Karnataka – ivory inlay work in rosewood, for instance, used to make everything from the classical instrument, the *veena*, to a rather grandly utilitarian coffee table. Or the chiaroscuro effect again, of *bidri* work from Bidar, gold or silver wire inlaid in zinc and copper alloys. Pitchers, spice boxes and bangles are graced by these dainty traceries, motifs origi-

Schoolboy woes.

nally introduced by Persian metal workers brought to India in the 15th century. **Kaveri**, the government arts and crafts emporium on M.G. Road, is an obligatory stopover. Transient shoppers can carry back the likes of a couple of packets of finely fragrant Mysore coffee, and a vial or two of aromatic sandalwood oil. It is not unheard of to have them stocking up on leather clothing and modish cotton ready-to-wear, Bangalore being one of the garment export industry's hubs.

Excursions: Since even a city like Bangalore needs occasional getting away from, several places within a radius of 62 miles (100 km) have become popular weekend retreats for jaded citizens. The Jindal health resort on the Bombay road caters more to the world-weary out-of-towner in search of organically pure overhauling.

Nandi Hills (38 miles/60 km) is a small hill station, yet another retreat for Tippu Sultan. With its excellent natural fortifications, which the Tiger of Mysore improved upon, it made the ideal hideout; the British under Lord Cornwallis tried to dislodge him from it, but were dissuaded after several enormous granite boulders were dropped on their heads.

Nandi Hills was popular with the British subsequently, too, and the commissioner Sir Mark Cubbon built the bungalow named after him at the highest point of the range. The view is magnificent, especially from the part of the battlements called Tippu's Drop, and there are enjoyable rambles to be discovered through the tree-covered hills. There are two Shiva temples, both well over a thousand years old, the one at the foot of the hill built by a queen of the Bana dynasty and extended by members of subsequent ruling houses, and the other on top built by the Cholas.

The **Banerghatta National Park** (13 miles/21 km) is a game sanctuary that is home to lions, bison, elephants, wild boars and other beasts.

Mekedata (61 miles/98 km) is a resort as beautiful and uninhabited as any nature lover could wish, where the **Wayside shrine.**

Kaveri river surges fiercely through a deeply chiseled gorge a mere five yards wide on top, enough for a goat to leap over; hence the name, which means just that – Goat's Leap.

Bangalore today: From the air, Bangalore has a definite metropolitan breadth and reach; it is India's fifth largest city, after Bombay, Delhi, Calcutta and Madras, extending over 61.3 sq miles (159 sq km). It is still quite green, even if – as some people say – Madras is more verdant and Delhi has more flowers and parks. With the boom in progress, the city continues to surge upwards and outwards and its eight industrial belts burgeon with some 10,000 units, among them electronics and electrical engineering, aluminium and steel, machine tools and watch-making, and aeronautical and computer engineering units.

The concentration of scientific and technological calibre has always been formidable, well before the current revolution in computer technology. The Indian Institute of Science, started in 1914 with an endowment by Jamshedji Tata, the leading industrialist of the time, was the first institution to provide facilities for scientific research. After Independence, the establishment of several public sector enterprises spurred the development of technological expertise. This was further stimulated by research in such areas as laser and liquid crystal technology and achievements in aeronautics and telecommunications.

The multinationals have moved in – Kodak, Hewlett-Packard and Texas Instruments, drawn by the possibilities of the city's new avatar as an indigenous Silicon Valley. Leading national companies have been moving in from all over the country, confirming the potential of a city that seems to accommodate them all.

If Bangalore can be said to have an identifying characteristic, it is that of a tempered assurance: the new and the unfamiliar are acknowledged with a civilised responsiveness that is the city's most appealing, and hopefully most enduring, attribute.

Landscape over the Bangalore-Mysore road.

SRAVANABELAGOLA

The serenity that Sravanabelagola emanates derives from the simplicity of its ascetic inspiration and the grandeur of its scale (it is said to be the world's tallest monolithic statue).

The art historian Fergusson said of the monolith: "The statues of this Jain saint are among the most remarkable works of art in South India. One is astonished at the amount of labour such a work must have entailed, and puzzled to know whether it was part of the hill or had been moved to the spot where it now stands. The former is the more probable theory. The hill is one mass of granite about 400 ft (122 m) high and probably had a mass or two standing at its summit – either a part of the subjacent mass or lying on it. This the Jains undertook to fashion into a statue 58 ft (17.7 m) tall, and have achieved it with marvellous success. Nothing grander or more imposing exists anywhere out of Egypt

and even there, no known statue surpasses its height."

Sravanabelagola is wedged between two rocky hills called Indragiri or Vindhyagiri and Chandragiri. The translation of Sravanabelagola is "the white pond of the ascetic". This most probably refers to a pond that once existed where the present temple tank now is, at the base of the Indragiri hill. The ascetic is Bhagwan Bahubali, also known as the Tirthankar Sant Gomateshwara, whose huge statue dominates this little village. This is the holiest of all Jain places of pilgrimage.

Note the simplicity of the carving at Sravanabelagola, and contrast it later with the ornate and complex sculptural work in the temples of Belur and Halebid.

Indragiri looms as the visitor enters Sravanabelagola, and the steps leading to the summit are cut into the rock face. The visitor passes a temple as the climb begins, which is dedicated to Adinatha, father of the Jain saint whose monolith is at the peak of the hill. Climb yet higher, past another temple, and the town of Sravanabelagola is spread out below, with panoramic views of the surrounding districts and the azure Kalyani tank. The small hill of Chandragiri from here, crowned by a slender pillar and the tomb of the great emperor Chandragupta Maurya, a patron of Jainism. Climb past a stone gateway, and the head of the monolith is visible, silhouetted against the bright blue sky: serene, he seems to float in eternity.

The visitor then enters a court, where there are more shrines to Jain saints, and a beautiful sculpture of Kushmandini Devi with an oval cup in her hands. The visitor arrives at the base of the statue, its immense legs rising from a platform on which priests devoutly perform their rites, dwarfed by the mammoth monument. Jungle vines climb up around the legs of the saint, to signify the perfect concentration he attained during his penance.

Sravanabelagola has a history dating back to the 3rd century BC, when it is said that the emperor Chandragupta Maurya, having renounced his king-

Left, colossus of Gomateswara at the Mahabhisheka ceremony, held once every 12 years. Below, Adinatha, a Jain Tirthankara, inside a shrine at Sravanabelagola

dom, came here with his guru, Bhagwan Bhadrabahu Swami. The emperor is believed to have died by penitential starvation.

During the course of time, Bhadrabahu's disciples established Jainism all over the south. This religion found powerful royal patronage and reached its zenith between the 4th and 10th centuries. It was during the reign of the Ganga king Rachamalla that the statue of Lord Gomateshwara was erected, having been sculpted by Aristanemi in AD 981.

Bahubali and Bharata were the sons of Adi Tirthankara Vrishaba Deva, the Jain ruler of a kingdom in northern India, who renounced his throne to become the first saint of the Jains. His renunciation sparked off a bitter war for succession between his two sons, and Bahubali emerged the victor after a long and bloody duel. In his moment of victory, Bahubali realised the futility of violence and worldly success, which inspired him to give all his worldly possessions away to his brother Bha-

rata. So began his 1,000-year penance in the forest.

Thousands of Jain pilgrims from all over the world attend the Mahamastakabhisheka ceremony which is performed once every 12 years. The last was conducted in 1981. The culmination of this spectacular ceremony is the anointing of the statue by priests from a specially erected scaffolding above the image. They pour down thousands of pots of milk, curd, *ghee*, saffron, coconut milk, poppy seeds, almonds, gold coins and other substances, each of which carries a special significance. The sight of the monolith's features being inundated and changing colours with every application is indeed a memorable one.

No single person can be credited with the building of Sravanabelagola. It was built over the period of a millennium and a half by saints, rulers, chieftains, merchants, artists, scribes and pilgrims, who developed it gradually into the centre of pilgrimage that it is today.

In no other Digambara Jain centre in

Thousands of pilgrims from around the country assemble for the great ceremony of Lord Bahubali.

India are there as many temples covering as wide a time span as at Sravanabelagola. The earliest dates back to the 9th century AD, while the most recent was built less than 100 years ago.

The carving of the Tirthankaras is an art that follows the strictest rules and regulations. No ornamentation of any kind can be attributed to the sculpture, whose entire demeanour has to follow the strictest codes of simplicity, in keeping with the Jain ethos. The face must not turn to the left or right, though the figure may be depicted sitting or standing. The rigid, sitting yogic posture is called *Paryankasana*; the standing, meditative posture is called the *Kayotsarga*. All the 24 Tirthankaras have identical features, though the first Tirthankara, Adinatha, is sometimes portrayed with long hair. Yaksas and Yaksis, attendants of the Tirthankaras, can be depicted in flexed postures and with attributes in their hands.

In addition to the main statue of Lord Bahubali are the Small Hill with archways and inscriptions at its summit, the Bhadrabahu Cave where many monuments are enclosed – the Chandragupta Basti, the Kattale Basti, the Bhandari Basti and the Akkana Basti which are built in the Hoysala style. There are well preserved frescos in one of the temples, documenting Jain history.

There is a large and valuable collection of old bronzes, some dating back to the 10th century in the Basti temples in the Math. Observe the relief carvings on the pillars of this temple.

At the base of the hill is a long row of shops selling mostly tourist junk, from fluorescent images of Lord Bahubali to plastic toys. A few stone carvings are the only worthwhile purchases.

Hassan: Hassan is probably the most convenient point from which to visit Sravanabelagola, Belur and Halebid. There are no places of interest in Hassan, but as it is the town with the most to offer by way of accommodation and transport, it would be logical to stay here. The tourist office here could assist in making reservations for Belur and Halebid, should you wish to spend the night there.

Belur: In contrast to the grandeur and simplicity of Sravanabelagola, is the small town of Belur. Located on the banks of the river Yagachi, Belur used to be the capital of the Hoysala empire before it was shifted to Dwarasamudram, over 800 years ago. Today it is a sleepy little town with attractive vistas around it, with memories of its past glory reflected in the **Chennakeshava temple**. This structure was built in AD 1116, the age when the great cathedrals of Europe were being erected. It was built in observance of the victory of the Hoysalas over the Cholas in the great battle of Talakad. King Vishnuvardhana commissioned this temple, and it took 103 years to complete. The facade of the building is intricately carved with sculptures and friezes. The inside is even more richly carved on its panels and pillars.

The Belur temple is one of the finest examples of Hoysala architecture. It was designed by Jakanachari, a notable sculptor of the period, though the signatures of other sculptors too can be dis-

Right, Narasimha, one of the 12 incarnations of Vishnu, Halebid.

cerned. Legend has it that Jakanachari left his wife and young son in quest of fame, and that when he had completed his most perfect work, an enormous Ganesha, its consecration was delayed by a young boy who pronounced the idol unfit for worship. In front of a huge crowd, the distressed sculptor challenged the boy to substantiate his statement, saying that he would cut off his arm if proved wrong. The boy picked up a stick and struck Ganesha's navel which split open to reveal a frog squatting inside the damp stone. The stone was obviously defective, and it would have been a desecration, in Hindu tradition, to have allowed the image to be worshiped. The sculptor therefore cut off his arm, only to find that the boy was his own forgotten son, who had learned the art of perfection.

Legends aside, the temple was built in commemoration of the Hoysala king Bittiga's victory over the Cholas. The actual temple is built on a star-shaped plinth, climbed by a short flight of steps. The first thing that strikes the visitor is the compact scale of the structure. In comparison with the towering edifices of most temples in India, the Belur temple is definitely small. It is when one gets close enough to notice the astounding wealth of detail in its sculpture that one realises its uniqueness. Around the base are 650 carvings of elephants, each one in a different configuration. Distinct themes embellish the rows above, mainly taken from the *Ramayana* and *Mahabharata*.

The Hoysalas were a martial race, but that did not interfere with their interest in culture, as is apparent from the highly developed forms in their music, dance and art. During times of peace and prosperity, they lived a life that encouraged the appreciation of all things beautiful, and talent in the arts was definitely something to be promoted. Healthy competition flourished amongst artists, who were allowed to sign their creations – something not usually found in Indian art.

Rulers who commissioned the building of temples did so in fulfilment of a

Chennua-kesava temple, Belur

vow, or for the promise of victory on the battlefield. Their art was infused with an extraordinary complexity. Regard for the proportions and rules that governed the art of sculpture is apparent in every carving. If you were to insert a thread into the pupil of an eye on one of the sculptures, it would emerge through the nose. Suspend a taut string from the forehead of a dancer and it will fall straight to an uplifted toe.

There is not a portion of the structure that has been left uncarved, and yet the effect is not overwhelming. There is a flow to the subject matter, like a story frozen in stone unfolding before you and coming to a definite conclusion. If you were to spend about 10 hours a day studying the workmanship, it might take the best part of 2 weeks to complete your survey.

After studying the 38 ornamental figures, which range from mythological themes to erotica, you enter the temple. An inky blackness envelops you, and if the electricity has not failed, you will see the hand-lathe-turned filigreed pillars, each distinct and astoundingly beautiful. It is said that the main Narasimha pillar once revolved on its own centre of gravity, but neglect and misuse have taken its toll. The jewelry on the sculptures is movable, and the delicate carvings are quite awe-inspiring in their perfection.

There is a sensuously smooth and polished platform where the Queen is said to have danced in praise of Krishna, Lord Chennakeshava. The four bracket figures on the ceiling celebrate feminine beauty, and the model for each of these was the Queen, Shantala Devi. Consort to King Vishnuvardhana, she was a woman of rare beauty and talent, and was considered responsible for the flourishing of art and culture during this period, as is discernible from these carvings. There was active participation by women in public affairs, and a high degree of sexual freedom.

The **Veeranarayana temple** lies west of the main Chennakeshava temple and is much smaller. There are exquisite carvings of various Hindu

Hoysalesvara Temple, Halebid.

gods, and around the temple are small shrines dedicated to Kappe Chenniga-raya, Soumyanayaki and Andal. Remember to get a guide to take you around the temples. These shrines are an experience in themselves and a must for collectors of minutiae.

Halebid: The original name of this city, the ancient capital of the Hoysalas, was Dwarasamudram, "gateway to the sea". After its sack by the Delhi Sultanate, it came to be known as Halebid, "old capital". There were many temples and palaces here, but few survived the invasion.

The magnificent **Hoysaleswara temple** is very similar to the temple at Belur, though different in detail work. It is set on the same star-shaped platform ascended by a short flight of steps. The palace once stood nearby, connected to the temple by a passage. A Nandi bull, the mount of Lord Shiva, stands guard at the entrance. This temple is about 800 years old, although not wholly in ruins. Only one bracket figure remains, though the relief carvings on the walls

are as profuse and complex as at Belur. The stellar base with the emblem of the stylized lions and elephants which seem to support the temple, signifies stability.

Among the carvings are scenes of many historical battles, of the child Krishna's frolics, Shiva and Parvati's embrace and Ravana hoisting Mount Kailash. The famous Queen Shantala makes another appearance here (she seems to have inspired every sculptor in her domain).

The Hoysalas, traditional enemies of the Chalukyas, ruled this part of the Deccan between the 11th and 13th centuries. They rose to prominence first under leadership of their ruler Tinyaditya and later under king Bittiga, better known as Vishnuvardhana. It was during this latter period when the Hoysalas established their supremacy that the temples of Belur and Halebid were built.

The Jain faith had been predominant up to this time, under the patronage of the Chalukyas and the Gangas. Bittiga himself was a devout Jain until he came

Dancer and accompanists Hoysalesvara temple.

under the influence of the saint Ramanuja, who converted him to the Vaishnavite faith; he then took on the name
Vishnuvardhana. Bittiga encouraged
one of his generals, Gangaraja, to re-
build the Jain temples that had been
destroyed by the Chola invaders, adherents of the Shaivite creed. There are
records showing Vishnuvardhana's tolerance for other religious sects, of
grants made to temples of other faiths,
and of pilgrimages undertaken to Sravanabelagola even after his conversion.

It is difficult to reconcile Halebid
now with what it used to be in its days of
glory; when it was the capital of the
Hoysala empire, it was crowded with
travellers and royal visitors from distant
lands, and teeming with life and activity. The cause of its decline was the
invasion of the city by Alauddin
Khilji's general in 1310.

The famous novelist R.K. Narayan
tells of the legend of the curse which destroyed Halebid: "The extinction of
Halebid or Dorasamudra was due to the
curse of a woman. The king's sister had

come on a visit to the capital, bringing
with her two sons, who were handsome.
One of the King's wives attempted to
seduce the young men, and was re-
pulsed. Enraged by her failure, she
reported to the king that the boys had
tried to molest her. The king immediately ordered his nephews to be impaled
and their bodies to be exposed at the city
gates. The mother, i.e. the King's sister,
was cast out and the citizens were forbidden to give her shelter. She wandered the streets, maddened by all this
injustice, cursing her brother and his
kingdom. She was given help and admitted only in the Potter's street, and
that is all that is left of the capital today,
the only remnant of a grand empire.
Although the human habitations of
those times have disappeared, the
temples built by Vishnuvardhana and
his successor stand to attest once more
to the grandeur of the Hoysala reign and
their artists."

The Hoysaleswara and Kedareswara
temples attract visitors by the thousand
every year. The detail of the friezes are
more complex than those at Belur. Says
Fergusson of this temple, "...From the
basement to the summit, it was covered
with sculptures of the very best class of
Indian art. The Hoysaleswara temple is
perhaps the building on which the advo-
cate of Hindu architecture would like to
take his stand. Unfortunately, it was
never finished, the works having been
stopped after they were in progress for
more than 86 years. No two facets of the
temple are the same; every convolution
of every scroll is different. No two
canopies in the whole building are alike,
and every part exhibits a joyous exuberance of fancy...".

Halebid has no particular local handicrafts, though little stone idols and a few
terracotta pieces make good mementos.
The tourist's best bet is the excellent
picture postcards sold at the museum
annex for about a rupee (which touts try
to sell you for twice the cost). The
Archaeological Survey of India maintains a small gallery within the premises
of the Hoysaleswara temple with a collection of stone sculptures, including a
splendid Ganesha.

The enchant-
ess Mohiniat
her toilette.

MYSORE: IMPERIAL ESSENCE

Every year on a certain day in October, as the sun sets on Mysore, the florid lines of the Maharaja's palace spring into incandescent relief against the evening sky. Every detail of the building – the fluted pillars, the cupolas, the minarets, the arched canopies, the onion domes and the campanile above them – is etched in light. All around the palace and beyond as well, the silhouettes of the great public buildings start to glitter in unison with millions of tiny bulbs, making the city a metaphor for the triumph of good over evil: this is Dussera, the celebration of the slaying of the demon Mahishasura by the goddess Chamundeswari.

So it continues for the next 9 days. Each day, prayers are offered to the deities of wealth, power and learning, the nine sacred incarnations of the female principle, Shakti. And each nightfall, should you make your way to

the top of nearby Chamundi Hill, you will be dazzled by the city's resplendence. The celebrations reach their peak on the 10th day, Vijayadashami, the Day of Victory. This marks the end of the rains, when new ventures can begin: artisans pay homage to the implements of their trade, and businessmen open fresh ledgers for the new financial year ahead.

The day used to have a martial significance as well. It is also known as Ayudha Pooja, or the worship of weapons, the start of the season of war when rulers set off on new campaigns of acquisition or got on with finishing old ones interrupted by the monsoon.

At the appointed time the procession moves out of the palace, a cavalcade of uniformed soldiers, caparisoned horses and elephants, dancers and floats, accompanied by brass bands thumping out sometimes incongruous but always infectious medleys of Indian and Western tunes. The palace guards and the Mysore Lancers march by in opulent uniform, and the Camel Corps, each rider's dour mount swaying in step. Costumed folk-dancers swirl past in riotous rhythm, and trundling along at intervals in makeshift stateliness are the floats, each bearing its tableau.

In a parade a mile long, the main attraction is undoubtedly the state elephant. Monumental in its golden accoutrements, anklets, bells and chains, with its trunk and body graphically painted, the impressive beast carries a gold howdah, in which is placed the image of the city's patron goddess, Chamundeswari. The Maharaja himself once sat on this howdah, leading the procession, a custom now gone the way of other regal prerogatives. However, for the thousands who have come to see it, some from afar, it remains a spectacle evocative of a time when the city was indeed a royal capital, with all the attendant pomp and paraphernalia of a monarchy.

The parade ends at the Banimantap, about 2 miles (3 km) from the palace, in front of the Bani tree worshipped as the embodiment of Shakti. Since homage to Shakti is central to the celebration of

Dussera, it was the monarchical custom to offer prayers here and then shoot an arrow into the air as a gesture of victory. No longer; the celebration now ends on a more secular note with a torchlight parade by the State Police. The grand finale comes with the fireworks when the sky, like the city beneath it, is drenched with radiance.

The crowds leave, and Mysore goes back to being a sheltered city of quiet beauty and amicable climate. It lies in a valley 87 miles (140 km) to the south-west of Bangalore. Tree-lined avenues and sumptuous parks make it a contemplative setting for the courtly architecture that houses civic and institutional routine.

Mysore is a place of remembered fragrances – sandalwood, incense and jasmine, the individual aromas of craft, prayer and femine adornment. To speak of the last is also to summon up associations with silk in all its sensuous, textured variety. Local industry – the government sandalwood and silk factories, the many homes where *agarbathis*, or incense sticks are made – sustains these traditional links.

In the streets that lead out from **Statue Square**, where the statues of former kings Krishnaraja and Chamaraja Wadiyar stand under a golden canopy, is a welter of little shops replete with objects in wood, stone and brass, saris and shawls in silk, perfumes and powders, furniture and coffee beans. On Sayyaji Road, the government emporium, **Kaveri**, retails all the products from the state's handicrafts sector.

Mysore has always fostered a spirit of learning, and academics pursue their studies at establishments as diverse as Manasagangothri, the University of Mysore and the Oriental Research Institute. Its seclusion still appeals to the retired and the elderly, even while industries set up shop, contractors build repetitious residential complexes, ready-to-wear department stores and video libraries proliferate and traffic increases exponentially.

This is because Mysore, despite the thin end of the wedge of modernisation,

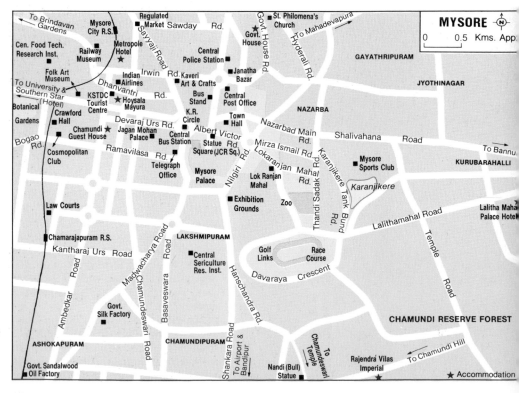

is still very much what history made it. Now a city with a population of 260,000 at last count, it has been the capital of various dynasties from the time it was mentioned as Mahishmati in India's great epic, the *Mahabharata*.

Mysore was ruled by the Wadiyar dynasty from 1399 almost uninterruptedly till Independence, except for the 38-year-rule of the Muslim warlord Hyder Ali and his son Tippu Sultan in the 18th century. The destiny of the Wadiyars has in large measure shaped the city's identity. If it seems at first a city only of palaces, there is further the vitality of Mysore's art, music and dance and the crafts of perfumer, florist and carver which flourished under their patronage.

The dynasty's founders, Vijaya and Krishna, two brothers of the Yadava family, came to Hadinadu, as Mysore was then called, on a pilgrimage from Gujarat. According to one story, Vijaya rescued the local king's daughter from the unwelcome attentions of a rival king. Her grateful father gave him the princess in marriage and made him heir to the title of Wadiyar, or ruler.

The Wadiyars were, by and large, responsible rulers, so much held in esteem by their subjects that when Mysore acceded to the Union of India the then Maharaja, Jayachamarajendra Wadiyar was unanimously favoured as the state's new Governor. The family still live in a portion of the main **Mysore Palace**, cloistered from the eyes of the thousands of tourists who pad by on bare or stockinged feet through the public areas. It is an extravaganza of a structure, embellished with detail on every conceivable surface. To call it overblown would be to deny the ingenuousness of a sensibility that delighted in ornamentation for its own sake.

The palace is basically representative of the Indo-Saracenic school, though the architect Henry Irwin (who designed many public buildings in Madras) indulged his client's whims with a potpourri of Hindu, Islamic and Moorish styles. Thus the building flaunts arched canopies reminiscent of Rajput

Mysore palace, illuminated for Dussera.

palaces and onion domes in the Mughal fashion, surmounted by an unmistakably European campanile. There is a heady mix of cupolas, minarets, balconies and porches, everything tricked out with meticulous carvings of scrolls, flora and fauna, so much so that an early European visitor was heard to mutter, "All curves and carving, there is not an inch of repose on its surface."

Inside is just as grandiloquent: the handsomely proportioned halls and corridors have marble floors and carved mahogany ceilings, stained glass and mosaics. Hunting trophies abound and antique weapons decorate the walls. There are great chandeliers, massive doors wrought in silver, carvings in ivory and other materials, and much elaborate inlay and stucco work.

There is the **Durbar Hall** and the **Kalyana Mandap**, the wedding chamber, with its painstakingly recorded murals of bygone Durbar processions, and the distinctive paintings of Hindu gods and goddesses by the famous Raja Ravi Varma of Travancore. The palace

has a throne worthy of its setting. Made of figwood, initially overlaid with ivory and finely wrought with mythological figures, it was subsequently plated with gold and silver. The throne's gold content is said to weigh about 616 lbs (280 kg), which alone imparts to it a definite curiosity value. The royal elephant throne, as it is called, was apparently gifted in 1699 to a Wadiyar monarch by the Mughal emperor Aurangzeb.

A city of palaces: There are three others, apart from the old fort which sequestered the previous Mysore Palace within its moat before it burned down in 1897. Two of them function as luxury hotels, **Lalitha Mahal** at the foot of the Chamundi Hill and **Rajendra Vilas** at the top. The former was built in the 1930s for those of the Wadiyars' guests who, unlike their indulgent but abstemious hosts, drank alcohol and were not vegetarian. White colonnades surround its two stories and a staircase of Italian marble sweeps up from the foyer where today's guests of the Indian Tourist Development Corporation register.

Cheerful shanty hut and staid Mysore University in the background.

Rajendra Vilas, with its echoes of the Italian style this dynasty seems to have favoured, was formerly the summer palace, also used at other times of the year as a devotional retreat.

The third palace is the **Jaganmohan**, about a mile to the west of the main palace, housing the **Chamarajendra Museum**. It was built in 1861 for the king's wedding, after which the members of the family, compulsive collectors all, began to store their many antiques and curios there, eventually opening it for public viewing. A visit affords an examination of the assortment of trifles that amused royal minds: a set of medieval playing cards, carvings on rice grains, a French clock with toy soldiers to mark the time. Apart from such curiosities, the museum has interesting Mughal and Rajput art, paintings by Raja Ravi Varma and a commendable collection of sculpture and brassware.

Further still to the west is the **Folk Art Museum**, an engrossing storehouse of implements, dolls, costumes, furniture and articles of daily use, their shapes, surfaces, colours and textures reflective of centuries of ethnic craftsmanship. Among the objects of interest is a giant 200-year-old plow which probably needed a dozen oxen to pull it, a canopied pedestal festooned with scarab beetle wings for the elephant god Ganapati, and a cradle with a smart bamboo harness to secure its occupant around the waist.

At the **Oriental Research Institute**, India's art of the written word is manifest. Over 60,000 palm-leaf manuscripts in Sanskrit, Kannada and the other major South Indian languages are lovingly preserved, some of them dating back to the 3rd century BC., and their texts range from dissertations on philosophy, literature and statesmanship to the sciences.

Similarly, the **National Archaeological Survey** has its epigraphical department in the city, with more than 10,000 inscriptions garnered from monuments all over India.

The **Museum** by the railway station

Neighbours: temple adjacent to Mysore Palace.

Silk – Art And Craft

For generations before the advent of powerlooms and chemical dyes, the sons of the silk weavers of Bangalore would be taught to develop a feel for the fabric. The elders would show them how to fashion strings for their kites from leftover silk warp threads tied in weaver's knots. As they grew up, they learnt to make colours from vegetable dyes: yellow from powdered jackfruit wood, red from sandalwood tree bark, indigo from the indigo plant. Without graph paper to plot their designs on, they learnt to weave the

scale: there are references to silk apparel in the *Mahabharata* and *Ramayana*. Tippu Sultan was enamoured of its tactile opulence, its shimmering tones, its seductive fluidity. He recognised the potential of sericulture, with its high value and low volume, and as an export commodity which could be exchanged for arms and ammunition to fuel his war machine. After much searching, his envoys found a South Chinese species of silkworm producing a yellowish yarn, which they brought home to cultivate. Under his supervision sericulture flourished in Bangalore, Kollegal, Channapatna and Dodballapur and Mysore.

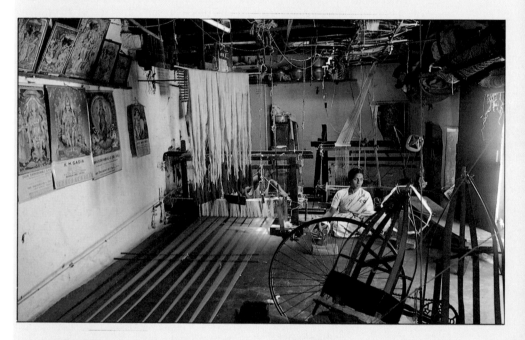

traditional motifs of elephants, peacocks, trees and flowers, in the traditional repeats.

Today's weavers still use the handloom, though dyes are often chemical, designs are no longer woven from memory (many are modern prints – especially on chiffon), and cotton weavers are switching to silk, since it pays much better and Karnataka silk is treasured around the world (8.4 million sq yds/7 million sq m are exported a year).

The beginnings of Karnataka's silk industry lie in an inspiration of Tippu Sultan, although silk had been used by the nobility for centuries before he cultivated it on any

The Depression of the 1930s hit sericulture. The industry recovered during World War II, when Karnataka's silk was suddenly in demand again, this time for parachutes. Since the War, the silk industry has grown to the extent that today Karnataka produces about 5,317 tonnes of yarn annually, about 65 percent of India's total output. About 70 percent of this is consumed by the other states, so that many of the splendid *saris* from Varanasi, Kanjivaram and Lepakshi are in fact woven from Karnataka yarn.

There are basically five kinds of silk: soft silk, crepe, georgette and chiffon, dupion and spun silk. The first three are distinguished on the basis of the twist count of their yarns. Twisting of fibres strengthens yarns and varies texture. Yarns used for soft silk bestow á smooth finish and are more lustrous than the high-twist yarns which create the textures of crepe and georgette. Dupion yarn is reeled from two cocoons, which gives the fabric its coarse, slubbed surface. It is often erroneously referred to as raw silk. Spun silk is spun like cotton from the waste left when yarn is reeled. It figures a great deal in furnishing fabrics, like the Channapatna variety woven into carpets.

Traditional *saris* are still woven from soft

the Devanga community which traces its origins to the Vijayanagara period. They once wove *angavastrams*, the mantle used to clothe temple deities – hence *dev* (god) and *anga* (body). Traditional colours, designs and patterns prevail, though amidst them can be seen concessions to modernity. The Molkalmuru *sari* is one of contrasts in deep colours – red, indigo, snuff and pink.

The motifs used are to some extent general, such as the sacred *rudraksha* bead, the mango or paisley, and the lotus. Another symbol of veneration is the temple design where an architectural detail of the temple itself becomes a motif. Ornamentation is en-

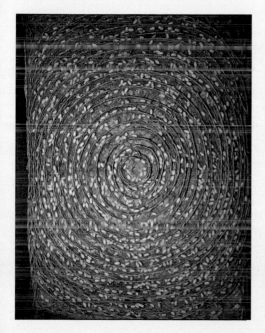

silk. These have an appeal that goes beyond the comeliness of the fabric; it derives from colours and motifs particular to each style. Circumstances conditioned the evolution of regional styles. Molkalmuru in north Karnataka is exemplary. In the arid region where the village is situated, frequent drought compelled many farmers to look to other livelihoods; weaving, already a part-time occupation, was the natural choice. This combined with other factors to form the nucleus around which weavers from other areas were drawn to settle down in Molkalmuru.

The silk weavers of Bangalore come from

hanced by gold thread, *zari*, used in the motifs and in various configurations on the *sari* body, border and *pallu* (the end piece of the *sari*), of stripes of diverse widths, checks, and the *butas* (dots).

In a craft with products so geographically diverse, what distinguishes one type of silk from another, apart from the motif and colour, are features like the way patterns are repeated, how the *pallus*, borders and bodies are connected, and even the way a *sari* is folded. The inspiration that informs every metre of silk in an age of mass production, gives it a universal appeal.

offers a collection of rolling stock redolent of a dated grandeur, upholstered according to lavish regal notions of how travel was to be undertaken.

Mysore Zoo is a verdant, sprawling zoo, where the emphasis is on simulation of the natural environment. Within its moated enclosures, you can see the white tiger, lions, a gorilla, and a cheetah. Close to the city, near Srirangapatnam, is the **Ranganathittu bird sanctuary**, where hundreds of migratory birds swoop down onto ancient trees spread over the rocky islets dotting the Kaveri.

One compulsory halt for all the tourist buses is the **Brindavan Gardens**, about 12 miles (19 km) outside the city. This is the site of the Krishnarajasagar reservoir, created when the adjoining irrigation dam, Karnataka's largest, was built across the Kaveri river. The dam is notable because it was constructed from stone and mortar, without the use of cement, the public gardens because they extend a concept. Musical fountains bathed in candy-coloured light rise and fall in synchronicity with the recorded music of either Ananda Shankar or, more mundanely, Paul Mauriat. Chromatically abloom, the gardens descend in manicured terraces, margined by water courses in the Islamic fashion. (Incidentally, inscriptions testify to Tippu's attempts to build a dam at the same spot.) In a niche beneath the ornate parapets on the rear face of the dam stands a statue of the river goddess, holding a pot from which water spills as symbol of prosperity and perhaps as a reminder that without the 44,000 million cu ft (1,245 million cu m) of water behind, the gardens might not be such a lush reality.

Chamundi Hill towers over 1,320 ft (400 m) over the city and is named for the royal family's deity, who once delivered the people of the area from the buffalo-headed demon Mahishasura. The legend has it that after she killed him she took up residence on the hill. Having no desire to attract the evil eye once again, the inhabitants took the sapient step of naming the city they

loved so much after the demon himself. Hence the name Mahishasura, referred to in the *Mahabharata* as Mahishmati, and still elsewhere as Mahishamandala. His statue stands at a roundabout on the road to the **Sri Chamundeswari temple**, scowl in place, scimitar in one hand and an enormous cobra firmly gripped in the other. Just beyond is the temple, with its colossal pyramidal *gopuram* built by Krishnaraja Wadiyar III, who also made an endowment of a fabulous gold gem, carved with 30 Sanskrit verses, called the Nakshatramalika.

Descending the hill, either by road or down a flight of a thousand steps which has the virtue of being 5 miles (9 km) shorter – long-winded Mysoreans climb up and down it all the time on their way to the temple – you pass the 16-ft (4.88 m) monolith of the seated **Nandi bull**, Shiva's chosen carrier, a 17th century work of devotional art carved from one enormous boulder with loving attention to detail patent in everything from the bell around its neck to the anklets above each massive hoof. The

statue is immediately emblematic of the old Mysore to every Indian and to most travellers it remains the most enduring of the many images of the city.

The citadel in the stream: Its strategic position as an island in the middle of a river has been to Srirangapatnam's advantage several times through its history. It has also worked against it, since the fact has unhappily brought it to the covetous attention of every ruler in the region. For a period of about 3 centuries, from the 15th century when the fort was first built on the island till the end of the 18th century, Srirangapatnam suffered the virtue of its location as various rulers strove mightily to oust whoever happened to be entrenched on it at the moment. The years from 1638 to 1799 in particular saw the island under siege seven times, the last by the British who finally vanquished its occupant, Tippu Sultan. Since then, this battle-fatigued island has been left more or less to itself.

It is odd that in this picturesque town with its mausoleums, cemeteries (including the **British Garrison cemetery**

nterior of Tippu's summer palace, Daria Daulat Bagh.

and the graves of the troops of Tippu's French allies) and commemorative monuments (the obelisk in the Fort that marks where Tippu Sultan fell and the memorial to the soldiers who died in the final siege), the only ghost story you are likely to hear is the one concerning Scott's Bungalow.

Colonel Scott supervised a gun factory on the island when the British occupied it. One day he came home to his bungalow to find his wife and child dead from a sudden attack of cholera. Disconsolate, he threw himself into the river that ran outside the garden. For years, his ghost rose from the river at night and wafted forlornly up to the bungalow, looking for his loved ones.

Most of Srirangapatnam's buildings and monuments were constructed by Tippu Sultan, known as the Tiger of Mysore for his ferocity and tactical cunning. His insignia was tiger stripes and everything, from his throne to his dagger, featured either a tiger's head, claws or teeth. (Apparently, tigers also functioned as summary dispensers of justice and he kept a cage of these beasts to punish the occasional miscreant, such as the tax collector who had come up short.) He proclaimed himself Sultan in 1782 after the death of his father Hyder Ali, a former commander under the Wadiyars who had wrested power from his employers.

Tippu was an inspired warrior and commander, his troops trained by the French whose revolutionary ideals he sympathised with to the extent that he referred to himself briefly, if whimsically, as Citoyen Tippu. He then proceeded to give the British, who had dismissed this as the mere antics of a temporary Francophile, a bad fright by inviting Napoleon, then in Egypt, to come to his assistance – an offer not taken up.

Daria Daulat: When not embroiled in conquest or defence, Tippu ruled his island capital well and built upon it with a fine aesthetic judgement. He indulged himself with a summer palace he built in 1784, called Daria Daulat Bagh – the Garden of the Wealth of the Seas. Made

Tiger stripes, Tippu's insignia, carpet the floor of his tomb.

of teak, it looks exquisitely cool, an Indo-Saracenic structure painted forest-green and set in formal Islamic gardens. The restraint of its elegant facade nicely balances the extravagance of its interior.

Large wall murals, still vivid in hue, detail (with maybe a slight bias) the lives and times of the ruler and his family. There is one with the Mysore soldiers, French comrades in arms alongside, dashingly portrayed in contrast to their stodgily depicted British opponents. One room serves as a museum chock-a-block with personal trivia: a gold-embroidered tunic Tippu once wore, his coin collection and some Western paintings and engravings.

Sri Ranganatha Temple: When Thirumalayya, a governor serving in the Ganga Kingdom, built the Sri Rangunatha temple in AD 894 on an island in the Kaveri river, 10 miles (16 km) from Mysore, it was uninhabited and dense with jungle. Three centuries later came a chieftain Thimmanna, anxious to put to constructive use a cache of buried treasure he had unearthed. He built the island's fort with the temple structure and improved upon it. For this, as a gesture of secular stonework, he also used materials he had garnered from a stupefying pillage of 101 Jain temples.

These architectural efforts, three centuries apart, explain the melding of the temple's Hoysalan and Vijayanagaran styles. Representations of Vishnu cover the pillars, ceilings and domes, and at the temple precincts is a juggernaut donated by Hyder Ali, a truly secular man. In the sanctum, recumbent under the hood of Adisesha, the seven-headed serpent, is the image of the god after whom the island and its oldest structure were named.

Jumma Masjid: Two hundred steps lead to the top of each of the slender minarets on the Jumma Masjid, both overlooking the fort area. Epigraphs in Persians record the 99 names of Allah and date the period of construction of the mosque to AD 1787. Tippu, a devout Muslim, offered *namaz* in the hall with its foil arches.

Fort: The British breached the Fort's

southwest wall and demolished the Lal Mahal, Tippu's palace; most of the remaining fortifications have since then crumbled away. The Elephant Gate, the dungeons where the river surged in to lap at the unfortunates who were chained there, the obelisk on the spot where the great general fell: these are the fragments left.

Gol Gumbaz: On Tippu's tomb in the Gol Gumbaz, the inscription says, "The light of Islam has left this world, a martyr for the faith of Mohammad." His father Hyder Ali is buried here, and his mother (born a Hindu) too. Splendid rosewood doors inlaid with ivory lead indoors, where Tippu's favourite tiger stripes band the walls. Glossy pillars of black hornblende offer a contrast to the cream walls and the superb dome, with its minarets in four corners. Traditional gardens define the approach to a mausoleum that has been inevitably compared to the Taj Mahal, though it is much smaller and more austere. On the island which Tippu Sultan died so valiantly for, its beauty is entirely appropriate.

Somnathpur: This is the site of the **Prasanna Chennakesava Temple**, with the star-shaped base characteristic of Hoysala temple architecture. Of the three most famous Hoysala temples in Karnataka, this was the last to be built, in AD 1268. It is situated in a somnolent village about 22 miles (35 km) from Mysore city, a short distance and a trip well worth making to see the degree of sculptural and structural precision that the art of temple-building could attain.

The temple was the creation of Janakachari, perhaps the era's finest architect and sculptor, who is believed to have so excelled himself in its design and execution that the gods themselves were tempted to steal it. But as they caused the building to rise heavenward, the resourceful Janakachari disfigured some of the carvings on the outer walls. Seeing its perfection thus marred, the celestial ones coveted it no longer and let it go. The temple sank back onto the ground with a thud that dislodged its flagstaff, awry ever since – the one flaw in an edifice of perfection.

The diversions of legend aside, history relates that the temple was commissioned by Somnath, a minister of the Hoysala king, Narasimha III, from whom he received a handsome sum of 3,000 gold pieces for his many charitable works. A devout man, Somnath used the money to build the temple in homage to his family deities – Chennakeshava, Janardhana and Venugopala – in the village that its elders named after him. Janakachari used soapstone in the construction of the building, since it is both easy to work with and wear-resistant.

Unusually for a Hoysala temple, there are three shrines, one for each member of the trinity. In the main one facing the entrance, the images of the sentries still stand guard, though the idol of Lord Chennakeshava it once housed disapppeared long ago. The northern shrine still has its image of Janardhana, and the southern that of Venugopala. Both have halos carved with the 10 incarnations of Vishnu. The latter idol is particularly symmetrical:

Star-shaped plinth of the Kesava temple, Somnathpur.

holding a flute, it stands with nose, navel and supporting foot in precise alignment.

Each shrine has its tower and multi-pillared hall that opens out onto a central square called the *navrang*, where songs and dances were performed in worship.

Since the superstructure is not as tall as those of most South Indian temples, all the carving is at a comfortable eye-level – marvellously articulate carving, with a variety of facial expressions minutely rendered.

The exterior walls are frescoed with narrative passages from the *Ramayana*, the *Mahabharata* and the *Bhagavatha*, laid out so exactly that each segment ends at a door. Vivid with detail, no two frescoes are alike, and some extend right around the temple. The carvings ascend the temple walls in seven rows of distinct motifs. At the bottom, in symbolic support, is a row of elephants and next, one of equine and floral forms, which support in turn the scenarios from the epics.

Row No. 4 is of the avatars of Vishnu, and above that, a seated lion, emblem of the Hoysala dynasty. The second highest line has representations of Lord Narasimha and finally, a tier of swans and crocodiles. Stripped of ornamentation above this, the wedge-shaped shafts of the *gopurams* end in the Vysara style, derivative of both the Dravidian and the Orissan temple *gopurams*. (The latter ends in a point, unlike the former.)

The occasional contradictory detail presents itself: a depiction from the *Bhagavatha*, for instance, on the exterior of the middle shrine has a palace set in Mathura (the birthplace of Krishna), framed by coconut palms which do not grow in North India. Another frieze from the *Mahabharata* has a row of camels, animals rarely seen in the South or in illustrations of the epic.

These idiosyncratic touches were certainly deliberately introduced and left there, perhaps like the flagstaff, never straightened after that failed essay in divine larceny.

Bands of friezes cover the exterior walls of the Kesava temple.

COORG, MANGALORE AND UDUPI

About 156 miles (250 km) from Bangalore, located in the Western Ghats, lies **Kodagu**, formerly known as **Coorg**. The British, with their propensity for nostalgia, dubbed it the Scotland of India, probably for its misty green slopes and lush forestation. Today, Kodagu is primarily an agricultural center, with cash crops of coffee, rice and oranges supported by cardamom, pepper and other spices.

The Kodavas constitute the main population of Coorg, and are a martial race with distinct ethnic and cultural characteristics. The concept of the clan amongst them is a powerful institution that many credit with having preserved the Kodava culture for centuries. The clan or *okka* is an exogamous group: marriage within the same *okka* considered tantamount to incest. Kodavas practise the cross-cousin marriage system, which is a distinct trait of tribal ethnic communities. Women occupy an exalted place in the family hierarchy, and remarriage from widowhood is encouraged. Many women run estates single-handedly, and local legends often have heroines occupying the central role.

Most explanations on the origin of the Kodavas are fairly colourful but have never been authenticated or proved. One such school considers them descendants of the Greeks. Alexander the Great, in pursuit of world domination, had sent his infantry down the west coast of India. Having travelled deep into the south, the Greek soldiers decided to settle where they were. These Mediterranean strangers are credited with the founding of the race. Another story attributes Kodava ancestry to Arab migration, based on the similarity of the traditional costume, especially the head-kerchief and the long black robe worn to this day – known as the *kuppia* to the Arab *kuffia*.

Coorg's manicured neatness comes as something of a surprise to the traveller who has experienced the untamed landscape of India. Coorg is a region of scattered hamlets and villages separated by distances varying between 3 miles (4.8 km) and 30 miles (48 km). The capital is **Madikeri** or , a picturesque little township at an elevation of over 5,000 ft (1,525 m) above sea level. Access there is by road, as there are no air or rail services beyond Mysore. From Bangalore, the best way to travel and the most comfortable is by private taxi, which allows you the freedom to move around within Kodagu. Alternatively, bus services ply between Bangalore and different areas of Kodagu on a regular basis.

The township of Mercara is itself worth a ramble. Streets dip and rise as they follow the hilly terrain. It is a charming, old-world town dotted with pretty cottages all around and panoramic views which come upon you unexpectedly. Winding lanes meander off the main streets and if you are fond of walking, there are excellent prospects and mountain trails to follow. **Tadiyendamol**, the tallest peak in the

area, is a beautiful climb and you can view the distant horizon of the Arabian Sea from the top. Trekking at the Nagarhole National Park can be organised with the permission of the Chief Wildlife Warden. In the centre of Mercara is the **Madikeri fort**, a 19th century building of no particular distinction. Within its walls lie the local prison, a temple, a small museum and various government offices.

The temples of Kodagu are more interesting, ranging from primitive hero stones set up under banyan trees to multi-roofed ethnic architecture. There are three temples you must see in Kodagu. The **Omkareshwara** temple, dedicated to Shiva and built by Lingaraja in 1820 in the centre of the township, is an unexpected mix of Gothic and Islamic styles. It is built around a central pool teeming with fish that you can feed. The **Bhagamandala** temple has been built at the confluence of three rivers, the Kaveri, Kanike and Sujyothi. It is built in the Kerala style and houses a variety of smaller shrines dedicated to various gods. Five miles (8 km) up the hill from Bhagamandala is the source of the river Kaveri with the **Talakaveri** temple built around it. In October, on Kaveri Sankaramana day, thousands gather at this little temple to witness the miraculous rise of the fountainhead, when water gushes up at a predetermined moment.

There are two picturesque waterfalls. The **Abbey Falls** are near Mercara and quite an agreeable place for a picnic. The **Iruppu Falls** are where the Laxmanthirtha descends, and lies on the route from Gonikoppal to Kutta.

Nagarhole National Park: Magnificent natural forests stretch as far as the eye can see. Rosewood, teak, sandal, silver oak and other trees make up this thick jungle, teeming with the flora and fauna of the region. Jeeps and elephants are available for transport and guided tours. You can go directly to this reserve forest from Mysore or Hunsur. Forest lodges provide fairly decent accommodation and food on a *prix-fixe* basis.

Mangalore: The Western Ghats have

The beautiful township of Mercara, Coorg.

to be traversed if you travel to Mangalore from Bangalore, and the journey snaking down the hairpin bends is spectacular. As the descent begins, Mangalore becomes visible, ensconced on the coast. This maritime city has always been significant, for it was a major seaport and shipbuilding centre in Hyder Ali's time. Today it is a business and commercial centre and the major port of Karnataka for the export of coffee, spices and cashew. Mangalore has a turbulent history of conflict for possession of this important port. These influences are still apparent in the cosmopolitan attitude and diverse religions that exist here.

You can visit the **Sultan's Battery**, the old lighthouse. Climb **Kadri Hills** for a spectacular vista, and view temples like **Shri Yogeshwar Math**. The **Dharmathsthala** and **Shringeri** temples are nearby, the Mangalore Port is outside of town, and of the old forts, only the ones constructed by Basavappa Nayak and St Sebastian built by the Portuguese stand as relics of their times.

A beautiful 10th century temple to the goddess **Mangaladevi** co-exists with splendid churches and mosques. Visit **St Joseph's Theological Seminary**, the ancient **Church of the Most Holy Rosary** at Bolar, which was founded in 1526, and the **St Aloysius College Church**, which has a magnificent Biblical fresco on the walls and ceiling painted in 1889.

Among the remarkable mosques are the **Jumma Masjid** in the Bunder, built centuries ago by the Arabs, and the **Idgah** mosque at Lighthouse Hill whose construction is attributed to Tippu Sultan at the end of the 18th century. The saint Shah Amir is entombed at the **Shamir Mosque** at Dongerkery.

Mangalore is a good base for a trip down coastal Karnataka. Inviting beaches easily reached by a good coastal road dot the area both above and below Mangalore. Seafood enthusiasts will appreciate the variety available in local restaurants. Styles of cuisine are varied, and it is possible to eat Continental food at most of the better hotels.

Mangalore clay tiles, still widely used for roofs, lend a rustic charm to the hill town.

Local cuisine is spicy, with a lot of coconut gravy used in the preparation. Good vegetarian food is available from a host of Udupi cafeterias.

The Hotel Manjarun and the Moti Mahal both have bands and dance floors in their restaurants. Cinemas are at every corner. Try to catch the local theatre form Yakshagana, a stylised and elaborate dance that tells the stories of the ancient epics.

Beaches: Mangalore is indifferent and polluted as beaches near ports normally are. While here, you should plan to go further up or down the coastline.

Malpe, 6 miles (10 km) from Udupi and Manipal, has beautiful silvery beaches. Fishing, boating and bathing facilities are available.

Ullal, 3 miles (5 km) from Mangalore, has a resort called Summer Sands, 42 beach cottages set amidst casuarina groves. You could spend a day here. It is a pretty place, though the service and the food are fair to middling.

Marawanthe, just over 5 miles (9 km) from Coondapur between the river and sea coast, has good swimming facilities. You can canoe down the river and explore the hinterland.

Bhaktal: Up the coast from Mangalore, this used to be the major port of the Vijayanagara empire. There are Portuguese ruins to explore and old temples from the Vijayanagara period to visit.

Karwar: About 325 miles (520 km) from Bangalore, this is a beautiful seaside town that Vasco da Gama is reputed to have visited. The fort at Sadashivgad, Devgad island and the lighthouse are of some interest. The nearby coastal villages of Binaga and Araga have good beaches.

Around Mangalore

Dharmastala: The impressive Manjunatha temple, Jain *bastis*, and a 45 ft (14 m) high statue of Lord Bahubali.

Venur: The ruins of a Mahadeva temple, a statue of Lord Bahubali 35 ft (11 m) high on the banks of the Gurupur, installed in 1604, and Jain *bastis*.

Mudbidri has 18 *bastis*, the oldest of

The monsoon arrives in Mudbidri.

which is the Chandranatha temple with its 1,000 richly carved pillars.

Karkala: An ancient and venerated religious township with a statue of Lord Bahubali, installed in 1432.

Jog Falls: About 217 miles (348 km) from Mysore, where the Birur railway line terminates quite near the coast, are Jog Falls, the highest waterfall in India. The river Sharavati makes a spectacular drop of 810 ft (253 m) in four distinct cascades known locally as the Raja, Rani, Rover and Rocket. The dry season detracts from the grandeur of the falls and, in the monsoon, mist totally obscures the view. They are at their best just after the monsoon, when the arching rainbows are beautiful.

Udupi: Up the coast from Mangalore lies the 13th century seat of Madhavacharya, the great religious leader. The temple at Udupi is an impressive institution with a beautifully bejeweled statue of Lord Krishna. The elaborate religious rites performed at each day's *puja* have remained unchanged through the centuries. Several festivals are held here throughout the year. Under the patronage of the *swamis* of the eight *maths*, religious centres, Udupi is a centre for higher learning through all the educational institutions and colleges that were opened under their sponsorship, and funded by their educational trusts.

Food: The famous *masala dosai* has its origins in Udupi, and a whole school of South Indian cuisine takes its name from this town. Today, in the most far-flung corners of India you will see the inevitable "Udupi Tiffin Room" or "Udupi Brahmin Hotel", a name synonymous with inexpensive vegetarian food.

You must sample the *masala dosai*, a crisply fried pancake of fermented rice stuffed with a mix of spicy potato and onion. Try the *idli*, a steamed rice cake that can be eaten with lentil and mint chutney or *sambar*. Other dishes to ask for are the *rava dosai*, *puri palya*, *uthapam*, *vada sambar* and the paper *dosai*, which is an outsize *dosai* with the crisp consistency of paper.

Foothills of the Western Ghats.

LEGACY OF THE DECCAN KINGS

Beyond the Western Ghats is the northern plateau, where the Malaprabha, the Ghataprabha, the Krishna and the Doni rivers intermittently vein the boulder-spiked landscape as they make their way to the east. This is where the early Islamic empires of Karnataka established themselves, creating in the span of their existence the superb examples of Deccani architecture that command such universal regard. These are the great buildings whose design came from the cultured synthesis of the Delhi and the Persian schools of Islamic architecture.

The Islamic approach brought innovations: the use of the arch, the employment of mortar. Muslim mathematical and scientific building formulae were often applied by Hindu craftsmen, which resulted in more flexible interpretations of the original Persian traditions, no less memorable for being re-sponsive to ethnic inspiration. In fact, what happened sometimes, as in the case of the **Karim-al-Din Mosque** in Bijapur, was that old temple pillars were used in some constructions.

Belgaum: Like so many other South Indian towns before post-Independence industrialisation altered their profiles and demographics, **Belgaum** had two main areas. There was the old quarter where the cotton and silk weavers still dwell, their lives paced to the tempo of their looms. The tempo was set many generations before the British came and built the spacious, tree-lined cantonment, the other main section of the city, with its own unhurried rhythms in counterpoint.

Belgaum's history followed much the same pattern as other towns of the region, submitting as a matter of course to different Hindu and Muslim rulers and then to the British. The reminders of dominion are few and scattered; the **fort** near the heart of the city where Mahatma Gandhi was incarcerated and the **Masjid-Sata** mosque are worth visit-

Prayer wall: part of the Muslim legacy of the Deccan.

ing, as are the two **Jain temples** and a **watchtower** with a view which has not yet been obscured by the fast-changing skyline. Local history celebrates the story of Rani Chennamma of Kittur, a nearby village. She was one of India's first freedom fighters, a ruler whose resolute opposition to British domination made her a heroine, still commemorated locally in song and story.

When the ruler of Kittur died, leaving the Rani childless, she sought to nominate a nephew to the throne. The British collector Thackeray (a relative of the 19th century author), who had his eye on this wealthy principality, used this as an excuse to march on the fort. This was a mistake: the Rani and her troops held the British off; Thackeray was shot dead and his head impaled on a spear and paraded in triumphant procession.

Determined more than ever to get their hands on the fort and, more important, its treasury, and goaded by their recent defeat, the British attacked again, led by Sir Walter Elliot. This time they won and the Rani was taken prisoner.

She lived the rest of her life in captivity, dying five years later at the age of 50.

Around the Bijapur battlements: The story of the Adil Shahi dynasty began in the 15th century with the death of the Sultan of Constantinople. It was a time when pragmatic scions often asserted their conviction that one male heir in each generation was sufficient. The Sultan's widow, knowing this full well, had their second son Yusuf spirited away out of his brother's reach, and the young boy's long journey brought him to India. He was 17 years old, resourceful and adventurous. Sold to a minister in the powerful Bahmani kingdom, Yusuf rose above his circumstances to become the Adil Khan, the Governor of Bijapur, a Bahmani territory in the northwest of Karnataka.

The Bahmani dynasty was in decline, and in 1489 Yusuf asserted his independence of it to pronounce himself Adil Shah. For the next two centuries, the Adil Shahis reigned from Bijapur, a succession of rulers whose legacy was the architectural tradition that inspired

brahim Rauza, Bijapur.

so many generations of master builders, its influence unmistakable too in the Indo-Saracenic style of the Raj.

Yusuf Adil Shah set about fortifying Bijapur with a wall 6¼ miles (10 km) in circumference, one that still stands in good repair, with its expansive moat and crenellated battlements. You can see how commanding its reach was over the arid, arduous environs, and how well the great ordnances must have guarded the approaches. On a bastion named for its ornamental stone lions is the **Malik-e-Maidan**, "the Lord of the Plains", reputedly the largest medieval cannon in the world. Ten elephants, 400 oxen and much manpower were needed to draw it all the way from Maharashtra. It is shaped like a lion's jaws and throat devouring elephants. A small tank of water would be handily placed so gunners could immerse their heads and spare their eardrums when this tremendous gun was fired. In reassuring contrast to its capabilities is the legend which holds that if you touch the gun and make a wish, it will come true.

While the remnants of armaments and fortifications confirm dynastic prowess, the city of Bijapur affords proof (very little of it in perfect repair) that Deccani architecture was at its most civilised under the Adil Shahis. You could spend days wandering around these buildings, over 30 in number, their austerely elegant silhouettes detailed with the precise mathematics of the Islamic style. The most distinguished of these are the Gol Gumbaz, the Ibrahim Roza, the Jami Masjid, the Anand Mahal and the Mehtar Mahal.

The Gol Gumbaz: If is fitting that the dynasty's last principal structure should be a mausoleum, it is equally appropriate that is also the most visible. The massive rotundity of the Gol Gumbaz dominates the eastern skyline near the station, the first silhouette the railborne traveller sees.

In 1626 its builder, Muhammad Adil Shah, inherited from his father a kingdom shot through with such factional instability that he, perhaps presciently, devoted much time and resource to

The Gol Gumbaz: Asia's largest dome

building his own mausoleum. It is surmounted by a dome built in 1659 that is second to none but St Peter's in Rome, being a mere 5 m smaller in diameter. It rests on intersecting pendentive arches over an enormous square hall, the largest floor space in the world covered by a single dome.

Four octagonal towers buttress the structure, each seven storeys and with its own small dome. They open on top onto the legendary Whispering Gallery that runs round the inside of the central dome, all but invisible from below. Its accoustics are incredible, and you will receive playful injunctions to beware of what you say up there: no matter how hushed the voice, it will echo, on and on. Entombed below with Muhammad Adil Shah in splendid conjugal impartiality are his wife and his favourite courtesan.

Across the town to the west is the **Ibrahim Rouza**, built by Ibrahim II, the sixth ruler of the dynasty who ascended the throne in 1580. He built it for his wife, though he predeceased her and is buried there too. With its enclosed garden containing a mosque, it provided much for emulation and envy: the architects of the Taj Mahal studied it before embarking upon their own illustrious task, and the Gol Gumbaz was another inspired attempt to surpass it. Adjectives are rendered superfluous by an inscription on a wall which says, "Heaven stood astonished. When [the Ibrahim Rouza] rose from the earth, another paradise was created. Its every column is as graceful as the cypress tree in the Garden of Purity."

Within the citadel Ibrahim II also built the **Anand Mahal**, the Palace of Joy, and the **Taj Baori** in the *zenana*, the ladies' quarter, named for his wife Taj Sultana.

The **Mehtar Mahal**, to the east of the citadel, is not a palace as its name would lead you to expect. According to one source it was built for the sweepers of the regal household. The relief work around the doorways, on the balconies and the ceilings, proclaims a pride in workmanship that was as much the patron's as it was the artisan's.

Ruins of Bidar, one of the Decca Sultanates.

The years after the founder Yusuf's reign were tumultuous. When Ali Shah (Ibrahim II's predecessor and uncle) came to rule in 1557, he achieved a stability of sorts only after defeating the Hindu Vijayanagara empire in 1565 in alliance with three other splinter states from the erstwhile Bahmani kingdom. In thanksgiving for his victory, he began to build the **Jami Masjid**, a mosque whose magnificent proportions are balanced by its understated ornamentation, the exception being the *mihrab* festooned with gold leaf calligraphy, its stunning niches with *trompe l'oeil* books, censers and floral arrangements.

The comparative tranquility of Ali Shah's reign also afforded him the time to build himself an enormous durbar, the **Gagan Mahal** or Sky Palace, and the **Mecca Masjid**, a miniature mosque for the women of the court, both within the fortress walls. He also strengthened the city's defences and implemented its waterworks, the latter a far more important undertaking in that parched area.

In 1686, the Adil Shahi empire succumbed after an 18-month siege by the Mughals, the last in the series of assailants the dynasty had to fend off throughout its life. With no food or ammunition and his forces decimated, the 19-year old Sikander, the last of the Adil Shahis, opened the citadel gates to Aurangzeb.

Learning in Gulbarga: Gulbarga features the burial place of a Muslim saint, and a temple dedicated to a Hindu savant, both of them scholars whose humanity attracted thousands of adherents to their philosophy. Khwaja Bande Nawaz was from Delhi, a disciple of the religious teacher Hazrat Khwaja Peer Naseeruddin Mahmood Chirag. Fleeing from orthodox persecution in the north, he was invited to Gulbarga by the Bahmanis, the royal house that ruled the Deccan during the 13th-15th centuries.

Scholastic deliberation was encouraged at their court, and respected astronomers and mathematicians taught at the schools and colleges these rulers started. The state coffers paid teachers' salaries and students' stipends, and Sultan Muhammad Shah II himself **The great mosque at Gulbarga.**

delivered regular lectures following a timetable that allotted particular days for logic, mathematics and rhetoric. Unlike his predecessors and successors, he could afford to do this since his 19-year reign was the most peaceful, as well as the longest.

Muhammed II spoke fluent Arabic and Persian, apart from Dakhni (Deccan) Urdu, the language of the new Islamic aristocracy of the South. Arabic came to India through commercial trade between its west coast and the Middle East. The founder of the empire claimed regal Persian ancestry in the loftier, more nebulous reaches of his family tree (his immediate origins certainly were much more modest).

Like Khwaja Bande Nawaz, Persian scholars flocked to the Bahmani court, disarmed perhaps by a ruler like Muhammed II with his intellectual attainments and inclination to teach. The saint-scholar lived in Gulbarga for over 20 years and among the 100 or more books he wrote are the first essays in the new Dakhni Urdu. His beliefs in universal peace and brotherhood drew thousands of followers; today, on the Urs, his annual feast, just as many flock to his brocade-bedecked tomb on the eastern side of Gulbarga. In the adjacent mosque is a venerable library of works in all the three languages this devout man had mastered. Today it is the temple cart procession in April from the temple dedicated to Basaveshwara that attracts 100,000 pilgrims to its precincts near the Gulbarga Tank. This philosopher's name endows several colleges and in this city of 2 million, the teaching of medicine and history, of the sciences and the arts continues.

The most majestic place of learning was the **Madrasa** in the nearby town of Bidar, where the Bahmani kingdom shifted in 1428. Though ravaged, the architectural and decorative details of its ruins are sufficient to explain why the architectural historian Percy Brown wrote that it "might have been bodily moved from Samarkhand". Founded by the Persian Muhammad Gawan, a minister at the Bahmani court, the original institution contained lecture halls, a library and a mosque, and dormitories and rooms for at least 300 students of Islamic theology and the arts.

It rises within the 15th century sandstone fort, strategically placed to monopolise the landscape. In its precincts activity bustles around the new buildings juxtaposed chock-a-block with charmingly timeworn *mahals* and mosques.

Before the visitor leaves Gulbarga, however, he would be well advised to enter its sprawling fort and see the **Jami Masjid**, a 14th century mosque designed by a Moorish architect. His references are obvious: the 38,000 sq ft (3,420 sq m) building has been based on the mosque in Cordova. What is remarkable is that the roof spans the entire courtyard, something never accomplished in South Asian Muslim architecture. Dome after dome crowns the prayer hall, and below arched columns are so placed that the pulpit is seen from every angle, and the accoustics so keen that everything said from it is just as easily heard.

HAMPI

Hampi is perhaps the most beautiful and evocative of all the ruins in Karnataka. There is a brooding, mystical ambience to the landscape – bleak, barren and strewn with boulders, the desolation offset by the magnificent remnants of a once-powerful empire.

The Vijayanagara empire was one of the largest in the history of India. Though there are diverse opinions on the founding of the empire, most historians agree that the Sangamas were the first ruling dynasty of this kingdom. The Telugu princes Harihara and Bukka in the 14th century extended their kingdom from the Tungabhadra right up to Trichinopoly in the south. A hundred years later, the empire reached its zenith under Krishnadeva Raya, who controlled the whole of the peninsula south of the Krishna river.

For two centuries the glory of this kingdom was boundless. According to Nicolo Conti, the Italian merchant, the city of Vijayanagara was just 8 miles (13 km) in circumference and its ruler was the most powerful in India. In another instance, the Portuguese traveller Paes who visited Vijayanagara in its golden age described it as being as large as Rome, with the palaces of its kings being larger than the castles of Lisbon. He recorded that it was the most flourishing city in the world and had more than 100,000 dwellings.

A Muslim envoy, Abdul Razaq, visited the capital in 1443 and wrote, "Vijayanagara is such that the pupil of the eye has never seen a place like it and the ear of intelligence has never been informed that there existed anything to equal it in the world. The audience hall of the king's palace is elevated above all the rest. In the long bazaars, flowers are sold everywhere. The people could not live without flowers and they look upon them as quite as necessary as food. The jewellers sell publicly pearls, rubies, emeralds and diamonds. In this agreeable locality, as well as in the king's palace, one sees numerous streams and

channels formed of chiselled stone, polished and smooth."

The notable rulers of this dynasty were Deva Raya II (early 15th century), Krishnadeva Raya and his successor Achyutadeva Raya (early 16th century). Krishnadeva Raya (1509-29), brother of Vira Narasimha, was the greatest ruler of Vijayanagara. He dominated the Bahmanis and contained the threat from the king of Orissa, another traditional enemy. His army advanced further to the north and his empire stretched from Konkan in the west to Waltair in the East and Cape Comorin in the south. Some islands in the Indian Ocean also came under his influence.

The Vijayanagara kings were great promoters of culture. As is apparent even from these ruins, the arts flourished under their patronage and they gave equal attention to the development of new techniques in agriculture, warfare, waterworks and civic building.

Textiles and mining flourished. Craftsmen and merchants' guilds played an important role in the economic system. There were 300 ports in different parts of the empire and trade relations were maintained with Burma, the Malay Peninsula, China, Arabia, Abyssinia, Portugal and islands in the Indian Ocean. The chief exports were textiles, rice, iron and sugar, while the imports included horses, elephants, pearls, copper and Chinese silk. Ships built in the Maldives were used for carrying cargo overseas.

Although Vijayanagara was essentially a Hindu kingdom, the rulers permitted the practice of other religions and they themselves following a variety of Hindu cults. The better known are the cults of Virupaksha, Krishna, Vittala, Rama and Venkateshwara. Thus, Hampi had a diverse population with a rich blend of cosmopolitan cultures.

By 1565, the Muslim Sultanates had declared war and defeated the Vijayanagara military commander. The king, together with his court and treasury, escaped southward. The abandoned city was sacked. Left in smouldering ruins, Vijayanagara was never to be occupied again.

eft,
e 22 ft
.7 m) tall
olossus of
arasimha
Hampi.

The splendour of Vijayanagara has never been entirely lost, for even in the ruins you can glimpse its past glories. Ruins of ancient temples are found to this day in towns and villages around Hampi. Plans are now underway to protect the site. The Indian National Trust and the Archaeological Survey of India are together making an effort to conserve what is left and to preserve it for the future.

The natural setting of Vijayanagara offered protection from invaders, since the capital had rocky ridges on three sides and the river on the fourth. The Tungabhadra flows through a rocky gorge which dominates the north, and extensive plains stretch to the Sandur hills towards the southwest.

On the south bank of the Tungabhadra, on rocky outcrops overlooking the ravine, are the main temples. This, the sacred axis of the city, is said to have existed before the founding of the kingdom.

The urban core of the city was fortified from invasion, and was separated from the sacred centre by an irrigated valley, through which ancient canals and waterways still run. There is evidence of habitation at the urban core, with temples, gateways, tanks and wells, most of which are in ruins or buried under the earth. It was probably here that the majority of the city's population lived, with different areas being assigned to the Jains and Muslims.

In the southwestern section of this core are structures enclosed by high granite walls. This was obviously the royal enclosure, because of the wealth of architecture associated with the court and military activity. The Mahanavami festival was the most important annual event and the Vijayanagara rulers celebrated its rituals here.

In the plains towards the southwest were the suburban areas of the city. Fragments of earlier fortifications are in evidence here, which indicate that the city itself was guarded by a series of concentric protective walls. These walls had gateways set into them that led to the centre of the city.

The 9th century Virupaksha temple is still used for worship.

The elaborate defence system around Hampi suggests that the capital was planned as a gigantic fortress. The natural granite ridges have granite fortifications built upon them. Doorways and entrances are set into the fort walls and roofed with beams or corbeled brackets. **Bhima's Gateway**, one of the best preserved arches from this series, has beautiful ornamented corbels. An alternative design seems typically Islamic, with four archways raised high to form a dome. The gateways were fronted with courtyards enclosed by thick walls. All traffic passing through to the city was monitored here.

Hemakuta Hill: To the southern side of the village of Hampi, in the sacred center, are the temples on Hemakuta hill. These temples predate the Vijayanagara empire, and it is thought that they date from the 9th and 10th centuries. This was the first seat of power of the Vijayanagara kings, who built the later fortifications. These are constructed in the medieval Deccan style, using granite as the main material. This style is distinguished by unembellished exteriors, towers resembling stepped pyramids and terraces with gallery seating. Two or three temples were grouped together. Legends inscribed on the temples indicate that these shrines were dedicated to the god Shiva.

Temple Complex of Virupaksha: Pampa, a primitive goddess symbolising the Tungabhadra river, and her consort Virupaksha, also known as Pampapati (another aspect of Shiva) were the original divinities of the area, well before the establishment of the Vijayanagara empire. They appear to have post-dated the empire as well as pre-dated it, because it is the only temple at Hampi to be still used as a place of worship. An annual festival is held here to commemorate the marriage of Virupaksha and Pampa which attracts several thousands of pilgrims from all over the country.

The structure of the complex attests to its growth over the centuries, with ancient Chalukya and Hoysala shrines forming the heart of the layout, and later

additions forming the periphery. There are two main courtyards here, both accessible through towered gateways, one of which is over 160 ft (50 m) high. The hall leading up to the principal sanctuary has finely detailed columns with carvings of animals, while the ceiling is painted with the legends of Shiva. A colonnaded street leads out of this temple, which ends in a badly damaged monolith of Nandi.

The Monoliths: Towards the south are two granite boulders carved with images of Ganesha, the elephant god. One of these is enclosed in a temple with very tall columns while the other stands within an open hall. Further south is the notable Narasimha sculpture that has been carved out of a single boulder. There is a monolithic *lingam* in a chamber to the north.

Krishna Temple Complex: Krishnadeva Raya is said to have worshipped at this assembly of shrines. It dates back to AD 1513 with the installation of a Bala Krishna (the infant Krishna) image. The 16th century standard layout has been followed here, with the sanctum sanctorum surrounded by colonnades and set within a large enclosure. There is an unusual Islamic-style granary in the south court. Yet another feature of interest is the plaster figures along the east gateway.

Matanga Hill: Climb this hill for an imposing panoramic view of the city of Hampi. It is named after a sage who is believed to have protected the monkey gods Sugriva and Hanuman. However, in spite of these associations with the *Ramayana*, the temple on the hill is dedicated to a savage aspect of Shiva. (In the epic, Hampi is mentioned as Kishkindha, the domain of the monkey chiefs with whom Rama planned the crusade to rescue Sita from the demon king Ravana.)

Immediately beneath the hill, on the south bank of the river, is the Kodandarama temple, dedicated to Rama and still popular with followers.

Tiruvengalanatha Temple Complex: The temples are set within a double-walled enclosure with two sets of towered gate-

Frieze of dancers and warriors under training.

ways. Erotic sculptures decorate the columns within the open halls near the main gateway. Unfortunately the temples which make up the central part of this complex have been badly damaged and the chariot pathway leading out of the temple is now a field for paddy cultivation.

Sugriva's Cave: Close to the temple complex listed above is a site overlooking the river, where a crevice between two colossal rocks is believed to be the cave where Sugriva hid Sita's jewelry after she was kidnapped by Ravana.

The 16th century musician Purandaradasa, whose works are performed even today, is associated with a columned hall on the river bank. You will see the stone pylons of a bridge that once connected the two banks of the river Tungabhadra.

Vittala Temple Complex: Experts consider the Vittala complex to be among the finest examples of existing sculpture from the Vijayanagara period. Dated to the 16th century, this exquisite group of temples stands within the main courtyard. Built on a low elevation, the temples form an elegant pattern, while the tower is constructed out of brick and plaster. The hall in front has superb carvings of rearing animals while the detached columns are carved out of a single slab of granite. The brackets are intricately carved and support beams of immense spans. The ceiling is sumptuously carved with floral and geometric designs.

To the east of this hall is the famous stone chariot of Hampi, styled as a miniature shrine. Close by is another columned hall with intricate sculptures which was probably used on ceremonial occasions.

Along a path by the river is an interesting structure known as the **King's Balance**. Ruling kings were weighed against grain, gold or money for distribution to the poor, usually on their birthdays.

Raghunatha Temple Complex: Malyavanta hill, associated with the Ramayana epic, is a shrine dedicated to Rama, Sita and Lakshman. Two shrines and a

arvings
relief of
ishnu the
reator
below), and
anuman the
monkey-god
below right).

colonnaded hall are set within high walls entered through gateways that blend into the granite outcrop. Images of the deities are carved on a large boulder inside the temple that also projects through the roof, forming a sort of natural tower.

There are several Shaivite shrines to be found here too. Behind the Ragunatha temple are two rows of *lingams* and Nandis cut into the rock face of a natural crevice.

The Hazara Rama: This was the state chapel for the ruler and is situated significantly between the royal court and residence. It dates from the early 15th century and is finely detailed. Within the central hall are superbly carved basalt pillars that display the various incarnations of Vishnu. There are three rows of sculptures around the exterior walls that vividly tell the story of the *Ramayana*. There are two gateways outside with continuous friezes on the outside walls of the enclosure. They depict elephants, dancing girls, soldiers and horses which were presumably viewed by royalty during ceremonial worship.

Area of Royal Performance: Remains of civic buildings, the basement of a huge 100-column hall which might have served as a hall of justice, stepped stone platforms from which the king might have viewed the Mahanavami festival and other structures probably linked with the religious rituals and administrative functions of the court can be seen here. The state treasury is believed to have been situated here. Several wells, aqueducts and tanks with stepped stone sides have been discovered here which leads to the conclusion that the royal bath was an important ceremony. The queen's bath is located here, built in the Islamic style, a square water basin surrounded by a vaulted corridor. Beautiful filigreed balconies are cantilevered over the water.

Close to the Ramachandra temple is the *zenana* or women's quarters. A variety of Islamic inspired structures stand here, the most famous of which is the Lotus Mahal. This is thought to best represent the Vijayanagara courtly style

which was a skilful blend of Hindu and Islamic architectural forms.

Eastward of this enclosure are the famous elephant stables, a row of 10 chambers with high vaulted entrances in different styles centralised around a two-storeyed pavilion. A nearby arena might have been the site of military and athletic tournaments.

The Royal Residence: Recent excavations, which show that this was the area where large palaces once stood, are of particular interest as they fill in the gaps in the history of Indian architecture. Only stone basements, plaster floors and rubble walls now remain. Many Islamic-style gazebos and watchtowers are to be seen in this area.

There is a Virupaksha temple here very similar to the one at Hampi. This was probably a private shrine for royalty. After the sack of Hampi, this temple was almost buried and has been wrongly assumed to have been underground, whereas recent excavations show that it was definitely within the precincts of the royal residence.

Right, lady conversing with parrot, love's messenger; Hampi. Below, pillared dance hall of the Hazara Rama temple.

CRADLE OF TEMPLE ART

The rocks from which the temples of Badami, Aihole and Pattadakal have been hewn are part of the oldest land formation on earth, the Gondwana Plate. The lava that spewed from Archaean Age volcanoes cooled into rock formations which geologists say are a thousand million years old. Along the Malaprabha river on the northern Karnataka plateau, the land is red sandstone, planed and contoured into cliffs and gorges. On one strategic eminence 3 miles (4.8 km) from its banks and in the canyons beneath is the town of Badami, earlier known in Sanskrit as Vatapi. Just as Mysore derived its name from the demon Mahishasura, Badami is named after the demon Vatapi who met his doom when he was eaten by a ravenous sage. Five miles (8 km) from Badami is Pattadakal, and about 8 miles (13 km) down the river Aihole – three towns whose stone temples stand testimony to the great architectural heritage of the Chalukya dynasty.

Like many dynasties, the Chalukyas had a mythological explanation for their name and origin, recounted by Bilhana, the court poet of Vikramaditya, the fifth Chalukyan emperor. The god Indra once came to Brahma in supplication, while he was at his morning devotions. The world, he said, had become so wicked that there was no man left to make offerings to the gods or perform any of the Brahminical sacrifices. Could Brahma not create a godlike being, righteous and valorous enough to rid the world of its sinfulness? In response, Brahma caused a valiant warrior to spring forth from the cupped hollow of his palm, his *chaluka* – a man endowed with the power to protect the three worlds, and it is to him that the Chalukyas traced their ancestry.

The extent of the Chalukyan empire was what originally defined the territorial concept of Karnataka. Their name was known throughout India: some authorities say that a cave painting at Ajanta testifies to their being known as

far away as Persia. The Chalukyan predominance spanned 2 centuries, from about AD 547 to 753 . According to the Chinese traveller Hieun Tsang, who visited Karnataka in AD 641 during the reign of Pulakesin II, the Chalukyas were a proud and martial race. A tenline poem lauding their valour is inscribed on a large boulder near the nearby village of Tattukute. Hieun Tsang also observed that the great Chalukyan commanders and their warriors went into battle well intoxicated, with their elephant-mounts similarly primed for combat. The penalty of defeat was to be made to wear women's clothing, a dishonour deemed worse than death.

On the whole, the Chalukyas were enlightened, tolerant and actively concerned with their subjects' welfare. Prolific builders, they oversaw a major transition in medieval religious architecture – the shift from brick and wood construction to stone and rock. Though Badami, Pattadakal and Aihole bear the mark of empires and rulers who came after the Chalukyas, from the Rashtrakutas who ousted them upto the Marathas of the 15th century, it was the Chalukyan accomplishments in excavated and structural temple architecture that gave these monuments their identity. The first ruler, Pulakesin I, proclaimed his supremacy over the region with an Ashvamedha – the traditional rite of sending forth a riderless horse arrayed in royal colours and insignia, to roam where it wished; those who let it wander unchallenged through their territory were presumed to have acknowledged its master's sovereignty. He then set about building fortifications and excavating the rock-cut temples.

Badami Cave Temples: The cliffs of Badami have four rock-cut temples, three Hindu and one Jain. The former follow a plan which influenced the design of many structural temples built in Karnataka. A flight of steps leads up to a pillared verandah, behind which is a hall, with the *garbha griha* carved into the back wall. The exteriors of the temples are unadorned, save perhaps for a row of figures along the plinth

Left, the goddess slaying Mahishasura, Durga temple, Aihole.

beneath the verandah. Inside, figures from religion and myth, carved in relief, cover walls, pillars and ceiling. The felicity of execution captures in stone live movement with all its energy and grace.

The largest and most ornamental is **Cave No. 3**, dedicated to Vishnu, with an inscription that testifies to its excavation by Pulakesin I's second son, Mangalesa, for his older brother who ruled before him. The verandah at the top of the steps has at one end a four-armed figure of Vishnu, seated on the Ananth Naga, the serpent whose five hoods spread protectively over his crown. At his feet is the bird Garuda, his mount. This is the Vaishnavite avatar of Chaturbhuj. Another incarnation shows him as the cosmic boar, Varaha, four-armed also, a lotus in one of his hands bearing the earth goddess Prithvi, "relaxed in charming and complete resignation", as the art historian Zimmer described it in *The Art of India and Asia*. At the verandah's other end is Vishnu in his avatar of the eight-armed dwarf Vamana. Barely discernible on the ceilings are what probably are Karnataka's first Hindu paintings. (Weathering, neglect or vandalism – whatever the cause, the toll on the monuments in these towns is disheartening.) The other caves are smaller, though equally arresting: the transition from daylight to near-darkness as you enter is dramatic, as the wealth of sculpted imagery becomes perceptible through the gloom. The Jain temple on top of a cliff is more modest than the rest, being merely an early essay in rock architecture.

The structural temples at Badami represent the second developmental stage of Chalukyan architecture after Aihole. The **Malegitti Shivalaya** on the northern hill and **Mahakuteshvara temple** at Mahakuta 3 miles (5 km) away are in the Dravidian style, while those at Aihole and Pattadakal are an amalgam of the Dravidian and North Indian Nagara styles. To the east, more structural temples fringe the **Agastyathirtha tank**, known for its curative powers. In the monsoon, water plunges

Muslim tombs in Badami.

214

from a rocky ledge into the tank named for the sage Agastya Muni who once meditated by a sacred pool on the cliffs above and was revered for curing a king's leprosy. The man-made lake is also called Bhuthanath after Shiva, Lord of the Spirits. His appropriately forbidding visage regards the worshipper from within the confines of the temples' inner sanctums. Stylistically they are distinguished by towers and finials derived from the technique of the antecedent Kadamba empire.

Aihole: This is referred to as the cradle of Indian temple architecture. There are over a hundred temples scattered around the village, their silhouettes and layouts anticipating the sophistication of the later constructions at Belur and Halebid. Culled from contemporary northern and southern styles, the temples nonetheless exhibit the hallmarks of the Chalukyan style – its lavish door-frames and plinth mouldings, octagonal finials and roofs.

The **Lad Khan temple** is possibly the earliest, having been built in the 5th century. Its name comes from a Muslim noble who once inhabited it. Originally used for royal weddings and assemblies, it is a low, flat-roofed building with a porch on its eastern side. The river goddesses Ganga and Yamuna, popular icons of the 4th-century Gupta dynasty, flank the entrance. Over the cella at the back is a square, flat-roofed superstructure, in effect forming a two-storey sanctum. The roof itself echoes the earlier wooden structures, though the influence of its jointing technique of grooved stone slabs can be seen in subsequent Chalukyan design.

The **Durga temple** exemplifies another stage in the progression of the discipline. Sculpturally resplendent, it is notable for its semi-circular apse, elevated plinth and the gallery that encircles the sanctum. However, its *shikhara* or roof, again in the northern Nagara style, seems to have been an architectural after-thought. It was not named after the goddess Durga, as is often thought, but because of its proximity to the fort (*durg*) wall. The interior

Rock-cut Vishnu No. 4, Badami.

abounds with images of Shiva and also of Chamundi, the patron goddess of Mysore, in the process of dispatching the buffalo-headed demon.

The sculpture of Vishnu in the **Hutchimalli temple** depicts him seated in a posture much like that affected by Chalukyan kings, with the difference that he is ensconced atop a large cobra. The structural innovation in this temple is the vestibule (*antarala*) that connects the *garbha griha* and the main congregational hall.

The **Ravalphadi cave** is Aihole's only excavated temple, again dedicated to Shiva. Though similar in layout to the Badami caves, the representations of Vishnu and Shiva (such as the depiction of Ardhanarishwara, the dual aspect of Shiva and his consort Parvati) are somewhat more delicately detailed.

Compared with the voluptuousness of Hindu temple craft, the two Jain and Buddhist temples of Aihole are ascetic. The roof still standing over the remains of the austere **Megutti** (or hilltop) **Jain temple** covers the sanctum within

which Mahavira sits, serene in perpetuity. The temple affords a view of the sleepy village below. A little way down is the Buddhist temple, its desolation highlighted by bats that occasionally swarm into chittering flight under a ceiling graven with the image of the Enlightened One.

Pattadakal: This was the last Chalukyan capital before the empire was supplanted by the Rashtrakutas, a feudatory family that rose to become the next major dynasty. It is where the Chalukyan kings were crowned, and the temples they built here express the complete maturity of their craft.

Temples are found clustered at the foothills, built in both the Dravida and the Nagara manner, with the Virupaksha, Mallikarjuna, Sangameshwara and Galaganatha temples in the former style.

In front of the **Virupaksha temple** is an independent Nandi *mandapa*, carved from green stone. The temple itself was built in AD 740 by Queen Lokamahadevi, its *vimana* (the tower over the **Ravanaphadi, Aihole**.

216

sanctum) an eminent example of Dravidian design. The building's plain and fine proportions indicate just how much the discipline had progressed from the constructions at Badami. Sculpture narrating epic and myth has been employed here to lavish effect.

The earliest in the Nagara group is the **Papanatha temple**, though much of the Dravidian influence is discernible in its elevations. Two axial halls precede the *garbha griha*, the first with an open porch for the congregation, and the second an *antarala* controlling access to the sanctum.

So many places of worship in so many gatherings, so much to ravish the eye and excite the curiosity of the beholder – the flow of form, line and silhouette in the sculpting of hall and portal, the fastidiousness of detail: the cumulative impact can be overwhelming. The Hindus saw the temple as a metaphor for the human body: the tower symbolising the head, the sides the arms, the pillars the legs and the sanctum the womb. Associations of daily routine add resonance to the significance of handed-down legend. For instance, on the way between Pattadakal and Badami is Mahakuta where the devout come to wash away their sins in the Kashi Tirtha spring.

Outside the temple at nearby Banashankari, named after the local goddess, is the hallowed tank into which she was transformed. Inside the temple, her eight-armed form, borne by a gold lion with jaws ferociously agape, confronts her devotees with a compelling stare.

Pulakesin I built the fort on the hill overlooking Badami, using not merely the location to advantage but also the enormous boulders that lay around. This building material was pliable enough to work upon but strong enough to provide durable shelter, not merely for their builders but also for the objects of their veneration. It must have been formidable, back-breaking work as R.K. Narayan observed, it certainly would have been a lot easier to have them built on the plains, though posterity would have been the poorer for it.

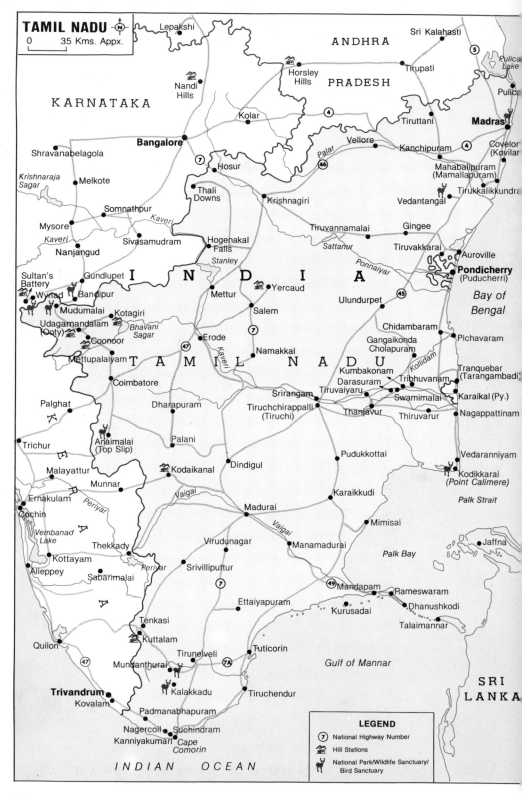

TAMIL NADU

0   35 Kms. Appx.

KARNATAKA

ANDHRA

PRADESH

Lepakshi

Sri Kalahasti

Horsley Hills

Tirupati

Pulicat Lake

Nandi Hills

Pulicat

Kolar

Madras

Bangalore

Tiruttani

Kanchipuram

Covelor (Kovilar)

Shravanabelagola

Vellore

Hosur

Mahabalipuram (Mamallapuram)

Krishnaraja Sagar

Melkote

Thali Downs

Tirukkalikkundra

Palar

Somnathpur

Krishnagiri

Vedantangal

Kaveri

Mysore

Tiruvannamalai

Gingee

Kaveri

Sivasamudram

Hogenakal Falls

Nanjangud

Stanley

Tiruvakkarai

Auroville

Sultan's Battery

I N D I A

Pondicherry (Puducherry)

Gundlupet

Yercaud

Sattanur

Ponnaiyar

Wynad

Bandipur

Mettur

Salem

Ulundurpet

Bay of Bengal

Mudumalai

Kotagiri

Udagamandalam (Ooty)

Bhavani Sagar

Chidambaram

Coonoor

Erode

Namakkal

Gangaikonda Cholapuram

Pichavaram

Mettupalaiyam

T A M I L   N A D U

Kaveri

Kumbakonam

Kollidam

Tranquebar (Tarangambadi)

Coimbatore

Darasuram

Tribhuvanam

Dharapuram

Srirangam

Tiruvaiyaru

Swamimalai

Karaikal (Py.)

Palghat

Tiruchchirappalli (Tiruchi)

Thanjavur

Thiruvarur

Nagappattinam

Palani

Anaimalai (Top Slip)

Pudukkottai

Vedaranniyam

Trichur

Kodaikanal

Dindigul

Kodikkarai (Point Calimere)

Malayattur

Karaikkudi

Palk Strait

Munnar

Vaigai

Ernakulam

Periyar

Madurai

Mimisal

Jaffna

Cochin

Vembanad Lake

Virudunagar

Manamadurai

Palk Bay

Thekkady

Vaigai

Kottayam

Srivilliputtur

Periyar

Mandapam

Rameswaram

Alleppey

Sabarimalai

Ettaiyapuram

Kurusadai

Dhanushkodi

Tenkasi

Talaimannar

Quilon

Kuttalam

Tirunelveli

Tuticorin

Gulf of Mannar

SRI LANKA

Mundanthurai

Trivandrum

Kalakkadu

Tiruchendur

Kovalam

Padmanabhapuram

Nagercoil

Suchindram

Kanniyakumari

Cape Comorin

INDIAN OCEAN

LEGEND

7 National Highway Number

Hill Stations

National Park/Wildlife Sanctuary/ Bird Sanctuary

TAMIL NADU

Tamil Nadu is situated at the southeastern end of the Indian peninsula. With an area of 50,193 sq miles (130,000 sq km) and a population of over 48 million, it is one of the country's larger states. The official language is Tamil, an ancient classical language with a rich body of literature.

Tamil Nadu has three distinct agro-climatic zones: the mountainous ridge of the Nilgiris that runs along its western boundary; semi-arid plains dependent on the monsoon and on tank and tube-well irrigation; and the alluvial Kaveri basin. Paddy, millet, sugarcane, pulse and bananas are the main crops, besides extensive coconut groves and tea and coffee plantations in the hills. The state has a long coastline with many beaches, estuaries and lagoons. The Marina beach in Madras is reputed to be the second widest in the world. South India's major hill stations – Ootacamund or Ooty, Kotagiri and Coonoor – are all located in Tamil Nadu.

Tamil Nadu, as its official emblem indicates, is the temple state of India. The history of South India temple architecture and sculpture begins with the Pallavas who ruled large parts of South India from the dawn of the 5th century to the last quarter of the 9th century. The Cholas, who supplanted them and ruled till the middle of the 12th century, were also great temple builders. They added the concept of the *gopuram* or gateway to Dravidian temple architecture. In later years the ornate *gopurams* in the enclosed temple premises increased in number and size and sometimes overshadowed the main shrine. In addition, pillared halls and long colonnades were added to the temples built by the later Cholas and their successors, the Pandyas and Nayaks who ruled the far south from Madurai

The British, too, left Tamil Nadu a rich architectural legacy in structures like Fort St George, and several Victorian Gothic buildings like the Egmore railway station, the High Court, the Senate House and the San Thome church in Madras. Since the British were longer in Tamil Nadu than anywhere else in India, there is a widespread familiarity with the English language, a convenience to visitors. Tamil Nadu is a rapidly developing state where the old and the new dwell harmoniously together: modern factories and offices along with age-old Carnatic music and dance forms and a flourishing tradition of art and literature.

Preceding pages, annual celebration of the marriage of Shiva and Meenakshi, Madurai.

GATEWAY TO THE SOUTH

Madras, capital city of Tamil Nadu and "Gateway to the South", is many things to many people. One of India's four leading metropolises, this city of 70 sq miles (180 sq km) and 4 million people has been variously described as "The Queen of the Coromandel", "The First City of Empire", "City of Shrines", "City of Tradition and Culture", "City of Graciousness and Spaciousness", and even as "A Withered Beldame Brooding on Ancient Fame". It is this variety that makes Madras one of the most fascinating cities in India.

As Indian cities go, Madras is not ancient. It was founded only 350 years ago, the first of the cities of Britain's Age of Empire. But as it grew, it took within its bounds many an ancient town and port of the Coromandel, and is today a curious amalgam of Coromandel – ancient, imperial and modern.

The Coromandel is India's legendary southeastern coast. But in the past, when the Arabs and the Chinese, the Romans and the Greeks came to trade in its ports, and when ancient Chola and Pallava kings took the culture of Hindustan from here to the lands now called Southeast Asia, there was no Madras. That city was born in the age of modern trade where Vasco da Gama's explorations led.

The Portuguese and the Dutch, the British, the French and the Danes all sought the riches of Coromandel, its textiles and cordage, its dyes and timbers and spices, and the wealth of its hinterland. In fact, it was the quest for "excellent long cloath better cheape" that led to the founding of Madras.

When British trading posts north of the area now called Madras came under pressure from the Portuguese and the Dutch, Francis Day, an East India Company trader, and his local broker, the *dubash* Thimanna, sailed south to prospect for a better settlement. What the local governor of the declining Vijayanagara Empire was willing to

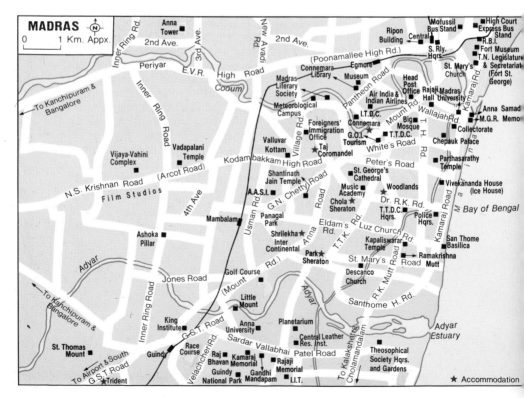

part with was a sandy spit of surf-wrecked beach, three miles long and a mile across at its widest, protected on two sides by rivers and on the third by the angry sea. It was on that land grant of July 1639 that Day and his superior, Andrew Gogan, and their *dubashes* built a fortified "factory", which they christened on St George's Day, April 23, 1640 – Fort St George.

The tiny settlement, Britain's first Indian bastion, was the nucleus from which an empire grew. And Madras' role in that growth is the stuff of history. There is no field in the development of modern India to which the city has not contributed. To explore that contribution is to walk down the corridors of history in a city that, as the circumstances of history changed the face of a nation, has returned to its beginnings as a quiet "Gateway to the South".

The relics of British rule in India are not all that remain in Madras. Here are ancient legends and symbols of much older faiths, of cultural traditions and ways of life that have changed little over

the centuries. Here is also a graciousness and a spaciousness that few metropolises anywhere in the world possess. But that does not prevent Madras from being a vibrantly alive metropolis where the bustle of industry and commerce, politics and modern entertainment vie equally for the attention of the business and the holiday traveller. Both will find Madras rewarding.

Fort St George, where the city began, is the place from where any discovery of Madras must begin. Like most other forts in India, this one too is an ancient monument. But unlike in most of them, life flourishes within its walls during the day and even on Sundays – government and the military, the administration and church-goers, all have something to do within its precincts.

A stroll through the Fort's walls reveals that its buildings look almost the same as when Clive and Pitt, Wellesley and Hastings lived and worked there. Much of Fort St George as it is today was built over 125 years, growing from one small rhombus-shaped building

named Fort House by Cogan and Day, fortified by four walls into 42 acres (17 hectares) of streets, buildings and parade grounds. Outside its fortifications, the Fort developed another 58 acres for its field of fire, much of which is parks and quarters now.

When the first major construction in the Fort began, a few years after its foundation, the designation of **Fort House** was conferred on another building constructed to the east of the original Fort House. That second Fort House, where the earliest governors of Madras lived, is the oldest surviving British construction in India. But it survives as the core of a building that was expanded several times over the years. The last great additions in the early 20th century provided the **Secretariat** and **Legislature** of the Tamil Nadu Government with their handsome classical appearance, facades embellished with gleaming black pillars.

The main gates of the Fort today open on the Secretariat and the Legislature, whose splendid **Assembly Hall** may be visited with the permission of the Speaker's office. To the south of this handsome symmetrical block is the second oldest surviving British building in India and the oldest Protestant church in Asia, the historic **St Mary's Church**. Constructed in 1680, it is now an ancient monument tended carefully by both the Archaeological Department and an enthusiastic congregation.

It was first built as a rectangular box with an arched, cannonball-proof roof; the towers, steeples and curved flights of steps were added over the years to make it the St Mary's of today – in its tree-shaded setting, one of the loveliest monuments of the British rule in India. Part of its courtyard is paved with tombstones brought here from the British cemetery in Madras, just north of the Fort. Amongst them is the tombstone of Elizabeth Baker, its inscription of the date of her death in 1652 making it the oldest British tombstone in India.

Within the wood-embellished, multi-pillar St Mary's are records and registers, tombs and memorials, paintings

Below and below far right, Madras Marina: vendors of trifles.

and silver-plate, each with a story to tell: of Elihu Yale, who helped found the church, and was married in it, and whose contributions helped found Yale University in the USA; of Robert Clive who married Margaret Maskelyne here; of Job Charnock who had his three daughters, born of an Indian mother, baptised here before he went on to found Calcutta; of Arthur Wellesley who was best man at a wedding here; and of Hastings and his Maid Marian who worshipped here before they became man and wife. Everywhere in St Mary's are touching reminders of the men and women who founded an empire that was to last 200 years.

Across the road and to the west of it is **Clive House**, an imperially handsome building in which Clive, one of the heroes of the Carnatic Wars, lived in 1753 with his bride. Next to it, also part of government offices now, is what was known as **Writers' Building**, once lodgings for newly arrived writers (clerks) from England. Among them was Clive and it was in this building that he made the first of his many attempts at suicide. Just a little to the south of these two handsome buildings is **Wellesley House**, its crumbling state a sad memorial to the man who was responsible for consolidating much of the British Empire in India.

Northwards are the Parade Grounds where many a magnificent parade and rally were held, before and after Indian independence, as well as a multi-storey, glass-and-concrete modern horror that can be temporarily avoided by turning east and admiring a later **Fort House** which the army maintains in 18th-century splendour, and **Fort Museum**.

Just by the museum and overlooking its cannon is the **Cornwallis Cupola**, moved from the Parade Grounds. A statue of Cornwallis greets visitors entering the museum. The museum, a treasure trove of British South Indian memorabilia, is housed in what was built as the **Public Exchange**. Warehouses and the city's first bank occupied the ground floor. On the first floor, what is now a wooden-floor art gallery was once the coffee shop where the merchants and officials of Madras met daily for gossip, coffee and trade.

To the south-east of the museum is the country's tallest flagpole, about 150 ft (45.7 m) high, which goes back to 1687 when Governor Elihu Yale hoisted the first Union Jack over the first British settlement in India. Today the Indian tricolour flutters over its classically designed bastions and ramparts, with towering walls and massive wooden gates – a memorial to impregnability.

The Marina: The best way to see Madras is to follow the four roads that lead out of the Fort. First take the road south, to "ancient Meliapor" of which Camoens sang. Then move westwards to the road to the Mount. Still further west is the ancient road to Poonamallee, whose governor deeded Madras to "John Company". Finally, move to the road north, the newest of the four.

The road south begins at **Fairlands**, by the War Memorial, where the government plans to develop a year-round entertainment park. But till that happens, the liveliness of an Indian exposi-

tion – with the vaunted achievements of government added – are offered here from mid-January till well into April. Then begins **Marina** promenade with the beach drive which was developed 150 years ago by a Governor.

Marina begins with the **Anna Memorial** commemorating C.N. Annadurai, who led the Dravidian movement to political power and changed the social and political structure in Tamil Nadu. Beside it is being constructed a memorial to M.G. Ramachandran, a film star beloved of the masses, and Annadurai's main vote-getter. Almost a decade after his mentor's death "MGR" came to power himself, the first film star to make it from a studio set to the leadership of a state in India.

Another part of the Madras experience begins across the road from the memorials. The Madras skyline is mainly made up of the buildings of the University and those further south, of Chepauk Palace. Both display an architectural style termed the Indo-Saracenic, where Hindu and Muslim elements were amalgamated by Britons brought up on the Gothic, Classical and Regency architectural styles. The results, as in the case of **Senate House**, the oldest university building (1879), can be spectacular.

No less striking is the tower that links the two halves of **Chepauk Palace**, once the home of the Nawabs of the Carnatic whose notorious extravagances led to the British acquisition of South India.

Presidency College, the first collegiate educational institution in South India, is the last of the Indo-Saracenic contributions to this skyline. Then come more Victorian contributions: **Ice House**, now a women's hostel called Vivekananda House, but once an intriguingly circular-styled storehouse for ice imported from Boston, and **Police Headquarters**, which was earlier a vast, Regency-style Masonic hall.

Across from Marina is Governor Grant-Duff's promenade of walks, gardens and drives, now embellished further with sculpture and lighting. Be-

Once known as Ice House in the Raj, it was a store for ice shipped from Boston. Today, it is a women's home.

yond it is one of the most magnificent beaches in the world, washed by the famed Madras surf. Bathing is not advisable here, though getting one's feet wet is everyone's favourite dare when strolling along the beach. Sunbathing is strictly taboo – staid Madras would never stand for it.

The towers of the faithful: Marina ends where the Town of Thomas begins. But a little before them, off the Marina, is Triplicane, Mylapore's suburb of "the sacred lily tank". The ancient tank is still there, though the lilies are few. But a thing of beauty is its Vaishnavite temple dedicated to **Lord Parthasarathy**. Dating to mid-8th century, it is the oldest building in the city with much of its original construction intact.

Not far from the Parthasarathy Temple is the beautiful **Wallajah** (Big) **mosque** which the Nawabs of the Carnatic bequeathed to Madras 200 years ago. Nearby is **Amir Mahal**, the home of the Nawabs, visitable by invitation.

Beyond Triplicane and the Marina lie Mylapore and San Thome. Mylapore was one of the great ports of the Pallavas in the 7th and 8th centuries, but its traditions go back 2,000 years and more as one of the South's leading cultural and religious centres. The Portuguese arrival in the 16th century pushed Mylapore back far from shore and the great **temple of Kapaleeswarar** had to be rebuilt where it now is. The magnificent sculptures within the temple and all over its towering *gopuram* are among the most spectacular sights in Madras.

All around the Kapaleeswarar Temple, in narrow lanes and bylanes, life is little changed from the traditional. The clothes and some of the comforts may be of the 20th century, but customs, household worship, food habits and festive occasions go back centuries.

Mylapore is one of the busiest parts of the city, with its tiny old houses built in traditional style, Hindu religious organisations, and busy bazaars selling much that is traditional – "temple jewellery", floral decorations and the glittering silks that adorn Bharata Natyam dancers. But unlike the bustle in the more commercial parts of Madras, there is a more gentle air to Mylapore, a more patient attitude to the crush all around, almost a serenity amid the rush of traffic and the push of crowds.

The Portuguese may have appropriated Mylapore's shore and called it San Thome, but long before them there was a Thomas in Mylapore, and the Town of Thomas was what it was called by the ancient Nestorians. One of the most enduring legends of South India, fervently believed by millions of all faiths is the legend of Thomas Didymus, the Apostle who doubted. So much is this legend an article of faith for most South Indian Christians that Thomas was decreed the Apostle of India in 1972. The culmination of that legend is in **San Thome Basilica**.

Though following the trail of Thomas in Madras is to wander a bit off the road south, much of it is in ancient Mylapore where, legend has it, he preached every day. Thomas lived in a cave on **Little Mount**, at one end of Mylapore. From there he would walk every day to the beach at Mylapore, resting a while and

preaching in the groves where the Portuguese later built **Luz Church** and **Descanco Church**. But the biggest crowd would wait on the beach to hear him, and it was on this site that he was buried after his martyrdom. The Portuguese found an old Nestorian church on the spot and the tomb of Thomas within. Moving the Apostle's remains further inland, they built another church over the new crypt. In 1898 the magnificent basilica of today was built on the ruins of the first Portuguese church. Its towering steeple, its ornate interior, its magnificent stained-glass windows telling the story of Thomas, are all counterpoints to the simple crypt from which the remains of the Apostle have been moved to Ortona in Italy.

The story of St Thomas would be incomplete if the trail he trod through Mylapore is not followed southwestwards to **St Thomas' Mount**, just outside the city and near the airport. It was here that he fled to from the cave in Little Mount and where he later died. The lovely little Portuguese church here, with its relics of the saint and its steps for the faithful, is one of the most serene in Madras. The view of Madras from here is spectacular.

The Reaches of the City: Once the road south reached the city limits at the Adyar River estuary. Dry for most of the year but occasionally in spate during the monsoons, the Adyar is little noticed except by historians, nature lovers and washerfolk. To historians it is the river at which a handful of French-trained troops stopped the Nawab's army, demonstrating the possibilities of Empire for any small but disciplined army. To bird-watchers the **Adyar Estuary** is a protected area of river, dunes, islands and woods that is home to small fauna and bird life, much of it migrant during the winter.

The city has, however, now spread way beyond the Adyar River and now takes in Adyar and Guindy. Adyar is the headquarters of the **Theosophical Society** founded in 1882, dedicated to the quest for truth through the interaction of all faiths. It is a major Indological re-

The famous Theosophical Society headquarters

search centre, set in hundreds of acres of garden and scrub forest. The Society boasts some magnificent buildings, houses typical of Madras of another age, shrines of all faiths and an internationally famous library with a priceless collection.

However, the greatest attraction for the public is in the gardens of the Society – the second biggest banyan tree in the subcontinent, 200 years old and more and, with its spreading branches shading 5,000 sq yd (4,180 sq m) of space. It is often used for meetings and discourses. The main trunk of the tree was uprooted during a freak storm in 1989, but was replanted and has begun to show signs of revival.

The Society's acres stretch from the main road south to **Elliot's Beach** on the Coromandel shore. Once an exclusive beach for the sahibs of colonial Madras, it is now a stretch of fun and leisure for the new colonists who occupy Adyar and beyond. By the beach is the **Ashtalakshmi temple**, one of the country's only two shrines on the shore

dedicated to the goddess Mahalakshmi.

The road south branches left at the Theosophical Society to lead to the beach and the road to Mahabalipuram. To explore the rest of the city, keep going straight on until you reach Guindy, once the country homes of the squires of urban Madras. Today, Guindy's only retreat is **Raj Bhavan**, the Governor's mansion, to the east of which stretches its private forest reserve, the only National Park within a city anywhere in the world. Permission is needed to view Raj Bhavan even from the outside, but **Guindy National Park** may be driven through on payment of a fee. This protected sanctuary is home to herds of spotted deer, blackbuck and a wealth of bird and small wildlife. Several acres of this vast wooded estate of the Governor have been taken over, rather sadly for conservationists, for a variety of purposes. The **Indian Institute of Technology**, one of the premier educational institutions in the country, has a spacious wooded campus. Next door are the **Snake Park**, a children's

park with its mini-zoo, and **memorials** to **Gandhiji**, **Rajaji** and **Kamaraj** – respectively the Father of the Nation, the Madras Prime Minister who became free India's first Indian Governor-General, and the first Tamil political leader from the grassroots level.

The Road to the Mount: Mount Road, Madras' main thoroughfare which refuses to get used to being called Anna Salai, was once the mall to the Mount of St Thomas and the cantonment, bungalows and sanatoria that surrounded it. On either side, till well into the early years of this century, were the "garden houses" of the elite of Madras. Today it is a modern commercial mall where the expansive homes of the past are fast giving way to multi-storey blocks. Snaking out of the city past St Thomas' Mount, the road leads to India's two most modern airports and then, as National Highway 45, to the heartland of the Tamils and beyond.

Leading out of the Fort, Mount Road crosses the man-made island watched over by the statue of Sir Thomas Munro

and begins to veer southwest at **Government Estate**. The mansion where Madras' governors once lived in regal splendour is beginning to fall apart, but connected to it by a courtyard is the handsome banqueting hall built by the second Lord Clive to commemorate his father's victory at Plassey and the Madras Army's victory at Seringapatnam a generation later. Now called **Rajaji Hall**, the building has lost its imperial glitter but is still the venue for important official functions.

Mount Road now becomes a commercial stretch till it reaches the suburbs, and along its early reaches are some of the city's oldest commercial landmarks and vestiges of the age of empire. Here are the offices of *The Hindu*, a paper as indispensable to the educated Madrasi as his cup of morning coffee. Then there are **Higginbotham's**, the largest bookshop in the country, **Spencer's**, a pale shadow of the department store that was once among the best in Asia, and the **Connemara**, once the city's finest hotel and distinguished by its blend of tradition with urbane modernity.

Wherever commerce was in days past, clubland was never far away. More or less across the road from these three landmarks are the vestiges of the first buildings of the **Madras Club**, the "Ace of Clubs", a memorial to the British elite's need to unwind amidst splendour and spaciousness, and the Ionic lineaments of the **Cosmopolitan Club**, where Indians followed the track the British pioneered. Not far from these splendid buildings is a school and college, some of whose buildings and grounds were part of the estate where the Begums of the Carnatic lived. Bringing this busy stretch to an end are the **Horticultural Gardens**, a riot of colour during the season for a hundred years and more, and **St George's Cathedral**, a magnificent replica of St Martin's-in-the-Fields, London.

To the north of the busiest part of Mount Road are many of the newer landmarks of the city, most of them 100-150 years old. On Pantheon Road, where the **Pantheon** was home to pub-

Detail of Kapaleeswarar temple in Mylapore.

lic entertainments in Arthur Wellesley's day, are Madras' magnificent **Museum**, rich in bronzes, Buddhist antiquities and arms, the **Connemara Public Library**, one of India's four national libraries to which every book published in India must be sent, and the **National Art Gallery** and its newer wings, home for the best Indian art, past and present.

Not far from here is the campus of the Director of Public Instruction with its magnificent gateways, dating back to when it was the college of Fort St George, where the officials of the Company learnt language and governance. Part of this campus houses the handsome Indo-Saracenic building of the **Madras Literary Society**, a treasure-house of old books. Next door are **Doveton House**, where Tippu Sultan's sons may have been held hostage but which they certainly visited when they were wards of Sir John Doveton, and the **Meteorological Centre**, whose commemorative pillars and benchmarks are the oldest in Asia.

Nearby are **Valluvar Kottam** and the **Archives**. The former is a huge auditorium dominated by a 101-ft (31 m) tall temple chariot, in whose construction the ancient skills of Chola and Pallava artisans were revived. It is a memorial to Thiruvalluvar, the great philosopher-saint who laid down in immortal verse a code of ethics for the Tamil people.

The Old Towns: George Town lies beyond the Archives, the Indo-Saracenic splendour of **Egmore Railway Station**, the lively **Kirk of St Andrew's** with its towering steeple, domed roof and many-pillared circular nave, the **College of Arts and Crafts**, the gleaming white of the Municipal Corporations's splendid **Ripon Buildings** a vivid contrast to the striking red of **Victoria Public Hall**, an auditorium out of the gaslight era, the **Central Station**, the imperial *hauteur* of **Memorial Hall** and the palatial magnificence of the **Southern Railways Headquarters**. Once called "Black Town", the Indian town that existed outside the walls of the first "White Town" in Fort

Billboards along Anna Salai.

St George, it is now the commercial heart of Madras.

The road north from the Fort is a quicker way of reaching George Town. This road runs past perhaps the most magnificent Indo-Saracenic complex in the city, the **High Court** and **Law College** campus. The pillar of the city's first lighthouse and the obelisk marking the grave of Elihu Yale's son David, the last memorial of White Town's first cemetery, are landmarks that tend to get lost amidst the handsome pillars of justice. This campus was the Fort's very first Black Town, the first Indian settlement in the new town of Madras. When it was razed to create an esplanade providing the Fort's guns a clear field of fire, the new Black Town began to develop. The boundary of that esplanade is still to be seen in a pillar at the southeast corner of George Town, by **Dare House** where 200-year-old Parry and Company is headquartered. **Parry's Corner** at the junction of what was Esplanade Road and North Beach Road is dedicated to the man who founded the company that is the second oldest modern business house in India.

Landmarks on this road to the north, the eastern boundary of George Town, are the handsome Indo-Saracenic buildings of the **State Bank of India**, successor to the first modern bank in the country, and the **General Post Office**. Beyond is the handsome Regency **Bentinck's Building**, built for the first Supreme Court of the Presidency, their eastern bastion **Clive Battery**, now providing homes for harbour officers, and the earliest railway buildings in the city at Royapuram. On this stretch too, abutting the harbour, is **Burma Bazaar**, a row of tiny shops where hard-to-get luxuries from abroad and Indian imitations of them are bargained for by hordes every day.

Behind North Beach Road is an 850-acre warren, almost square in shape, which is **George Town**, the banking and wholesale trading centre of Madras. Developed in the classical gridiron pattern, George Town's narrow streets were meant for a more leisurely age.

Iridiscent streetscape, Burman Street.

Today they are by day one of the busiest parts of this populous city, and the experience of its jostling crowds is something a visitor should not miss. By nightfall, George Town empties and, as the shops on roadsides close, lights go on above them in what are veritable mansions behind shabby exteriors.

In George Town are the oldest temple and mosques of British Madras and the churches of the first Protestant missionaries. The twin **Chennakesavarar** and **Chennammallikeswarar** temple, the first "Town temple", and the beautifully kept **Armenian Church**, are not to be missed, if time does not permit a tour of all the important shrines in George Town. Another engrossing experience is **Kothawal Chavadi** at dawn, when the trucks begin to arrive with the day's supplies of fruit and vegetable for sale and distribution throughout the city.

Of all the experiences in this historic city, George Town could well be the one that lingers on long after others are forgotten. Here, as in Fort St George, the visitor is closest to the soul of the city.

Shaivite devotee.

The tradition of culture is to be found everywhere, in flower-bedecked, bejewelled women in rich *saris*, in the shrine rooms in every home, in the *kolam* designs drawn before every house at dawn and in the city's auditoria. Classical Carnatic song and Bharata Natyam dance, dance-dramas, theatre and religious discourses flourish in rich cultural variety throughout the year — more so during the season of the annual Music Festival, from mid-December to early January, when the tradition started by the Madras Music Academy 60 years ago makes all the city a stage, it sometimes seems.

Madras also offers year-round sport in comfortable surroundings for those seeking other forms of entertainment. Cricket, whether on the streets or in a stadium during a test match, is an aspect of Madras life worth sampling. The city is the tennis and chess capital of India, and you can enjoy a good game of both in the clubs where they are played; clubs also offer temporary membership and facilities for swimming, billiards, squash, bridge, golf, rowing and yachting. Racing is a 6-month winter-to-spring sport on one of the best-kept race courses in the country.

Eating out is also an experience that is different in Madras. The usual "Continental", Chinese and North Indian cuisines found all over India are available here. But to experience the flavour of South India's varied cuisines, try the Udupi vegetarian food in places like **Woodlands** and **Palimar**, the Chettinad non-vegetarian in places like **Ponnusamy's** and **Raintree**, the South Indian Muslim in places like **Buhari's** and the numerous "specials" that have become fast foods in Madras and delicacies elsewhere – the *vadais* (savoury doughnuts), *dosais* (wafer-thin rice pancakes) and *idlis* (steamed, fluffy rice-cakes).

If you still have the energy to shop after all those food, there are no better buys in the country than the rich thread and gold-bordered Kanchipuram silk *saris* (easily made into dresses) and the fabulous array of cottons and handmade household linens.

MAHABALIPURAM

Madras, Mahabalipuram (now officially renamed Mamallapuram) and Kanchipuram form the "Golden Triangle" of South India's travel circuit. The road to Mahabalipuram is an enjoyable all-day trip, with its 38-mile (60-km) drive offering variety and stimulation every few miles.

Just outside Madras lies the village of **Tiruvanmiyur**, which houses Kalakshetra. When the celebrated dancer and scholar Rukmini Devi Arundale took the ancient dance form of Bharata Natyam out of the temple and gave it a new respectability, she went one step further: she made up her mind that others who followed her would learn the art in a school that would be world-renowned. Today, students from all over the world come to Kalakshetra not to learn only Bharata Natyam but also Carnatic music and those ancient crafts of the Coromandel, namely weaving and dyeing. The age-old *gurukulam* system of education is still followed, and many classes are conducted in sylvan surroundings.

Artists' Village: Also in Tiruvanmiyur is the ancient **Marundiswarar temple**. Built by those great temple-builders, the Cholas, in the 11th century, it has a wealth of stone sculpture. About 6 miles (10 km) beyond it is **Cholamandal** with its unique **Artists' Village**, an experiment in cooperative living. Within this artists' commune by the sea, the best of South India's painters live and work. The art gallery exhibits contemporary art the year round, but visitors are likely to find the prices of the craftwork displayed separately more alluring. The income from craftwork is what allows many of these artists to keep on painting. An open-air theatre among the sand dunes stages avant-garde theatre, poetry readings and dance recitals from time to time.

The next stop, a few miles further along, is the **VGP Golden Beach Resort**. Its cottages amidst casuarina groves have made it the most popular weekend outing for residents of Madras. The groves and beach have had film decor from South India's famed "historicals" and "mythologicals" imposed on them, and every corner is a cinema set replete with creations in wood, granite, metal and plaster-of-paris. Practically every Tamil filmmaker is eager to shoot at least one scene in these picturesque gardens to ensure a successful film.

A few miles beyond Golden Beach, the backwaters of **Muttukadu** offer a variety of boating facilities as well as a luxury hotel, Fisherman's Cove, on **Covelong Beach**, built on the remains of an old Dutch fort whose walls have been landscaped into the hotel grounds. Covelong offers a fairly safe bathing beach (except during the monsoons, June-August, October-January) as well as a variety of water sports, including windsurfing.

Taming the wild: About 3 miles (5 km) further along is the **Crocodile Bank**, run by Romulus and Zai Whittaker. Rom Whittaker, founder of the Snake Park in Madras, answered a call to save the vanishing crocodile of India and has more than 3,000 muggers and gharials in the Bank, all of them bred on the premises, as well as several other crocodile and lizard species from other countries as exhibits. But he has not lost touch with his first love, and the tribal snake-catchers' cooperative he promoted has a corner where hundreds of cobras, kraits and vipers are reared in pots and regularly "milked". The venom, sent to anti-venin institutes to be made into vaccines, provides the cooperative with a handsome income; the small fee to watch "milking" operations at fixed times daily also helps swell the kitty.

Silver Sands, another beach resort, is a few miles further on. Then comes the briefest of introductions to Mahabalipuram, **Tiger Cave**. Left unfinished, like much of Mahabalipuram, Tiger Cave was obviously meant to be the stage for a regal open-air amphitheatre. Sculpted tiger heads frame a tiny stage in a casuarina grove which must have been in the first stages of being chiselled

Left, pastoral vignette in stone, Mahabalipuram.

out of the rock when work was interrupted. The rest of the theatre is as unfinished, but the exquisite details of the tigers' faces offer the best possible preview of what awaits the visitor a few miles further on.

Mahabalipuram may be a modern beach resort in the making, but all else in the tiny village by the sea is dwarfed by a dream world of Tamil art that awes even the uninitiated. Here is an open-air museum of sculpture in living rock which has few parallels in the world.

The *pièce-de-résistance* of this monumental art exhibition is undoubtedly **Arjuna's Penance** or the **Descent of the Ganga**, the world's largest bas-relief, 764 ft by 288 ft (27 m by 9 m) and one of the major masterpieces of Indian art. It is a beautiful composition of hundreds of celestial beings, humans and animals, all hurrying to a natural rock cleft that divides the giant stone canvas. Dominating the scene is a 16 ft (4.9 m) long elephant leading a procession of elephants to the scene of the penance by the cleft, where Arjuna

stands on one leg to propitiate Lord Shiva to help him win back the kingdom of the Pandavas.

The best-known landmark of Mahabalipuram, however, is the **Shore temple**. Standing by the sea, now protected by a wall that hides its facade but saves it from the elements that are fast eroding it, this twin-spire is pure poetry in granite in its perfect proportions and wealth of sculpture. It is also unique in that it includes shrines for both Shiva and a Vishnu in repose.

The other wonders of Mahabalipuram are the *mandapams*, each a cave scooped from a hillside of solid rock and ornamented with pillars and sculptured panels that are an integral part of the excavation, and the *rathams*, monolithic rock-cut shrines that have inspired generations of South Indian temple-builders.

In the **Krishna mandapam**, the serenity of a pastoral scene is ensured by Krishna protecting all God's creatures from a storm's fury with his massive umbrella, the Govardhana mountain. In **Bharata Natyam lesson, Kalakshetra.**

the **Varaha mandapam**, Vishnu in his incarnation as Varaha the boar bursts from the ocean clutching the rescued Earth Goddess. And in the **Mahishasuramardini mandapam**, the goddess Durga, an amazon astride a lion, battles the powerful buffalo-headed demon, Mahishasura.

The five *rathams*, named after the Pandava brothers, the heroes of the Mahabharata, and their wife Draupadi, are part of an amphitheatre of art. Each temple is incomplete, yet each remains an architectural gem. Also in this arena are a magnificent elephant and an exquisite Nandi, the sacred bull.

There are four other *rathams*, the **Trimurti cave**, and the **Adivaraha temple**, where worship still continues, and scores of individual pieces of sculpture, of *yalis*, monkeys and other mythical and living creatures. There is also a smaller man-made open-air museum of scattered sculptural treasures retrieved from around the site. In tribute to the skills of the ancient sculptors, a college of sculpture is run in the township, not only granting degrees but turning out some excellent work.

City of temples and silk: Just thirty-seven miles (60 km) west of Mahabalipuram is **Kanchipuram**, one of the seven sacred cities of the Hindus and one of the oldest towns in South India. But before "Kanchi" is **Thirukkalikundram**, half-way house on the road from Mahabalipuram. Here, atop the 5,000 ft (1,525 m) high Vedagiri hill, is a sculpture-rich Shiva temple. The view from the hilltop is spectacular, but many pilgrims make the steep climb to the top to see the two vultures that come without fail every noon to feed on the consecrated food spread for them by the temple priests.

Kanchipuram, the "golden town of a thousand temples", has about 125 officially-recognised shrines, all of them centuries old. Dating back to the early Cholas of 200 BC, Kanchipuram was successively capital of the Cholas, the Pallavas and the Rayas of Vijayanagara. The height of Kanchi's glory was when it was capital of the far-flung

Bas relief of the Descent of the Ganges, Mahabalipuram.

empire of the Pallavas from the 6th to the 8th centuries, when Mahabalipuram and Mylapore were its great ports. All that is left of that glorious era are its magnificent temples.

The **Ekambareswarwar temple**, a fairly new temple dating to the 16th century, is the largest of the Shiva temples and sprawls over 20 acres and more. It has a magnificent 1,000-pillared hall and a towering *gopuram*, at almost 6,000 ft (185 m) one of the tallest in South India.

The **Kailasanathar temple**, over 1,000 years old, is a Pallava creation dedicated to Lord Shiva. The narrow cells linking its courtyards have paintings and sculptures dating back to the 7th and 8th centuries, narrating the story of Shiva.

The **Kamakshi temple** is dedicated to Parvati, "the goddess with the eyes of love", who playfully blindfolded her consort Shiva and had to do penance for her mischievousness. She was eventually forgiven by him at the spot where the temple rose.

A perfect specimen of Pallava temple-building is the **Vaikuntanathar Perumal temple** dating back to the 8th century. A unique frieze narrates the history of the Pallavas and the battles they fought against the Chalukyas. Of note here are three sanctums, one atop the other.

A relatively recent temple is the **Varadarajaswamy temple**, with beautiful pavilions in its courtyard, a splendid 100-pillar hall that is a work of art and a 100-ft (31 m) tall 7-storey *gopuram* of rare beauty. Some of the most beautiful sculpture in all Kanchipuram is to be found in this temple.

The richest saris in India: Kanchi's other claim to fame is its silk, renowned for more than 4 centuries. Vibrantly contrasting colours, borders woven in gold thread, with traditional motifs such as peacocks, parrots, mangoes and leaves, and of silk that is woven to last make these the richest *saris* in India and certainly the most sought after. The *saris* are priced according to their weight, taking into consideration the

Entrance to the Krishna Mandapam, Mahabalipuram.

substance of the silk and the extent of the gold thread.

A unique system of weavers' cooperatives makes and sells Kanchi *saris*. Shops are on the main street, and shopkeepers are as pleased as the weavers in the bylanes are to display their range and show the art and skills that have been handed down over the genera-tions. The cooperative showrooms sell silk and cotton *saris*, as well as silk by the metre, stoles and scarves.

The drive of 37 miles (60 km) back to Madras from Kanchipuram can now be relieved with a stop at the **Vandalur zoo**, about two-thirds of the way to journey's end. The new Madras zoo in the making is taking into consideration all aspects of modern zoo-keeping. Keeping the animals and birds in large enclosures as close to natural settings as possible means that the visitor has to trek for miles.

The Kailash Temple, Kanchipuram.

Beyond Vandalur are several ancient villages: Pallavaram, Kunrathur, Thiruneermalai, Tirusoolam – all with 11th and 12th century shrines. **Pallavaram**,

site of several prehistoric finds and antiquities, **Tambaram** with its tree-shaded campus of the Madras Christian College, the new airport at **Tirusoolam** and the old army buildings and the Mount itself at **St Thomas' Mount** are brief halts on the drive from Vandalur into the city.

The best way to plan this whole journey is to start after early breakfast in Madras and spend a whole day on the road to Mahabalipuram, halting there for the night. Then spend another day at the giant open-air museum and getting your feet wet. After another night in Mahabalipuram, leave in time to reach Thirukkalikundram by 11 a.m.

Luck with the eagles or not, get to Kanchi for a late lunch and an evening temple tour. Stay over for the night and silk-shop the next morning, before driving back to Madras at leisure after lunch, taking in Vandalur Zoo and other points along the way. A leisure trip for the visitor like this can make the Golden Triangle of the South a truly enjoyable experience.

TEMPLES IN THE DELTA

The river Kaveri starts as little more than a trickle among the hills of the upper reaches of Karnataka. It meanders slowly down to the plains, gaining in width and strength, and cuts across several districts of Tamil Nadu before debouching into the Bay of Bengal. It is a lifeline: the Tamils, who developed a culture of their own over 2,000 years ago, recognised the role played by the river in their economic life, and they worshipped it as a goddess, celebrating it in song and story. All along the banks of the river there are holy towns and hamlets, and innumerable temples. However, the river really comes into its own as it creates a vast delta right in the middle of the Tamil Nadu coast.

It is difficult to demarcate the precise area of the delta, but for practical purposes it lies between Chidambaram, near the coast where the river enters the sea, and Tiruchirapalli, 125 miles (200 km) inland south. This is rice country: paddy fields, with almost every few miles a temple tower rising out of the green expanse. Most of these temples were built by the pious Cholas. The visitor can reach Chidambaram by road or rail from Madras in 6-7 hours. It is an even shorter journey from Pondicherry, especially by road.

The best place to start this temple tour is **Chidambaram**, where the celebrated **Nataraja temple** – the temple of the Dancing Shiva – is situated.

Chidambaram too has a story about its origins. The god Shiva performed his cosmic dance after humbling several conceited *rishis* (sages) who believed they had acquired extraordinary powers through their rigorous austerities. Other sages, as well as the gods and goddesses, begged to see the dance, and Siva agreed to dance for them in the forest of Thillai (another name for Chidambaram). The situation acquired an additional piquancy when the guardian of the forest, Kalika Devi (in reality Shakti, the consort of Shiva), challenged him to a dance contest. By performing movements which she as a modest woman could not, Siva defeated her. He concluded his performance with the dance of bliss. In response to the *rishis'* request, Shiva dances the cosmic dance for all time to come in Chidambaram, as depicted in the beautiful bronze idol in the temple.

The dance has many mystic interpretations: as a famous scholar said, it is a symbol of god's rhythmic play as the source of all movement within the cosmos; it releases the souls of men from the snare of illusion; and that it is actually within the heart of the individual.

The iconography of the figure of the dancing Siva exemplifies these concepts. Nataraja holds a drum in his hand: with the beat of this drum, he brings all creation into being. The deer he holds in the other hand stands for the nimble and leaping mind of the individual. The tiger-skin he wears is the skin of egotism which he has killed. The river Ganga whom he has trapped in his matted locks represents wisdom, which is cool and refreshing. He stands on the demon of illusion (*maya*) on one foot, while the other is raised to represent a state of transcendental bliss. Other symbols stand for the concept that the ego or self must be destroyed if man is to be master of himself.

The Nataraja concept must have exercised the imagination of artists down the centuries until it found its finest interpretation in the hands of the Chola craftsmen, who repeated it untiringly in bronze and stone. The sculptor Rodin considered it the most perfect expression of movement, while Einstein said that all his thoughts on the structure of the world and its movements found lucid expression in the image of Lord Nataraja.

Much of the temple as seen today was built by the Chola emperors. Massive *gopurams* soar over great entrances. There are several shrines in the temple complex, including one for the god Vishnu. The sanctum sanctorum enshrines the god in his dance pose. Adjacent to it is the sanctum of the goddess, whose name here is Shivakamasundari, "the beautiful woman who evoked the love of Shiva". An unusual shrine is one without an image in it; this is known as the secret of Chidambaram – the implication being that god is to be found everywhere, and especially in the heart.

The roof of the temple is gold-plated. As befits a temple dedicated to the god of dance, poses of the classical Bharata Natyam are sculpted around the shrines and on the gateways. Scholars consider these to be in their entirety a veritable encyclopedia of Bharata Natyam.

Chidambaram is a somewhat cluttered town, completely dominated by the temple; rice fields outside the town take away a little from its drabness. Visitors and pilgrims are the principal contributors to the local economy. Besides the temple, the town's other claim to glory is the modern Annamalai University, located in the eastern part of Chidambaram. The university, founded over 50 years ago by a philanthropist, conducts courses in arts and sciences, as well as in technology, medical sciences and agriculture.

Though the Tamil Nadu Tourism Department provides reasonable accommodation in its guest house, most visitors would probably prefer to move on after seeing the temple. The best way to travel from here to Thanjavur (Tanjore) and Tiruchirapalli (Trichy) is by road, but there are frequent bus services in every direction.

The road from Chidambaram to Thanjavur passes through villages and small towns, all of which have temples, but the one stop that must be made is **Darasuram**, just outside the bustling town of Kumbakonam.

Darasuram has a magnificent Shiva temple, the **Airavateswarar temple** built by the Chola king Raja Raja II in the 12th century. Because of neglect and poor maintenance over the centuries, much of the temple has crumbled, but what remains reveals a gem of Chola architecture and sculpture. The main shrine with an 85-ft (26-m) tall *vimana* (superstructure) and the shrine of the goddess are in a fair state of preservation. The entrance hall is shaped like a chariot, and the steps lead-

Celestial musicians.

ing up to it give out musical notes. The exuberance of the sculptures makes one wonder what the temple must have been like in its heyday. Sculptures and remnants of paintings create a whole world of dancers and acrobats, and depict a variety of scenes from everyday life. It was known as "the temple of perpetual entertainment".

Kumbakonam has a large number of temples, some of them quite imposing in appearance, but they are of religious rather than artistic importance. Before leaving the area, however, the visitor is well advised to make the short trip to **Swamimalai**. There is an ancient and sacred temple on a small hill here, but the real attraction of Swamimalai is that it is one of the places where bronzes are still made by traditionally trained artisans. These men reach the heights of excellence achieved by their Chola ancestors, following the same rules, pouring the molten metal into carefully crafted moulds and giving the finishing touches by hand.

As the road winds past small villages,

paddy fields and temple towers in the distance, we reach **Thanjavur** in just over an hour's time. Even at a distance the magnificent tower over the sanctum of the **Brihadeesvara temple** can be seen. Unlike other temples in the south, the entrance *gopurams* of this temple (aptly called the Big Temple), are dwarfed by the *vimana* over the sanctum. The *gopurams* are over 90 ft (27 m) high, and are exquisitely sculpted. They lead to a vast courtyard in which the main temple stands, guarded by two enormous *dwarapalakas* (sentries) carved out of single stones, with disarming smiles in spite of their fearsome teeth. Separated by a corridor and facing the sanctum is a *nandi* (bull), Shiva's favourite vehicle.

Inside the sanctum stands a *lingam*, symbol of the god Shiva, which is reputed to be the largest in the country. The corridors around the sanctum in which devotees circumambulate, going from left to right, have many sculptures as well as Chola fresco paintings which were recently discovered.

The *vimana* over the sanctum is a pyramidal structure, soaring 216 ft (65 m) above a platform nearly 100 ft (30.5 m) square. A beautifully carved octagonal cupola with a glittering finial called a *kalasa* 12½ ft (3.8 m) tall, and covered by gold-plated copper, crowns the *vimana*. The cupola itself, carved out of a single stone, is gigantic in size.

The sides of the *vimana* are covered with beautiful sculptures and numerous niches, small pillars and balcony windows frame many of the carvings. The *vimana*, a slender pyramid in shape, has been so accurately constructed that its shadow never falls on its base. The total effect is one of indescribable magnificence. An eminent scholar considered it "unquestionably the finest single creation of the Dravidian craftsman", while the *Encyclopedia Britannica* describes it simply as "the grandest temple in India". The size of the compound is so overwhelming – 500 ft by 250 ft (150 m by 75 m) – that even on busy days the atmosphere in the temple complex is one of serenity.

Right around the corridors are as many as 250 *lingams*. There are also some subsidiary shrines, of which the beautiful **Subramanya temple** deserves special mention. The Big Temple was built by the great Chola emperor Raja Raja I, towards the end of the 10th century. The Subramanya temple was a later addition and was probably built by one of the Nayak kings of Madurai. This is a small and exquisite temple, full of sculptural ornamentation.

From the temple, the next logical stop is the **Palace** to the northeast. Remnants of the fort that surrounded the palace can still be seen, and a 190-ft (58-m) high lookout remains in good shape. Members of the former royal family of Thanjavur continue to occupy some apartments in the inner recesses, but for all practical purposes the palace is now used mainly as an art gallery and to house the Saraswathi Mahal Library.

The **Art Gallery** was set up almost accidentally around 1951. The story goes that a beautiful statue of Brahma was lying uncared for in a village, but **Entrance to the Great Temple.**

TANJORE PAINTINGS

While temples were adorned with metal and stone images and mural paintings on the walls and corridors, the icons for domestic worship were a little different. Throughout South India the houses of both rich and poor are adorned to welcome the gods. The front is swept and cleaned every morning, and the women of the house, the unrecognised artists of India, render intricate *kolam* designs on the floor with white rice paste, chalk and flowers. The main door lintel is often decorated with mango leaves and flowers. Within the house a special nook, shelf or room is set aside for prayer. The deities of the family are kept here and worshipped every day with flowers, incense and oil lamps. The deities were either sculptures in metal (bronze or silver), wood or clay, or painted images; today, calendar pictures and postcards are frequently added to the family pantheon. The genre known as Tanjore paintings grew out of this demand for household images.

The "Tanjore painting" is a generic term for many styles; there are paintings from Karnataka, from Sholapur in Maharashtra, wrought on wood, cloth, or on glass after it was introduced in the 18th century. It is mainly practised today in the districts of Trichy, Kumbakonam, Pudukottai and others in Tamil Nadu. Traditional artists skilled in sculpture or painting were commissioned to make the images to the exact size, specifications and budgetary considerations of the customer. They could be asked to do a painting of Krishna as a child, or one of him

Above, Tanjore painting of Krishna sporting with milkmaids.

as a grown man, for each form of the deity has a special significance.

In some styles the artist stretched and fixed a cloth over a plank of wood. The design, usually consisting of the figure of the main deity, consorts and minor figures on either side, was then traced onto the cloth. As in sculptures, the deity was shown standing, sitting or lying, on a lotus or throne or on his animal mount (*vahana*). The figures were framed by a flat background of colour, often a brilliant red, around which decorations of mango leaves, flowers and (later) draped curtains were added.

The drawing was finally embellished with relief work with a paste of glue and chalk to highlight jewellery: crowns, necklaces, garlands, belts, bracelets and anklets, and sometimes the border designs as well. Onto this the artist pressed beaten gold leaf, often punched with fine designs. In the Tanjore area uncut diamonds, rubies and emeralds were added or, if the customer's purse did not permit this extravagance, semi-precious or artificially coloured stones.

The colour palette of Tanjore paintings is derived from pigments with a predominance of red, blue, black and white. Each colour had its codified symbolism, as in Kathakali dance makeup where every character is portrayed in a specific colour. Paintings on glass were less expensive, and portrayed patrons as well as the deities. The subject matter varied greatly in these paintings depending on the period when they were made. Court scenes, amorous couples, top hats and dancing shoes, sofas and flower vases began to feature in later paintings for the first time, just a step away from the vivid calendar pictures, truck art and plastic kitsch that has flooded the market today.

when someone tried to remove it and take it away, the villagers went up in arms. An imaginative Collector of Thanjavur (the administrative head of the district) heard about this, went to the village, and persuaded the villagers to let him take it away to Thanjavur to be displayed in a good public location. It was set up at the entrance to the present art gallery. The Collector also began to retrieve sculptures from decaying temples and abandoned locations, and soon he had an art gallery on his hands. Over the years the collection grew, and a separate collection of bronzes was added to the gallery. As Brahma is the Creator in the Trinity, it is apt that he should have been responsible for the creation of the art gallery. Today the gallery houses some of the most beautiful sculptures of the Chola period, mainly from the 9th to the 14th centuries, and a magnificent collection of Chola bronzes, including some unique representations of Shiva as Nataraja.

The sculptures include free-standing pieces (many of them from the temple in Darasuram mentioned earlier) as well as groupings. One of the most beautiful of the ensembles shows Shiva as a handsome mendicant, making the chaste wives of several *rishis* fall in love with him. The *rishis'* wives had become arrogant because their husbands were noted for their penance and austerities, and Shiva decided to chasten them. It is extraordinary how the sculptor, with a tool as simple as a chisel, managed to depict so many delicate nuances of love and desire on the faces of the women.

A recent addition to the art gallery is the **Rajaraja museum** which houses Chola artifacts, many excavated from the site of the palace of Rajendra Chola at Gangaikondacholapuram. These include coins, terracotta objects, carved conch shells and metal vessels and measures.

The **Saraswathi Mahal Library** is housed in another part of the palace. The Maratha rulers of Thanjavur in the 17th and 18th centuries were enlightened monarchs who patronised art and cul-

Below left, veena player Below, penitent with pierced tongue and fire offering, Murugan festival, Tanjore.

ture. The greatest of them, King Serfoji, started the Library. An engaging and infinitely curious intellectual, he collected not only manuscripts and illuminations but also books in many European languages. There are over 40,000 items in the collection, and they include rare books on the arts and sciences, many of them on palm leaves. Serfoji's advisor and confidant was a missionary named Schwarz, and the church he built for the priest in 1779 to the east of the palace is still in use.

Thanjavur is a small town, easy to get around in. January is a good month for a visit, as the visitor can also take in the annual music festival in **Thiruvayaru**, seven miles away, in honour of the saint-composer Thyagaraja.

Before going on to Tiruchirapalli, the visitor should consider going out of his way to see **Gangaikondacholapuram**, about 40 miles (64 km) from Thanjavur. This elaborate name means 'the City of the King Who Conquered the Ganga' (Ganges), and commemorates the triumph of Raja Raja's son Rajendra.

He invaded the north and conquered many territories, reaching the Ganges in the process. On his return he built a city, and a temple which is almost the equal of the Big Temple in Thanjavur. Some even assert that the sculptures in this temple are superior. But the visitor would have made this a quick trip with the return journey planned for the same day; there are no amenities in the shabby village which is all that remains of a grand 11th century city.

Tiruchirapalli (Trichy) is about an hour away from Thanjavur, by road or by rail. It has an airport from which one can fly to and from Madras and Madurai, and the more affluent traveller may prefer to fly to Trichy and tour from there. Trichy is another historical town, the capital of the Chola rulers for a period. Approaching by road, rail or air, the first thing we see is the **Rock Fort**, 300 ft (90 m) high, which dominates the landscape. At its summit, alongside a rock which looks from certain angles like a bull with a raised head, is a Ganesha temple, a popular place of

Walking on burnt coal, Murugan estival.

worship in spite of the steep climb involved. There is also a 100-pillar *mandapam* which was used for music concerts and religious discourses. The top of the rock affords a fine view.

The main attraction of Trichy is actually across the Kaveri river on the island of Srirangam, 3 miles (5 km) away. Srirangam is a temple-town sacred to the god Vishnu. He is depicted in the sanctum as **Ranganatha**, in a reclining posture on his five-hooded serpent, Adisesha. The temple is practically a town in itself, with several residential streets within its 1 sq mile (1.6 sq km) compound, not to mention a number of shopping streets. Srirangam is one of the holiest temples for devotees of Vishnu, and its annual winter festival (December-January) attracts thousands of them. It is a rather confusing complex, since it was built over the centuries. Surrounded by crumbling granite walls, with 21 ornamental towers of no particular merit, it presents difficulties for the uninitiated visitor, though he can wander around freely in most parts of the temple. The main charm of Srirangam is that it is a live temple – in some respects even more so than the Madurai Meenakshi temple.

The two main features of the temple are the shrine dedicated to Krishna, the **Venugopala temple**, and the equestrian statues in one part. The carvings of *gopis* (pastoral maidens who loved the god Krishna) in the Venugopala temple are remarkable. The *gopis'* faces expressively depict the many aspects of love, and their figures are rendered with unusual sensuousness. The equestrian statues, obviously made during the Nayak rule in Madurai, are carved on monolithic pillars, and are so vibrantly realistic that they seem ready to take off any minute. On the way back to Trichy, the visitor might take note of the **Siva temple** of Jambukeswaram in **Tiruvanaikkaval**. This is a holy temple which is not open to non-Hindus; they may, however, walk into the compound where some interesting sculptures of animals dating back to the 16th century have been carved on walls and pillars.

Trichy rooftops from the Srirangam temple.

Trichy is a busy industrial, commercial and educational centre. It has a sizable Christian and Muslim population, and there are churches and mosques worth visiting. It is not a town to get around easily, being long and meandering, but if the visitor knows where he wants to go, he can be guided.

Pudukottai, 30 miles (50 km) from Trichy by road, is usually considered off the tourist route, but it has some attractions to offer. It was a princely state for 30 years until 1948, and developed its own courtly traditions. The Rajas were great patrons of the arts, and music and dance flourished in the tiny state. The city itself is of no great interest. The palace is a grand building but it is now used for government offices. The principal inducement to visit Pudukottai is its Government Museum which is very well maintained, though housed in a shabby building.

The tourist sights lie outside the town of Pudukottai at varying distances. A few miles before Pudukottai on the way from Trichy is **Narthamalai**, about a mile (1.6 km) off on the right side of the road. Here on the scarp of a hill stands the **Vijayalaya Chelesvaram temple**, one of the earliest Chola temples built by Vijayalaya, the first Chola ruler of the period. A small temple, it nevertheless includes all the facets of the Chola style of temple architecture that came to full bloom in Thanjavur and elsewhere. It also marks the transition from the earlier Pallava style to the Chola style.

Near to Narthamalai is a Jain cave in **Sittannavasel**, scooped out of the top of a hill, and decorated with frescoes, in the style of those found in Ajanta and Ellora. Despite their age, it is still possible to see how beautiful the colours of these flowers, birds, fishes and animals must have been.

Within a distance of about 18 miles (30 km) from Pudukottai, there are a number of small villages, such as **Kudimiyamalai**, **Kunnadarkoil** and **Kodumbalur**, all of which have small but remarkable temples constructed by the Pallava and Chola rulers, and filled with exquisite sculptures.

Gopurams of the Trichy temple.

THE COAST OF COROMANDEL

India's historic coast of Coromandel once stretched from Ganjam in Orissa, the kingdom of the Kalingas, to Point Calimere (Kodikkarai) in the land of the Cholas. The East India Company and the Age of Empire shortened that stretch to what is about half the coast of modern Tamil Nadu, and tacked on to it, so to speak, the half which the Portuguese once called the Fisheries Coast.

There is no more fascinating strand in the whole of India than this 560-mile (900-km) stretch from a little north of Madras to Land's End at Kanniyakumari. One day the promised East Coast Highway will open up its beaches and rich cultural, historical and natural heritage to the charter-flight tourist. But at present, it is still an adventure getting to many of the places that demand a visit on this coast and in its immediate hinterland. For travellers willing to accept a shortage of "mod cons", this adventure occasionally takes them away from the coast, but these detours include some of the more worthwhile places.

The traveller on today's Coromandel coast can begin with a day trip north of Madras to **Durgarayapatnam**, an ancient port by the northern end of Lake Pulicat, that was known to Francis Day, founder of Madras, as Armagaon. It was while he was serving as a factor here that Day began to search the coast further south for a better site. At the opposite end of the lake from the ruins of this early British settlement and the inevitable cemetery nearby are the better preserved ruins and cemetery of Fort Geldria, established by the Dutch in 1609 at **Pulicat**.

The tranquil Lake Pulicat and the backwaters which join it, as well as the southern and northern reaches of the **Buckingham canal** offer boating, fishing and picnic spots. The 400-mile (650-km) long canal connects Kakinada in Andhra Pradesh with Markanam in Tamil Nadu and was once navigable along its entire length, but today, the high cost of desilting makes this pos-

sible only on stretches. One such span is from the northern reaches of Madras to the rice-bowl town of Nellore in Andhra Pradesh, about 125 miles (200 km) by slow boat, a journey for the hardy and the patient to enjoy.

On the road back to Madras is the ancient village of **Tiruvottiyur** with its several temples dating to the 8th and 9th centuries, among them the **Aadipureswarar temple**, a splendid example of Chola architecture. Madras and the splendours of Mahabalipuram have been described earlier. We will move south and explore Cholamandalam, the stretch of Coromandel that the Cholas called their own.

South of Mahabalipuram is **Sadras**, the ruins of the early 18th century Dutch fort providing shelter for picnickers, and its lovely, almost deserted beach inviting sunbathers. As in Mahabalipuram, swimming is reasonably safe except during the monsoon, but remember: there are no lifeguards along this stretch of beaches, so you swim at your own risk. Sadras or Sadraspatnam, to

Pulicat Lake
Pulicat
Tiruvottriyur
St. Thomas Mount — Madras
Injambakkam
Muttukkadu — Cholamandal
Tirupporur — Covelong (Kovilam)
Palar
Tirukkalukunram — Mamallapuram (Mahabalipuram)
Sadras
Vedanthangal

C O R O M A N D E L

Bay of Bengal

Marakkanam
Tiruvakkarai — Auroville
Pondicherry (Puducherry)
Ponnaiyar — Cuddalore
Porto Novo (Parangippetai) — Pichavaram
Kollidam — Tirumullaivasal
Poompuhar
Tranquebar (Tarangambadi) — Karaikal (Py.)
Nagore
Nagappattinam — Velankanni
Kaveri — Thanjavur — Vedaranniyam
Tiruchchirappalli (Tiruchi) — Kodikkarai (Point Calimere)
Manora

C O A S T

Karaikkudi — Mimisal
Tondi
Palk Bay
Dhanushkodi
Madurai — Rameswaram
Vaigai — Mandapam — Pamban
Sethukarai — Kurusadai
Kilakkarai

F I S H E R I E S   C O

Tuticorin — Gulf of Mannar
Tambaraparani
Tirunelveli — Tiruchendur
Kulasekarappattinam

Kanniyakumari
Cape Comorin

0   30 Kms. Appx.

give the old port its full name, is now within the nuclear complex, but passes are given when asked for.

Lack of good roads enforces a brief but delightful detour to **Vedanthangal**, inland and westwards just to the west of National Highway 45, one of the best bird sanctuaries in South India. From October to March, but especially in December and January, just after the rain, the trees in the 30-hectare wetland are covered with birds and their nests. Over 100,000 migratory birds descend on Vedanthangal every year from as far north as Siberia.

Further south and again west of NH-45 is 700-year-old **Gingee fort**, one of the most magnificent military sites in the South with its battlements stretching over three hills. A Vijayanagara fort that the Marathas, the Mughals, Arcot and the French added to over the battle-scarred years, Gingee has within its walls several richly carved temples, a palace and a harem, a mosque, an audience hall, a gymnasium and granaries. It had an interesting system of plumbing and water storage, the remnants of which can still be seen. Towering over all of them is Rajagiri, a steep hill 180 ft (150 m) high, "which nature hath made secure and art impregnable".

Doubling back to Tindivnam junction on NH-45, the journey east to Cholamandal begins. Just before you reach the coast, you can pause to go back 20 million years in time into the Miocene Age. The small fossil park at **Thiruvakkarai** exhibits huge logs that ring like metal when struck by a hammer and chips of wood that sink when placed in water. The slopes of the nearby ravine are covered with similar logs, relics of that age when the now almost bare Eastern Ghats were a magnificent mountain range covered with majestic trees. In the neighbourhood are several prehistoric burial sites. Pondicherry and Auroville, described elsewhere, are close by.

Another lovely beach is the one at Tegnapatnam, **Cuddalore**, once watched over by Fort St David. As Governor of the fort, Elihu Yale named it as much after the young son he buried in Madras as after the patron saint of his native Wales. Little remains of this major fort whose existence gave the British the foothold they needed to wrest Madras from the French in the 18th century and establish the Indian Empire. Clive learned the art of war here and his old house is now the Collectorate. Fort St David's walls have bungalows built on them, by the 200-year-old Madras commercial house, Parry & Co.

Parry's own buildings in Cuddalore town could be something out of *Beau Geste*; indeed, in the early 18th century they housed the East India Company's Deputy Governors in the **Factory House**. Next door is Christ Church, consecrated in 1767 and to all intents and purposes a "Company church"; here lies Thomas Parry, one of the founders of modern Indian commerce. Not far from Cuddalore inland is **Nellikkuppam**, where the Parry's sugar mill, one of the oldest in the country, and its club and staff quarters give visitors an ideas of that old British institu-tion, the "Company town". Ask Parry's in Madras for the grand tour of Cuddalore and its environs; they will be happy to oblige, so proud are they of their commercial heritage.

Parry's were also once in **Porto Novo**, further south. It was once one of Portugal's finest harbours in the east, and vestiges of the fort can still be seen. One of the country's foremost marine biology research stations is located here, the institute affiliated to Annamalai University in the nearby temple and university town of Chidambaram.

Porto Novo offers boating in its bay and backwaters, but this is more enjoyable and better organised in adjacent **Pichavaram**. The backwaters here are fringed by the finest mangrove forests in the country and provide hundreds of sheltered boating trails, the tree canopy overhead offering much to excite the birdwatcher as well.

From here on to Point Calimere, almost the entire hinterland is the heart of the Chola country: here are the finest temples in all India, almost every vil-

Rajgiri from Gingee citadel.

lage boasting a magnificent shrine. Elsewhere in this volume, the temples of Chidambaram, Thanjavur and the rest of Cholanadu are described in detail. On the coast, however, is the splendid temple at **Tirumullaivasal** – an appetiser for the magnificence that lies in the hinterland beyond.

Now the traveller is in the rice bowl of Tamil Nadu, the delta of the sacred river Kaveri. In this land of sparkling green fields of paddy and groves of coconut and mango is **Poompuhar** on the coast, the once great port of the Cholas known as Kaveripoompattinam, "the Flower of the Kaveri". It was from here that South Indian culture went across the seas, and it was here too at this port which the Greeks and Romans first called, making it an international emporium. Archaeological "digs" and a museum telling in bas relief the story of glories past are reviving a town that (like so many others on this coast) had gone to sleep after the Cholas, woken briefly and gone to sleep again after the early Europeans.

Another such town is Tarangambadi, "the Village of the Dancing Waves". More popularly known as **Tranquebar**, it was a Danish settlement that made a considerable contribution to Indian printing and education. The ramparts of Dansborg Fort, built by Ove Gedde around 1620, are crumbling. The deserted Tranquebar Mission premises, church and cemetery are not as well preserved. This was the first Protestant mission to establish a foothold in India, and it was here that the missionary Bartholomeus Ziegenbalg gave to India Denmark's greatest contribution: the printed word.

Not far from here are three pilgrim towns within commuting distance of one another, all demonstrating the tremendous religious tolerance that has prevailed on the Coromandel. In each of these towns are shrines of different religious sects, the best known in each of them visited by people of all faiths though held dearest by their own adherents. Karaikkal, once French and now part of Pondicherry territory, has many relics of the French age, but the town's

Rocky signposts mark land's end.

254

chief attraction is the **Sanneswarar temple**. The temple is a rarity, one of the few temples in the country dedicated to Saturn. At Nagore, the place of the Naga trees, five minarets and a golden dome glitter in the sun above the 500-year-old tomb of the Muslim sage Hazrat Mian Sahib. At this shrine Hindus offer their hair in penance and people of all faiths seek miraculous cures from bathing in the shrine's tank, **Peer Kulam**. In the huge church of **Velanganni**, dedicated to Mary, with its towering steeple visible for miles around, people of all faiths light tall candles and beseech the Virgin Mother to demonstrate that the age of miracles is not past. Hindus, Muslims and Christians all walk this short stretch of Cholamandal every year, confident that the divine guardians of these shrines will not reject their pleas, whatever their creed. There are few better examples anywhere in the world of the unity of all faiths.

Vedaranyam, just before journey's end at Point Calimere, is called Dakshina Kailasam and is one of the sacred places of the Hindus. It is also associated with the story of Rama, as one of the places where he stopped on his return from Lanka. The Archaeological Department tends a mound near here where the footprints preserved in the rock are said to be those of the hero of the *Ramayana*. Salt pans stretch as far as the eye can see all around the temple and, many years ago, Congress volunteers marched here defying the British salt regulations. The march, duplicating Gandhi's Dandi March which began India's historic Satyagraha campaign, is commemorated here and draws its own share of pilgrims.

A few miles further on is the sanctuary of **Point Calimere**. In the last quarter of the year, migratory birdlife finds a haven in the 30,000 acres of salty marshland. But none of this birdlife can compare with the 30,000 to 50,000 flamingoes that suddenly swoop down on the swamp, turning it into a black-streaked white and blushing pink sea, before departing again as suddenly. It is a sight for the gods and a fitting signa-

Pillared temple hall, Rameswaram.

CHETTINAD

A 2-hour drive east of Madurai or south of Tiruchchirappalli leads into the heart of Chettinad, the land of the Chettiars. The 78 villages left of the original 96 remain a fascinating study for those interested in architecture and artisanship, faith and culture, banking and investment, antiques and jewellery, comfort and cuisine.

An ancient merchant community, the Chettiars were renowned in the 19th century as the bankers of South India. But their financial reputation and their wealth were both earned overseas, in Burma, Sri Lanka, Malaysia, Indo-China, Singapore and the Indies. The riches earned abroad were always brought back to the ancestral villages from which the Chettiars went forth – and there, in the parched wilderness of scrub, they built mansions the like of which are rarely found in India. They also made Chettiar hospitality and philanthropy known all over the country.

To the newcomer travelling from village to village, the block-long mansions emerge

almost like gigantic mirages from the swirling dust. A greater surprise awaits him inside. Pillars of teak or satinwood or gleaming black granite are to be found by the score in every house, and intricately carved doors of solid teak. Marble from Italy appears to have been favoured for much of the flooring. The walls are gleaming white, and a secret process in the finish makes them velvet-smooth to the touch. As final touches, the deserted mansions are hung with chandeliers, fittings and paintings worthy of a palace.

For nearly a century before Independence, each house was filled with kitchenware of brass and stainless steel, with cupboards, mattresses and pillows and anything else an establishment might need in quantities fit for an army. The strongest safes in the house would keep silverware and traditional jewellery of gold and diamonds, rubies, emeralds and pearls, every bit fit for royalty.

But all that was in the years from the late 19th century till Independence. The winds of change that first stirred India also brought independence to the countries where the Chettiars had made their fortunes. The new nationalism brought in its wake a Chettiar exodus; they had to return home to an uncertain future with only their material possessions to fall back upon.

The Chettiar, however, is hardy and resourceful, and forsook banking and financing – the traditional means of earning a living – to become successful professionals and industrialists. But the wealth required to maintain the homes no longer exists. Today almost every Chettiar village is deserted, large numbers of its splendid houses pulled down, most of the rest becoming ghostly homes, maintained at a fraction of the standards that once prevailed. To make survival possible, many a Chettiar family has had to sell off its family possessions in bits and pieces. The antique shops in the bylanes of Karaikkudi, the largest Chettiar village, still have treasures from those houses.

To go through these decaying mansions is to marvel at the wealth that went into them and the achievement of the untrained local artisans who built them. If you were lucky enough to attend a Chettiar wedding, now reduced to just a day from the week-long celebration it used to be – you would wonder what the hospitality, constrained by circumstances now, would have been in the past before Chettiar fortunes fell low.

ture for the bounty they have lavished on this coast.

Around the corner from Point Calimere, the Palk Bay begins to curve inwards. Along this coast, bathed by calmer seas than on the Coromandel, are the ports from which migrant labour went from India to Sri Lanka: Athirampattinam, Thondi and Devipattinam. The last-named is also associated with the legends of Lord Rama. By Devipattinam's temple there are nine stone pillars in the sea where Rama is said to have worshipped the nine planets. Where the bay curves out and opens onto Palk Strait is **Mandapam**, a major marine research centre. Plans have been drawn up to develop islands off Mandapam as beach resorts and a marine park.

Across the bridge from Mandapam is the sacred island **Rameswaram**, one of the holiest places of the Hindus. Several places in the island are associated with the epic hero, Lord Rama. It is believed that the two *lingams* in the sanctum of the magnificently sculpted **Rathna-**

swamy temple were installed on this spot by Rama himself. The temple, it is said, took 350 years to complete, and its crowning glory is a magnificent 4,000-ft (1,220 m) long pillared corridor that surrounds the main quadrangle.

The **Kothandramar temple** on the island, with its bronzes of the heroes and heroine of the *Ramayana*, and **Gandhamadhanam hill**, where Rama's footprint is enshrined at the site of Hanuman's leap to Lanka, are other places the pilgrims visit in Rameswaram. But to the traveller from abroad, the awe-inspiring temple and some of the finest virgin beaches in the world are the main attractions of this island in the sun.

Rameswaram is connected to the mainland by road and rail. Looking over the road bridge, travellers will see huge boulders in the sea: these are in fact an extension of Adam's Bridge, the mythical land link between India and Sri Lanka. A ferry service once served as the link between Rameswaram and Talaimannar, but now it awaits more propitious times for revival.

Left, abandoned stately home of Chettinad. Below, Vivekananda Rock, where three oceans meet.

Back on the mainland south of Mandapam lies the Fisheries Coast. Here fishing villages vie with one another to build a bigger church with a taller steeple, often with spectacular results. These villages once sent out the divers who made the Gulf of Mannar renowned even in Roman times for its pearl fisheries.

Today ports like Kilakkarai and Sethukarai are almost deserted, but the fortunes of **Tuticorin**, the Thoothukudi of the Tamils, have revived. Its new port is one of the most modern in India, and has helped develop an industrial hinterland. Every once in so many years, Tuticorin organises a small pearl fishery and although the yields are poor, it helps to keep a diving tradition alive. Many a boy in Tuticorin will put on a bare-skinned diving exhibition for a visitor for a small consideration.

South of Tuticorin is the shore temple of **Tiruchendur**, perched on a rocky ledge that falls sheer to the ocean. One of the six abodes of Lord Muruga, the temple is more than 1,000 years old.

Few temples elsewhere in India are more scenically located, and even few more beautifully built. Near Tiruchendur are also other well-known temple towns, such as Alwar Thirunagiri and Sri Vaikundam.

And so to Land's End, Cape Comorin, where three seas meet and where the shore temple to the virgin goddess, Kanniyakumari, stands. It is one of the sacred places of the Hindus; all those who bathe in the Ganges and worship at Varanasi must bathe in the waters off **Kanniyakumari** and worship the goddess to complete the pilgrimage and attain salvation. The temple is a magnificently sculpted structure and the goddess in its sanctum a creation of rare beauty.

Kanniyakumari also has significant memorials. The **Gandhi Mandapam**, built in Kalinga style, commemorates the immersion of the ashes of Mahatma Gandhi, the Father of the Nation, in the waters by the temple. In the large hall is a statue of the Mahatma and above his head is an opening in the roof through

Kanniyakumari: Church of Our Lady of Ransom, protectress of fisherfolk.

which every 2 October, his birthday, sunlight streams to light up his brow, symbolising the light of freedom. The other memorial, dedicated to Swami Vivekananda, is built on the rock 656 ft (200 m) from shore where he meditated in 1892 before taking the message of Vedanta, the Hindu philosophy, to the West.

The church of Our Lady of Joy, which Francis Xavier founded in the 1540s, the beaches with their celebrated sands and rocks in seven colours, the rising and setting of the sun, and of the moon on full moon nights, are some of the discoveries that could make a casual traveller stay longer in Kanniyakumari than he first planned.

Not far from Kanniyakumari, mainland India's southernmost point, and up the small stretch of the western coast that is in Tamil Nadu, are one or two places that beckon the traveller. The temple in **Suchindram** is a storehouse of some of finest specimens of temple art and sculpture in the country. The dancing girls no longer perform their offices for the gods, but the music to which they danced finds echoes in the musical pillars that have been sculpted in the north corridor out of single blocks of granite. When the cylindrical rods of the pillars are tapped, musical sounds are heard, each pillar producing a different note.

Nagercoil, with its several temples and churches, and the inviting beach at **Colachel,** overlooked by the Circular Fort, are breaks on the way to **Padmanabhapuram**, Tamil Nadu's legacy from Kerala. A splendid fort and pagoda-style palace are the attractions of this small town where the Maharajas of Travancore used to holiday. The museum in the palace has a fine collection of murals, stone sculpture and woods of medicinal value. All around is lushly tropical vegetation, a contrast to the disciplined fields and groves of the Kaveri delta and the aridity of the rest of the coast. Adding the point to the exclamation mark, Padmanabhapuram emphasises the variety of the coast of Tamil Nadu.

Village deities care away evil spirits.

MADURAI

City of Sweetness, Temple City, City of Festivals – these are among the better known epithets of Madurai, a hoary and fabled city with a history that goes back to the pre-Christian era. Its origin is believed to be sacred: an early Pandya king, hearing reports of celestial beings coming down to earth to bathe in a certain tank and worship Shiva, caused a temple to be built there in which a *lingam* was installed. A city came up around the temple. When it was to be named, Lord Shiva appeared and blessed the people. Drops of nectar fell from the coils of his hair onto the city; from this it derived its named Madhura-puri, City of Nectar.

Madurai was the capital of the Pandya kingdom until the 10th century. It was a commercial centre and business entrepôt, trading with many countries including China, Greece and Rome. Megasthenes, writing in the 3rd century BC, bears testimony to Madurai's grandeur and prosperity; so does Marco Polo, 15 centuries later. Madurai flourished under the Pandyan kings until the Cholas overcame them in the 10th century. The Pandyans regained power in the 13th century, only to lose their kingdom to the hordes of Allauddin Khilji, then Sultan in Delhi. The Muslim rule was in turn ended by the Vijayanagara emperors. The new rulers left their far-flung territory in charge of governors, called the Nayaks, who in time became the de facto rulers. It was during their reign that the magnificent temple and other buildings were constructed. The Nayak rule lasted until the middle of the 18th century, when the British gradually took over.

Through its vicissitudes Madurai has remained a great city, its temple a magnet for pilgrims from all over India. The tradition of literary Tamil in Madurai dates from pre-Christian times, with successive academies (Tamil Sangams) serving as the nerve-centre of Tamil culture. The Madurai temple, in a sense, symbolises all that being a Tamil

means. Even today, when the city has a population of over a million, the temple's presence can be felt everywhere in Madurai.

Myth and legend take concrete form in the city. The **Meenakshi Sundareswarar temple** (commonly known as the Meenakshi temple) in the heart of Madurai is probably the biggest temple in the country, both in area and in the number of structures within a single compound. The area of the temple, an approximate square about 800 ft (245 m) by 750 ft (228 m), contains a multitude of shrines, halls and colonnades. It is believed there are 33 million sculptures in the temple. While this figure might be an exaggeration, there are a sufficient number to keep the visitor occupied for days.

The primary deity in the temple is not Shiva, but his consort Meenakshi. Though the temple was originally established around the *lingam* that Indra, the king of gods, is said to have found in this area, it was consecrated to Meenakshi, daughter of a Pandyan king, who was wooed and won by Shiva. (Meenakshi and Sundareswarar are among the names by which Shakti and Shiva are known.)

At first glance, the outstanding features of the temple are the four towers at the four points of the compass, soaring between 140 to 160 ft (43 m to 49 m). There are other towers inside the temple complex also, but the four corner *gopurams* are the most striking. These are essentially entries into the temple; more precisely, they surmount the huge entrances which are about 60 ft (18 m) high. Each *gopuram* is adorned with numerous sculptures of gods and goddesses, people, animals and birds. The tallest of the towers, the southern one, can be climbed for a small fee. The visitor will encounter both grimy steps and bats, but he will be rewarded with a spectacular view.

The towers were renovated about 3 decades ago, and new sculptures replaced several old ones; everything was gaily – or garishly – painted, as was the custom in the old days. Many were dismayed by what they considered the

eft,
rain to
Ootacamund.

vulgarity of the new painted sculptures, but time has a way of restoring the balance. Over the years, wind and weather have softened the sculptures so that they look as beautiful as the old ones must have been. It should also be remembered that without binoculars, these sculptures are seen from a distance of at least 60 ft (19.7 m).

But the sculptures inside the temple are, for the most part, on eye level. It is customary to enter a temple by its eastern entrance, but in the Meenakshi temple the eastern entrance with its magnificent tower is permanently closed, though it is the oldest. Some centuries ago, a temple servant committed suicide by flinging himself from the top of the *gopuram*. Since then, visitors enter the temple by an adjacent gateway which has no tower over it. This leads to the **Ashta Shakti mandapam**, a hall with sculptured pillars which represent the various aspects of the goddess Shakti, as well as scenes from some of the miracles – there are 64 of them in all – that Shiva performed in Madurai.

Shops selling the paraphernalia that devotees need for worship flank the hall. Next to this hall is the **Meenakshi Nayakkar mandapam**, also known as the **Yali mandapam** because on each of its 110 pillars is a carved *yali*, a mythical animal somewhat akin to a griffin. This hall has a votive lamp-holder with 1,008 lamps, which are lit on festive occasions and present a spectacular sight.

The **Chitra gopuram**, adjacent to the Yali *mandapam*, is the tallest tower within the temple. It has seven storeys covered with sculptures, and leads into a passage which has a sculpture of Shiva as a mendicant. Next is the **Potramaraikulam** (Tank of the Golden Lotuses) and the magnificent colonnade which surrounds this reservoir. The colonnade has an assortment of sculptures and paintings all around, most of them depicting Tamil poets and poetry, and the various aspects of the temple. From the colonnade, the steps lead down to the tank in which the god Indra is believed to have bathed. All round the year, devotees take a dip in its holy waters.

The celebrat
Meenakshi
temple
gopurams,
Madurai.

Passing by the **Rani Mangammal mandapam**, and the **Oonjal mandapam** (so called because it has an *oonjal* or swing on which golden images of Shiva and Meenakshi are placed every Friday and rocked to the chanting of hymns by the priests), the visitor comes to the **Kilikkoondu mandapam** (Parrot-cage Hall) which has not only caged parrots but another set of huge monolithic pillars, each depicting a character from mythology and the epics. On the western side of this hall a three-storey tower leads to the shrine of the goddess; non-Hindus are not admitted here. While the sanctum houses the idol of Meenakshi, the shrine comprises two concentric corridors and several halls and galleries.

A tower north of the Parrot cage *mandapam* leads to the shrine of **Sundareswarar**. The first thing the visitor encounters here is a huge monolithic figure of the elephant god Ganesha, which is supposed to have been unearthed when the Mariamman Teppakulam was being excavated. The most important part of the shrine is the **Kambattadi mandapam** around the flagstaff in front of the sanctum. It is difficult not to indulge in superlatives when describing any part of the Madurai temple, but the temptation becomes acute when contemplating the magnificence of the monolithic sculptured pillars in this hall. The most beautiful of them all depicts the god Vishnu giving away his sister Meenakshi in marriage to Sundareswarar. Other spectacular sculptures are those of Shiva in an acrobatic dance pose and Parvati in the aspect of Kali (Earth Mother). Beyond this *mandapam* is a three-storey tower marking the entrance to the sanctum of Sundareswarar. Non-Hindus are not allowed to enter the sanctum.

The **Ayirakkal mandapam** the 1,000-pillar hall which lies to the east of the sanctum is one of the great glories of the temple. There are actually 985 pillars, and they are a riot of sculptures, depicting gods and goddesses as well as human beings. The hall now serves as a museum of bronzes and other artifacts,

The float festival in Madurai.

as well as paintings and photographs which delineate Tamil culture and architecture, and selected episodes from mythology.

The Meenakshi temple is no museum piece; it is a vital, living temple. Devotees worship at its many shrines several times a day. There is a festive atmosphere all the time: in fact, there is a festival at least once a month, the most important among them being the **Chitra festival** (April-May) to celebrate the wedding of Meenakshi and Sundareswarar. This festival draws over 100,000 devotees from different parts of India. The temple is also a living entity in the sense that people live out their lives in its premises: weddings take place, classes are held, people eat and sleep there and run the numerous shops it houses.

Across the east gate is another architectural marvel, the **Pudhu mandapam** (New Hall). It is a large rectangular hall, supported by 124 sculpted pillars, each over 20 ft (6 m) high. The pillars are most intricately carved, and no two are alike. During the Chitra festival, the idols of Meenakshi and Sundareswarar are kept here for a while. Unfortunately, except during the festival, Pudhu *mandapam* is cluttered with all sorts of shops, and it is difficult to view the sculptures, except those on the outside. An unfinished tower east of Pudhu *mandapam*, heroic in conception – its base measures 210 ft by 120 ft (64 m by 36 m) – is yet another legacy of Nayak construction.

There are several other temples in Madurai which are worth seeing. The **Koodal Alagar**, a Vishnu temple, may be as ancient as the Meenakshi temple, and it has beautifully carved stone lattice windows.

The visitor should also make a special effort to see another Vishnu temple, the **Kallalagar temple** in Alagarkovil, about 12 miles (20 km) to the northwest of Madurai. It is located on a hill in the forest, and has some splendid sculptures depicting the various incarnations of Vishnu. It is also the place from which Vishnu is supposed to have trav-

Below and below right, details of Thirumalai Nayak palace.

elled to Madurai, crossing the river Vaigai on his way to the temple to give his sister Meenakshi away in marriage to Sundareswarar.

The splendour of the Nayak rule in Madurai is evident in the remains of the **palace of Thirumalai Nayak**, the most famous king of the Nayak dynasty. The palace originally occupied an area of nearly 1,000 ft (300 m) by 700 ft (213 m), and consisted of many splendid apartments and galleries, as well as gardens, tanks and fountains. Much of it is gone now, but for the great audience hall, a three-sided pavilion about 220 ft (67 m) by 110 ft (33 m); the courtyard, supported by pillars 60 ft (18 m) high and 12 ft (3.6 m) in circumference; a dome over 60 ft (18 m) high, unsupported by girders or rafters. These indicate the magnificence of the palace as it must have been. Some of the original apartments still remain, and a museum has been set up in one of the halls. *Son et lumiere* shows which portray vividly the Nayak period in Madurai's history are held every day.

Yet another Nayakar legacy is the **Mariamman Teppakulam**, one of the biggest and most beautiful tanks in the country. The tank is at Vandiyur, in the eastern part of the city. The great Ganesha in the Meenakshi temple was found here when the earth was being dug up for use in the construction of the palace and the temple. Rather than leave a big hole in the ground, Thirumalai Nayak converted it into a tank, and set up an engineering system by which it was fed from the waters of the river Vaigai, north of the city. Unfortunately, the tank now remains dry much of the year due to the absence of the monsoons, but water is usually let in for the float festival, a colourful occasion when a decorated and illuminated float goes around in the gentle waters of the tank. There is a many-tiered pavilion in the middle of the tank which is accessible by boat.

Today, Madurai is a bustling and populous industrial and commercial city. It has large textile mills, automobile ancillary industries, and a variety of small-scale industries. Traditionally it was a town of weavers, who still continue to produce rich textiles in both silk and cotton.

Before leaving Madurai there is one stop the visitor should make. This is the **Mahatma Gandhi Memorial**, in the Tumkum Palace in Tallakulam, in the northeast part of the city. The Memorial offers an overview of the Mahatma's life through paintings and a variety of memorabilia. Some of his possessions are preserved here, but the *pièce de résistance* is a model of the hut in which Gandhiji lived in Sewagram. It plays his minimal personal belongings, a replica of his bed, and other furniture. The Tumkum Palace was built in the late 17th century by a great queen of the Nayak dynasty, Rani Mangamma. It is a relatively simple structure on two levels, with a cupola on top, but it has great dignity. An air of peace surrounds the palace, set in the middle of a well-kept garden. In the period of British rule it was known as Tumkum Bungalow, and occupied by successive Collectors of Madras.

THE HILL STATIONS OF TAMIL NADU

The holiday resorts of Tamil Nadu are all in the hills, a hangover from the days of the Raj when the British took to plateau and hilltop to escape the heat of the plains. Old habits die hard, and the hill stations are even more crowded these days during the "Season", from late March to mid-June. At other times of the year, the weather may not be so balmy, but if the visitor is willing to cope with drizzles and showers, bright moments of sun that vanish into various shades of dull grey, sweaty mornings and bundled-up evenings, the hill resorts are ideal for those who seek the leisurely, stay-put holiday away from the madding crowd.

Southwest of Madras is **Vedanthangal** and 62 miles (100 km) to the west is the sacred Arunachala Hill of **Thiruvannamalai**. The hill temple is one of the largest shrines in South India, sprawling 25 acres (10.1 hectares) and more over the hillside and entered through a giant gateway over which towers a 200-ft (60-m) high, 11-storey *gopuram*. During festival time, the sacred beacon lit on the hilltop can be seen for miles around. At the foot of the hill lived the late Sri Ramana Maharishi, the philosopher-saint. The serene *ashram* he established is now visited by mystics, philosophers, seekers and believers from many nations.

A long drive northwest of Thiruvannamalai brings you to **Hogenakkal**, whose waterfalls are the central attraction around which an inexpensive holiday resort and health spa are being developed. The waters of the falls are said to have medicinal properties – an added incentive to bathe under one of Nature's most glorious showers. A massage with mineral oils, available from scores of local masseurs, is an invigorating part of the bathing ritual. Another exhilarating experience is boating in the "rapids" at the foot of the falls. The boats, frail coracles made of hide, ensure a water-bobbing experience rather than a boating one.

Southeast of Hogenakkal is the commercial centre of **Salem**, and up the winding roads to the east of it is **Yercaud** in the Shevaroy Hills. Set in coffee and orange country, it is the first of Tamil Nadu's hill stations on this journey. The sleepy old school town is only being rejuvenated as a holiday destination, and the visitor has a choice of wandering through tree-shaded estates, trekking along mountain trails, strolling around the lake or fishing in the local streams. The several apiaries around supply delightful fresh honey.

Bhavani Sagar, southwest of Salem, is being developed as a picnic spot by the government. The dam here is the longest multi-purpose dam in the world, five miles in extent. It is also the halfway house between Salem and the industrial centre of Coimbatore, from where begins the climb into the Nilgiris, the Blue Mountains. **Coimbatore**, the centre of black-soil cotton country is known as the Manchester of South India for its concentration of textile mills. Northwest of Coimbatore are the Nilgiris. The climb into the hills begins at **Mettupalayam** and offers both the visual pleasure and the thrill of driving along switchbacks. But the hill road is in fact perfectly safe and drivers who use it have a healthy respect for the rules of the mountain road.

A more exciting way of getting up to **Ooty** or **Udhagamandalam**, as it is now called, is by the Toy Train. A tiny narrow-gauge train with two engines takes you up in a series of switchbacks. At times the train seems to be clinging to the edge of the mountain, at others it chugs comfortably through the middle of small hill villages, proceeding all the while at walking pace but providing a scenic thrill around every bend. It is possible to saunter alongside the train as it is chuffing up.

Ooty has much to offer the visitor all year round. The botanical gardens are a blaze of colours during the annual flower show in May, and a delightful excursion during the rest of the year. Trout are plentiful in the rushing, crystal-clear mountain streams. The magnificent golf course seems an extension

Left, devotees haul their sacred burden through the streets of Madurai during the annual festival.

of the emerald-green downs which, alas, are being despoiled. The large lake offers hours of boating pleasure. Peaks and falls await exploration: Dodabetta, the highest peak of them all, Snowdon Peak, Elk Hill, Cairn Hill, Fern Hill, Glen Morgan Lake and Mukurti Fall.

The resort offers racing during the season and club life, if you have a host at the Ooty club where snooker was born, a fact immortalised on the wall of the billiards room. There's Charing Cross – remember, the locations were named by the British – where you stop and gossip. Ooty is also tea country, and a visit to a tea estate is easy to arrange; to stay takes a little more effort. The headquarters of the United Planters' Association of South India (UPASI) in Coonoor is always helpful in arranging such visits.

Two thousand feet (600 m) below Ooty's elevation of 7,500 ft (2,250 m), and with temperatures a little warmer than Ooty's 10-20°C, is **Coonoor**, surrounded on all sides by hills and slopes of tea, with old colonial houses. Like

Ooty, Coonoor offers a park (Sim's), a lake, waterfalls (Low's) and a peak (Tiger Rock), picnic spots, mountain trails and clubs. It is also a research centre, with several experimental fruit farms and the Pasteur Institute. Tea auctions are held here and in the nearby cantonment town of **Wellington**, named after the hero of Waterloo, who as the young Wellesley earned his spurs in the Madras Presidency. Wellington is the home base of the Madras Regiment, the oldest unit in the Indian Army, and houses the Staff College of the defence forces. Both have fine libraries and museum pieces, immaculate campuses with magnificent buildings and clubs that boast a fine table. A stroll around is not frowned upon, but an invitation will help a visitor enjoy the more all that the two campuses have to offer.

To the east of Ooty, at 6,500 ft (1,950 m), is **Kotagiri**, the first hill station in the Nilgris, now being revived as a quiet little holiday resort. Nearby are **Kundah** and **Pykara**, picnic spots developed alongside hydroelectric projects,

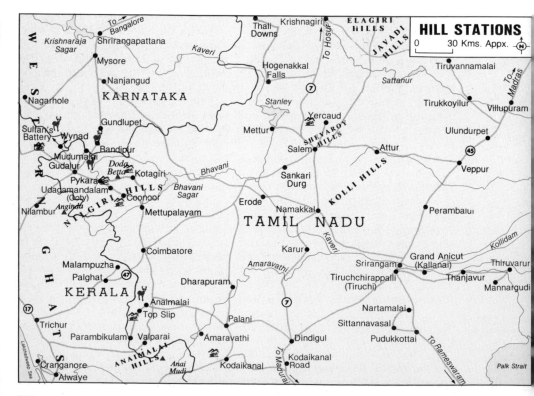

and to the north of Ooty is **Mudumulai**. This is Tamil Nadu's biggest wildlife sanctuary, contiguous with Karnataka's Bandipur and Kerala's Wynaad.

Mudumalai has a wealth of wildlife, deer, wild boar, monkeys and birdlife. Occasionally an elephant herd may be seen and, with some luck, a tiger, a leopard, packs of wild dogs or any of a variety of resident reptiles. The pride of Mudumalai is its gaur, the Indian bison, nearly decimated by disease in the past but now seen again in numbers. Game-watching can be indulged in from the comfort of car, van or jeep, in the company of a game ranger. A more adventurous way of spotting animals is to book a seat astride a Forest Department elephant. For all its apparent scariness, it is very safe, as the elephant-guide knows exactly what he is doing.

Back in the plains, heading south of Coimbatore, you reach the lower slopes of the Annamalai Hills, from where a climb takes you to **Top Slip**, the main camp of the Annamalai Wildlife Sanctuary. Here are some of the thickest rain forests in South India and some of the finest game in the country, but it is difficult terrain to get around in, and a knowledgeable guide would be needed.

East of **Pollachi** is **Palani**, a major pilgrim centre and main base for the journey into the tea hills and game sanctuaries of the Annamalais. Its hilltop temple is the most renowned of the six abodes of Muruga, the son of Shiva. Its festival in April brings thousands from Tamil Nadu, carrying religious relics on their heads or shoulders; they trek all the way to Palani and then climb the 659 steps to the 450-ft (135-m) high peak in a spontaneous expression of fervour.

South of Palani and not far from it, in fact on the southern crest of the Upper Palani Plateau, at an elevation of 7,000 ft (2,100 m), is the other famed hill station of Tamil Nadu, **Kodaikanal**. Smaller than Ooty and less congested, Kodaikanal owes its development to American missionaries working in Tamil Nadu and northern Sri Lanka. Looking for a rest station and sanatorium, they chose "Kodi" in the 1840s,

Ooty's pleasant slopes: a haven for the Raj.

but it was only after the British Governor Sir Charles Trevelyan's visit in 1860 that the site began to develop as a hill station. It has clubs and an observatory, splendid waterfalls, forests and natural spectacles such as the Pillar rocks. Kodi's pride is its lake, which offers boating and a 3-mile (4.8-km) circumambulatory promenade. Its park, somewhat less spectacular than Ooty's, is at its best during the fruit and flower show in May. A better flower show is laid on by nature when the Kurinji blooms once in 12 years, carpeting the hillside with its pale blue. The next bloom is due in 1994.

From green Kodi, the traveller moves into the parched deep south to reach a few delightful oases in the foothills of the Western Ghats. About 1,000 ft (300 m) above sea level is the quiet spa of **Kuttralam**. Set midst low hills and forests, Kuttralam is renowned for its five waterfalls and bracing climate. June to October is when the Cittar river cascades down the rocks and the waterfalls are at their best. Bathing in the mineral-rich water and breathing the salubrious air is a great restorative.

In another picturesque forest setting a little southwest are **Papanasam falls** and its temple whose deity absolves all sin. Together they make Papanasam an important pilgrim centre. Just east of here is the **Mundanthurai** sanctuary, sited on the slopes (2,000 ft/600 m) of the Papanasam hills and now one of Project Tiger's 18 reserves. To the east of this reserve and near Tirunelveli is the **Kalakad** Sanctuary, now incorporated administratively as part of Mundanthurai. Deer and four monkey species of the South – the Nilgiri langur, the common langur, the bonnet macaque and the endangered lion-tailed macaque – are found here. With luck, a tiger or leopard may be sighted.

From Kalakad to the temples of **Tirunelveli** and the churches of **Palayamkottai** is only 20 miles (32 km). And from there a splendid National Highway gets you back to Madras via Madurai and Tiruchchirappalli, both with airports.

Below, Nilgiri vista: the Blue Mountains. Right, coffee blossoms and berries.

TEA AND COFFEE

Tea has traditionally been a product of China, in whose literature the beverage first finds mention millennia ago. China had the world monopoly on tea until the middle of the 19th century, when the plant was accidentally discovered growing wild in Assam. Major Robert Bruce, who noticed it in 1823, and his brother Charles, were pioneers in the development of the tea industry in India. As the land was hospitable to the growth of tea, quality seeds were imported from China by the Imperial Government of India, and sown in upper Assam in 1834. The first consignment of eight chests of Assam tea was sent to London in 1838, and auctioned on January 10, 1839. The 150th anniversary of this event was celebrated in London in January 1989 when selected Assam teas from well-known gardens were auctioned.

The earliest tea plantations in South India were developed in the Nilgiri hills between 1859 and 1869. Unlike in Assam, tea in South India tends to grow on hill slopes; the higher the elevation, the better the flavour. Tea plantations stretch all the way from the Nilgiri hills to the southern parts of Kerala.

Tea is an agro-industry, processing its raw materials, namely the green leaf, in factories situated on or near the plantations. The manufacturing process consists of curing the green leaf, rolling and fermenting it, and drying and grading. This is the orthodox way of manufacturing the leaf and the dust, though many innovations in the process have been introduced. Tea is a growth industry, and by AD 2000, production is expected to reach a million kg.

Coffee made its advent in India in the 17th century, nearly 200 years before tea, and that too under Indian auspices. An Arabian saint, Hazarat Shahi Janab Allah Mogatabi, popularly known as Baba Budan, sowed seven coffee seeds he had brought from a pilgrimage to the holy places of Islam. The seeds were sown in the hills in Karnataka, which still bear his name. Karnataka continues to be the largest producer of coffee, followed by Kerala and Tamil Nadu. The two major varieties grown are the Arabica and the Robusta. The fruit crop gathered is pulped in the pulper house, and the separated coffee seeds are dried and sent to the curing works. The process is simple, compared to the sophisticated processing of tea. Today, multinational corporations have set up factories to manufacture instant coffee in India. It is estimated that by AD 2000 India will grow close to 300,000 tonnes of coffee.

The legacy the British planters left behind is a splendid one. A tea plantation is a thing of beauty, and the plantations remain a significant part of the Indian national wealth. With their neatly laid out rows of tea on the slopes, the winding roads and the colonial bungalows, they are constant reminders of British organisation and British esthetics.

Coffee country is also scenically beautiful. In the coffee blossom season, the stretches are decked with a mass of white flowers, wafting a heady fragrance for miles around. When they turn into green berries and then into red fruits, it is yet another cropping season for coffee. Among the amenities the plantation country affords is ample opportunity for cross-country hiking along mountain trails, fishing, hunting and motoring. A number of game sanctuaries in the South, including Mudumalai and Thekkady are located near the plantations.

PONDICHERRY

Pondicherry was the former capital of the French territories in India. Its history was one of constant conflict, first with the Dutch, then with the British, who attacked the French in India whenever there were hostilities between England and France in Europe. They occupied Pondicherry several times, and during one such period, from 1761 to 1765, they razed the town to the ground, leaving unscathed just a few places of worship. It was only from 1816 that Pondicherry enjoyed a period of stability and peace. The city which we now see came up gradually, literally on the ashes of the old one. Today it is the administrative capital of a Union Territory which also includes former French enclaves elsewhere in the South – Mahe in Kerala, Yanam in Andhra and Karaikkal, also in Tamil Nadu.

Pondicherry lies within an oval boulevard which girdles the entire

town. Within the oval, streets are laid out running east to west, and these are bisected by streets that run from north to south. The layout of the town is thus (except for the later additions) a series of squares and rectangles, which makes it easy for the visitor to find his way around. The French reserved the seafront for their homes and offices, and laid out five streets parallel to the beach on which they built fine mansions. This was known as the *Ville Blanche* or White Town, and demarcated by a canal from the *Ville Noir* or Black Town. In the course of time the canal dried up, and now unfortunately serves as a dumping ground for garbage.

Pondicherry is located on the east coast of South India, 100 miles (160 km) south of Madras. It is routine for guidebooks to describe Pondicherry as "a sleepy French provincial city", an impression based almost entirely on recollections of the sea front, which looks vaguely Mediterranean, and of the former White Town where the streets tend to be quiet and clean, and high-walled compounds protect gracious old buildings set among shady trees. Pondicherry today is a bustling town with a population close to 700,000. Over the years the French influence has declined, but enough remains to mark out Pondicherry as different. The French have an active cultural presence. Their language is still spoken extensively among old-time residents and French citizens of Indian origin. A number of streets still bear their original French names, commemorating famous generals: Rue Suffren, Rue Law de Lauriston, Rue Mahe de la Bourdonnais, for example. Bastille Day is still celebrated with all the fervour one would see in France.

The best way to get to Pondicherry is by car or bus from Madras. There are several buses a day, some air-conditioned, the roads are good, and the travelling time is about 4 hours. There is a daily railway connection with Madras, but the journey is long and tedious. An airstrip has been built in Pondicherry but has not yet been commissioned. Pondicherry also has bus connections

Preceding pages, squirrel scrutinises rapt devotee at the Aurobindo *samadhi.* **Left,** war memorial honours French dead, **Pondicherry.**

with a number of other towns in Tamil Nadu. The weather is hot and humid for most of the year, but pretty equable from November to March. Warm clothes are rarely required.

It is fortunate that quite a few of the sights in Pondicherry are in the old White Town or nearby. The visitor cannot do better than to start with the **Raj Nivas**, the residence of the Lieutenant Governor of Pondicherry, even if one can do little more than peer at it from the outside. It is a handsome 200-year-old building which was once the residence of the redoubtable Marquis Joseph-François Dupleix, a great governor and builder of Pondicherry. It represents the best of the period's French and Indian style of architecture, a fusion not in the least jarring. The furniture is French in style with carved Indian motifs (a kind still to be seen in many old houses in Pondicherry). There are several stone sculptures in the garden, the most prominent of which is a representation of the god Vishnu in his incarnation as a boar.

The Raj Nivas faces **Government Park**. This is the old **French Place**, renovated and somewhat Indianised. It is a pleasant site, with well laid out paths and lawns. A number of sculptures, most of them brought back from Gingee after some long-forgotten war, add to the attractions of the park. The park also boasts a few fountains, one of them dating back to the time of Napoleon III, and a mysterious monument at its centre about which different tales are told. Several government offices, the Pondicherry Legislative Assembly, the Tourism Department, and the Romain Rolland Library are located on the streets around the park.

The **Romain Rolland Library** is well worth browsing around. With over 60,000 volumes on its shelves, it represents a catholic collection of French and English books, many of them rare. The **Pondicherry Museum** is an adjunct to the library, though located a few blocks south in Rue Romain Rolland in the old premises of the library. The museum has an outstanding collection of arti-

facts, especially relating to all aspects of the French Indian past. It has attempted with some success to recreate a French ambience in one section where the rooms are furnished in French style, and decorated with paintings, marbles, mirrors and clocks. The atmosphere is very much that of an elegant French home of the early 19th century. A display of antique armaments and weapons makes for another interesting section. The museum also houses rare bronze and stone sculptures from the Pallava and Chola periods in Indian history, and Roman artifacts excavated in nearby Arikamedu. Its prize exhibit is the bed that Dupleix slept on when he was Governor of Pondicherry.

From the Government Park, a short distance eastward is the beach, dominated by a 13 ft (4 m) statue of Mahatma Gandhi in his familiar walking pose, stick in hand. Tall sculpted stone pillars, probably again from Gingee, encircle the statue. Slightly to the north of the Gandhi statue is the Memorial raised by the French in honour of the soldiers from French India who died in World War I. This is a poignant piece of art, the centrepiece of which is a soldier with his head bent in reverence. Moving scenes are engraved on the back of the monument, which is a large rectangular slab. It is surrounded by beautifully maintained lawns and hedges.

The beach in this part of Pondicherry is narrow, but pleasant and clean. For about 4 miles south, this is a very good place to swim. The boulevard in front of the beach here, known as **Goubert Salai**, is wide and well-maintained and provides a promenade for jogging, walking or simply sitting, both morning and evening.

Going south along the boulevard, the visitor soon reaches the **lighthouse** and the new **pier**. At this point, where the coast begins to curve, a magnificent statue of Dupleix, which originally stood on the pedestal now occupied by the statue of Gandhi, has been re-erected. Set in the middle of a small and beautifully manicured children's park, the statue dominates this part of the

Facade of the French colonial Sacred Heart church.

beach as much as the Gandhi statue does the northern end.

Before turning back into the city the visitor can follow the boulevard, which now becomes the South Boulevard, all the way to the Botanical Gardens. The major attraction on this road is the **Church of the Sacred Heart of Jesus**. Gothic in style and serene in atmosphere, it has some noteworthy features: three large stained-glass panels that tell the life of Jesus, and many handsome arches that span the nave. Further along the boulevard on the southern side is the **cemetery**. Those interested in monuments will find several interesting tombs with marble decorations from Europe. The **Botanical Gardens** mark the end of the South Boulevard and the beginning of West Boulevard. Set up in 1826, it has grown over the decades to become one of the best botanical gardens in the South, with unusual and exotic plants from all over the country and abroad. An interesting little aquarium is an adjunct to the Gardens.

Getting back to the beach front area again, the visitor comes upon a statue of Joan of Arc on Rue Dumas, set as usual in a garden (which, however, is not as well maintained as it should be). A universal symbol of resistance, the Maid of Orleans is shown in an appropriately heroic pose. A short distance away is the church of **Notre Dame des Anges**, a striking structure with twin square towers. Built around 1865, the church boasts a rare oil painting of Our Lady of the Assumption, another gift from Napoleon III.

At the northern end of Rue Dumas is the French **Institute of Indology**. Established in the mid-1950s by an eminent French Indologist, Dr Jean Filliozat, the Institute has expanded its scope to include various scientific disciplines. It is now an internationally renowned research organisation and provides an abiding link between France and India, since it works in cooperation with several French universities and research organisations. The French Government maintains the **Alliance Française**, located at the southern end

of Rue Dumas, which promotes French culture and the teaching of the French language. It has a well-equipped library of French books and periodicals, and organises shows of French cinema, music, theatre and art.

The most eminent Indian in the history of Pondicherry was Ananda Ranga Pillai. He was Dupleix's trusted confidant and trade agent, and he enjoyed unlimited powers and prestige in his time. His more important claim to fame lies in his diary, covering the period 1736-60. It is a storehouse of information not only about the French rule in India, but also about the social customs and manners of the period. **Ananda Ranga Pillai's house** on Rue Rangapoulle has been converted into a museum which is a must for the visitor. Architecturally it is a fusion of the French and Indian styles – a graceful building, lavishly furnished and decorated. It gives the visitor an understanding of how an 18th century Indian nobleman lived in Pondicherry.

The visitor moves on to what might be called the Indian part of Pondicherry. Rue Rangapoulle branches off Jawaharlal Nehru Street, the main shopping centre of the city. The stretch from the canal to West Boulevard is filled with shopping areas, restaurants, teashops and pubs with names like Jolly Bar. One can do no better than just flow along with the traffic, and encounter something new at every street corner.

The last stop for the visitor is **Aurobindo Ashram**, the best-known landmark of Pondicherry, the presence of which is felt in every part of the town. Sri Aurobindo, after whom it is named, was an accomplished scholar in English and several European and Indian languages. After a stint of teaching, he plunged into the freedom movement with great fervour, but was eventually disillusioned about obtaining any immediate results. He was imprisoned by the British three times but never convicted. His mind gradually moved towards the spiritual, and during his last period of imprisonment he began to practise yoga intensely. In 1910 he re-

Conserving the surplus from nature's bounty.

tired from politics and found political asylum in Pondicherry, where he continued his spiritual discipline of yoga, in search of a complete realisation that would unite spirit and matter. A few disciples joined him in this quest, but it was not until the Mother, born Mira Alfassa in Paris, joined him, that the Ashram began to be organised. Sri Aurobindo soon retired into the exclusive practice of yoga, leaving it to the Mother to guide the disciples and the way of life of the Ashram.

Sri Aurobindo died in 1950, and the Mother in 1973. Their **Samadhi** in the main Ashram is the focal point of all disciples and followers. (The main Ashram buildings are in the block bounded by Rue de la Marine and Rue Giles.) The tomb has two chambers, one above the other, in which lie the remains of Sri Aurobindo and the Mother.

The Ashram, in addition to practising its primarily spiritual vocation, also provides scope for concrete practical activity for its followers who come from all over the world. These include all spheres of enterprise, from construction and farming to shoe making and laundering. It has a large library, of course, and an active publishing programme. It would be difficult to describe all the activities of the Ashram. The visitor is advised to go to the Reception Centre in the main building to obtain the guide to the Ashram. Those who stay in one of the Ashram guest-houses are issued special passes which enable them to visit Ashram installations that are out of bounds to others.

Auroville, the City of Dawn, is a logical extension of the aspirations that Sri Aurobindo and the Mother had for mankind. It is intended to be a future-oriented international city where all persons of goodwill can come and live together in peace and develop all aspects of life, "obeying only one authority – that of the Supreme Truth". Auroville is a voluntary commune, 6 miles (10 km) northwest of Pondicherry, where around 800 individuals from 28 nations live. Though it is eventually expected to be an integrated city for a population of 50,000, construction in Auroville has not been following a logical pattern. It does indeed look like a city of the future with its near-surrealistic architecture, the result of diverse experiments in building materials, techniques and styles.

Auroville has as its core the **Matrimandir**, the spiritual centre of the city, for meditation on the divine consciousness. Its universality is symbolised by an urn in its amphitheatre which contains earth from 124 countries and all the states of India. **Bharat Nivas**, intended to be a centre for Indian culture, arts, products and cuisine is not yet complete. Auroville, built on arid land, has cultivated a considerable portion, and has constructed small dams, wells and other sources of water supply, planted many trees. It produces nearly half the food supply for its residents. The institutions and structures in Auroville are spread out and it would be quite difficult to look around without a car. Upon arrival in Auroville, the visitor should go to the Information Centre at **Promesse** for guidance.

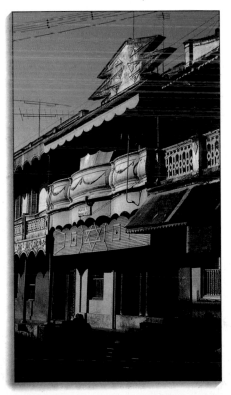

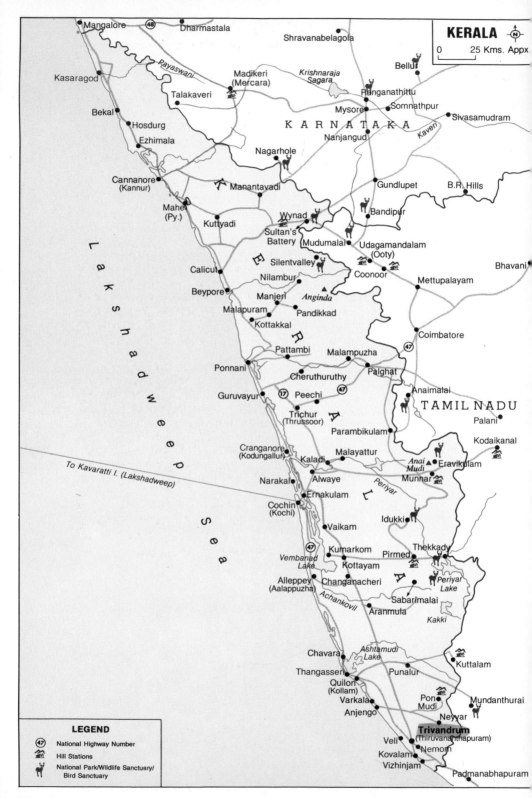

Just over 15,500 sq miles (38,800 sq km) in area, Kerala is a long (360 miles/576 km) and narrow (averaging 30 miles/48 km, and not broader than 75 miles/120 km) strip along the southwestern tip of India. The narrow ribbon of palm-fringed beaches gives way inland to the highlands of the Western Ghats, rising to 5,000 ft (1,525 m) at their highest point in the state. No less than a quarter of the area is covered by forests, with more than 600 identified varieties of trees. With an annual rainfall exceeding 100 inches (2.54 m) in several districts, it is green and lush throughout the year. Paddy fields and coconut palms cover the plains, while up in the hills there are plantations of arecanut, cardamom, rubber, pepper, tea and coffee.

Today, with its 25 million people, Kerala is not only one of the most densely populated of all Indian states, but also the most advanced in terms of family planning and literacy. The official language is Malayalam. The people of Kerala have traditionally been distinguished for their ingenuity and daring. The Malayali diaspora has taken its people virtually to every inhabited continent of the world, but their link with their beautiful home state invariably remains strong.

Whilst the majority of Kerala's population is Hindu, one third is Christian – Syrian Christians, converted in the early years of this millennium, and Roman Catholics, converted in the 16th century. There is also a sizable population of Muslims of Arab descent and converts. There was once also a thriving Jewish population in Cochin, dwindled since the establishment of the state of Israel. All of these communities generally co-existed harmoniously; paradoxically, though Keralites are religious, they pride themselves on their rationalist tradition and have more than once elected Communist governments.

Kerala is rich both in the bounty of nature and in the creations of man: beautiful beaches and rivers, hills and forest sanctuaries, forts and palaces, monuments and memorials, shrines and festivals, and a fascinating heritage of art and culture.

Preceding pages, Kerala's most spectacular event: the Onam boat races.

THE BEACHES OF TRIVANDRUM

Once, long, long ago, the sage Parasurama hurled his battle-axe into the sea and renounced all war. The waters parted and the receding sea threw up a lovely tropical paradise in the furthest southwestern reaches of India.

It was to this land of spices, timber and ivory, a land that traders called the "treasure trove of the East", that the biremes of King Solomon and the faith of St Thomas came, and the Arabs, the Jews and the Chinese, the Greeks and the Romans, and – following Vasco Da Gama's route – the Portuguese, the Danes, the Dutch, the French and the English. What they found was one of the world's most hospitable regions.

Judaism, Christianity and Islam found a haven in Kerala first came in India, long before they went westwards. The visible symbols of the contributions made to Kerala by the great religions of the world are their shrines found everywhere, their festivals celebrated by all, and the peace in which people of all faiths have lived for 2,000 years.

The main entry point into Kerala is Thiru-anantha-puram, or what is called **Trivandrum** today: the abode of the sacred snake Anantha on which Lord Vishnu, the Preserver, reclines. It is also one of the loveliest capital cities in the country, small, green and clean.

The **Sri Ananthapadmanabhaswamy temple** dominates Trivandrum. This ancient Vishnu temple with a seven-storey *gopuram* is a splendid example of Dravidian temple architecture, to which the barest embellishment of the purely Keralite variety has been added. Exquisite stone carvings and pavilions with beautifully sculpted pillars – the Kulasekhara Mandapam and the temple corridor are eye-catching – abound in this temple which overlooks a tranquil tank, the **Padama Theertham**. The image of Lord Padmanabha reclining on Anantha is viewed through three doors opening on the sanctum.

Legend has it that the temple was first

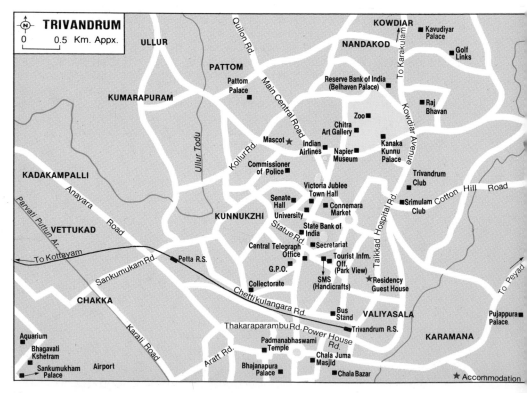

built to house an idol found in a nearby forest. Over the years the temple grew, till in the 18th century the princely state of Travancore, the southernmost part of Kerala, was dedicated to its deity. Since then, the rights and the possessions of its rulers belonged to the deity, and the Maharajas of Travancore were considered only the regents of the deity. They rebuilt the present temple in 1773. It is open only to Hindus, and only at specific times. All those entering its precincts have to conform to its code of attire. Despite the entry restrictions, the temple beckons every visitor to "the city on seven hills" and a drive around its square will offer glimpses of both a glorious architecture and a fervent faith.

The visitor will not find similar restrictions in Trivandrum's most beautiful Public Park. The setting for the magnificent **Zoo**, the **Napier Museum**, the **Sri Chitra Art Gallery** and **Observatory Hill**. The colourful red-and-brown Museum has a collection of South Indian bronzes, Keralite ornaments and costumes and a model of a *tharawad*, the traditional home of a Nair community joint family.

The Art Gallery has several masterpieces from Japan, China, Indonesia, and from other parts of India, including Rajput and Mughal miniatures, and replicas of work from Ajanta, Bagh and Tanjore. But the pride of its collection is the work of a native son, Raja Ravi Varma of Travancore. A painter of the Academy style favoured in the 19th and early 20th centuries, Ravi Varma was considered the finest artist in India in that era. His paintings of the mythology of religion are reflected today in the scores of religious pictures found in every Hindu home and workplace. But among Ravi Varma's finest work were his portraits and scenes from real life. The section in the Art Gallery named after him also has many items of Ravi Varma memorabilia.

The sprawling Botanical Gardens with their wealth of exotic plant life, the Zoo and the Aquarium are the second part of an all-day outing in the heart of the city. In this small, compressed area,

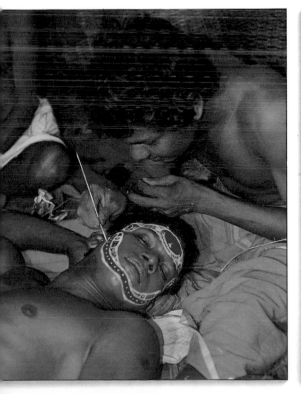

the fascinating display ranges from art and culture to flora and fauna.

The highlight of the Public Park complex is the Napier Museum, its many gables and sloped roofs fusing the traditional architecture of Kerala with the British Colonial style of the early 20th century. This blend is to be found in many of Trivandrum's palaces and public buildings. These include the **Kaudiyar Palace**, home of the Maharajas of Travancore, other palaces in the Fort, most of them now public offices, the Legislative Chamber and the Secretariat, the Victoria Jubilee Town Hall and the University buildings. Visitors interested in architecture might also like to meet Laurie Baker, a British architect, who has now made Kerala his home, and is propagating a low-cost style of architecture that blends the traditional with the modern.

Trivandrum is also developing as a science research centre and there are several national research laboratories in the city. Many of them welcome visitors – with prior permission, of course. Visiting the Space Research Centre, however, is likely to be more difficult.

Trivandrum offers the traveller more than sightseeing. **Shanmukam beach** by the airport is a pleasant, clean stretch, but not really a bather's beach (for that one has to go further afield). Trivandrum offers several yoga institutes and daily demonstrations of the famed martial arts of Kerala Kalaripayattu the best known of them that are said to predate *kung fu* and other Far Eastern forms of stylised combat. There are also several organisations which stage daily recitals of the ancient Kerala masked dance-drama, Kathakali. Superb masks in brilliant colours, gorgeously ornate costumes that weigh as much as 80 lb (40 kg), the oil-lit atmosphere and storytelling in mime and gesture make this an experience not to be missed in Kerala. The occasional Mohini Attam recital, a graceful dance full of seductive lyricism, is perhaps easier to appreciate, but the rich and dignified stylisation of Kathakali make it an art form that transcends the charms of pure rhythm.

Below left, Padmanabhapuram palace. Below, backwaters church.

Trivandrum – and indeed all of Kerala – offers a variety of handicrafts with its ivory and wood carving, and its delicate lacework. For shoppers or window-shoppers, **SMSM Handicrafts Emporium** near the Secretariat offers a variety which makes it a must on every visitor's programme.

Most visitors to Trivandrum, however, come in quest of its beaches, and Kovalam, 9 miles (15 km) to the south, is internationally famed.

Idyllic Kovalam, a sheltered natural bay with a broad, dazzling white palm-fringed beach offers five-star facilities as well as yoga, meditation, Ayurvedic massages and Kathakali in the dim flickering light of traditional temple oil lamps. There is ample secluded space for sunbathing, safe bathing in the placid blue waters of the bay, trips out in catamarans for those who want a dip in the deep, skin-diving and other water sports and there are several hotels that offer up-market comforts.

Round the corner from the bay, there are several cottages and guest houses for the traveller who seeks adventure rather than comfort while on holiday. Here anything goes and life can be rugged, but many like it that way and Kovalam draws such a crowd too.

The **Veli Tourist Village**, on the other hand, is more of a family resort. The backwaters form a broad lagoon, fenced off from the sea by a sand bar that is a beach. Surrounding this idyllic body of water, no more than 10 ft (3 m) deep anywhere, are coconut groves and low hills covered with lush greenery. The Tourist Village offers boating in a variety of craft, safe bathing in the lagoon, sunbathing on the beach beyond and a dip in the sea. The gardens surrounding the infrastructure of the Village have been landscaped to make picnicking enjoyable, while the hillocks provide enough challenge to make hiking a favourite holiday recreation.

Until Independence and the reorganisation of the princely states, much of this coastal strip was part of the erstwhile kingdom of Travancore, now southern Kerala. It is not surprising to

Bovine overhaul in river.

find in **Padmanabhapuram** a palace of the Maharajas of Travancore. Padmanabhapuram, 34 miles (55 km) from Trivandrum, was once the capital of Travancore; now it is a village in decline, with only its preserved 17th century palace and museum of interest. **Puvar**, the ancient Ophir with which King Solomon traded, is now a fishing village with few relics of its past; **Colachel** has a Danish fort and a superb beach and **Suchindram**, a magnificent temple.

Nearer Trivandrum and to its northeast is the Neyyar Dam. The Shivananda Yoga Vedanta Ashram here has an annual yoga meet that attracts practitioners from all over the world; it also holds year-round classes.

The Neyyar reservoir is set in a wild life sanctuary where elephants, wild dogs, wild bears, monkeys and a rich variety of birds can be spotted. A crocodile hatchery and a deer park have also been opened by the side of the reservoir.

Another sanctuary further on, just 6 miles (10 km) short of Ponmudi, is the

Peppara Wild Life Sanctuary in the Cardamom Hills. This too is elephant country, and rich in birdlife as well.

Every Indian state must have a few hill stations for vacationers to beat the heat of the southern plains. Kerala is no exception and has quite a few. Of them Ponmudi, the "golden crown" of the Golden Valley, is Trivandrum's own hill station. About 35 miles (60 km) northeast of Trivandrum, and located at 3,500 ft (1,066 m) in the Cardamom Hills by the Tamil Nadu border, Ponmudi is unspoilt, refreshingly cool and mist-shrouded almost the year round. It is surrounded by tea estates and hill ranges covered with forests. A visit to Ponmudi offers one the delights of trekking in these forests, of wandering in the tea estates, and discovering the flora and fauna of the hills.

Offering further enrichment to that experience are **Anjengo**, north of Trivandrum, the East India Company's first settlement on this coast (1684), **Aruvikkara**, just outside Trivandrum, and **Varkala**, a major pilgrim centre 34 miles (55 km) north of Trivandrum.

The English cemetery and other relics of the past in Anjengo will interest the historian, the beach will entrance others. Aruvikkara is a picnic spot but is better known as a pilgrim centre. Varkala is one of Kerala's major Hindu pilgrim centres. The Janardana temple here is believed to be over 2,000 years old. Its bell is said to be from a 17th century Dutch sailing ship, whose captain gifted it to the temple when his prayers were answered. The mineral springs here are much sought after for their curative properties. There is a nature cure centre nearby.

In an eastern suburb of Varkala is **Sivagiri Hill**, where Shri Narayana Guru, the philosopher-saint, established an *ashram*. The *ashram* and the Guru's *samadhi* (sanctified tomb) attract those in need of spiritual guidance as well as those paying their respects to a great social reformer. Two water tunnels link the waterways of Trivandrum with those of Quilon. Varkala's beautiful beach makes the town a resort, spa and pilgrim centre, all in one.

Left, Kovalam's enticing beaches beckon bathers. Right, sleeping it off.

THE BACKWATERS OF KERALA

A special delight Kerala offers is the trip on a slow boat through its forests and its palm-shaded back-waters and canals, enjoying magnificent scenery all along the waterways and stopping to admire what history and religion have left in many towns and villages along the way. Motor-powered launches provide regular passenger services, but the same experience in a covered country boat is far more pleasurable and authentic. The design of these boats goes back to the Chinese influence on this coast.

It is possible to make a backwater journey from Trivandrum to Kodungallur, a distance of nearly 155 miles (250 km), or from Trivandrum to Kottayam, a distance of about 110 miles (175 km). But both journeys really start from the ancient town of Quilon (Kollam), about 44 miles (70 km) north of Trivandrum.

Once a major international entrepôt known to the Phoenicians and the Ar-abs, the Romans and the Greeks, the Chinese and the Persians, **Quilon** is still a major commercial centre in Kerala. Together with two other important trading centres, **Alleppey** and **Kottayam**, it forms a triangle that is not only commercially affluent but also unspoilt in heritage and natural surroundings.

Beautifully situated in the midst of coconut groves on the southern banks of the vast **Ashtamudi Lake**, the Lake with Eight Creeks, with its shore-level promontories of red laterite and china clay, Quilon is a picturesque town, and its commercial activity seems a world away. Cashewnut is its main business now, but medieval sailors from east and west came to Quilon in search of spices, timber, fauna, ivory and textiles. The Chinese established a trading settlement here as far back as AD 9. They also exchanged envoys during the time of Kublai Khan, and left behind a heritage of fishing nets fixed to poles, cargo boats covered with thatch, and many shards of exquisite chinaware that have been excavated in and around Quilon.

Fishing for a livelihood.

Chinnakkada, the busy bazaar that is the heart of Quilon, the **Thirumullavaram beach** and the park and beach at **Kochupilamoodu** are places to visit in this town associated with the origin of the present Malayalam era in AD 825. So is the Roman Catholic cathedral, the history of which goes back to the creation of the first Roman Catholic See in India, when Friar Jordanus was consecrated Bishop in 1530.

About 2 miles (3 km) north of Quilon is the historic town of **Thangasseri** where you can picnic among the relics of its European past or frolic on the beach in the shadow of the old lighthouse, one of the earliest built in British times. The old Portuguese, Dutch and English cemeteries have many a tale to tell; the remains of the Portuguese and Dutch fortifications are memorials to a glorious past; and the old British Residency is now a lovely guest house on the shores of the Ashtamudi Lake.

North of Quilon, 53 miles (85 km) away, is **Alleppey**, the "Venice of the East", situated on the Vembanad Lake, the longest lake in India. A maze of canals and a network of bridges give this busy commercial town its descriptive sobriquet. Alleppey is known for its coir, the retted fibre of the coconut husk, and for black pepper. Coir yarn, coir mats and matting, and a wealth of other coir products are manufactured in Alleppey and are good buys.

August-September is the season of Onam, the famed harvest festival of Kerala. This is the best time to visit the backwaters of the state. The colourful water carnivals, the gaily clad women and their graceful dances, the ornate and bright-hued floor decorations (*kolam* and *rangoli*) using coloured powder or, more beautifully, flowers, and the festive spirit everywhere, make all of Kerala a lively place at this time of the year. But what sets apart the backwaters country and makes its festivities even more joyous are the *Vallam Kallis*, the boat races.

The Nehru Trophy Boat Race Day, held at Alleppey on the second Saturday of August every year, sees the most colourful event in Kerala. There are races for a variety of boats, but the biggest race of the day is the one for the *chundan vallams*, the giant snake boats. Each boat is over 100 ft (30.5 m) long, with raised snake-like prows, and is gaily decorated. With crews of more than 100 men rowing in perfect rhythm to traditional boat songs, the race has become part of an unforgettable drama for the thousands who line the banks to cheer themselves hoarse. There is nothing like it anywhere else in India – except at other boat race centres in the backwaters country of Kerala. It is no wonder then that the Sports Authority of India has set up its Kayaking and Canoeing Centre here to train young oarsmen to international standards.

About 31 miles (50 km) southeast of Alleppey, near the town of Chengannur, is **Aranmula**, where the second of the most famous boat races is held. Aranmula, on the banks of the placid river Pamba, is a pilgrim centre where the temple is dedicated to Lord Parthasarathy – Lord Krishna in the role of charioteer to Arjuna – and its boat race is part

of the temple ritual. The annual commemoration of the deity's installation is celebrated on the last day of the week-long Onam festival. It is on this auspicious day (in August-September, though the day changes from year to year according to the Malayalam calendar) that the snake boats race against each other on the river Pamba, thousands of singers churning up the calm waters of the river with their short oars that plunge in and out of the waters in time to the chanted beat.

Other boat races are held in Kottayam, but almost every backwater in this part of Kerala celebrates Onam by taking to the water. The Cochin and Kottayam races are of recent origin and are more in the nature of sport than of religious ritual. But at Payipad, 2 miles (3 km) from Haripad, where there is a famous temple of Lord Subramaniya, the races are associated with the temple festival. The 3-day festival starts on Onam day, and on the first 2 days snake boat processions are held on the Acharkovil river. The third day is race day, the climax of the festival.

Approximately 15 miles (25 km) as the crow flies from Alleppey is the prosperous town of **Kottayam**. In fact, it is the first town in India to attain 100 percent literacy. A major commercial centre of Kerala, Kottayam lies in the foothills of the Western Ghats, beautiful backwaters to its west and scenic, fertile mountains to its east. A major centre of the trade in rubber, tea, coffee, pepper, cardamom (Kerala is the original home of cardamom), and other produce from the plantations to its east, Kottayam's prosperity is echoed in the city's facilities.

A major educational and Malayalam publishing centre, Kottayam is a city of handsomely built schools, commercial complexes and civic facilities. It also has the most successful writers' cooperative in India, and its publishing activity is phenomenal. But Kottayam has a strong spiritual side to it too. There are several sects and divisions of the Syrian Christian faith due to the influence of history over the years, and many

Thaiyyam dancer painted to represent Chamundi.

292

of them have their episcopal seats here.

The best known churches are the historic **Valia Palli** and **Cheria Palli**, both with colourful frescoes enriching their dim interiors. In the 9th century Valia Palli, there are Pahlavi inscriptions and a stone cross said to have been carved by St Thomas. This cross, it is believed, came from the first church Thomas founded in Kerala, in Kodungallur.

The 90 miles (150 km) to Kottayam from Trivandrum can be covered by road or rail. Six miles (10 km) to the west of Kottayam is **Kumarakom**, now being developed as a holiday resort. If the backwaters route is taken from Alleppey, Kumarakom, lying on the eastern shore of the Vembanad Lake, is only 6 miles (10 km) away from the coastal town.

The islands on the lake across from Kumarakom are home to a large variety of migratory birds. The birds can be watched from the comfort of Baker's Bungalow or other vantage points on the lake's shore. The Kerala tourist authorities have taken over the mansion and have done well to preserve much of its yesteryear charm. The *punkahs* still hang from the ceiling, but no one manually operates those cloth-on-woodframe fans any more. They remain, like much else in Baker's Bungalow, symbols of another age.

Another 6 miles (10 km) north of Kottayam is **Ettumanur**, famous for its Shiva temple. Beautiful murals on the inner and outer walls and some superb sculpture in the temple are the special features of this ancient shrine. Non-Hindus are prohibited from entering the temple precincts.

Northwest of Ettumanur, about 15 miles (25 km) along the road to Cochin, is **Vaikom**, where there is another famous Shiva temple. Here, too, non-Hindus are not allowed to go beyond the temple gates. About 25 miles (40 km) beyond Vaikom is Cochin-Ernakulam, one of Kerala's most attractive tourist destinations in its own right; but the backwaters country has a special charm of its own.

COCHIN

Cosmopolitan **Cochin**, the commercial capital of Kerala, glories in the title of "Queen of the Arabian Sea". A city of peninsulas and islands with a mainland centre, Cochin has a magnificent natural harbour, almost in the middle of the city, created by the underwater Malabar mudbanks that ensure calm waters.

Cruising around the islands through the backwaters extending to the south and the east from the sea and skirting the harbour is one of the many delights Cochin has to offer. Motor launches from jetties on mainland Ernakulam will take you to Fort Cochin and Old Cochin on the southern peninsula, and around the islands.

Factories producing coir goods and frozen shrimp are found in all these islands in the backwaters that are part of the huge Vembanad lagoon. **Gundu Island**, the tiniest of the islands in the lagoon, nestles in a small bay that dents the biggest island of them all, Vypeen. It has a model coir cooperative, the only building on its five acres. Visitors are welcome to watch the coconut fibre being woven on looms into beautiful mats and fashioned into other household articles.

Vypeen and Vallarpadam: At Narakkal, on **Vypeen**, is the famous **Veliyatta Parambil temple**, where trial by ordeal, using molten metal, was practised until 200 years ago. There is also a Shiva temple nearby that celebrates Shivaratri handsomely. At the other end of the island, Pallipuram, almost overlooking Kodungallur, is a Portuguese fort. Together with the one in Kodungallur, the fort must have ensured that no unwanted vessels sailed up the narrows here.

Vallarpadam, a large island to the northeast of Gundu, is home to an ancient church dedicated to St Mary. The miracles she is believed to have performed over the years bring the faithful in their numbers on an annual pilgrimage to this old shrine. To the east of Vallarpadam is beautiful **Bolghatty**,

with a Dutch palace at its southern tip, built in 1744 in the Dutch-Kerala style. Until 1947 it was the residence of the British Resident to the court of Cochin. The situation of the palace is enchanting, but it is not very well tended as a government-run hotel.

South of Bolghatty, and across the main channel leading into Cochin harbour is the most important part of Cochin, **Willingdon Island**. This is a man-made island, created in the early 20th century with sand dredged from the harbour. It serves as the headquarters of India's Southern Naval Command. One of the major Indian seaports, it also houses the airport, railway terminus and several government offices. To land or take off from Cochin airport is an experience comparable to arriving at Kai Tak airport in Hong Kong: one seems to be headed for the water either way, uncertain of the outcome till one is actually firmly on land or high above the clouds.

Almost as spotlessly clean as Willingdon Island is Old Cochin, the peninsula comprising Fort Cochin and ancient Mattancherry. Its history predates its Western conquerors. Some of the most interesting buildings in India are to be found here – old Portuguese, Dutch and British architecture, preserved as a striking contrast to styles in the rest of Kerala.

A rich heritage from the past: What is most distinctive about Old Cochin, especially viewed from the sea, is its skyline. Giant contraptions that seem to be from another world dominate the coast all around the Fort: these are the Chinese fishing nets, unique to this part of Kerala and living symbols of a centuries-old Chinese influence on this coast. The palm-woven, broad-brimmed conical hats the fishermen wear are yet another reminder that the Chinese had a thriving settlement in this part of India. So are the roofs of many buildings in Kerala turning up slightly at the corners, *cheena* firecrackers that explode with a thunderous noise, and clay jars distinctly in the Chinese style. However, it is the giant Chinese fishing nets, similar to those used in Southeast Asia, that at-

Left, timeless backwaters bearing fishing craft.

tract every visitor, especially those with cameras.

These fishing nets are as effective as they are dramatic. Ingeniously constructed, these giant cantilevered fish traps comprise coconut trunk platforms on elephantine teak-log legs stuck solid in the beach, and supporting teakwood frameworks and extended poles from which hang giant nylon nets. The net, tied to four poles that link it to pulleys and counterweights, is lowered into the water by ingenious use of the counter-balancing rocks and then hauled out of it 15 minutes later by a team of four manning each platform. By pulling on the rope with the counterweights, the team raises the net to platform level; then one of the team members climbs up one of the poles from which the net hangs and scoops the catch into a basket, and back goes the net into the water again.

Except during the May-August monsoon season, the nets are worked throughout the year. When in use they seem a throwback to another techno-logical era and of limited effectiveness in this day. But as a way of life, as traditional symbols of a historic past and as a sight that rivets the attention of any visitor to Cochin, they are permanent features of the Kerala scene that few would wish to vanish.

Behind the Chinese fishing nets are garden houses, stately office buildings and tree-lined lanes of another age. The occasional multi-storey building has made some inroads into the 18th and 19th century street facades, but generally Fort Cochin still looks much the same for decades.

The oldest church in India: St Francis's of Cochin is the oldest European church in India, its change from Catholic chapel to Protestant shrine a reflection of Cochin's history. On Christmas Day, 1500, just two years after Vasco da Gama had landed near Calicut, the Portuguese were granted the right to trade on the Cochin coast. Three years later, Alphonso de Albuquerque built a stockade of coconut trunks lashed together with coir ropes on the site of

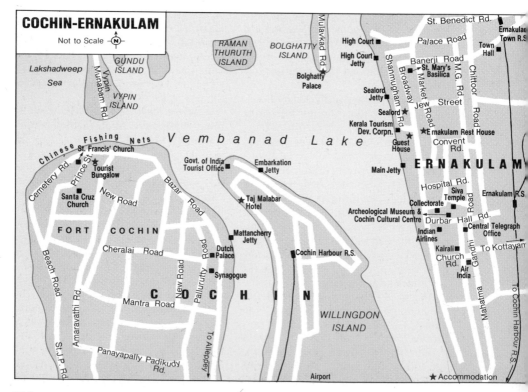

today's Fort. There, in Fort St Emmanuel, five Franciscan friars built the chapel of St Bartholomew. After Admiral Almeida negotiated a more permanent settlement here in 1506, stone-and-mortar buildings were constructed, including the church of St Anthony, consecrated in 1516 on the site of the earlier chapel.

Vasco da Gama, who had returned to the east as the Governor of the Indies in 1524, died on Christmas Eve that same year during a visit to Cochin. He was buried in St Anthony's Church, and the original rails and tombstone still mark the spot where the great navigator was buried. His remains were taken to Lisbon in 1538, but in this church the man who discovered the route to the Indies in 1497 is not forgotten.

It was in 1663 that St Anthony's passed into Dutch hands and became a Lutheran church, remaining so long after Cochin came under British control in 1795. In the middle of the 19th century it became an Anglican church and acquired its present name, St Francis's.

The church has several antiquities, including a wealth of records. Some of its prized possessions are a palm-leaf title deed the local Raja gave the Portuguese in 1503, the *Doop Boek* – a Dutch baptismal register dating to the days the church became Protestant – and stately *punkahs*, those ancient cloth-on-wood-frame fans that had to be manually pulled. Not far from St Francis's Church is Santa Cruz Cathedral, a Roman Catholic church of a later age. The paintings in the cathedral are particularly beautiful.

Mattancherri Palace: Around the corner from the church and the battlements, and facing Willingdon Island to the west, is the Mattancherry jetty. Beside it, more of Cochin's fascinating 16th-century history is revealed: the **Mattancherri palace** was built by the Portuguese in 1555 and gifted to the Raja of Cochin. Built in an amalgam of Portuguese Colonial and Kerala styles, it was extensively renovated in Burgher Bungalow style by the Dutch in 1663, as a sincere token of their regard for Cochin

Chinese fishing nets, Cochin.

royalty, and it became known as the Dutch Palace.

The Rajas of Cochin were crowned in the palace's Durbar Hall; today it is their portrait gallery. In these ancient rooms are 17th-century murals on the walls that relate in vibrant colour the story of the epic *Ramayana*. Palanquins, coronation robes, furniture, weapons and the woodwork in the palace are other relics to be admired during a tour of the building.

The same compound houses two temples used by the Cochin royalty for worship, the **Bhagavathi temple**, and the circular, stupa-like **Krishna temple** reflecting the Buddhist influence that existed in Kerala until the 8th century. Sharing a wall with the Krishna temple is one of the most interesting parts of Cochin, the **Mattancherri Synagogue** and **Jew Town**.

Legend dates Jewish trade with Kerala from the times of Solomon and Nebuchadnezzar. The stories of Doubting Thomas speak of Jews who followed the same trade winds from West Asia and settled here long before his arrival. Certainly there would have been Jewish settlements after the Roman destruction of the Second Temple in Jerusalem in AD 70, and records of AD 370 speak of over 10,000 Jews living in and around Musiris, the Kodungallur of today.

There are not many of these Asian Jews (locally called the "Black Jews") left, but they still have three synagogues open for worship in Kerala: two in Ernakulam, mainland Cochin, and one in Parur. Two synagogues in Mattancherri, one in Chennamangalam and another in Mala are now closed. One of the two synagogues in Ernakulam is the biggest in Kerala and claims to have the oldest copy of the Old Testament in the world, stored in a gold-plated box. These synagogues were built when the Black Jews fled Portuguese persecution in Cranganore and sought the protection of the Rajahs of Cochin in the mid-16th century.

It was to Kerala's hospitable shores that the Sephardic or "White Jews" also

Ginger warehouse in India's spice bowl.

came in the early 16th century when the Inquisition drove them from Spain and Portugal. They were joined by their Ashkenazy kin from Central Europe and together, for social and cultural reasons, they formed settlements separate from the Black Jews in Kerala. That separation continued even when they fled Portuguese persecution in Cranganore and settled in Cochin, establishing what is called Jew Town.

There are less than 100 White Jews in Jew Town and Fort Cochin today (most have migrated to Israel), but they still try to maintain the ambience of the "town" they founded, a street or two of picture-postcard houses out of another age, in 17th century Dutch and traditional Kerala style. Here is the best maintained synagogue in India, built in 1568, rebuilt in 1664, two years after the Portuguese depredation, and restored 100 years later.

Exquisite, hand-painted Chinese tiles, no two of which are alike, pave the floor, and the gleaming embellishments in the synagogue make it one of the most striking places of Jewish worship anywhere. Its treasures include ancient scrolls of Mosaic law in the tabernacle, golden crowns given by the Maharajas of Travancore and Cochin, silver lamps presented by the first British Resident to the court of Cochin, and the copper plate grant from the Rajas that enabled the Jews to call Kerala their home. A congregation still faithfully gathers here, for wherever 10 adult male Jews assemble services can be conducted. The Sabbath is still celebrated, as are Purim and Passover and all the other Jewish festivals. Such celebrations are what make Jew Town and its synagogue a living symbol of the tolerance with which the Malabar coast received all religions.

A symbol of faith: Not very far from the Mattancherry synagogue is the "leaning" **Coonen Cross**, symbol of another faith that endured. Tying themselves to this cross, the Thomas Christians revolted against the Latinisation of their Church by the Portuguese in 1653. They took the Oath of the Coonen Cross

Union demand with literary tag.

to resist the Roman Church and to remain true to the patriarchy of Antioch and the Syriac rites they had practised long before the Western world had heard of Christianity.

Cochin has several well-organised museums and theatres. Perhaps the most interesting of these is the **Museum of Kerala History and its Makers** in Edappally, on the road to Alwaye. Starting with Neolithic man, the Museum narrates the story of Kerala – St Thomas, Vasco da Gama, the Rajahs and the scholars – in models and in sight and sound.

The **Parishath Thamburan Museum** in Ernakulam has a fine collection of 19th century paintings, copies of ancient murals and sculpture and memorabilia from the Cochin royal family's collection. A complementary collection is found in the **Hill Palace Museum** in Tripunithura.

Kathakali (*katha*-story, *kali*-play), the 400-year-old dance-drama form that once used to bring Hindu mythology alive in Kerala's Hindu temples, is now staged in Cochin's art centres and auditoria. At least three performances are held every night: at the Cochin Cultural Centre, at the See India Foundation and at Art Kerala, all in Ernakulam. Here visitors are welcome backstage to watch the dancers put on their elaborate make-up, to examine their costumes that weigh up to 88 lbs each, and to marvel at the masks. Once the performance starts, it is a thrill of a different kind, trying to follow the drama accompanied by drumming and stylised dancing.

Beaches with an atmosphere: Cochin also has beaches, but they are not the best in Kerala. What they do have is atmosphere, the air of a more leisurely and gracious age. Nowhere is this more evident than in the **Malabar Hotel** on Willingdon Island. An old world hotel of the 1930s, the Malabar (now run by the Taj group) still remains, for all its modernisation, a hostelry of a more expansive and gentle age. The Bolghatty Palace could have achieved the same ambience, but government pro-

The beautifully preserved Pardesi synagogue.

prietorship and trade unionism have made it a soulless shell.

Across the lagoon is **Ernakulam**, a contrast to Cochin in its modern bustle and commercial activity. Away from its market-place, there are a few places of interest around Ernakulam. **Tripunithura**, the seat of the former ruling family of Cochin, is about 6 miles (10 km) southeast of Ernakulam. There are several palaces here, including the **Hill Palace**, now a museum. The **Sri Purnathrayeesa temple** also draws crowds.

About 4 miles (7 km) east of Tripunithura is **Chottanikkara**, famed for its **Bhagavathi temple**. And about 3 miles (6 km) south is **Mulanthuruthi**, a major centre of the Jacobite Syrian Christians. Their 700-year-old church has several beautiful frescoes that date to its earliest days.

From Ernakulam, the National Highway heads northeast to some of the most interesting places near Cochin that make a day's excursion or two. **Alwaye** is a major junction on the highway and,

though an industrial town, still has much to offer the traveller. A swim in the Periyar river here is an ideal way to cool off; in fact, the river makes the town a summer resort. The Shivaratri festival on the banks is a colourful celebration in which the devotees pay homage to the Shiva *lingam* on the sandbank. The Union Christian College here is the first college to have been started by Indian Christians, not foreign missionaries. And the tourist guest house, beautifully situated on the riverbank, is a splendid old palace.

Parur and Kodungallur: If you branch northeast from Alwaye, you are headed for **Parur**, one of the towns of Thomas and once a major Jewish centre, and then on to an interesting but little-remembered historical location. This is **Kodungallur**, known as Musiris to the Greeks and Cranganore to the Europeans. It was also known as Mahodyapuram to the Cheraman Perumals who ruled from here. The **Cheraman Paramba**, near the **Thrivanchikulam temple**, is believed to be the site of the

Perumal rulers residence, the **Allal Perumkovilakam**.

The oldest mosque in India: The **Bhagavathi temple** nearby attracts thousands for its Bharani Festival in March-April. The mosque here, behind its modern facade a Kerala temple look-alike, is the oldest in India, its history predating the Mughal influence in the north and the Deccan. Even older is the Christian connection of Kodungallur; it was at nearby **Kottappuram** that St Thomas is believed to have landed, and the St Thomas Church here claims antiquity since then. In modern times, Kodungallur offers the remains of a Portuguese fort and a beach in its lee.

This is a tourist destination that is undeveloped but full of possibilities; among its riches are the backwaters, since Kodungallur is practically at the furthest extremity of the Vembanad Lake. Taking the slow boat back to Alwaye or from Cochin to Kodungallur is an exhilarating experience.

From Alwaye, the northeast branch of the road runs to **Kaladi**, on the banks of the Alwaye river. This is the birth-place of the great 8th century Advaita philosopher and religious reformer of India, Sri Shankaracharya, and is a major pilgrim centre. One of the two temples here contains an image of Sri Adi Shankaracharya as Dakshinamurthy, the other an image of the Sringeri Mutt's tutelar deity, Saradamba. Near the **Saradamba temple** is another temple, with an idol of Lord Krishna, believed to have been installed by Shankaracharya himself.

A newer temple is the **International temple** of Sri Ramakrishna, the *swami* commemorated in a life-size marble statue and in a splendid library. On the road to the temples is the **Sri Adi Sankara Keerthi Sthamba Mandapam**, a 150 ft (45.7 m) tall, nine-tier octagonal tower, commemorating on each floor Sri Shankaracharya's life and his work in words, symbols and pictures.

A few miles beyond Kaladi, at the top of a hill 2,000 ft (610 m) high, is a shrine dedicated to St Thomas. The footprints in the rock at **Malayattur** are said to be his. The help of St Thomas, who is believed to have meditated here and built a shrine in this wilderness, is invoked every year by thousands of pilgrims. The Malayattur Perumal festival in March/April is one of the biggest Christian festivals in South India.

A little to the south, near **Perumbavur**, is a rock-cut temple, Jain in character but Hindu in ritual. From the **Kallil temple**, 120 steps lead to a statue of Mahavira cut out of rock. Westward, off Kothamangalam on the Ernakulam-Munnar road, lies the **Thattekkad Bird Sanctuary**. The only bird sanctuary in Kerala, it encompasses both the Periyar river and teak plantations, just the right setting for a wealth of birdlife including hornbills, rollers, parrots, water birds and migratory species.

The bird sanctuary, the shrines of various faiths, the historical monuments, the rivers, lagoons and backwaters, the beaches, parks and museums make Cochin an experience of Kerala in miniature. But beyond Cochin and Kodungallur is northern Kerala, a different world awaiting discovery.

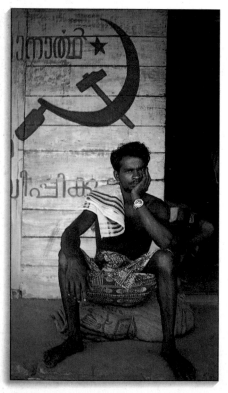

Left, Kerala has a strong Marxist tradition. Right, trainees in Kalarayipattu, Kerala's ancient martial arts.

THE HIGH RANGES

East of Kottayam lies plantation country: rolling estates of tea and coffee, rubber, cardamom and pepper, interspersed with forests and game reserves. The Western Ghats north of the Periyar river are the High Ranges, locally called the Annamalais – the Elephant Hills – with Anai Mudi, at a little short of 10,000 ft (3,000 m) the highest peak in the South. Below the Periyar are the Cardamom Hills, not so high but thickly forested and developed only in their southernmost reaches.

Ponmudi in the southern Cardamom Hills is the only hill station of note near Trivandrum and has already been mentioned. The High Range, however, is altogether more interesting; it offers not just a day's excursion in the country, but a whole holiday out in the open. At one time, travellers had to rough it out in this country, but now "mod cons" are easily available. It is still not the easiest of country stretches to travel in, but offers visitors an enjoyable experience.

The road that goes east from Kottayam to the Periyar Wild Life Sanctuary, about 75 miles (120 km) away, is a driving experience in itself. The road winds up the mountains, climbing through a carpet of tea bushes, estates of tall rubber trees and gardens of coffee, cardamom and pepper. A good place to rest during the drive is the pretty little hill town of **Peermade**, about 47 miles (75 km) out of Kottayam. The club here is something out of a picture postcard, a splash of colour surrounded by a carpet of tea-green, and set amidst rolling hills of all shades of dark green, misty purple and smoky blue. Now you are in the High Range and travelling at heights that average 7,000 ft (2,100 m) and more, about the height of the tallest peak in the Cardamom Hills.

Just south of Peermade is **Sabarimalai**, the abode of Lord Aiyappa, but it has to be approached from a road going south from Kottayam and curving up to the Pamba river. A 3-mile (5-km) trek from the river through thick forest brings you to the hill temple in the wilderness to which the faithful come from all parts of South India.

During the main festival season in December-January, the 4-hour trek often takes longer because of the throngs on the path. Pilgrims, most of them men, take strict vows that restrict them to a life of austerity for 40 days or more. During the days leading up to the Sabarimalai festival, a common sight in South Indian cities is the large number of men wearing black or saffron and sporting the beards that proclaim the vows they have taken of further self-denial. Few women make the pilgrimage, so onerous are the taboos tradition binds them to if they are to worship at the hill temple.

The road continuing east from Peermade takes the visitor to a place away from the temple in the wilderness and the sanctity that surrounds it. But in the forests and meadowed hills around the man-made Periyar Lake the visitor finds devotion of another kind. Here, in a vast area of nearly 8,608 sq ft (800 sq m), at heights ranging from 3,000 to 6,500 ft (900 m to 1,950 m), it is the preservation of wildlife that is sacred.

Road to Lake Palace: The road from Peermade joins the road from Madurai in Tamil Nadu at Kumili, and snakes through the eastern reaches of the park to reach Thekkady, overlooking the lake. This is the base camp for the **Periyar Wild Life Sanctuary and Tiger Reserve**. Accommodation ranges from deluxe comfort to ordinary dormitories, but if you have the choice, try to get a room in the **Lake Palace**; it may be a little spartan, but this erstwhile palatial watch-hut of the Maharajas of Travancore offers a serenity that cannot be matched by the crowded Thekkady lodgings.

Treetop lookouts for those who want to catch a glimpse of game by night – or even during the day – are few and far between in the reserve, but offer good watching, especially if your Forest Ranger is on the job. The more conventional method of game-spotting is to take a couple of hours in the morning and a couple more in the evening in one of the many launches that slowly circle the lake.

Forest rangers help you to spot distant game, but in this finest of elephant sanctuaries in India, you do not need much help to spot the herds of elephants. Herds of 20 to 30, sometimes more, are often spotted slowly meandering up and down the hillside, gambolling in the water or swimming across small necks in the lake to cross over to the other side. Often a ranger will take a boat up to within a few feet of a herd in the water, and the elephants continue to frolic – that's how safe they feel at Periyar. This place is a paradise for the wildlife photographer.

Spotted deer and sambar, the Indian bison and a variety of waterbirds are not difficult to come by. You need luck to spot a bear, leopard or tiger, or birds of rare species. But the experience of the cruise – at sunrise or sunset – is by itself an extraordinary one; and the anticipation of an unexpected animal or herd round the next bend can be a nail-biting experience.

In addition, Crusoe Island (12 miles / 19 km), Manakavala (6 miles/10 km), Mullakudy (80 miles/129 km), Periyar Dam (9 miles/15 km) and Thannikudy (24 miles/38 km) are short day-long picnic excursions from Thekkady. Back at Kumili, the twisting mountain road heads north for the highest ranges and the biggest plantations.

Munnar is your destination, only about 44 miles (70 km) away, though the twisting road makes it seem miles further. But there is one stop before that in this rugged terrain, and that is **Idukki**. Idukki means "narrow gorge" and that is exactly what the Periyar river gushes through to the west of the Kumili-Munnar road. On either side of the river, creating the gorge, are **Kuravan** and **Kurathi**, hills which according to folklore, are gypsy lovers who were turned into granite rocks because of a curse. Bridging the gorge is the magnificent Idukki arch dam, set against densely wooded hills and valleys traversed by a hundred rushing streams. The dam is surrounded by beauty in many forms: wilderness, man-made gardens, and the Idukki wildlife sanctuary. The flora and fauna in the sanctuary are similar to that in the Periyar sanctuary, but there are fewer facilities for game-spotting.

Heading towards **Munnar**, the road twists its way to Devikolam, the nearest town of any sort, and then you are a company town surrounded by plantations. British companies owned most of the large plantations here, with the exception of one Indian, Kannan Devan, who owned plantations even during the heydays of the Raj. The most important planter in the High Range today is Tata Tea, which oversee almost every public facility in the vicinity.

Munnar is situated at the confluence of three rivers, at a height of about 6,000 ft (1,800 m). It is the highest town in Kerala and lies at the heart of tea country. It has some of the biggest tea estates in Kerala and on either side of the High Range. Beyond lies Anai Mudi and the rich tropical forest of the Annamalai Sanctuary in Tamil Nadu, and the **Eravikulam National Park** in Kerala. **Elephantine ablutions.**

Access to the Park is now controlled by Tata Tea, who are assisting the Kerala Wildlife Department to protect the flora and fauna of the region.

The Nilgiri tahr in Eravikulam are among the rare breed of mountain goats in the world. Until a few years ago the species was fighting a losing battle for survival; now herds of 30 and more can be seen at a time. In the park, and around the estates in the Annamalais, elephants move across the border; Nilgiri langurs, lion-tailed macaques and other monkeys abound; sambars are often seen; wild dogs regularly trace the path of their prey; and with the new consciousness of conservation, even a leopard or tiger can be spotted.

A visit to Munnar is doubly rewarding: the visitors now see more game than ever before; and they also experience the flavour of life on a plantation and at the High Range Club where the planters socialise on weekends. Rugby is no longer played in the High Range Club, but golf is. There is plenty of fishing in the icy rapid streams.

An opportunity to stay on a tea estate should not be missed. Your every need is attended to in large, comfortable bungalows. But outside, life can be hard. Work at the estate means hoeing and pruning tea bushes to keep them green and to allow them to flush again. Pluckers with nimble fingers carefully but swiftly pick "two leaves and a bud" and flick them over their shoulders into their baskets. The leaves are taken to the factory and cured meticulously. All this is part of a day's work on a plantation, a domain different from the urban work environment in India. Seeing a tea-taster at work, swilling a gulp of the brew and spitting it out and repeating the process down the line, might give you a better idea of what goes into getting that cup of tea somewhere far, far away.

To return to Cochin from Munnar is to come down to earth; but you will find that the world is not such a dull place after all. Cochin, a beautiful harbor town, also has much to hold the visitor's attention.

Tea bushes amid wilderness.

TRICHUR
AND CALICUT

Trichur, 33 miles (53 km) from Alwaye on the national highway, is considered by many to be the cultural capital of Kerala. Three state academies – the Kerala Sahitya Akademi (literature), the Sangeet Natak Akademi (music and drama) and the Lalit Kala Akademi (visual arts) – have their headquarters here, the School of Drama run by the University of Calicut functions from Trichur, and the Kalamandalam Art Academy, the nerve centre of Kathakali, is not far away.

The name Trichur is an anglicised version of the Malayalam Trissivaperur, meaning the "Town with the name of Lord Shiva". The town is built around an elevated area, called the "round", in the centre of which is the **Vadakkunnatham temple**, a typical example of Keralite architecture with exquisite wood carvings. It contains the shrines of Paramashiva, Parvati, Sankaranarayana, Rama and Krishna. Legend has it that the temple was founded by the sage Parasurama who carved Kerala out from the sea.

The Trichur temple celebrates the famous *Pooram* festival every year in April. A spectacular affair, it involves a procession of 30-40 caparisoned elephants, amid the fanfare of the *Panchavadya*, five traditional Keralite musical instruments. A lavish display of fireworks goes on till dawn. The Pooram fireworks are considered the most magnificent of their kind in India and perhaps in Asia.

All those interested in the performing arts should visit **Kalamandalam**, about 18 miles (30 km) from Trichur on the Trichur-Shoranur highway. This academy was founded by Kerala's renowned poet, the late Vallathol Narayana Menon in Cheruthuruthi on the banks of the river Bharathapuzha and imparts training in Mohini Attam and Ottam Thullal.

Kathakali was traditionally the preserve of men, but now women also perform the dance. The themes have also changed with the times, and the latest innovation is Shakespeare's *King Lear*, stylised in Kathakali form; a Kalamandalam troupe recently toured Europe and performed *King Lear* to appreciative Western audiences.

North of Trichur, about 18 miles (30 km) away, lies **Guruvayur** with its famous Sri Krishna temple, considered the most sacred Hindu religious centre of Kerala. Though the origin of the temple is shrouded in mystery, there is no doubt that it existed from the 16th century at least. Legend says that the consecration of the idol was done by Guru, the preceptor of the *devas* (gods), and Vayu, the god of the winds, and so the place came to be known as Guruvayur. Lord Krishna, who is the deity installed in the temple, is also known as Guruvayurappa.

There are regular *poojas* every day before dawn and at twilight, to which thousands of devotees flock. A large number of Hindu weddings are solemnised here. Non-Hindus are not permitted within the temple. The devotees

Left,
solitary
tusker.
Right,
Silent Valley.

give large donations in cash and kind, including grain, vegetables and *ghee* (clarified butter). The temple has a big elephant yard to stable the many elephants presented by the devout. The annual **Ulsavom** or temple festival at Guruvayur is spread over 10 days in February-March, starting off with an elephant race. There is a colourful elephant procession and a performance of Krishnattom, the precursor of Kathakali as an art form. There is another festival in November-December when concerts of famous musicians are held at the temple.

Palghat, at the base of the Western Ghats, is a busy trading town 49 miles (79 km) from Trichur. It is the capital town of the district which is considered one of Kerala's rice-bowls. It has a well-preserved fort built by Hyder Ali, Sultan of Mysore, which now houses government offices.

A 9 mile (14 km) drive from Palghat takes you to the **Malampuzha dam** complex. The dam has been built across the Bharatapuzha river, near the foot-hills of the Western Ghats. The vast lake, with its many varieties of fish, offers boat cruises while the dam has an attractive terraced garden with statues created by Kerala's well known sculptor, Kanai Kunhiraman.

Wildlife in Silent Valley: Driving north from Palghat on the Coimbatore-Cannanore National Highway, you finally reach **Attappadi**, a tribal centre. Anthropologists will discover the lifestyle of the Irulars, Mudugars and Kurumbars of interest. Another 7 miles (12 km) and you reach the **Silent Valley**, which is one of the few tropical evergreen rain forests left in the country. Elephants, tigers, wild dog, flying squirrels and lion-tail macaques are found in this valley, in addition to a wealth of plant life. Entry into the area is regulated by permits issued by the Forest Department.

Getting back to Mannarghat to rejoin the National Highway, you can drive on to **Nilambur** about 37 miles (60 km) away, passing through extensive rubber plantations. Nilambur serves as the

Rural buffalo race in Chittali.

headquarters of an important forest division in Kerala. Here you can visit the finest man-made teak plantations in the world, almost a century old, and pause for a break at picturesque picnic spots such as Nellikuthu.

From Nilambur you can go to Calicut through Moplah country to **Malappuram**, the district headquarters. Both towns have ancient mosques where the annual *nerchas* or festivals are colourful affairs. On the parallel road, which is the main highway, is the Calicut University at **Chelari** southeast, the picturesque town of Mamburam, on the banks of a small river. You pass on via Feroke which has a flourishing tile industry on the banks of the river Chaliyar, to Calicut 7 miles (12 km) beyond

Calicut, Kozhikode in Malayalam, is 7 miles (12 km) from Feroke. It was once the dominant port of the Malabar coast, and known to the Phoenicians and the Greeks for its export of spices and cloth. This town gave to the English language the word *calico*, after a type of cotton material. The first colonial adventurer from the West, Vasco da Gama, landed at Kappad, 8 miles (14 km) north of Calicut. The Zamorin Raja welcomed him and followed him the same trading rights as had been given to many other foreigners, but Portuguese ambitions made conflict inevitable. The Zamorin's navy composed of intrepid Moplah Muslim seamen, put up a stiff resistance under his able admirals, the Kunhali Marakkars. The Portuguese were succeeded by the Dutch and then by the British, with a short French presence in between. One can see vestiges of their presence over the entire Malabar coast.

Calicut is a crowded city with narrow streets spilling over with more than half a million people. It still is an important trading centre for spices, coconuts and several other produce. There is the **Pazhassi Raja museum** managed by the State Archaeological department and also the **Krishna Menon art gallery and museum**.

Islam in Kerala: Though early Kerala history lacks authentic records, there is reason to believe that Islam came to Kerala in the 7th century AD through interaction with Arabs who had been plying their trade for centuries with what they called Malabar. It is still believed by many that the last ruler of Kerala, Cheraman Perumal, was attracted to the tenets of Islam and sailed to Jeddah to meet the Prophet. He was converted to Islam, called himself Tajuddin and married the sister of a great sailor and teacher by the name of Malik Bin Dinar. The first mosque was established at Kodungallur and Malik Bin Dinar is said to have established nine other mosques which are still extant. Among them are the ones at **Chaliyam**, near Beypore, **Kollam** near Quilandy, Madayi near Cannanore and Ezhimalai on the way to **Kasargode** – all seaside towns, testifying to the close connection between maritime trade and the advent of Islam. The Kerala Muslims, called Moplahs, grew as a community by intermarriage with Arab traders and the gradual spread of their religion by precept and practice, never by compulsion. That explains the kind of communal harmony one notices throughout the state.

From Calicut one can drive 34 miles (55 km) eastward to the **Wynaad plateau** 2,000 ft (610 m) high. Wynaad is known for its plantations of coffee, cardamom, pepper and rubber. **Lakidi** en route is a quiet place of great beauty with hill streams and the **Pookote Lake** which is a scenic picnic spot.

Wynaad is a separate district with headquarters at **Kalapetta**. There is a famous Jain temple here (in fact Kalapetta was once the stronghold of the Jains), and natural caves in nearby **Edakkal** with prehistoric carvings. The highway branches off at Chundale, one leading to Ooty and the other to Mysore. The last town in Wynaad, called **Sultan's Battery**, was built by him. A parallel highway in Wynaad connects Mysore with Tellicherry and Cannanore, passing through Manantodu and the extensive Avalam farm and wildlife sanctuary.

Very close to Calicut lies the major fishing harbour of **Beypore** at the mouth of the river Chaliyar. Once

SPICES OF THE ORIENT

Variety is the spice of life – so goes the old adage. But a variety of spices – in food, at least – also adds flavour to life. The ancients, more than two millennia ago, obviously believed this. Ever since man began to cross the high seas, he has sought the good things of life. The Phoenicians and the Greeks sailed to the shores of India to gather the spices of Ind. Indian pepper and cardamom were highly valued. The trade was mainly with the western coast of South India, specifically Kerala. Musiris – now Kodungalloor, and Ophir – present day Beypore, were ports of call even from the days of Solomon. Pepper was called black gold and highly-valued – as much as the yellow metal and precious stones for which they were bartered.

Cardamom was also another highly prized item. Today it is a popular seasoning ingredient for Indian curry dishes; cardomom seeds produce a camphor-like aromatic flavour. The small green fruit is abundantly grown in the forests of the Cardamom Hills.

Intrepid Arab sailors were regular visitors to the "Malaibar" coast to buy spices long before the advent of Islam. The beaches of Kerala were busy entrepóts for the spice trade. The trade continued through the centuries and exists even today, though the modes of trade, and the men behind it, have suffered a sea change.

Though pride of place goes to pepper and cardamom, other spices such as dried ginger, garlic and turmeric are also in considerable demand. Then comes what are called minor spices – dry chillies, coriander, cumin and fenugreek.

With the revolution in modern packaging, the demand for Indian spices is being catered to by a sophisticated packaging of ground and mixed spices, under a variety of brand names, as Indian Curry Powder. Leading Indian manufacturers and even subsidiaries of multinationals have entered the field of "instant foods".

India produces approximately 80 percent of the world's cardamom, and of this, 60 percent is grown in Kerala. Similarly, pepper (black gold) has been the largest foreign exchange earner among India's cash crops. Both cardamom and pepper are commodities with widely fluctuating prices which stimulate the gambler's instinct among the operators on the commodities exchange. Many fortunes have been made and lost on account of this, though the actual grower of the spices gets little of the benefit from a steep price rise.

Along with spices, another product that merits attention is the cashew. Though it is not, strictly speaking, a spice, it is in popular demand the world over. The cashew has an interesting history in India. It was introduced by the Portugese, one of the few lasting benefits of the Portugese incursion into India. It is not only grown widely in Goa but also in Kerala where it is a valued cash crop which earns foreign exchange.

The cashew workers of Kerala, mainly in Quilon, are among the most skilled in the world. Many countries in the world prefer cashew kernels (even from Africa) to be processed and re-exported from India. Cashew nuts are an important ingredient in South Indian vegetarian dishes as well as in some meat delicacies. The cashew fruit yields a potent liquor called *feni* which is a specialty of Goa and no wine tippler should leave the country without tasting it.

known to the Arabs and the Greeks, Breypore is being revived as a port. It boasts a boat-building yard which has been building vessels for the Arabs from the Gulf and Kuwait for centuries.

The northern highway from Calicut passes through the suburb of West Hill which has a small army barracks. About 10 miles (15 km) away is **Kappad beach** where Vasco da Gama landed, once a quiet village with a picturesque seashore. Now building activity is in full swing to convert its 275 acres (111.3 hectares) into a tourist resort with cottages, a health club, sauna bath, swimming pool and other facilities.

As you drive northwards from Calicut you pass **Quilandy**, where there are families who can trace their descent from Arab settlers and **Badagara**, an important trading centre. Just off Badagara is **Lokanar Kavu**, the home of the Kurups who were heroes of *Vadakka Pattu*, the Northern Ballads. They are exponents of the ancient martial art of *kalari payattu*, which is older than *kung fu*. With the aid of sticks and staves and the thin steel foils known as *urumi*, they can fend off a host of antagonists with superb gymnastic skill. Northward from Badagar you reach **Mahe**, formerly a French enclave and now administrately part of Pondicherry.

Old world charm: About 3 miles (5 km) further north lies **Tellicherry**, a sleepy municipal town with an old world charm. The fort, built by the East India Company in the early 18th century, is at the beach, from where one can contemplate the beauty of the Arabian Sea. Tellicherry has the distinction of being the nursery of Indian circus. All the major circus troupes in India are dominated by Tellicherry artistes who have been trained from childhood in the gymnastic arts, thanks to the pioneering effort of the late Keelari Kunhikannan Gurukkal. Tellicherry now boasts a Circus Academy and Gymnasium built near the beach.

Northwards, 18 miles (29 km) away, lies **Cannonore**, once the capital of the Kolathiri Rajas and also the seat of the Arakkal Rajas, the only Muslim ruling family in Kerala. **St Angelo's fort**, built by the Portuguese in the 16th century, is a landmark to be visited. About 31 miles (50 km) north is **Ezhimala** on a high promontory overlooking the sea with a beautiful beach. The place has been taken over by a Naval Academy. On the way lies **Taliparamba** where there is a snake farm.

About 62 miles (100 km) north of Cannanore on the National Highway lies the fishing centre of Kasargode. The Muslims of the town are considered expert seamen, with a reputation of intrepidity and adventure. **Bekal fort**, some 6 miles (10 km) from Kasargode, is worth a visit. Situated on a jutting beachhead high above the shore, at a strategic curve on the coast, this huge fort, built of red laterite by a Kannada chief, must have served as a vantage point to look out for naval marauders. Bekal fort houses a tiny travellers' bungalow where you can stay by previous reservation. Beyond Kasargode, you cross the Netravati river by the long Ullal bridge and enter Mangalore, the busy port of Karnataka.

Toddy tapper.

LAKSHADWEEP ISLANDS

Thirty-six tiny islands with a total land area of only about 8 acres (3.2 hectares) constitute the archipaelago of Lakshadweep, the smallest of the States and Union Territories of India. However, the geographical area including the lagoons adds up to approximately 1,035 acres (419 hectares), and the territorial waters to almost 5,000 acres (2,023 hectares).

Until 1956, the islands formed part of the state of Madras, and were known until 1973 as the Laccadive, Minicoy and Amindivi Islands.Only ten of the islands are inhabited. They are, in descending order of size, Minicoy, Androth, Kavaratti, Kadmat, Agathy, Ameni, Kiltan, Chetlat and Bitral. However, entry to many of the islands is restricted to protect the fragile ecosystem which consists of lagoons and land which is barely 6.6 ft (2 m) above sea level and the ocean. International tourists are permitted to stay only at Bangaram, which was originally uninhabited; Indians, however, can stop over at Kalpeni, Kadmat, Minicoy and the capital, Kavaratti.

India's coral islands: The islands are located between 8° and 12°N and are about 200 miles (340 to 350 km) away from the Kerala coast on the Indian mainland. The Lakshadweep cluster are India's only coral islands. The archipaelago boasts 12 atolls, three reefs and five submerged banks. Almost all the atolls have a northeast-southwest orientation with magnificent lagoons in between, opening out to the sea through one or more channels. The climate is tropical throughout the year, with a maximum temperature ranging from 35° to 38°C and minimum from 17° to 18°C. The monsoon arrives in May and it rains till the end of September. During this period, the islands are closed to tourists.

Lakshadweep's chief attraction lies in its unspoilt and virtually unpopulated sandy beaches, its verdant coconut groves and its crystal-clear lagoons which range in colour from pale aquamarine to dark lapis lazuli. These lagoons are shallow, calm and safe for swimming. They abound in a variety of brilliantly coloured tropical fish. For the more adventurous, the Society for Promotion of Recreational Tourism and (SPORTS) provides snorkelling equipment to enable tourists to investigate the enchanting coral reefs.

Unspoilt and inviting: Lakshadweep's other attraction lies in the fact that it is one of the few spots on earth untouched by the march of time. There are no sophisticated luxuries or distractions: the islanders, who were recently exposed to TV, returned their sets deciding that they were better off without them! There are few places more inviting than these islands for a "get-away-from-it-all" holiday.

Apart from the up-market Bangaram Tourism Resort run by the Casino Hotel in Cochin, the accommodation available on the other islands is sparsely furnished tourist huts. If the visitor is stopping off at Bangaram, perhaps the best

Preceding pages, Lakshadweep is India's coral trove. Left, Island belle.

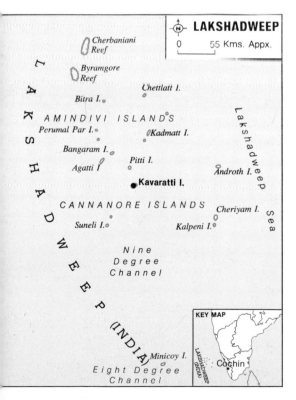

LAKSHADWEEP

0   55 Kms. Appx.

Cherbaniani Reef

Byramgore Reef

Chettlatt I.

Bitra I.

AMINDIVI ISLANDS

Perumal Par I.

Kadmatt I.

Bangaram I.

Pitti I.

Agatti I.

Androth I.

Kavaratti I.

Lakshadweep Sea

CANNANORE ISLANDS

Cheriyam I.

Suneli I.

Kalpeni I.

Nine Degree Channel

(INDIA)

KEY MAP

Minicoy I.

Cochin

LAKSHADWEEP (INDIA)

Eight Degree Channel

way to visit the islands is to stay on board the ship. The new *M.V. Tippu Sultan* which the administration has chartered from the Shipping Corporation of India provides very comfortable accommodation for its passengers. Aboard the vessel are 6 four-berth cabins, 2 two-berth cabins and economy-class dormitory accommodation up to 16 people.

For those visitors wishing to explore the islands from Cochin, the journey by ship to the closest island, Kalpeni, takes 15 hours. The tourists are taken to Kalpeni on the first day, Minicoy on the second and Kavaratti on the third, and the ship returns to Cochin on the fifth day. Vayudoot also operates regular flights to Agatti, the closest inhabited island to Bangaram, from where passengers are taken to the resort complex by motor-launch.

Language, people and customs: The population of Lakshadweep is relatively high, around 50,000. Most of the islanders are of Keralite descent – originally Hindu, as the prevalent systems of caste and of matrilineal inheritance bear out. The language spoken on all the islands except Minicoy is a dialect of Malayalam. Mahl is normally spoken in Minicoy which is close to and has historical links with the Maldive group of islands. Ninety-six percent of the population is Muslim, Islam having been brought to the islands by Hazrat Ubaidullah in the 7th century. (It is therefore inadvisable to visit the islands during Ramadhan).

Coconut cultivation and fishing are the chief occupations of the inhabitants who are contented with their simple lifestyle. There is virtually no industry other than producing and processing coir. Coconut shells are also used in making handicrafts and souvenirs. Till recently no banking facilities were available. Local transportation on the islands is also limited, and is mainly restricted to the movement of goods, and the ubiquitous bicycle is the usual mode of transport.

Island courtesy: The people of the islands are polite and friendly, and the

Island paradise in the sun.

level of education is among the highest in India. There is no crime of any kind on the islands and it is common to see even small children wandering around with gold necklaces around their necks without any fear of being robbed. In brief, the life of the islanders is informal and simple as befits the paradise they inhabit.

Kavaratti: Kavaratti is the administrative capital of Lakshadweep and has a sizable number of mainlanders, chiefly working for the Government. Ujro Mosque is worth a visit, as is the Aquarium which has a fine collection of ornamental fish and coral forms.

Kalpeni: Kalpeni is the first island that tourists on package tours are likely to visit. It has a spectacular lagoon and a beautiful bay. There are two uninhabited islands nearby which tourists can visit by boat.

Kadmat: This island has a beautiful lagoon, ideal for swimming. The tourist huts at Kadmat are in a better condition than those on the other islands.

Minicoy: Minicoy is the southernmost island of the archipelago and closest to the Maldives in both geography and culture. The lighthouse built by the British more than a century ago is worth a visit. Tuna fishing and boat-building are important occupations for the inhabitants in Minicoy.

Bangaram: This uninhabited island has been developed into an international tourist resort. Those planning for a long stay would be well advised to stay at Bangaram.

The advent of tourism has brought inevitable change to Lakshadweep and pressures on resources as well as society are likely to intensify. However, there is a sensitivity to these problems on the part of the local authorities and controls are being debated which are aimed at preserving the beauty and tranquility of this natural Eden.

Below, our little maids from Lakshadweep school. Following page, Gangaikonda-cholapuram lovers.

TRAVEL TIPS

GETTING THERE

BY AIR

Most visitors arriving in India by air usually touch down at Delhi's **Indira Gandhi International Airport** or at Mumbei's (Bombay's) **Sahar International Airport** and get connecting flights to the rest of India by Indian Airlines and, to closer destinations, by the new feeder airline Vayudoot. Each of the four southern capitals is linked to these two major entry points by at least two flights a day, but if the traveller misses the morning flight, he usually has a longer wait than anticipated because evening flights tend to run behind schedule.

The four capitals themselves are linked together by Indian Airlines flights at least twice a day and many of the major towns in the South are linked with their state capitals with once-a-day flights. Smaller towns in each state are often linked to their capitals by Vayudoot. There are flight connections to the following towns:

Tamil Nadu: Coimbatore, Madras, Madurai and Tiruchchirappalli (Indian Airlines); Coimbatore, Madras, Madurai, Neyveli, Thanjavur and Tiruchchirappalli (Vayudoot).

Karnataka: Bangalore, Belgaum and Mangalore (Indian Airlines); Bangalore, Bellary, Mangalore and Mysore (Vayudoot).

Kerala: Calicut, Cochin and Trivandrum (Indian Airlines).

Andhra Pradesh: Hyderabad, Vijayawada, and Vishakhapatnam (Indian Airlines); Hyderabad, Rajahmundruy, Ramagundam, Tirupati, Vijayawada, Vishakhapatnam and Warangal (Vayudoot).

Pondicherry: Pondicherry (Vayudoot).
Lakshadweep: Kavaratti (Vayudoot).

Madras is being developed as the major "Gateway to the South" and its modern airports, international and domestic, are among the finest in the country, a reflection of this intent. At present, British Airways flies in twice a week from London and there is a through New York-London-Madras Air India flight once a week besides daily Air India flights from Mumbei (Bombay) or Delhi that connect flights to and from the West. Eastwards, there are daily flights from Kuala Lumpur and Singapore, Malaysia Airlines System, Singapore Airlines, Air India and Indian Airlines providing the services. Malaysian Airlines System also takes in Penang once a week. Air Lanka and Indian Airlines link Colombo and Madras daily.

The only other southern cities with international flight connections are Trivandrum, which receives flights from Abu Dhabi, Colombo, Dhahran, Dubai, Kuwait, Male, Ras-al-Khaima and Sharjah (Indian Airlines and Air India), Tiruchchirappalli, which receives flights from Colombo (Indian Airlines and Air Lanka), and Hyderabad, which receives flights from Jeddah (Air India). The Government of India has relaxed its rules on air charters and Madras, Bangalore and Trivandrum, besides neighbouring Dabolim Airport in Goa, have been opened to sanctioned charter flights. But getting charter permission is still not easy. Several international carriers are also negotiating landing rights in Madras, and by 1991 Madras is expected to be as important an entry point as New Delhi and Mumbei.

NOTE: Though the State of Goa and the Union Territory of the Andaman and Nicobar Islands have not been included in this volume, both are part of several southern tourist circuits. Dabolim Airport in Goa is linked to Bangalore and Cochin by direct Indian Airlines flights as well as to Delhi and Mumbei. Port Blair in the Andamans is linked by direct Indian Airlines flights from Madras, Calcutta and New Delhi (via Bhubaneshwor). There is also a flight which continues from Port Blair to Car Nicobar.

WARNING: Passengers to Port Blair run the risk of being off-loaded despite holding confirmed reservations, depending on flying conditions and pay-load at the time; this is not surprising, because the planes have to carry their return fuel as well.

Indian Airlines charges are favourable compared to international prices. But cancellation charges on tickets bought locally can be very high nearer the day of departure.

Indian Airlines tickets are valid for 6 months. Indian Airlines also offers special fares for tourists from abroad under such schemes as **Discover India** ($400 for 21 days, unlimited destinations but only one halt, transfers excluded, in each city), **Tour India** ($300 for 14 days, unlimited destinations but only one halt, transfers excluded, in each city), **Indian Wonderfares – South** ($200 for 7 days to 11 South Indian destinations – a surcharge $100 for Port Blair – and other rules as stated above) and a 21-day **South India Excursion Fare** (30 percent off on Economy-Class US$ fare for tourists entering from Sri Lanka or the Maldives and visiting seven South Indian destinations).

Air India, India's international airline, has an excellent record for hospitality and service. Pleasant English-speaking air hostesses serve good meals on board, offering three different menus. Indian vegetarian is a particularly good introduction to a unique cuisine, but remember to state your meal preference when booking your ticket. This is in contrast to the domestic carrier, Indian Airlines. Its air hostesses do speak English, but tend to be brusque. The snacks and meals they serve on board are minimal, Indian and not particularly haute cuisine. No liquor is served aboard Indian Airlines domestic flights, though flights to neighbouring countries do serve liquor (with many a passenger making the most of it, sometimes rather annoyingly). The free baggage allowance on internal flights is 44 lbs (20 kg), but an additional 22 lbs (10 kg) is permitted for international passengers with First Class tickets and those travelling Executive Class on Airbus (A300) flights. Only one piece of hand baggage per passenger (barring handbags etc.) is permitted aboard. However, airlines officials tend to be helpful on both counts in *bona fide* cases.

TRAVEL ESSENTIALS

VISAS & PASSPORTS

Everyone entering India, including Indian nationals, requires a valid passport. Everyone needs an entry, tourist or transit visa to enter the country.

An **entry visa** is for a person visiting India for business or employment.

A **tourist visa** is issued to tourists for a 3-month period, to be used within 6 months of issue. Extensions for a further 3 months are considered by the Foreigners' Registration Office in New Delhi, Mumbei (Bombay), Calcutta or Madras or by the Superintendent of Police in district headquarters.

A **transit visa** valid for 15 days must be used within 3 months of issue – and is strictly for those passing through.

Visas are issued by Indian embassies, consulates-general, consulates, high commissions and deputy high commissions in the cities where they are located abroad. Foreigners staying over 3 months in India for business or employment must register themselves within 7 days of arrival with the nearest Foreigners' Registration Office. An exit endorsement from the registering officer is necessary for these persons prior to departure. No such formalities are necessary in the case of transit or tourist visa holders.

Special permits are necessary to visit the Andaman and Nicobar Islands with additional permits (from the Chief Secretary's Office, A & N Administration, Port Blair) for areas apart from Port Blair, Jolly Buoy and Cinque Islands. Permits are also necessary for visits to Lakshadweep: Indians are permitted to visit Bangaram I, Kadmat I, Kalpeni I, Kavaratti I and Minicoy, but foreigners may only visit Bangaram. Elsewhere in South India, permits are only required to visit the Tibetan communities and monasteries a few miles north of Mysore.

MONEY MATTERS

The unit of currency throughout India is 100 paise to the rupee. There are about 27 rupees to the pound sterling and about 17 rupees to the U.S. dollar at time of press.

Coins come in denominations of 5,10, 20, 25, and 50 *paise* and Rs. 1 and Rs. 2, while notes are in denominations of Rs.1, Rs. 2, Rs. 5, Rs. 10, Rs. 20, Rs. 50, Rs. 100 and the rare Rs. 500.

Major credit cards are accepted throughout the country in the above average hotels and restaurants and many of the better shops. Travellers' cheques are also accepted at these places. Encashing travellers' cheques, however, tends to take time, especially in banks, so change a few days' requirements at a time.

Any amount of foreign currency or travellers' cheques may be brought into India, provided the visitor declares it on arrival in the Currency Declaration Form. Such declaration will enable the visitor to exchange the currency brought in and take back on departure the unspent amount, provided encashment receipts from banks or hotels where money was changed are also submitted. Currency, however, must be exchanged only through banks or authorised money changers; to exchange currency by any other means is an offence. No Indian currency may be brought in or taken out except as travellers' cheques.

Indians and foreigners domiciled in India for over 90 days or who have worked in India during a 90-day visit need an income-tax clearance exemption certificate from the Income Tax Department in Delhi, Mumbei (Bombay), Calcutta or Madras, to leave the country.

TIPPING

Tipping is customary even if there is a service charge on hotel or restaurant bills. The conventional tip is 5 to 10 percent of a restaurant bill or of the amount on the meter of a vehicle on hire. If there is already a 10 percent service surcharge on the bill, the tip could be less than the conventional, but a tip is nevertheless expected.

The minimum tip these days is a rupee and that's what porters should be tipped per piece of baggage over and above the standard railway station or airport fee.

If staying as a house guest anywhere, tipping the domestic help is customary when you are leaving. If in doubt about the amount, ask your hosts.

WHAT TO WEAR

South India is warm throughout the year and light cotton clothing is quite sufficient. Sandals are recommended footwear. Evening attire tends to be quite informal, though a few clubs insist on shoes and ties. Evenings and early mornings from November to March get quite mild and a light cardigan might be useful. These mild evenings and mornings are like summers in the temperate zones and a cotton pullover or cardigan is recommended. Winters in the hills can get quite cold; although it doesn't snow in the South, heavy frosts and showers of hailstones are quite common – woollens, thick socks and shoes are advised.

HEALTH

No vaccination certificate is now required for entry into India, nor is there a medical check on passengers leaving the country. However, persons arriving from some countries in Africa and Central and South America that have been notified as yellow fever infected areas need valid international certificates of vaccination. Pets and plants brought in are subject to quarantine.

All good hotels serve boiled water. In many homes, too, you will get boiled water. But elsewhere, stick to mineral water, soda, well known aerated drinks or bottled or tetra-packed fruit juices – but here again make sure you are getting a branded product. A good rule is to choose hot cooked food, avoid salads and eat only fruit you've peeled.

CUSTOMS

Travellers carrying no dutiable articles and who do not have any unaccompanied baggage may pass through the Customs **Green Channel**. This, however, does not mean that you may not be stopped by a vigilant Customs Inspector. If you are then found to be carrying dutiable goods, the penalties are likely to be stiff. Therefore, if you are carrying any dutiable goods, or are not sure what is dutiable or not, it is best to take the **Red Channel** and inform the Inspector what you have. In many cases, a frank and friendly request to an Inspector will also result in minor dutiable goods being permitted free of duty, when it is obvious that trade is not the reason for the import.

The **Red Channel** must also be used by passengers who have unaccompanied baggage or who have dutiable valuables (such as cameras, binoculars, typewriters, personal computers, word processors, jewellery, etc.) that they plan on taking back with them. In the latter case, a Tourist Baggage Re-export Form (TBRE) has to be filled in and submitted at the time of departure. The form must be retained during the visit in the country and any goods entered in the form and not re-exported will involve the payment of penalty duties.

A visitor may bring in, free of duty (and with the promise of re-export in specific cases) the following items, besides personal effects:

Personal jewellery, one camera, one mini-cinematograph camera and limited film for both, portable radio and recording equipment, one musical instrument, a portable typewriter, audio-visual aids, professional equipment, a pram, sports equipment and gifts to the value of Rs.500. Two hundred cigarettes or 50 cigars or 7.5 oz (250 gm) of tobacco, and alcoholic liquor up to 28.5 fl oz (950 ml) may also be brought in duty-free.

The import of dangerous drugs, live plants and gold or silver in the form of bullion or as ancient coins is strictly prohibited.

When leaving, goods brought in on the promise off re-export may be re-exported if the documentation (TBRE) is right. Free export of souvenirs, handicrafts, Indian silk and cotton materials etc. is also permitted. Gold jewellery made in India and not exceeding Rs.2,000 in value, and other jewellery made in India and precious stones bought in India, both together not exceeding Rs.10,000 in value, may also be taken back by a visitor without prior permission. The export of antiquities and art objects over 100 years old and animal and reptile skins in any form (including shoes and handbags) is banned.

All railway stations have porters, and officially sanctioned porters wear badges. A rupee may be the official rate per piece of baggage, but something more is generally expected.

Free baggage trolley service has been introduced in some of the larger railway stations and in most of the airports. Free porter service is also available at most airports, but a substantial tip is expected.

At bus terminals, no official porter service is available, but there are hangers-on (watch your luggage!) who are willing to oblige in such cases. Most official porters are, however, reliable.

RESERVATIONS

All Indian Airlines reservations are computerised, at least in the main offices of the Airlines, and fewer errors now occur. Railway bookings are also computerised in the main cities, but bookings made at smaller stations tend to be chancy. Reservations for long-distance bus travel are best done at the main bus depots. However, it is wisest to use the services of a travel agent of repute to ensure reservations and get reliable local transport.

Leading travel agents like Thomas Cook, Travel Corporation of India, SITA Travels, Cox & Kings, Mercury Travels, PL Worldways, Diner's Travel Service have offices in all the southern capitals as well as in most of the major towns and tourist destinations in the South. Both they as well as travel counters in the hotels will help with reservations.

ON DEPARTURE

Check-in time is two hours before an international flight, 1½ hours for domestic Airbus flights and one hour for other flights.

Security checks at airports can range from the strict to the perfunctory. Most of the bigger South Indian airports have scanning machines to check hand baggage, but in smaller airports manual searching continues. In most South Indian airports it is mandatory to identify on the tarmac any luggage you have booked in. Unidentified luggage will NOT be loaded on board, but here again Indian Airlines officials go out of their way to find the owners of unidentified baggage. Pen cells and other dry batteries are not allowed in hand baggages and are usually confiscated by security officials.

All passengers flying out from India are required to pay a Foreign Travel Tax at the airport/seaport of eventual departure. The tax is Rs.150 for travel to any South Asian country and Rs.300 to any other country.

GETTING ACQUAINTED

GOVERNMENT & ECONOMY

India is a union of semi-autonomous States and Union Territories. Each state has its own legislature, though its powers are limited to certain subjects. Each Union Territory too has its own legislature, but its powers are even more restricted. The residue powers in both cases are wielded by the Central Government through the House of the People (Lok Sabha, Parliament) and the House of the Elders (Rajya Sabha, Upper House) in Delhi.

South India comprises four of these States and, for the purposes of this volume, two Union Territories. The states are Tamil Nadu, Kerala, Karnataka and Andhra Pradesh, roughly what used to be called the Madras Presidency before India became independent, together with the "Princely States" of Hyderabad, Mysore, Travancore and Cochin. The Union Territories are Pondicherry and Lakshadweep. Present-day Pondicherry amalgamates four former French enclaves in South India; Mahe (in Kerala), Yanam (in Andhra Pradesh), Karaikal and the biggest of them all, Pondicherry (both in Tamil Nadu). Lakshadweep (once called the Laccadive Islands) is an island archipelago some way off the western sea coast which takes its name from the Indian numerical term *lakh*, meaning 100,000 and *"dweep"* meaning island.

The four States are fairly densely populated and each has several "A Class" towns, i.e. towns with a population of over 100,000. Pondicherry too is thickly populated, but has only one major town, Pondicherry, its capital. Lakshadweep is about the only part of the South with a scant population and no town to speak of. Kavaratti, its capital, is a tiny, separate island with a small, scattered population. Madras, the capital of Tamil Nadu, is the only metropolitan city in the South, but Bangalore, the capital of Karnataka, and Hyderabad, capital of Andhra Pradesh, are both faster-growing cities, with a population of over 3 million each. Trivandrum, the capital of Kerala, still has some way to go to reach that mark, but Kerala, where one town or village runs into another, especially in the Trivandrum-Cochin region, has a contiguous urbanised stretch along the coast.

The other important towns in Tamil Nadu are Coimbatore, Erode, Madurai, Salem, Tiruchchirappalli, Thanjavur and Tuticorin, and in Kerala, Alleppey, Calicut (Kozhikode in the vernacular), Cannanore, Cochin, Kottayam, Quilon and Trichur. The major towns in Karnataka are Bellary, Gulbarga, Hubli-Dharwad, Mangalore and Mysore, and in Andhra Pradesh, Guntur, Kakinada, Nellore, Rajamundry, Vijayawada, Vishakhapatnam and Warangal.

A good network of roads, railways and air routes connect all these towns, indeed almost the entire South. This is one of the best served parts of India, communications-wise.

TIME ZONES

The entire South follows Indian Standard Time, which is 5½ hours ahead of Greenwich Mean Time and 4½ hours ahead of British Summer Time. It gets dark quite early from October and the evenings are longer from April. The morning too brightens up later from October, and earlier from April.

CLIMATE

The South is warm throughout the year, except in the hill ranges of the Nilgiris, the Annamalais, the Cardamom Hills, the Western Ghats and the Shevaroys. But the region can also be very wet, especially if the monsoons are good.

Average temperatures in the plains range from 73°F to 90°F (23°C to 32°C) in Tamil Nadu and Pondicherry, 73°F to 85°F (23°C to 29°C) in Kerala and Lakshadweep, 66°F to 88°F (19° to 31°C) in Karnataka and 70°F to 92°F (21°C to 33°C) in Andhra Pradesh. Hill station temperatures tend to range from about 50°F to 65°F (10°C to 18°C).

The hottest part of the year is from April to June, the months preceding the southwest monsoon. Temperatures on some days can reach over 105°F (40°C) in Tamil Nadu and Andhra Pradesh and over 97°F (36°C) in Karnataka and Kerala. Both Kerala and Tamil Nadu are also particularly humid. The monsoons begin around 10 June and can last well into September. Kerala, Lakshadweep and the Karnataka coast, as well as the western hills of Tamil Nadu, are lashed by these monsoons, but the rest of the South gets only scattered showers or drizzles in bright sunshine.

From October to February/March it is mainly dry weather in many parts of the South, with temperatures ranging from 64°F (18°C) to 75°F (24°C) and hill stations like Ooty and Kodaikanal even registering 39°F (4°C). Tamil Nadu and the Andhra Pradesh coast, however, are the only parts of India that get rain at this time of the year; the northeast monsoon being most active from mid-October to early December.

Kerala, Lakshadweep and Tamil Nadu in the monsoon are experiences in themselves, but sea-bathing is ruled out by rough seas at this time of the year. The Tamil Nadu and Andhra coasts are also prone to cyclonic storms from October to December – and that can be an experience of another kind. But the rains notwithstanding, the best time to visit the southern coasts is from September to March with April and May included if you can bear the heat. The hills and plateau-cities of Bangalore, Mysore and Hyderabad and their environs are year-round destinations.

CULTURE & CUSTOMS

The South is where tradition is strongest in India, even in its cities. Much of its culture and traditions are visible in everyday life. And much of this has to do with the faith of centuries.

Most Hindu homes have *pooja* rooms – shrine rooms where members of the pan-theon of gods are displayed in portrait and sculpture and worshipped daily. Visitors are generally not welcome in such rooms, more especially when worship is going on or the sacred lamp is being lit in the morning and evening. Several Christian homes, especially in Kerala and in the deep south of Tamil Nadu, also have such shrine rooms.

Every Hindu home has its doorstep washed clean every morning and ritual designs traced on the ground as offerings to the Sun God. These designs – *kolam* – are generally done with rice flour, but sometimes coloured powders or flowers are used. To step out of the house before the day's *kolam* is drawn is considered inauspicious.

When giving a gift or paying out money and when receiving a gift or money, always use the right hand. This is also so when you decide to follow hosts who unabashedly observe tradition and eat with their hands. The right hand is the "clean" hand. Almost everyone eat with their hands at home and many do so outside as well, especially in the less luxurious restaurants. Hands are washed after a meal, not wiped on a napkin.

Meals are traditionally eaten off plantain leaves and at formal functions this is still the practice. But the ubiquitous china or metal plate is now becoming more common as tableware. However, the custom of taking several helpings of rice and flavouring each with a different mix in a preordained sequence – first, with *dhal* (curried lentils) and *ghee* (clarified butter), then with a thick gravy called *getti kolambu* followed by a thin gravy called *sambar*, then a peppery soup *rasam* and finally with curd or buttermilk – is a custom that continues in many South Indian homes, though the sequence is traditionally not as elaborate in Kerala or in most homes today.

Much of the south is vegetarian in habit and even non-vegetarians have what are basically vegetarian meals with just one dish either of chicken, mutton (really goat's meat) or fish, which is usually foregone on Fridays. Beef and pork are not eaten in most Hindu homes, and Muslims won't touch pork.

The times are changing, but in many Hindu homes a visitor is expected to leave his or her footwear at the entrance. This custom is mandatory in temples and shrine rooms, mosques and many ancient churches.

If you go out shopping early and happen to be the first customer in a shop, for you to leave without making a purchase is considered inauspicious by many shopkeepers. That first purchase assures the shopkeeper a good day and many a shopkeeper or vendor looks forward to a favourite customer being the day's first. Price is often not important in the case of the first sale and many bargains can be picked up if a rapport is struck between buyer and seller. Prices are fixed in most organised shops – especially in the case of branded goods. But in markets and in the case of non-branded goods, no sale is made without a haggle over the item.

Cleanliness is almost a fetish in the South and the daily morning bath is customary; certainly, the weekly oil bath is a ritual. The oil bath may not be necessary, but most people in the South expect visitors to be as addicted to the morning bath as they are.

Most women in the South still favour the *sari*, oiled and plaited long hair with jasmines in it and a moderate helping of gold jewellery. The modern college girl or the occasional career girl might be dressed in something Western, but, even here, revealing clothing is seldom worn. Dating is virtually unknown and most visitors asking for a date are likely to be rebuffed. Ballroom dancing in any form is also only for that microscopic minority of women considered sophisticated. And the occasional alcoholic beverage is drunk only by a fraction in that minority. Under these circumstances, weddings are naturally still arranged and continue to be as successful as ever.

The *pottu* – the vermilion (nowadays other colours have become fashionable) dot marked on the forehead every day – is customarily worn by all South Indian Hindu women and does not, as in the North, specially signify a married woman. The Hindu wife in the South is more likely to wear silver rings on her toes and a gold chain with a special pendant round her neck to signify her marital status.

"Please", "Thank you", "Sorry", "Excuse me" and similar expressions of politeness are rarely heard in the South. The absence of such polite usages should not be considered rudeness; it's just not a custom to use such terms. A welcome on arrival is generally "Come in" and a farewell is generally a "I'll go and come back," responded to with "Go and return." The palms of the hands, touching as though in prayer, is the usual sign of greeting and farewell.

It is important to realise that the South is perhaps the most tolerant, polite and friendly part of India, where no one ever seems to have the heart to say "No" or "I don't know" or "I can't do it." In these circumstances, almost any transgression by a stranger from abroad, short of a criminal act, is quickly overlooked and accepted with a smile. In that context, there isn't a more understanding part of India and a more perfect host you will come across than the South.

WEIGHTS & MEASURES

Grams and kilograms are the official units of measure but people talk as easily of pounds and ounces as they do of kilos.

Litres – remember, of petrol, not gasoline, for instance – are also official usage and are much more frequently talked of than gallons.

Though metres and kilometres are official, it is more likely to hear miles and yards – and even the forgotten furlong – being used in conversation. All institutions, shops and the government use the metric system and it's best to follow the form in official and business transactions, but be ambivalent in conversation.

Though the metric system is now used all over India, a few things are bought by traditional weight. Gold and silver, for instance, are sold by the *tola* in the more traditional shops, the unit being the equivalent of about 11.5 gm. Gems are weighed in carats; a carat is equal to 0.2 gm.

When Indians talk of large sums, they talk in terms of *lakhs* – a hundred thousand, and written "1,00,000" – and *crores* – ten million, or one hundred *lakhs*, and written "100,00,000". A billion is a hundred *crores* or a thousand million.

ELECTRICITY

Electricity in India is of the 220-volt, 50-cycle kind, but especially in these chronically power-short days, the voltage tends to fluctuate. A voltage stabiliser is advised for sensitive and expensive equipment.

If you have electrical equipment unsuited to Indian voltages, some of the bigger hotels will help with step-down transformers on request. Some even have built-in systems in the bathrooms to step down voltages. Hotels can also loan stabilisers for use with portable computers and typewriters.

Don't be surprised to find notices in the hotel room requesting you to use as little electricity as possible. One of the consequences of the Indian economic boom is that the infrastructure has not kept pace with it and power shortages are endemic. Virtually all reasonably good hotels and most offices and industries in the South have stand-by generators to counter "load-shedding", that is, power being switched off at local distribution points.

Water is often in short supply too in many places in the South, especially during summer, and most hotels request your cooperation to go easy on the water. Madras is particularly badly affected on both counts, water as well as electricity.

BUSINESS HOURS

Business hours tend to vary from area to area, but shops, mercantile establishments and industrial offices open around 9 in the morning. Government offices open about an hour later. Offices close between 4.30 to 5.30 p.m. depending on opening hours; an 8-hour day, or rather a 45-hour week, is in force. Saturdays are either half-days or full days depending on the week's schedule in individual offices. Sunday is a holiday. Central Government offices have a 5-day week (closed on Saturdays and Sundays).

Many shops, however, work a split day and work till about 1 in the afternoon before closing for a long lunch then reopening about 4 p.m. to work until around 8 p.m.

Cinema shows are at fixed times, usually 10 a.m., 3.30 p.m., 6.30 p.m., and 9.30 p.m., which is the last show. Around 11.30 p.m. is also closing time for restaurants. Most bars, where permitted, and taverns (arrack shops) close earlier, usually between 9 and 10 p.m.

HOLIDAYS

Sunday is the official weekly holiday throughout the South, but a few private establishments might close on Fridays. Other compulsory holidays are 26 January (Republic Day), 1 May (May Day), 15 August (Independence Day) and 2 October (Mahatma Gandhi's Birthday).

Other holidays generally follow the individual State Government's list, though many business establishments work during several of these holidays.

The main holiday seasons in the South are the week-long Pongal-Sankranthi period in mid-January, Dussera (ten days in September/October) and Diwali (a few days in October/November).

FESTIVALS

In a part of the country that is more religious than any other, almost every day seems to be a festival day. But some festivals are more important than others and are more elaborately and publicly celebrated. Also, not all festivals are religious festivals.

Visitors planning their stay in the South to coincide with some of the more festive occasions will enjoy something unique – reason enough to think ahead and time their holiday accordingly.

Perhaps the most glamorous South Indian festival is the **Dussera** celebration in Mysore over a period of 10 days in September/October. Once a festivity sponsored and graced by royalty, it is now a tourist extravaganza and a fun-fair for the public. Processions led by gaily caparisoned elephants, classical and folk music and dance programmes, fireworks displays and brilliantly lit public gardens in Mysore and at the Brindavan dam site, are all part of this glorious celebration, while the float and car festivals atop Chamundi Hill are among the highlights.

The Dussera festival is celebrated in most other parts of the south as **Navaratri** (Nine Nights), the highlight of these 10 days and 9 nights in September/October being the *golu* (doll) displays in homes, **Ayutha Pooja** in factories and homes when all implements of work are decorated and worshipped, and **Vijaya Dasami** when the implements are first put to use again and new ventures started.

As a festival of classical dance and music, the Madras music season in December/January is even better, but it lacks the colour of Dussera in Mysore, though the glittering saris of the women during evening recitals offer some compensation.

Pongal in Tamil Nadu, and **Sankranthi** in Karnataka and Andhra Pradesh in mid-January, are harvest festivals, the bounties of the gods offered back to them for their blessings. Pongal in Tamil Nadu is the most rustically charming of these festivals in the South, lasting almost a week. During that week, houses are cleaned and bonfires made of all that's not needed; rice – with milk and jaggery – is cooked in the open on open hearths and the resultant *pongal* is offered to the gods, cows are decorated and worshipped for the bounty they provide, and rounds of visits are undertaken in all the family's finery. In the deep South, near Madurai, cattle fairs and cattle "rodeos" are part of the festivity, these "rodeos" in several villages taking the form of cattle races, cart races and cattle-wrestling.

Doll displays in every houses are a feature of the three-day **Makara Sankranthi** in Andhra Pradesh each mid-January.

As festive as Pongal is **Onam** in Kerala in August/September. Once again, the harvest is the reason for celebration. Floral decorations catch the eye everywhere, but the greatest excitement is generated by the snake-boat races and other competitive water sports events in places like Alleppey, Cochin, Payipad and Aranumula. Folk dances, music recitals and cultural shows are also part of this happy festivity.

All the world loves a parade, and the southern capitals stage some grand ones on 26 January (Republic Day) and 15 August (Independence Day). The highlights of these parades are not so much the participants but the folk dances and the floats.

Deepavali (the northern Diwali) is another major festive occasion in the South. In the weeks leading up to Deepavali, the sari shops are packed with buyers and additional hordes of sellers. To visit a sari shop at this time is an experience, not the least to marvel at the dazzling arrray of silks in a fantasy of colour and design. Deepavali in the South is mainly a religious occasion, with temple visits followed by calls on friends and relatives with an exchange of sweets and savouries. Fireworks are also an integral part of the 2-day festivity. In parts of the South, where there are old settlements of people from the North, Deepavali is celebrated more riotously, with fireworks, dancing and feasts of sweets.

The **festival of Lord Ganesh** in September/October is also an important celebration in the South. The image of Lord Ganesh, getting grander by the year, is taken in procession through towns and villages before being immersed in the sea, rivers or tanks. Some of the most colourful celebrations are in Hyderabad, where Ganesh Chathurthi is preceded by the month-long **Batkamma** harvest festival.

Christmas and **New Year** in Kerala among the Thomas (Syrian) Christians is another unique experience, different in its sobriety from Christmas celebrations in the West.

Other festivals in the respective states are:

ANDHRA PRADESH

Chitra Festival, Araku Valley (March/April) – tribal dances.

Muharram and **Ramzan**, Hyderabad and Secunderabad.

Ugadi – Telugu New Year – (March/April).

KARNATAKA

Banashankari Temple Fair, Badami (January/February) – A 20-day festival and fair.

Gomateswara Festival (Mahamastakabhisheka), Sravanabelgola – Once in 12 years, the greatest Jain festival in the South. The next one will be in 1993.

Groundnut Fair, Bangalore (November/December) – The highlight of the groundnut season, with groundnut-eating competitions at the Bull Temple.

Karaga Festival, Bangalore (April) – Processions of believers wind their way balancing pots on their heads.

Purandaradasa Music Festival, Hampi (January/February) – In honour of the famed founder of Carnatic Music.

KERALA

Elephant March, Trivandrum and Trichur (January) – A new, tourist-oriented festival in which the focus is on scores of elephants.

Arat Festivals, Trivandrum (March/April and October/November) – 10-day temple festivals culminating in processions of caparisoned elephants to the beach and fireworks displays.

Malayattoor Festival, Malayattoor (March/April) – Hilltop celebration and fulfilment of vows at the shrine of St Thomas.

Pooram Festival, Trichur (April/May) – Processions of caparisoned elephants, fireworks, dance and music recitals are part of this temple festival.

Ulsavoms, Ernakulam (January/February) and **Trivandrum** (March/April and October/November) – temple festivals lasting 10 days.

PONDICHERRY

Firewalking festivals – Held several times a year in different temples, the devotees walking on live embers to fulfill vows.

Masi Magam, Pondicherry (February/March) – Deities from 38 temples are taken to the sea on full moon days for immersion and are joined in the water by thousands of devotees.

TAMIL NADU

Arupathumoovar Festival, Madras (March) at the Kapaleeswarar temple, Mylapore's 11-day festival when the 63 Tamil saints are taken in procession round the temple.

Float Festival, Madras (January/February) – This is the Mylapore temple's tank festival, marked by processions dominated by the temple chariot. Chariot and float festivals are common throughout the South and are part of the festivities of every temple.

Kanduri Festival, at the Islamic shrine in Nagore, and the Roman Catholic **Festival of Our Lady of Health** in Velankanni, both near Thanjavur, are thronged by people of all faiths seeking succour and miracle cures.

Meenakshi Temple festivals, Madurai – Float Festival featuring decorated floats in the Mariamman Tank bearing the deities (January/February); Lord Sundareswarar and goddess Meenakshi with pageantry and processions (April/May); and the **Arani Moolam** festival (August/September) marking the coronation of Lord Shiva as Sundareswarar.

Rajaraja Chola's Birthday, Thanjavur (October) – A celebration in memory of a great king.

Summer festivals, Ooty, Coonoor and Kodaikanal (April/May) – Month-long festivals of music and dance recitals, stage shows, dog shows, flower, fruit and vegetable shows, boat races and boat pageants.

Other important temple festivals are:

Chidambaram: June/July and December/January

Kanchipuram: February, March/April, May, June and November

Rameshwaram: February/March (10 days), and July/August

Srirangam: December/January

Srivilliputtur: July/August and December/January.

Thiruvaiyaru Music Festival, Thiruvaiyaru (January) – Homage in song to the saintly trinity of Carnatic music.

RELIGIOUS SERVICES

Hindu temples are generally open in the early hours of the morning and shortly after dusk in the evenings. All mosques conduct Friday prayers and also sound the call for worship throughout the day. There are Sikh *gurudwaras* in all the state capitals and in one or two other major towns in the South. There are also several synagogues found in the Cochin area of Kerala, but service is conducted regularly only in the Mattancherri synagogue.

Churches hold regular Sunday services as well as the occasional service on other days. Church services are listed in most English language newspapers on Friday or Saturday. Besides the Roman Catholic and Protestant churches, there are several churches in Kerala and a few in the other states which conduct services according to the Eastern (Antioch) Orthodox rites. Madras has an Armenian church open for worship but it does not conduct services.

Footwear should be removed before entering temples, mosques and *gurudwaras*. Some churches, especially those pre-dating the Portuguese, also request that footwear be left outside.

Photography is also prohibited inside most of these places of worship. Remember to put an offering in the box.

COMMUNICATIONS

MEDIA

NEWSPAPERS AND MAGAZINES

The 110-year-old English language newspaper *The Hindu* is published simultaneously in five regional editions and covers the entire South. A serious, well-edited newspaper with a national slant to the news, *The Hindu* is one of the best English-language newspapers in Asia. It is, however, likely to be short on local (regional) news, though it does carry a comprehensive diary of events every day. Its fortnightly magazines, *Frontline* and *Sportstar* (both strong on pictorial content), are among the country's most popular magazines of their type. Visitors from abroad are likely to find *Frontline*'s colourful features on places of interest particularly appealing.

The *Indian Express*, a daily also published in the four southern states, is more entertaining to read than *The Hindu* and has a definite anti-establishment slant. It is also stronger on local news, but with its moderate distribution network, its reach is nowhere near as extensive as *The Hindu*'s.

Despite their regional editions, both these papers are basically Tamil Nadu newspapers, being headquartered in Madras. The other English daily in Madras is the evening *News Today* that's raucous about local politics, but offers little else in the way of news. Better presented and with a strong local slant are Karnataka's popular *Deccan Herald* (from Bangalore) and Andhra Pradesh's *Deccan Chronicle* and *Newstime* (both from Hyderabad). Mumbei's (Bombay's) leading daily, *The Times of India*, has a Bangalore edition as well. The most literate part of India, Kerala, does not have an English daily of its own, though its Malayalam language dailies are among the newspapers with the highest circulation in the country.

The only regional English language magazines of any consequence are *The Week*, a newsweekly from Cochin, *Heritage*, a cultural and general interest monthly from Madras, and Madras' *Aside*, which has moved from being the country's first "city magazine" to becoming a political and film fortnightly that pays some attention to Madras and provides a fair amount of information about the city. *City Tab*, a tabloid weekly from Bangalore, attempts the same thing but is nowhere near as professional.

Hello Madras, a pocket-sized weekly aimed at visitors, is likely to be found in some Madras hotel rooms besides the bookshops. Not very strong on reading matter, the magazine is nevertheless full of the kind of information a visitor to the city might want.

The more popular all-India magazines like *India Today* (India's version of *Time* and perhaps the best magazine in South Asia), *The Illustrated Weekly of India*, and *Sunday*, as well as such special interest magazines as *The India Magazine*, *Discover India*, *Destination Traveller* (all connected with travel) and *Business India* and *Business World* (both business magazines) are available throughout the South and (apart from *Frontline*) are probably more easily available than those of the South.

RADIO & TELEVISION

Both radio and television are state-owned and of little to interest those who do not speak Hindi or the regional languages. Only about a tenth of the programmes each day are in English. Madras alone in the South has a second channel on TV, while the height of the Kodaikanal relay centre enables national programmes to be seen throughout almost the whole of Tamil Nadu. In the other southern states, television viewing is limited to around the capital cities and a few major cities with relay centres.

Radio and TV entertainment in rooms are now offered by even moderate quality hotels in major cities, the VCR bringing into your room a wide range of American and British films.

POSTAL SERVICES

Almost any town of consequence in South India and many a large village has postal and telegraphic facilities. The postal service is good – the authorities generally taking the trouble even to trace change of addresses. In many of the larger towns, the service offers additional facilities – such as **Quick Mail Service** (QMS), at no additional cost, to all district headquarters – and **Speed Post**, to and from major towns at rates lower than the several competitive courier services.

Postal rates at press time are:

Local letters: Rs. 60 for the first 10 gms and Rs. 40 for every extra 10 gm.

Inland letter forms: Rs. 0.50.

Post-cards: Rs. 0.15.

Picture post-cards: Rs. 0.40.

Foreign airmail: Rs. 6.50 for the first 20 gms to all destinations.

Foreign aerogrammes: Rs. 5.00

Airmail post-cards: Rs. 4.00

Poste Restante facilities are fairly reliable and are available at most large post offices. But clearly written (preferably in block-letters) addresses are essential. Correspondents are advised to use the family name: letters addressed to "Samuel Jones", *Poste Restante*, Madras might be filed under either "S" or "J"!

It is also advisable to hand over heavily stamped letters at post office counters for immediate franking; it's safer than using the post box.

Sending post parcels abroad involves wearisome procedures. Many government emporia and leading shops offer to post goods purchased from them; this is a facility that is generally reliable and can be availed of. To send a parcel yourself, it needs to be stitched into cheap cotton cloth and then sealed (there are often people sitting outside major post offices offering this service). Two customs forms also need to be completed. Once the parcel has been weighed and stamps affixed, make sure they are franked and a receipt of registration issued to you. All important or valuable material should be registered.

There are telegraph offices in many large towns open 24 hours. These combined with post offices observe day working hours only. The service is fairly reliable and quite inexpensive. Express telegrams are charged double the rate of ordinary telegrams. There is also a letter telegram rate – and with leisurely delivery schedules – that is offered for foreign telegrams.

TELEPHONES & TELEFAX

The telephone service is improving, but telex – and fax nowadays – is better. Direct dialling facilities are available to and from most larger towns in India and most countries abroad. Long-distance calls can also be booked through the operator, calls being clocked every 3 minutes. A demand service and a lightning service are also available at very much higher rates. Public call boxes are few and far between, but most large post offices and travel termini have them, though those available are rather outdated and cumbersome to use.

Both telex and fax services are reasonably priced and are quite efficient. Good courier services, to both local and international destinations are found in most large towns. DHL, Skypak, Federal Express (Blue Dart in India), UPS and IML all have offices in the major towns of South India.

EMERGENCIES

SECURITY & CRIME

The South is one of the safest parts of the country and violent crime is almost minimal. Walking on the roads late at night, even in the cities, is not a particularly risky proposition. But untoward incidents can occur, so always keep an eye on your property. Things like cameras, expensive and stylish windbreakers and other personal effects which are difficult to obtain in India are the first choice of snatch thieves; handbags, purses, briefcases are comparatively safe. It is advisable, however, to lock all valuables – including passports and travellers' cheques

– in hotel lockers, removing them only when needed.

Always report a loss to the local police. In many cases you'll get your items back intact. The police turnout in the South is generally tidy and efficient. The Madras Police has a particularly good record in crime detection.

In all major cities, the police are on emergency telephone numbers and respond quite fast. They are also quite helpful to foreigners, though communication – even in English – will pose a major problem with all those in the ranks and with junior officers. If you can get through to an Assistant Superintendent of Police or higher – especially in areas outside the urban – you are likely to receive more attention.

Despite police affability and efficiency, it is always advisable to insure your valuables, and there are several good insurance companies – all government-owned – in India. But if you have insured your goods at home, make sure that you are covered for loss in India or while in transit. If anything is lost, obtain a copy of the F.I.R. (First Information Report) from the police to support any insurance claim.

MEDICAL SERVICES

Most district headquarters and major cities have government hospitals. There are less well-equipped government hospitals in smaller towns. Nowhere in India are you really far from medical aid.

While the big government general hospitals in Madras, Bangalore, Hyderabad and Trivandrum are the best places in an emergency, the overcrowding and the resultant effect on standard of hygiene and cleanliness tend to put off most people who are finicky. The Railway Hospital in Madras has particularly good facilities for those with heart problems.

For those seeking cleaner hospitals, there are several private hospitals and nursing homes, many of international class, which charges rates that vary from moderate to expensive. Some of the better ones among these are:

The Vijaya, Apollo and K.J. hospitals in Madras, the internationally renowned CMC Mission Hospital in Vellore (100 miles/160 km from Madras), St John's and St Martha's hospitals in Bangalore and the Apollo Hospitals in Bangalore and Hyderabad.

There are scores of other good private hospitals in the South and your hotel physician will be able to advise you on them. Most of the better hotels do have physicians on call.

Most pharmacies close by 8 or 9 p.m. and open around 10 a.m. The 24-hour pharmacy is a rarity, but there are a couple in most major cities. Hotel staff will be able to help with names.

All major government hospitals have excellent emergency facilities. A few major private hospitals in the four capitals have also been designated by the government as emergency hospitals to treat victims of unnatural causes. While hotels, police and tourist offices will know which private hospitals will admit emergency cases due to unnatural causes, in cases of such emergencies on the road, it is safest to head for the nearest major government hospital.

Though medical aid is quite easily available in South India, it is not a bad idea to include in your travelling kit anti-diarrhoeal medication, an antibiotic or two, aspirins, something for throat allergies, an antiseptic, bandaids, insect repellents, water purification tablets and, in summer, salt tablets.

LEFT LUGGAGE

Most large railway stations, bus terminals and airports have safe left luggage facilities that charge moderately. Most hotels too will oblige those who've been their guests.

GETTING AROUND

MAPS

Using maps is still not an Indian habit, but map-reading is on the increase and several publishers have come forward to meet the demand.

The TTK Maps by TT. MAPS of Madras are the country's best and their series include city, state, and regional road maps and road atlases. But if you are looking for a A to Z of a city, forget it; not even TT. MAPS have got to that stage, though their maps are perfectly adequate for sightseeing and getting to all areas of a city. Another series of maps now available throughout the country are those published by Nelles Verlag GmbH of Munich. The Nelles map INDIA:4 covers the four South Indian states except a small portion of northern Andhra Pradesh that falls in INDIA:3. These maps are available at all leading bookshops throughout the country and in a few of the department stores in Madras.

Some major bookshops also occasionally have Survey of India maps, but these rather more detailed publications are unwieldy and have too much extraneous detail for their size. Maps and Agencies also has a series of state maps and is just getting into city maps.

State government as well as Central government tourism organisations also offer regional, state and capital city maps, sometimes free, sometimes for a small fee.

FROM THE AIRPORT

Most Indian airports are no more than about 9.3 to 15.5 miles (15 to 25 km) from town. This is certainly so in the South; in Cochin, you virtually land in the middle of the city, on Willingdon Island in the harbour lagoon. Getting to and from the airports is not difficult; there are both metered and private taxis available at both ends. There is

also an official coach service at most airports in the region which takes passengers for a nominal fee to and from the important hotels, the city centres and the railway stations.

At the four major airports in the South there are additional transport facilities besides the coach services. Prepaid private taxis are now available and cars can be hired not only for drops and pick-ups but also for daily travel. Taxis and "autos" are also available and are quite safe, but rates have to be negotiated. Starting with Madras, the prepaid public taxi is beginning to catch on.

Public bus services also pass by all airports and Madras airport has the added advantage of having, right across the way from it, Tirusoolam railway station, a halt for the electric trains of the city's commuter lifeline, every 5 minutes during peak hours and every 20 minutes during the rest of the day till 10 p m. The Madras suburban electric train service is a fast and quite comfortable way of reaching the major railway stations and some of the busier centres of the metropolis – though it doesn't go too near the "main street", Mount Road (Anna Salai).

Several of the bigger hotels have their representatives meet all flights at the international and major airports and lay on transportation for passengers booked with them or who would like to stay with them.

DOMESTIC TRAVEL

BY SEA: The days of the passenger liner are over, but cruise ships during the October-March season often touch Marmagao (in Goa), Cochin and Madras. Once in India, however, travelling by sea or inland waterways can be an excitingly different experience. Except during the monsoons from April/May to October there are regular connections by sea between Madras and Port Blair, Cochin and Kavaratti, and Mumbei (Bombay) and Marmagao.

Tours of the Lakshadweep Islands are regularly offered during the season, passengers shipping out from Cochin and staying aboard ship for the nights. The Mumbei-Marmagao coastal journey is a rare experience of song, dance and cuisine that reflects the average Goan's *joie de vivre*.

Speedy launches or slow boats of another age offer trips through the backwaters of Kerala, from Trivandrum, but more comfortably from Quilon, to Cochin and Kodungallur. The Buckingham Canal in its southern reaches north of Madras and through the southern half of Andhra Pradesh up to Kakinada, is also used by slow freight-carrying boats on which a ride can be "hitched" for a small fee. Parts of the Kaveri River in Karnataka and Tamil Nadu are also used for navigation.

BY RAIL

Wherever you go in the South, a railway station is not far away; all stations are connected to the state capitals, which, in turn are well connected with Delhi and Mumbei (Bombay). First class and Second class is what is offered on most of the lesser routes, but on long overnight trips and on the trunk routes Air-conditioned First class, Air-conditioned two-tier Second class and Air-conditioned Chair Cars are also available. The highest charge in Air-conditioned First class is about Rs. 175 for 100 miles/160 km.

Indrail passes are valid for a period of from 7 days to 90 days and allow unlimited travel during their term validity. The pass is no guarantee of seat or berth reservation which has to be made separately for every section of the journey, but foreign tourists have a preferential quota and benefit from it. An Indrail Rover Journey Scheme offers tourists special itineraries which can be booked in advance.

The South has no train comparable to the superfast trains of the north or the luxury of the Palace-on-Wheels. But a southern Palace-on-Wheels is being planned and some trains, such as the Brindavan Express (Madras-Bangalore), the Vaigai Express (Madras-Madurai) and the Blue Mountain Express (Madras-Coimbatore) are very good ones. A railway experience with a difference is the hill train from Mettupalayam (Coimbatore) to Ooty; a double-engined train that is pushed and pulled up a switchbacking route to the mountain top.

Check from which station your train departs. Madras, for instance, has south-bound trains leaving from Egmore and trains bound elsewhere leaving from Central Station. Reservations are computerised nowadays and consequently more reliable. Nevertheless, give yourself at least half an hour to find the seat or berth allotted to you. The reserva-

tions are listed both on the platforms and the train compartments an hour before the train is scheduled to depart, but stations are crowded and trains long, and you might find it difficult to reach your seat in a hurry. Compartment and seat/berth numbers are also marked on the tickets issued, but it is always safer to confirm these indicators on the platform.

Most long-distance trains offer meals, but the dining car has been replaced by a pantry car, so your orders are served at your seat. Most large stations also have refreshment stalls. They also have retiring rooms where accommodation is inexpensive, but prior reservation is recommended. Bed rolls on hire at a nominal fee for overnight journeys are available at most large stations. Bedding is provided with Air-conditioned First class berths.

BY ROAD

The South has one of the best road networks in the country: Tamil Nadu has the best highways, Kerala the prettiest narrow, tree-shaded roads, Lakshadweep no roads to speak of and Karnataka and Andhra Pradesh roads varying from the best to the most poorly-maintained. But no place in the South is too far away from the pavement and public transport.

Inter-State transport services especially between the state capitals and major towns are good, but in Tamil Nadu's city as well as *mofussil* (meaning that great area outside Madras) bus services are the best in the country. Kerala too has good bus services, but the vehicles are not as well-maintained as those run by Tamil Nadu's several state-owned transport corporations. Karnataka and Andhra Pradesh run bus services better than those available in most other parts of India, but they still have a way to go to catch up with Tamil Nadu in frequency, vehicle quality and comfort.

Several privately-owned luxury coaches on trunk routes provide more comfortable, sometimes even air-conditioned, transport on southern trunk routes and are quite inexpensive even by budget travel standards. However, the video programmes with volume on high can be a bit wearing on the system in those coaches which also offer "entertainment" during long journeys.

The Tourism Development Corporations of all the southern states and Pondicherry, as well as the Indian Tourism Development Corporation's (ITDC) local branches offer city, state and South India tours in luxury coaches with guides.

Metered taxis and scooter-rickshaws (called "autos") are available in most cities, but going by the meter is more the exception than the rule. Few taxis are in good condition and for short local trips the "auto" is preferred; given the traffic, it is often faster, the bone-jarring is no more than in taxis and the rates are much lower. Private taxis booked through hotel counters and travel agents are a more reliable and comfortable form of transport, but are more expensive. Most taxi drivers know some English.

Self-drive cars are not available, though bicycles are, but bringing in your own vehicle is not difficult, provided all relevant documents are in order and the vehicle is taken back with you when you leave.

A vehicle may be brought in duty-free for a period up to 6 months if it is accompanied by a *triptyque* or *carnet* from an internationally recognised automobile association or a club that is a member of the Alliance Internationale Tourisme, Geneva. In India, everyone drives on the left (or at least they are supposed to), but cars with left-hand steering are permitted, provided they carry clear signboards on the rear in English stating "Left Hand Drive".

Other road regulations are not very different from the international code. Road signs and distance markings are generally clear in the South, especially in Tamil Nadu; they are scant in northern Andhra Pradesh. Most signs are in English, though not always.

An adventurous way of travelling to India from Europe is by the land routes. Despite often hazardous conditions, several British and German companies continue to offer bus trips to India, and there are always the single car adventurers who travel east or west.

Good motels on the main highways are still few and far between, but plans are underway to establish one every 62 miles (100 km) on all major roads in the South by 1992. There are, however, government travellers' bungalows, dak bungalows and rest houses every 31 or 37 miles (50 or 60 km); they provide facilities ranging from the well-maintained to the uncared-for, but a roof and a bed are assured (if not already occupied), and meals can usually be provided to order. Fuel stops are also available every 31 miles (50 km) or so, though diesel is more frequently available than petrol.

The Automobile Association of South India's offices in the state capitals and most major towns, as well as its mobile patrols, offer motorists all help.

With bullock carts, cyclists and stray cattle still using the roads, and with lorry and bus traffic on the increase on roads meant for a more leisurely age, extra care must be taken while driving and speeds must be moderate. An average of 31 to 37 miles (50 to 60 km) on the main highways and about 40 mph (64 kmh) on secondary roads must be considered good and safe going.

If you are driving, remember a valid international driving licence or an Indian driving licence from any state is essential. So is third-party insurance from a company registered in India or from one with a guarantor in India. National Highways 2, 25 and 7 bring you from Delhi to Land's End at Kanniyakumari via Agra, Jhansi, Nagpur, Hyderabad, Bangalore and Madurai. National Highways 9 and 5 link Madras to Mumbei (Bombay) via Hyderabad. National Highway 4 connects Mumbei and Madras via Bangalore. National Highways 17 and 47 link Bombay and Trivandrum.

ON FOOT

With the beggar and tout menaces having reduced rather drastically, though they have not been completely wiped out, getting around on foot is neither wearying, difficult nor a nuisance. Pavements are slowly vanishing and so, as towns and cities burgeon with a growing immigrant population seeking the city lights, walking on the road is the norm. This practice becomes even more necessary in areas near slums, where the road edges and pavements are used as open-air latrines.

Walking in the crush of city centres and bazaars – as in George Town, Madras, and the Charminar area of Hyderabad – is quite an experience, but is relatively safe. The South is one of the most law-abiding parts of the country, but nevertheless watch your belongings, especially in such crushes; pickpockets exist, as they do everywhere else.

Walking the roads at night is quite safe, but here again the unexpected incident could happen. "Eve-teasing" or molesting women travellers is rare.

Hitch-hiking is not a common practice in India and even less so in the South. "Hitching" a ride on the highways, therefore, is likely to be difficult, especially for a traveller of scruffy appearance. But there has been many a hitch-hiker who has struck it lucky and even got a bed for the night, so it is not completely ruled out.

WHERE TO STAY

ACCOMMODATIONS

As in other parts of India, hotels in the South range from the luxurious "deluxe" to the inexpensive and ill-kept. Prices vary according to quality, but the best are cheaper than their equivalent in Mumbai (Bombay) and Delhi.

In the deluxe and five-star category, rates range from about Rs. 900 to Rs. 1,500 for a room. Mid-range hotels, most of them air-conditioned, charges between Rs. 400 and Rs. 800, while the better downmarket hotels charge between Rs. 200 to Rs. 350, much of the rate in this third category depending on whether you want an air-conditioned room or not.

These rates are purely indicative, but they are all for single occupancy. Most rooms are double-bedded and the rate for two in a room works out to only slightly higher (about 30 percent more), making such occupancy quite inexpensive for the comfort you get. Many hotels have lower off-season rates, those in hill stations often have seasonal rates and group rates are appreciably lower.

The State Tourism Development Corporation runs several small hotels and tourist bungalows, especially outside the metropolises and in tourist centres. This accommodation is quite inexpensive, around Rs.100 for a double room, but standards vary. Also, as in even the better government hotels, service tends to be a bit lethargic and sometimes even indifferent, especially when the larder is low.

Several state government tourist hotels provide dormitory accommodation. Some state governments also run youth hostels with dormitory accommodation. In other places, a bed for the night can be as little as around Rs.10. Young groups might be able to cope with the problems of such accommodation, but for those used to certain standards of comfort, dormitory accommodation is not recommended. The YWCA and YMCA have hostels in most of the major cities. The YWCA hostels are generally better kept.

All foreign visitors are expected to pay their hotel bills only in foreign currency, preferably by travellers' cheque.

Most hotels offer laundry, dry-cleaning and telephone services, but restaurants are unlikely to be found in the cheaper hotels - especially those labelled "lodges" – and bars are unlikely to be found even in many mid-range hotels. Incidentally, the word "hotel" is often used in the South to mean a restaurant and a "military hotel" is a non-vegetarian "hotel" of the more ethnic and cheaper variety.

Central air-conditioning is still a rarity in India, so most of the smaller hotels have air-conditioned (A.C.) and Non-A.C. rooms, the A.C. rooms being equipped with window-type air-conditioners. But though air-conditioning might not be available, a television set in the room with cable television through is often available in such hotels.

Besides all these accommodations, there are countless government travellers' bungalows throughout the South – most meant for officials on tour, but willing to put up sudden arrivals if accommodation is available – and even more *choultries* (bedless dormitories) run for pilgrims by temples and various charitable institutions. Accommodation in either facility is unbelievably cheap, but whereas government accommodation can sometimes be excellent and is always at least tolerable, the majority of *choultries* are not recommended for the visitor from abroad.

Government travel counters are ever ready to oblige with information about accommodation. Unfortunately, most of those who man them are not too aware of the standards foreign visitors demand. Travel agents are to some extent more reliable.

For accommodation in the wildlife sanctuaries, check the section on "National Parks & Sanctuaries."

ANDHRA PRADESH

FIVE-STAR

Ashok Bhaskar Palace and **Krishna Oberoi**, Road No 1, Banjara Hills, Hyderabad 500034, Tel: 222121, Tlx: 0425-6931 OBH IN; and **The Park Hotel**, Beach Road, Vishakapatnam 530023, Tel: 63081, Tlx: 0495-230.

MID-RANGE

Mount Pleasant Cottages in Horsley Hills are quiet retreats. **The Banjara Gateway** (Taj Group) Road No 1, Banjara Hills, Hyderabad 500034, Tel: (0842) 222222, Tlx: 0425-6947 GATE IN, Fax: 0842-222218, is beautifully located and has recently been renovated. It will soon be worthy of five-star status.

The Ritz is an old Palace run to seed and the **Rock Castle Hotel**, Road No 6, Banjara Hills, Hyderabad 500034, Tel: 33541/3, amid spacious gardens, is out of the Raj era; both are slow on service.

Kandhari International, M G Road, in Vijayawada, Tel: 61311, Tlx: 0475-271, is pleasantly efficient. **The Dolphin**, Dabagardens, Visakhapatnam 530020, Tel: 64811, Tlx: 0495-316 is ideally moderate.

INEXPENSIVE

The vegetarian **Ashoka** and **Dwarka** in Hyderabad, **Baseraa**, in Secunderabad, **Bhima's Deluxe** for its vegetarian fare in Tirupati, the luxury **VIP Cottages** up the hill in Tirumala, and the convent cottages and **South Eastern Railway Rest House** in Waltair.

KARNATAKA

FIVE-STAR

Welcomgroup Windsor Manor Sheraton, 25 Sankey Road, Bangalore 560052, Tel 79431, 28031, Tlx: 0845-8209 WIND IN, Fax: 0812-74941. **Taj Residency**, 41/3 Mahatma Gandhi Road, Bangalore 560001, Tel: 568888, Tlx: 0845-8367 TBLR IN, Fax: 0812-563548 and **The Holiday Inn**, 28 Sankey Road, Bangalore 560052, Tel: 79451, 77931, Tlx: 0845-2354, in that order, in Bangalore.

The ITDC's **Ashok Hotel** is short on service and the Taj's **West End**, Race Course Road, Bangalore 560001, Tel:29281, 74191, Tlx: 0845-2337, 2283 WEND IN, Fax: 0812-27610, a beautiful old garden hotel, is ideal for visitors seeking a leisurely holiday (the cottages here are particularly recommended).

The new **Gateway Hotel**, (Taj Group), 66 Residency Road, Bangalore 560025, Tel: 0812-573265, Tlx: 0845-2567 LUX IN, Fax: 0812-573382 is centrally located and promises to be good value.

In Mysore, the ITDC's **Lalitha Mahal Palace**, Mysore 570011, Tel: 26316, 27650, Tlx: 0846-217, gives you palatial rooms, moderate service, antique bathrooms and public facilities. The less expensive quality inn **Southern Star**, Vinobha Road, Mysore 570005, Tel: 27217, Tlx: 0846-256 QSSM IN, is a better bet, unless atmosphere is what you seek. In this category quality-wise, but very much less expensive, is a model of what can be done with little resources if you've the right man in charge is the **Kabini River Lodge** near the Nagarhole National Park.

MID-RANGE

The **Harsha**, No 11, Venkataswamy Naidu Road, Shivajinagar, Bangalore 560051 Tel: 565566, Tlx: 0845-2561, is tidy and good on food. The ITDC's **Hasan Ashok**, Bangalore-Mangalore Road, Hasan 573201, Tel: 8731/37 Tlx: 08306-201, manages to maintain some standards in Hasan, as do the government-run **Adil Shahi** in Bijapur and **Chalukya** in Badami, all in the middle of nowhere. The **Krishnarajasagar** at the Brindavan Gardens near Mysore would have been among the top of the list with its setting and atmosphere, but facilities and service have aged as badly as at the rather similar **Ritz Metrople**, 5 Jhansilakshmibai Road, Mysore 570005 Tel: 20681, 20871, Tlx: 0846-214 RITZ IN. **Welcomgroup Manjarun**, Old Port Road, Mangalore 575001, Tel: 31791, Tlx: 0832-316 WELH IN, in Mangalore is still to get into its stride, but **Valley View International** at Manipal 576119, Tel: 20285, Tlx: 0833-209 VVHC IN – with its keep-fit overtones – and **Summer Sands Beach Resort** at Ullal Beach, near Mangalore, are more appealing to the average holiday-maker. **Pariwar** in Gulbarga is clean and well maintained, but the cuisine is vegetarian.

INEXPENSIVE

Curzon Court, **Bangalore International**, **Chalukya** and **Woodlands** in Bangalore, (the last two are vegetarian), the KSTDC'S **Malpe Beach Resort** near Udupi, the **Vimlesh International** in Mangalore and the **Dasaprakash** in Mysore.

KERALA

FIVE -STAR

The **Taj Malabar** in Cochin, Willingdon Island, Cochin 682009, Tel: 0484-6811, Tlx: 0885-6661 MLBR IN, is probably the best place in the state. An old-style hostelry renovated.

The **ITDC's Kovalam Ashok Beach Resort** near Trivandrum is magnificently located and imaginatively built, its cottages especially rich in the ethnic touch. However, service is lackadaisical, fixtures don't always work and the food is not of the best quality – the riches of the sea being wasted – though all this can be forgiven for the beach and the setting.

MID -RANGE

The **Alleppey Prince**, A S Road, NH 47, Alleppey 688007, Tel: 3752, Tlx: 0884-202 JONS IN, **The Casino**, Willingdon Island, Cochin 682003, Tel: 6821, Tlx: 0885-6314 SAFE IN and the **Sealord**, Shanmugham Road, Ernakulam, Cochin 682031, Tel: 352682, Tlx: 0885-6643 TOUR IN and the **Luciya Continental** in Trivandrum are ef-

ficient, serve a good table and keep an eye on cleanliness.

But for a holiday with a difference, the **High Range Club** in Munnar (if accommodation is available), the KTDC's cottages in Ponmudi hill station, its **Garden House** at Malampuzha Dam and its **Aranya Nivas** on Periyar Lake's edge in the Sanctuary are recommended. All of them are endowed with splendid settings.

INEXPENSIVE

The **Luciya** and the KTDC's **Bolghatty Palace**, Tel: 35003 – for its location alone, if you are willing to put up with all other discomforts – in Cochin; the beautifully sited **Government Guest House** in Sultan's Battery, the **Casino** and **Luciya Place** in Trichur, the lovely old but ill-kept KTDC **Hotel Mascot**, Tel: 68990, Tlx: 0884-229 in Trivandrum and the **Anjali** in Kottayam. **The Tourist Bungalow** in Quilon, once the British Residency, is particularly recommended, its gardens are a delight.

PONDICHERRY

FIVE -STAR

The Ashram's **Sea Side Guest House** – its spotless cleanliness and magnificent view put this inexpensive and homely hostelry among those at the top of the list.

MID -RANGE

The **Pondicherry Ashok**, Chinnakalapet, Pondicherry 605104, Tel: 460/68, Tlx: 0469-239 is new and has still to make a mark, but the **Grand Hotel d'Europe** is old and survives only by serving the last vestiges of French cuisine. Better than both is the well-kept, centrally-located, vegetarian-only **Ashram International Guest House**.

TAMIL NADU

FIVE -STAR

If you can afford to commute to Madras, the **Taj Fisherman's Cove**, Chingleput Dist, Madras 603112, Tel: 04114-6268, Tlx: 041-7194 TAJM IN, Fax: 044-470070 at Covelong Beach on the way to Mammallapuram is the ideal place to stay in – the beach is lovely, the food is good, the cottage ethnic and the service satisfactory.

The Taj Coromandel, 17 Nungambakkam High Road, Madras 600034, Tel: 044-474849, Tlx: 041-7194, 6720 TAJM IN, Fax: 044-470070 in Madras may be more luxurious and better on service and food, but it doesn't have the beach-side hotel's atmosphere.

The Trident, 1/24 G S T Road, Madras 600027, Tel: 434747, Tlx: 041-26055, Fax: 044-434743 (near the airport) emphasising its garden atmosphere, and the **Welcomgroup Park Sheraton**, 132 TTK Road, Alwarpet, Madras, Tel: 452525, Tlx: 041-6868 WELC IN, Fax: 044-455913, are sleek, modern and efficient, vying with each other for top of the list in food; The Trident scores with its coffee shop, the Park Sheraton with its buffet, possibly the best in the country, certainly the biggest.

The renovated **New Carlton**, Lake Road, Kodaikanal 624101, Tel: 560/76 in Kodaikanal and the **Taj Savoy**, Ootacamund, Nilgiris Dist 643001, Tel: 0423-2572,2463, Tlx: 08504 207 SAHO IN, in Ooty, with its cottage and public facilities are splendid reminders of a more leisurely age.

MID-RANGE

The Sree Annapoorna, 47 East Arokiaswamy Road, R S Puram, Coimbatore 641002, Tel:47722, Tlx: 0855-447 is renowned for its vegetarian cuisine, though all else is moderate.

In Madras, the upmarket **Taj Connemara**, Binny Road, Madras 600002, Tel: (044) 860123, Tlx: 041-8197 CH IN, Fax: 044-860193 and **The Savera**, 69 Dr Radhakrishnan Road, Mylapore, Madras, Tel: 474700, Tlx: 041-6896 have had their day and don't offer value for money, while the **Ambassador Pallava**, 53 Montieth Road, Egmore, Madras 600008 Tel: 868584, Tlx: 041-7453, has still to match in service and food the ornateness of its public facilities.

Much less expensive but paying greater attention to cleanliness, service and food are the **New Victoria**, 3 Kennet Lane, Egmore, Madras 600008, Tel: 567738, Tel: 041-7897 VICKY IN, and the **Sindoori**, 24 Greams Lane, off Greams Road, Madras 600006, Tel: 471164, Tlx: 041-8859 SIND IN, with **Harrison's Hotel**, 154/155 Village Road, Nungambakkam, Madras 600034, Tel: 475271 trying to keep up with the other two. The vegetarian hotels like **New Woodlands**, **Ashoka**, **Palm Grove**, **Dasaprakash** and **Maris** are all still strong on cuisine, but all have fallen off on standards, indifferent service and a lack of consciousness about cleanliness being the worst drawbacks.

The ITDC's **Madurai Ashok**, Alagarkoil Road, Madurai 625002, Tel: 42531, Tlx: 0445-297 and **The Pandyan**, Race Course Road, Madurai 625002, Tel: 42470, Tlx: 0445-214 COSY IN, the ITDC's **Temple Bay Ashok Beach Resort**, in **Mahabalipuram** and the **Silver Sands**, Tel: 04113-228, Tlx: 041-8082 SAND IN, could all be better than they are. But good occupancy – due to lack of anything better – has brought with it complacency.

The Sangam, Collector's Office Road, Tiruchipalli 620001, Tel: 41514, Tlx: 0455-221 and **The Femina** (vegetarian), 14C Williams Road, Cantonment, Tiruchipalli 620001, Tel: 41551, Tlx: 0455-333 FMNA IN; **Fernill Palace**, Ootacamund 643004, Tel: 3910, Tlx: 0853-246 FERN IN (an old palace that is redolent with age), the Southern Star **Quality Inn**, Havelock Road, Ootacamund 643001 Tel: 3601, Tlx: 0853-249 QSSO IN and the **YWCA** accommodation in Ooty and the **Shevaroy**, Hospital Road, Yercaud Post, Salem District Tel: 288383 in Yercaud, all provide good value for money.

INEXPENSIVE

The Ritz, Orange Grove Road, Coonoor 643101, Tel: 6242 and **Hampton Manor** Church Road, Coonoor 645101, Tel: 6244 are both rather old-fashioned; TTDC's **Hotel Cape** in Kanniyakumari; **Madras International**, **Imperial** – both of which provide good food – **Shrilekha International** (vegetarian), the **YWCA Guest House** and **Broadlands**, a delightful guest house for the foreigner in Madras; the **Parisutham** in Thanjavur, the **Rajali** in Tiruchi and the TTDC motels at Ulundurpet, Ranipet and Krishnagiri are all functional and reasonably priced.

LAKSHADWEEP

Tourist quarters in Kavaratti and in Minicoy are rather minimal.

Note: This is only a selection of recommended accommodations from among the hundreds in each state. Always check with the main tourist information counters before venturing.

FOOD DIGEST

WHAT TO EAT

There's an infinite variety of ethnic cuisine to be found in South India, ranging from the rather bland, subtly flavoured Udupi vegetarian cooking of the Karnataka coast to the mouth-scorching non-vegetarian fare of Andhra Pradesh, from the coconut milk-based curries of Kerala to the richly spiced Nawabi food of Hyderabad. From district to district, or rather, from ethnic community to community, the cuisine varies in the South and the best of each of this variety constitutes some of the finest dishes in the world. Much of it, though, might not appeal to tastes that prefer fewer spices or more wine in cooking.

Another feature of South Indian cooking is that it is basically vegetarian; rice, the basic staple, being accompanied by a variety of vegetable preparations and an array of curries – dishes with gravies that are used to moisten the rice. Non-vegetarians usually add only a mutton or chicken or fish dish to this spread. Beef is generally cooked only in Christian and Muslim homes and pork only in Christian homes.

There is, however, a world of difference between home-cooking and fare served in restaurants. In fact, ethnic fare in most restaurants is limited to only a few kinds of cooking from this rich variety. Most of the bigger cities have several up-market restaurants specialising in Indian food (meaning North Indian "Mughlai" food), Western food or Chinese food, with several featuring all three on the menu. But very few of these restaurants offer South Indian fare for any meal except breakfast, though a few ethnic specialty restaurants are beginning to make their mark. For ethnic fare, you will have to visit the "vegetarian hotels" in these cities or, for non-vegetarian fare, restaurants that calls themselves "military hotels" or "non-vegetarian hotels".

Also calling itself a "hotel" is the ubiquitous Udupi restaurant. Udupi vegetarian "hotels" are found everywhere in the South – and now not only further north but even overseas. What's standard breakfast fare in the South – *idlis* (steamed rice cakes), *dosais* (wafer-thin rice pancakes, crisped or removed from the gridle soft) and *vadais* (savoury doughnuts) with accompanying chutneys and curries – all taste better when served in Udupi "hotels". So do "meals", helping after helping of rice, each with *ghee*, different curries and curd, all accompanied by a variety of vegetarian side dishes. The visitor should try buttermilk for a drink in these restaurants; it's a subtly flavoured thirst quencher.

Similar vegetarian fare is served in most of Tamil Nadu, Pondicherry and Karnataka but is souped up with peppers in Andhra Pradesh and enriched with coconut milk in Kerala. Kerala breakfast fare, however, is different, *idiappam* – a thin rice noodle preparation steamed as "cakes", *appam* - a coconut-milk-based pancake with a thick soft centre and *puttu* – a rice dish steamed in a bamboo hollow – the usual fare. All are also favourites in the deep south of Tamil Nadu and coastal Karnataka and, like Udupi breakfast staples, now often find themselves on 24-hour menus.

It's in non-vegetarian fare that marked differences emerge from area to area, the fiery hot Andhra chicken and mutton dishes a far cry from the less hot, more subtly flavoured soup-like *milligatawnys*, thick gravies, dry curries and *kurumas* of Chettinad. In like manner, the tamarind-rich sea food preparations – the *molies* and *karimeen* curries of the Malabar Coast in the west.

There's also nothing quite like South Indian coffee: freshly roasted seeds ground at home and their "decoction" obtained by filtering the riches drop by drop, the cup of coffee then being prepared by blending one part of "decoction" to three parts of milk. The local tea is nowhere near as good. Both are almost bought by the yard - or so it would seem, the way they are cooled in down-market restaurants by exchanging the contents between two containers held apart at arm's length.

For dessert, Kwality and Dasaprakash are the best ice creams and are rich in variety; try custard apple ice cream – it's delicious! Indifferent fruit salads are available everywhere. But there's little by way of specialty South Indian desserts; if almond *payasam* (*badhamkeer*) or fruit *payasam* (both creamy liquid desserts) is available, try not to miss it. If your visit falls during the mango season in late March to August – you should try feasting on the South Indian varieties; Nanganapalle is particularly delicious. The smaller species of South Indian bananas are also very tasty.

To taste the best of South Indian dishes, the small, rather shabby-looking "hotels" throughout the area are probably the best places to eat in. But hygiene is not a strong point in most of them. It is safer to patronise restaurants in hotels and government tourist establishments. Up-market restaurants and the fast-food outlets are now to be found in most major cities and in several smaller ones. Unfortunately, few of them serve anything out of the ordinary where South Indian food is concerned.

Here is a list of the places and the various types of dishes they serve.

WHERE TO EAT

ANDHRA PRADESH

Gulbarga

Partwar, Station Road – good Udupi fare.

Hyderabad

Banjara, Banjara Hills – the Mughlai barbecue is the best in town.

Kamat's – there are several outlets of this Udupi-style vegetarian chain in the city; the best branch is at Ravindrapati. Food at all outlets is inexpensive.

Medina, near Charminar – Hyderabadi cuisine at inexpensive prices – is particularly good.

Palace Heights – up-market multi-cuisine of standard variety, but the rooftop view is magnificent and the ambience opulent.

Tirupati

Bhima's – inexpensive Udupi-style fare, the breakfast menu is particulary excellent.

KARNATAKA

Bangalore

Casa Piccola, Residency Road – one of the few truly American-style fast-food "joints", serving excellent pizzas, burgers and milkshakes that are virtually full meals at fast-food prices. Imaginative, informal decor and easy prices. Highly recommended in a city full of fast-food restaurants.

Chalukya, near Racecourse – Udupi fare of good quality served in better than usual ambience.

Chinese Hut, Palace Road – excellent Chinese fare, mainly Cantonese. The "Drums of Heaven" are exquisite.

Coconut Grove, Spencer's Oakshott Place, (Behind M G Road) – excellent Malabar, Konkan, Coorg and Chettinad dishes, with draught beer available!

Kamat's – several of them in the city where the chain first began.

Mavalli Tiffin Rooms, Lalbagh Road – MTR is not to be missed. The finest Udupi style fare in the South and as much of it as you wish to eat at specified times. But be prepared to wait in the queue. Breakfast here – especially before 7 a.m. – should not be missed.

Memories of China, Taj Residency, M G Road – the buffet at lunch is possibly the best Chinese lunch in the country.

Prince's, Brigade Road – in the one city in the South where eating out is a long-time reflection of its cosmopolitan atmosphere, and where good restaurants meeting that demand have always flourished, the up-market Prince's stands out for quality, value for money, service and regal ambience. The steaks are about the best in the country. Table bookings advised. Diners – if couples – have free access to the popular disco next door.

Topkapi, M G Road – had everything going for it with its splendid rooftop location, but over the years its quality of food (multi-cuisine) has slipped, though it still has atmosphere and a glorious view.

Tycoons, Copper Arch, Infantry Road – good continental food.

West End, near Racecourse – poolside barbecue under the trees is recommended.

Mysore

Kamat's, Jhansi Laxmibai Road – another in that vegetarian chain that maintains uniform quality.

Dasprakash, J. Gandhi Square and Yadavagiri Road – Udupi cuisine, *dosais* a specialty.

Metropole, Jhansi Laxmibhai Road – for Western fare out of the Raj and where some old-fashioned standards are still maintained.

KERALA

Calicut

Beach Road – several small places here, ranging from fast-food to the more formal, serve a variety of non-vegetarian dishes from Kerala to South Indian and more international cuisine.

Indian Coffee House, Kallai Road and Indira Gandhi Road – a chain that serves the best South Indian "decoction" coffee and tasty snacks.

GH Road – Kerala Muslim cuisine in several places.

Cochin

Bharat, Darbar Hall Road – Udupi vegetarian of good quality.

Ceylon Bake House, M G Road, Ernakulam – good ethnic fare.

Dwaraka, M G Road, Ernakulam – Udupi as well as North Indian vegetarian, the latter of better quality.

Sealord, Shanmugam Road, Ernakulam – the rooftop restaurant provides a lovely view of the harbour, but the fare is moderate.

Kottayam

Aanjali – the *karimeen* (fresh water fish) curry is excellent.

Trivandrum

Luciya Continental – the best of the multi-cuisine hotel foods in the city.

PONDICHERRY

Pondicherry

Aurobindo Ashram Guest Houses, Goubert Avenue, Gingee Salai and Rue Romain Rolland – rather bland but nutritious vegetarian fare in ample quantities (cafeteria style).

Grand Hotel d'Europe, Rue Suffern – once famous for its French cuisine, vestiges of which still remain.

Transit, Rue Romain Rolland – an excellent new multi-cuisine restaurant in an area where several small Vietnamese restaurants serve "home-cooked" meals. Has a few French dishes on its menu but with 24 hours notice will produce a meal comparable to the best in the Grand's heyday.

TAMIL NADU

Covelong

Fisherman's Cove – the buffets, especially the one on Saturday night, are strong on excellent seafood, but prices are up-market.

Coimbatore

Annapoorna – excellent Udupi vegetarian, especially breakfast.

Madras

Amaravathi, Cathedral road and elsewhere – Andhra cuisine, pepper-hot and tasty, but standards of cleanliness are low.

Bahar, Cathedral Road – the barbecue is the best in town.

Cascade, Nungambakkam – the best Chinese food in town, but prices are steep.

Dasa, Anna Salai – Udupi fast-foods in an up-market ambience but at moderate prices.

Dynasty, Anna Nagar – moderately priced Chinese fare, better than most.

Dasaprakash, Poonamallee High Road – flagship of another Udupi chain; the dosai is reputable.

Imperial, Egmore; **Buhari**, Mount Road and Central Station – a chain serving non-vegetarian Muslim fare with a strong flavour of Kerala and Sri Lanka.

Kaaraikudi, Radhakrishnan Salai – Chettinad cuisine that's more Andhra in its flavouring. The ambience is ethnically appealing, but standards are only moderate as are the prices.

Maratha, Trident Hotel, near the old airport – the best up-market coffee shop in town; the Thai fare, the South Indian *thalis* (good value for money) and the varied Continental fare are all recommended.

Ponnusamy's, Royapettah – the best Chettinad fare outside Chettinad, and it's inexpensive too. But if you are fussy about cleanliness and eating decorum, it's best to take-away.

Raintree, Taj Connemara, Binny Road – the open-air ambience is superb in this up-market restaurant serving what's close to authentic Chettinad cuisine.

Residency, Park Sheraton, TTK Road – up-market, but the daily buffet is something to be experienced; it's possibly the largest spread in India.

Sagari, Chola Sheraton, Cathedral Road – the view at night is superb, there's a band in attendance, and the Chinese fare is adequate in this up-market rooftop restaurant.

Tic-tac – tasty and inexpensive Chinese and North Indian fast food.

Woodlands Drive-in, Cathedral Road – the only Woodlands that still maintains quality, but this restaurant in a horticultural garden is better on *channa-bhatura* (North Indian fare, comprising chick-peas and large puffed-up wheat "bread") than on its own traditional Udupi cooking.

Mabalipuram

Silver Sands – seafood can be good in its open-air restaurant of variable standards.

Madurai

Railway Refreshment Room – not quite as good as its Tiruchi counterpart, but better than most others for similar fare.

Harvey Mills Club – superb meals out of the heyday of the Raj, if you can get youself invited.

Ooty

Taj Savoy – good value for money at lunch and dinner buffets.

Trichy

Sangam, Cantonment – South Indian non-vegetarian fare is recommended.

Femina, Cantonment – vegetarian fare of good quality with excellent service.

Railway Refreshment Room – in the days of the Raj, one of the best places for imperial Western "staples" and a version of "rice and curry" from that era. Memories of that unique cuisine linger on.

Ulundurpet

Motel Emerald – Half-way house on the Madras-Madurai highway. One of the few Government establishments with pleasant surprises from its kitchen – if the larder is not empty.

THINGS TO DO

NATIONAL PARKS & SANCTUARIES

The list that follows details the main protected areas in the four states of South India. Between them they include some of the most important wildlife areas of the country, protect numerous endangered and threatened species and save much natural forest.

ANDHRA PRADESH

The largest of the four South Indian states, Andhra Pradesh, has a varied terrain with a rich and interesting population of birds and animals. Although it has 16 sanctuaries, including the large Nagarjunasagar Tiger Reserve, it has no area with national park status. While most of the sanctuaries have accommodation, the tourist infrastructure is limited and, in most cases, visitors have to make their own arrangements. For information, contact: The Chief Wildlife Warden, Saifabad, Hyderabad, AP 500004.

Andhra has a long and varied coastline with two great rivers (the Godavari and the Krishna) flowing west to east into the Bay of Bengal. There are mangrove forests along the estuaries, dry deciduous forest inland, and extensive open scrub stretching into the Deccan plateau. The southern half of the state, below the Krishna river, is largely thorn forest while the northern part is more teak dominated. Lake Pulicat is one of South Asia's largest lagoons and an important center for both resident and migratory water birds.

CORINGA SANCTUARY

Established in 1978, this area of 90 sq. miles (235 sq. km) in the delta region of the Godavari river is home to otters, fishing cats, the estuarine crocodile (*Crocodylus porosus*) and many water birds.

Best time to visit: November-March (summer temperatures up to 96°F/36°C)

Accommodation: rest houses

Contact: DCF (WL Management), Rajahmundry.

Nearest town: Kakinada (12.5 miles/20 km) with railhead. Accommodation and transport are available in the town.

ETURANAGARAM SANCTUARY

Established in 1953, this large sanctuary covering 313.5 sq miles (812 sq km) the core (85 sq miles/219 sq km)of which has been proposed as a national park. This dry deciduous mixed and teak forest near the borders of Maharashtra, Madhya Pradesh and Andhra is the habitat of many mammals (tiger, leopard, sloth bear, gaur, sambar, chousingha, chinkara, mouse deer, blackbuck and leopard cat) along with interesting birdlife. The forest department has both vehicles and machans for game viewing.

Best time to visit: May-March (up to 114°F/46°C); November-March are cooler and more pleasant months.

Accommodation: 8 guest cottages (22 beds); forest rest houses at Salvai, Tadavai and Eturnagaram town.

Contact: DFO, Warangal, AP 560 010.

Nearest town: Eturnagaram (10 miles/17 km)

Rail: Warangal (56 miles/90 km)

Airport: Hyderabad (140 miles/225 km).

KAWAL SANCTUARY

Established in 1965, this sanctuary covering 345 sq. miles (893 sq. km.) of dry deciduous hill forest with dry teak stands over uneven terrain has tiger, leopard, sloth bear, gaur and chousingha among others.

Best time to visit: February-May (up to 112°F/44°C)

Accommodation: 2 rest houses

Contact: DFO (WL), Jannaram, Adilabad Dist. AP 504 205

Nearest town: Jannaram (1/2 mile/1 km)

Rail: Mancherial (30 miles/60 km) Hyderabad (175 miles/280 km)

KINNERSANI SANCTUARY

Established in 1977 with a core area of 86 sq miles (222 sq km) and a buffer zone of 160 sq miles (413 sq km), this undulating sanctuary of mixed forest surrounding the Kinnersani Reservoir has a good range of mammal and bird species, which includes the tiger, dhole, leopard, guar, wild buffalo and sloth bear.

Best time to visit: November-June (summer maximum 120°F/49°C, drops to 50°F/10°C in January).

Accommodation: 7 small rest houses.

Contact: Wildlife Warden, Poloncha, Khamman Distt, AP.

Nearest town: Paloncha (7.5 miles/12 km)

Rail: Bhadrachalam Road (15 miles/24 km)

Air: Vijayawada (106 miles/170 km)

KOLLERU SANCTUARY

Established in 1963, this large bird sanctuary of almost 347 sq miles (900 sq km) wetland and marsh in a natural shallow depression surrounding Kolleru Lake, between the Krishna and Godavari deltas. Water, after the northeast monsoon, extends over 232 sq miles (600 sq km). Many migratory ducks and resident water birds and the famous pelicanry at the village of Aredu use the lake for feeding.

Best time to visit: late October-February
Accommodation: 5 huts; PWD resthouse at Eluru
Contact: DCF (WL), Rajahmundry, AP.
Nearest town & Rail: Eluru (12.5 miles/20 km)
Air: Vijayawada (40 miles/63 km)

MANJIRA SANCTUARY

Established in 1978, this small pocket of rain forest on the banks of the river Manjira is only 12.5 sq miles (20 sq km) in extent. Many water birds and mugger crocodiles; also two species of fresh-water turtles.
Best time to visit: November-February (cool), March-June
Accommodation: Small rest house
Contact: DFO (WL), Medak, AP
Nearest town: Sangareddy (2.5 miles/5 km)
Rail: Ramachandrapuram (15.5 miles/25 km)
Air: Hyderabad (34 miles/55 km)

NAGARJUNASAGAR SRISAILAM SANCTUARY (TIGER RESERVE)

Established in 1978, this sanctury of 1,374 sq. miles (3,568 sq km) is the largest of India's tiger reserves, with a core area of 463 sq miles (1,200 sq km). The reserve spans the Krishna river with a dam forming the Nagarjunasagar reservoir. The area is dissected by deep winding gorges which cut through the Mallamalai hills. A range of forest types, from dry scrub and dry mixed deciduous forests on the plateau to the west and south to moist valleys with bamboo and tropical thorn forest to the east. Since the sanctuary came under Project Tiger in 1983 a programme to relocate the village inside the core area is now under way. With the reduction of human interference and the stopping of grazing, this sanctuary could soon become a major park. A proposal in 1988 to give the core area of 463 sq miles (1,200 sq km) national park status is yet to be implemented. The range of animals includes the leopard, sloth bear, palm civet, wolf, striped hyena, in addition to the tiger. Also found are barking deer, nilgai, chinkara, chousingha, sambar, chital, langur, bonnet macaque and the Indian pangolin.

Best time to visit: October-June (summer maximum 108°F/43°C).
Accommodation: 3 guest houses next to temples within the sanctuary.
Contact: Field Director, Project Tiger, Srisailam Dist., Kurnool,AP 518 102.
Nearest town & Rail: Machesla (8 miles/13 km)
Air: Hyderabad (94 miles/150 km)

NEELAPATTU SANCTUARY

Established in 1976, this small water bird sanctuary at the coastal village of Neelapattu covers only 1.5 sq miles (4.5 sq km). The focal point is the village tank which, during the winter, becomes a large and mixed heronry.
Best time to visit: November-March
Accommodation: PWD rest house at Sulurpetta
Contact: ACF (WLM), Sulurpetta, Nellore Distt. AP.
Nearest town: Sulurpetta (10 miles/16 km)
Rail: Dorawai Satram (1 km)
Air: Madras (75 miles/120 km)

PAKHAL SANCTUARY

Established in 1952, this sanctuary of 339 sq miles (878 sq km) of forest includes a large lake. Interesting bird life and an extensive range of mammals.
Best time to visit: November-June
Accommodation: 2 guest houses
Contact: DFO (WLM), Warangal, AP 506010.
Nearest town: Narsampet (6.25 miles/10 km)
Rail: Warrangal (28 miles/45 km)
Air: Hyderabad 112 miles/180 km)

PAPIKONDA SANCTUARY

Established in 1978. Covers 228 sq. miles (590 sq km) of mixed forest on the banks of the Godavari as it cuts through the Eastern Ghats, with a core area of 85 sq miles (221 sq km). Many steep slopes of the Papikonda range give the sanctuary its name. Animals include tiger, leopard, chousingha and wolf and many water birds.
Best time to visit: November -June
Accommodation: 2 rest houses

Contact: DCF (WLM), Rajahmundry, AP.

Nearest town & Rail & Air: Rajahmundry (50 miles/80 km)

POCHARAM SANCTUARY

Established in 1952 on the banks of the Pocharam Lake on 50 sq miles (129 sq km) of bear, wolf, wild boar and chousingha with flamingoes and other water birds at the lake.

Best time to visit: late October-May

Accommodation: 2 bungalows

Contact: DFO (WLM), Medak, AP.

Nearest town: Medak (5.6 miles/9 km)

Rail: Akkannapet (9.4 miles/15 km)

Air: Hyderabad (72 miles/115 km)

PRANAHITA SANCTUARY

Established in 1980 along the river Pranahita on 52 sq miles (136 sq km) of mixed teak forest holding a few gaurs, tigers, leopards, sloth bears, chousinghas and others and a few water birds.

Best time to visit: November-May

Accommodation: 2 rest houses

Contact: DCF (WLM) Rajahmundry, AP

Nearest town, Rail & Air: Rajahmundry (50 miles/80 kim)

PULICAT SANCTUARY

Established in 1976, the southeastern mouth of this large lagoon is in Tamil Nadu. Of the 224 sq miles (580 sq km), about 193 sq miles (500 sq km) are in Andhra. Large flocks of flamingo, many migrant shore birds, and local residents are visible. Boats are available in the early morning.

Best time to visit: late October-March

Accommodation: small guest house

Contact: ACF (WLM), Sulurpetta, Nellore Distt. AP

Nearest town & Rail: Sulurpetta (5 miles/8 km)

Air: Madras (63 miles/100 km)

ROLLAPADU SANCTUARY

A small 1.5 sq mile (4 sq km) sanctuary of gently undulating grassland at the northern end of the Erramala range of hills. Established in 1985 to protect the 60-odd resident Great Indian Bustard there. A buffer zone

has been proposed but currently it has a large cattle and human population. Another rare bird breeding in the sanctuary is the Lesser Florican. Animals found in the sanctuary and buffer include blackbuck, wolf, jackal, fox and the blacknaped hare.

Best time to visit: May-June for minor nesting, and August-December for major nesting.

Accommodation: None at present but a visitors' centre with rooms has already been proposed.

Contact: Forester, Rolapadu Village, Nandikotkur Taluka, Kurnool Dist., AP 518 508

Nearest town and rail: Kurnool (25 miles/40 km)

Air: Hyderabad (154 miles/248 km)

SHRI VENKATASWARA SANCTUARY

A 196 sq mile/507 sq km sanctuary of which the 115 sq mile/300 sq km core area has been proposed as a national park. One of the few well preserved south eastern deciduous forests with several endemic species of both flora and fauna such as the red sanders trees and the golden gecko.

Best time to visit: November-February

Nearest town, rail & air: Tirupati

SIWARAM SANCTUARY

Established in 1978, this small sanctuary of undulating forest on the Godavari river near the Madhya Pradesh border is home to several species of mammals and birdlife.

Best time to visit: November-March

Accommodation: 3 rest houses

Contact: DFO (WLM), Jannaram, Adilabad Distt, AP. 504 205.

Nearest town: Manthani (3 miles/5 km)

Rail: Peddalpalli (19 miles/30 km)

Air: Hyderabad (187 miles/300 km)

By early 1989 other areas had been proposed as sanctuaries and some existing sanctuaries proposed as national parks. Many of the new sanctuaries are in the Eastern Ghats near the Orissa border. Among the areas proposed are:

Donubhavi National Park and Sanctuary. An area of 116 sq miles/300 sq km and

270 sq miles/700 sq km respectively includes the southern limit of sal forest interspersed with teak. Situated in Srikakulam District in the northern part of the Eastern Ghats near the Orissa border. Elephants traverse the area.

The GBM National Park and Sanctuary covering a total of 116 sq miles/300 sq km and 371 sq miles/962 sq km respectively in the Nallamallai hill ranges of Kurnool district. Mainly arid mixed deciduous forest with teak and bamboo. The area has a viable population of tiger, leopard, dhole, sloth bear, sambar and chowsingha.

Gudem-Marripakala National Park and Sanctuary. Another large area of 132 sq miles/341 sq km and 270 sq miles/700 sq km respectivly. With an altitude range of between 328 ft/100 m and 3,281 ft/1,000m this mostly moist deciduous forest is rich in both plants and the distinctive birds of the Eastern Ghats.

Lankamalai Sanctuary. A 116 sq mile/ 300 sq km sanctuary has been proposed in the Lankamalai range of the Eastern Ghats in Cuddapah District. On 14 January 1986 the Bombay Natural History Society rediscovered the Jerdon's or Double-banded Courser (*Cursorius bitoraquatus*), last recorded in 1900.

Sriharikota Island Sanctuary. This 8 sq mile/22 sq km proposed sanctuary for the saltwater crocodile and rare biotype is also the launch pad for India's space programme and could easily be a protected area.

KARNATAKA

Southern Karnataka in what was once Mysore State has long been famous for its rich and distinctive wildlife and magnificent forests. The great tracts of forest that remain today as a legacy of the management and concern shown by the Mysore rulers are noted for elephant, gaur and other large mammals.

Eleven of the 23 protected areas are within the rich (and vulnerable) Western Ghats. The forests of the Western Ghats contain many endemic birds and flora species. In the northern part of the state the dry thorn forests and scrub are home to different species. In the dry deciduous scrub of Ranebennur, the blackbuck and an increasing number of great Indian bustard are found. The bustard

has also returned to the scrub areas north of Bijapur, near the Maharashtra border.

BANDIPUR NATIONAL PARK & TIGER RESERVE

Established in the early 1930s with an area of 23 sq miles (60 sq km), the area was expanded to 266 sq miles (690 sq km) in 1974 and is now a total of 874 sq km. A further extension is proposed to the northeast. It is bounded on the northwest, west and south by the Nagarahole, Wynad and Mudumalai parks respectively. It has one of the best-planned road systems among Indian parks and provides excellent opportunities for game viewing, especially of elephants. The gaur population is on the increase after the 1968 rinderpest epidemic. The park is bisected north-south by the Mysore-Ootacamund road. The hilly landscape in the shadow of the Western Ghats is dissected by rivers and streams. Forest vehicles are available.

Best time to visit: March-July, September-October

Accommodation: forest lodges, cottages; forest rest houses at Kakanhalla, Mulehole, Kalkere and Gopalaswamy (Betta).

Contact: Field Director-Project Tiger, Bandipur Tiger Reserve, Aranya Bhavan, Ashokpuram, Mysore 570008. Tel:20901 or ACF, Bandipur National Park, Bandipur. Tel:30.

Nearest town: Gundulpet (12.5 miles/20 km)

Rail & air: Mysore (50 miles/77 km), Bangalore (136 miles/217 km).

BANNERGHATTA NATIONAL PARK

Established in 1974 with 40 sq miles (104 sq km) of undulating terrain with valleys and hills, only 17 miles (28 km) south of Bangalore. Mammal life is poor although the occasional leopard is seen, and also chital, wild boar and sloth bear. Zoo-born tigers have recently been introduced to a large enclosed area. A few elephants still traverse the area. There is also interesting scenery and fascinating birdlife. Popular attraction, especially during weekends.

Best time to visit: September-June
Accommodation: forest rest house
Contact: ACF, Bannerghatta National Park, Bangalore-83.

Nearest town, rail & air: Bangalore (17 miles/28 km). Bangalore bus nos 365, 366 and 368 go to the park.

BHADRA SANCTUARY

Established in 1974 over 189 sq miles (492 sq km) of the Bhadra river valley and ringed by the Bababudan range. Most of the valley is covered with moist deciduous forest. Roads are in poor condition and jeeps are needed. Large gaur population, with other animals such as the elephant, tiger, chital and sambar. Vehicles and forest guides available at Muthodi. There has been a proposal to upgrade the sanctuary to national park status.

Best time to visit: October-May
Accommodation: forest rest houses at Sukhalathi, Seegekan and Kesave booked through the Range Officer, Muthodi, via Mallandur PO, Chickmangalur Dist. PWD Bungalow and Circuit House at Lakkavalli Dam booked through the Asst. Executive Engineer, B R Project, Lakkavalli.

Contact: ACF, Wildlife Preservation Subdivision, 1st Cross Lane, Jayanagar, Shimoga, Karnataka 577201. Tel:2983

Nearest town: Shimoga (19 miles/30 km)
Rail: Tarikere (12.5 miles/20 km)
Air: Belgaum (151 miles/242 km), Bangalore (158 miles/255 km), Mangalore (135 miles/218 km)

BILIGIRI RANGASAMY TEMPLE SANCTUARY

Established in 1974 south of Mysore over 125 sq miles (324 sq km) and extended to 209 sq miles (540 sq km) in 1987. The sanctuary protects a southern spur of the Eastern Ghats and is a link with the forests extending from the Western Ghats. Elephants are occasionally seen on migration, gaur, chital, sambar and an occasional tiger. A local tribe known as the Soliga live in the neighbouring forest.

Best time to visit: October-May
Accommodation: A deluxe tented camp has been set up by Jungle Lodges & Resorts, 2nd Floor, Shrungar Shopping Centre, MG Road, Bangalore 560001. Tel:575195. Rest houses at K Gudi, B R Hills, Seematti and Bedaguli booked through the Deputy Conservator of Forests, Chamrajnagar, Mysore Dist 571313. Tel:59.

Contact: ACF, Wildlife Preservation SD, Mysore-4 (Tel: 21159).

Nearest town & Rail: Chamarajanagar (37 miles/60 km)
Air: Mysore (68 miles/110 km), Bangalore (156 miles/250 km).

BRAHMAGIRI SANCTUARY

Established in 1974 in southern Coorg near the border with Kerala. Borders Nagarahole National Park to the east. Currently 70 sq miles (181 sq km) of hill country with moist and mixed deciduous forest. It has been proposed to extend the sanctuary northwards to 109 sq miles (281 sq km) and give it park status. Animals which can be seen here are the elephant, gaur, tiger, mouse deer, chital and sambar.

Best time to visit: October-May.
Accommodation: none
Contact: ACF, Wildlife Preservation, Aranya Bhavan, Ashokpuram, Mysore 570008. Tel. 21159

Nearest town: Virajpat (24 miles/39 km)
Rail: Cannanore (Kerala) (47 miles/75 km)
Air: Mysore (84 miles/135 km)

DANDELI SANCTUARY

Established in 1975 and now covering 322 sq miles (834 sq km) of mostly moist deciduous forest; some teak and bamboo. The sanctuary once covered a huge area of (5,730 sq km) most of which was badly degraded. The area falls on the eastern slope of the Western Ghats. Fair road system. Large mammals including elephant, tiger, sambar, chital and occasional wolf seen.

Best time to visit: December-May.
Accommodation: 6 rest houses
Contact: ACF, Wildlife Preservation Subdivision, Dharwad, Karnataka. Tel: 40302.

Nearest town: Dandeli (1.25 miles/2 km)
Rail: Dharwad (31 miles/50 km)
Air: Belgaum (75 miles/120 km)

GHATAPRABHA SANCTUARY

Established in 1974, a small bird sanctuary of 11 sq miles (29 sq km). Mostly wetland next to the Ghataprabha river north of Belgaum.

Best time to visit: October-January
Accommodation: 4 small rest houses
Contact: ACF, Wildlife Preservation Subdivision, Dharwad, Karnataka. Tel: 40302
Nearest town & Rail: Gokak Falls
Air: Belgaum (51 miles/82 km)

KUDREMUKH NATIONAL PARK

A large park of 232 sq miles (600 sq km) formed in 1988 to protect the northern most extent of shola forest and an important lion-tailed macaque population. Other mammals found include tiger, leopard and gaur. The proposed 38 sq mile (100 sq km) Ammedikal sanctuary will link the park, along a narrow neck of Western Ghat forest, with the new **Pushpagiri Sanctuary** (42 sq miles/ 108 sq km) in Coorg (Kodagu) district to the south.

Best time to visit: September-May.
Accommodation: date not available
Contact: The Chief Wildlife Warden, Aranya Bhavan, 18th Cross, Malleswaram, Bangalore 560003. Tel:341993.
Nearest town: Kudramukh
Rail and air: Mangalore (63 miles/100 km)

MOOKAMBIKA SANCTUARY

Established in 1974 on the edge of the Western Ghats with a mixed semi-evergreen forest and tropical evergreen forest at higher elevations. Curently 95 sq miles (247 sq km) it may be expanded to 142 sq miles (367 sq km) to link up with Someswara sanctuary. Very high rainfall from early June. The tiger, sloth bear, lion-tailed macaque and chital are visible here.

Best time to visit: November-April
Accommodation: 2 bungalows (10 beds)
Contact: ACF Wildlife Preservation Subdivision, Jayanagar 1st cross, Shimoga, Karnataka 577201, Tel: 2983.
Nearest town: Bindur (15 miles/25 km)
Air & Rail: Mangalore (56 miles/90 km)

NAGARAHOLE NATIONAL PARK

Established in 1955 and expanded to its present size of 221 sq miles (573 sq km) in 1975. There is a further proposal to extend the park to 278 sq miles (721 sq km) and include the Masal Valley of Kakankote Reserve Forest and part of the upper Kaveri River valley to the north. Extremely attractive situation with the Brahmagiri hills in the distance. The Kabini river has been dammed to form a large and attractive reservoir which separates the park from Bandipur National Park to the southeast. The game viewing is excellent and well organised by the Kabini River Lodge. Large groups of gaur, elephant, the occasional tiger and leopard, chital and sambar are seen. Over 250 species of birds recorded. Park vehicles available.

Best time to visit: October-April
Accommodation: 2 forest rest houses (contact ACF-Mysore) and huts at Nagarahole booked through the Range Forest Officer, Nagarhole. Tel: Kutta 21; Kabini Jungle Lodge 14 rooms (double), with excellent facilities. Trained naturalists. Contact: Jungle Lodges & Resorts Ltd, 2nd floor, Shrungar Shopping Centre, MG Road, Bangalore 560001. Tel:575195.
Contact: Deputy Conservator of Forests, Wildlife Preservation, Aranya Bhavan, Ashokpuram, Mysore 570008. Tel: 21159.
Nearest town: Kutta (2.5 miles/7 km)
Rail & Air: Mysore (60 miles/96 km)

RANGANATHITTU
BIRD SANCTUARY

Established in 1940 near Tippu Sultan's capital of Srirangapatnam on six tiny islands in the Kaveri River 10 miles (16 km) north of Mysore. Boats available for hire. Nesting starts as early as June for many species. Scenically beautiful. A few crocodiles, otters and flying foxes (fruit bats) seen.

Best time to visit: June-November
Accommodation: 3 "Riverside Cottages' each with two rooms booked through KSTDC, Badami House, Opp City Corporation Offices, Bangalore 560002 Tel:221299
Contact: ACF, Wildlife Preservation Subdivision, Aranya Bhavan, Ashokpuram, Mysore 570008 Tel:21159.
Nearest town, Rail & Air: Mysore (10 miles/16 km)

RANEBENNUR BLACKBUCK SANCTUARY

Established in 1974 over 46 sq miles (119 sq km) to check the rapid decline of blackbuck in northern Karnataka. The wolf, fox, jackal and great Indian bustard can be found. Mostly dry scrub and open undulating ground with some eucalyptus plantation.

Best time to visit: May-December for Bustard; open throughout the year.

Accommodation: Rest houses at Gangajal and Ranebennur.

Contact: ACF, Wildlife Preservation Subdivison, Dharward, Karnataka Tel: 40302

Nearest town and rail: Ranebennur (2.5 miles/4 km)

Air: Belgaum (125 miles/199 km), Bangalore (185 miles/298 km)

SHARAVATHY VALLEY SANCTUARY

Established in 1974 over 166 sq miles (431 sq km) of the Western Ghats with wet tropical evergreen forest and semi-evergreen forest. The sanctuary is contiguous with the Mookambika sanctuary to the south. Has high rainfall from June. Chital, gaur, sloth bear, macaques and the occasional tiger seen.

Best time to visit: November-May

Accommodation: 4 rest houses (34 beds)

Contact: ACF, Wildlife Preservation Subdivision, 1st Cross Lane, Jayanagar, Shimoga, Karnataka 577201. Tel:2983.

Nearest town: Kagal (0.5 mile/1 km)

Rail: Talguppa (9 miles/15km)

Air: Mangalore (112 miles/180 km), Bangalore (230 miles/369 km).

SHETTIHALLY SANCTUARY

Established in 1974 on 152 sq miles (395 sq km) of mixed deciduous and semi-evergreen forest. Tiger, elephant, chital and sambar seen.

Best time to visit: November-May

Accommodation: 4 rest houses (20 beds)

Contact: ACF, Wildlife Preservation Subdivision, 1st Cross Lane, Jayanagar, Shimoga, Karnataka 577201. Tel: 2983

Nearest town & Rail: Shimoga (3 miles/5 km)

Air: Mangalore (118 miles/190 km), Bangalore (170 miles/273 km).

Other protected areas in Karnataka include: **Anshi National Park** (96 sq miles/250 sq km, Uttara Kannada dist.); **Adi Chunchanagiri Sanctuary** (Mandya dist.); **Arabititu Sanctuary** (5 sq miles/14 sq km, Mysore dist.); **Cauvery Sanctuary** (197 sq miles/510 sq km, Mandya & Bangalore dists.); **Melkote Temple Sanctuary** (19 sq miles/50 sq km, Mandya dist.); **Nagu Sanctuary** (12 sq miles/30 sq km, Mysore dist.); **Someshwara Sanctuary** (34 sq miles/88 sq km, Dakshina Kannada Dist.); and **Talakaveri Sanctuary** (40 sq miles/105 sq km, Kodagu dist.). Information on any of these areas and other protected areas can be obtained from: The Chief Wildlife Warden, Arnya Bhawan, 18th Cross, Malleshwaram, Bangalore 560003. (Tel: 31993).

TAMIL NADU

The parks of Tamil Nadu are mostly little-known, although their range is extraordinary - mixed deciduous forests of the Western Ghats, through the hot, dry plains, to the coastal and marine parks. Two biosphere reserves have been established: one at the Gulf of Mannar and the other in the Nilgiris. Most of Tamil Nadu receives both the monsoons, and the two rainy seasons severely limit game viewing. November to February are pleasant months to travel through the state.

ANNAMALAI WILDLIFE SANCTUARY

Established in 1976, it covers 323 sq miles (840 sq km) of the northern end of the Cardamom Hills and abuts other sanctuaries in Kerala on its Western border (forming a protected area of over 775 sq miles/200 sq km). It is certainly one of Tamil Nadu's finest wildlife areas with the large core area of 270 sq miles (700 sq km) proposed as a national park. The focal point, with tourist accommodation, is known as Top Slip. Rich, mixed deciduous forest with large rosewood and teak trees leading to temperate grassland at higher altitudes. Its main attractions are the lion-tailed macaque and the Nilgiri langur for which it offers a secure home, and both of which tend to stay in the evergreen sholas. Gaur can be seen near the Srichalippallam river. Elephant, chital, sambar, mouse deer and barking deer are all found here. Riding elephants and forest vehicles are available. Extensive birdlife.

Best time to visit: February-June

Accommodation: 5 rest houses and log huts, food and bedding available.

Contact: Wildlife Warden, 5 Round Rd., Mahalinga Puram, Pollachi, Dist. Coimbatore, Tamil Nadu 642001.

Nearest town & Rail: Pollachi (15.5 miles/25 km)

Air: Coimbatore (41 miles/65 km)

KALAKAD-MUNDANTHURAI TIGER RESERVE

Formed in 1987 by linking the Kalakad and Mundanthurai sanctuaries to create a single area of 309 sq miles (800 sq km) under Project Tiger. The tiger reserve is the southernmost range in India and has an extraordinary range of habitat. Dry teak forest merges into moist mixed deciduous forest and at lower levels tropical evergreen. The Mundanthurai area receives almost 120 inches (300 cm) of rain and there are still pockets of virgin rain forest. Excellent primate viewing with the bonnet macaque and common langur found throughout the sanctuary; the Nilgiri langur at Tarucvattampaarai and the lion-tailed macaque near the top of Valaiyar Hill. Tiger, leopard, sloth bear, sambar, gaur, slender loris, dhole and chital can also be seen. There is a proposal to extend the Kalakad sanctuary to the south.

Best time to visit: January-March

Accommodation: 2 rest houses (one overlooking the Tambaravarani River).

Contact: The Field Director, Kalakad-Mundanthurai Tiger Reserve, 64-B2-Vijayah Complex, TP Miles Road, Rajapalyam, Kamraja Dist., Tamil Nadu 626117.

Nearest town: Nanguneri (9.5 miles/15 km), Ambasamudram (6 miles/10 km)

Rail: Tirunelveli (25 miles/40 km)

Air: Trivandrum (Kerala) (88 miles/140 km)

MUDUMALAI SANCTUARY

Established in 1938 and now expanded to cover 124 sq miles (322 sq km) of mixed and moist-deciduous forests. The sanctuary is bisected by the road from Mysore to Ootacamund and bounded to the north by Bandipur National Park in Karnataka and to the west by the Wynad Sanctuary in Kerala. There is a need to extend the sanctuary to Barbetta in the east which would protect the elephant migration routes into Biligiri Sanctuary in Karnataka and the core area given national park status. There are good game-viewing and other facilities. Vehicles and riding elephants are available at Mudumalai. Excellent birdlife at the base of the Nilgiris at Masinagudi.

Best time to visit: March-June, September-October

Accommodation: Rest houses at Masinagudi, Theppakadu, Abhayaranyam and Kargundi; Jungle Hut, 3 miles (5 km) from Masinagudi has superb accommodation and food in friendly surroundings. Write to Mr and Mrs Joe Mathias, Jungle Hut, Bokkapuram, Masinagudi, Nilgiris, South India 643223 Tel: Masinagudi 40 (via Ooty). Bamboo Banks Farm, 11 miles (18 km) from the sanctuary also has comfortable accommodation and good food. Contact Mrs. S.T. Kothawala, Bamboo Banks, Masinagudi, Nilgiris, 643223. Tel: Masinagudi 22.

Contact: Wildlife Warden, Mahalingam Building, Coonoor Rd., Ootacamund 643001.

Nearest town: Gudalur (10 miles/16 km)

Rail: Ootacamund (40 miiles/64 km)

Air: Coimbatore (103 miles/164 km); Mysore

POINT CALIMERE SANCTUARY

Established in 1967, protecting 6.5 sq miles (17 sq km) of shoreline and hinterland that surround a saline lagoon. Part of the area is tidal swamp. Dolphins are also occasionally seen in the lagoon. There are numerous shore birds and waders, large flocks of both greater and lesser flamingoes. Blackbuck, chital, feral pig and bonnet macaques are some of the land mammals which visitors can see in the sanctuary.

Best time to visit: November-January

Accommodation: forest rest house (14 beds), food available on prior booking.

Contact: DFO, 281/1846 West Main Street, Thanjavur, Tamil Nadu 613009.

Nearest town: Vedaranyam (7 miles/11 km)

Rail: Kodikkarai

Air: Tiruchchirappalli (103 miles/165 km)

VEDANTHANGAL SANCTUARY

Protected for over 200 years, and first legislated protection in 1798 when shooting was prohibited. The sanctuary is extremely small and consists of a grove of trees growing in and around the village tank. There are a number of resident breeding water birds and many migrants. Can be visited in a day from Madras.

Best time to visit: October-February

Accommodation: Rest house with food available.

Contact: Wildlife Warden, 50 IVth Main Road, Gandhi Nagar, Madras 600020.

Nearest town: Maduranthakam (9.5 miles/15 km)

Rail: Maduranthakam

Air: Madras (50 miles/80 km)

There is a small preserve of only 1 sq mile (2.7 sq km) at Guindy in Madras city which also has a zoo and the Madras Snake Park. A Marine National Park in the Gulf of Mannar has been proposed as a biosphere reserve. Other sanctuaries are **Karikilli** (Chengalpattu Dist.); **Nilgiri Tahr Sanctuary**, **Pulicat** (Chengalpattu Dist.); and **Vettangudi** (Ramanathapuram Dist.). For further information contact: The Chief Wildlife Warden, 1710 Trichy Road, Ramanathapuram, Coimbatore 641045.

KERALA

Flanked to the west by the Indian Ocean and along the east by the Western Ghats, Kerala is well endowed with dense vegetation supporting a rich and varied fauna. Forest still covers 24 percent of the state and 5.9 percent is protected (3 national parks and 12 sanctuaries).

Road communication throughout the state is good and the major airports at Trivandrum (the state capital) and Cochin are connected to all major Indian cities. Both Cochin and Trivandrum are major rail termini. The weather throughout the year is pleasant with the monsoon arriving in late May and the wet period continuing up to September.

ERAVIKULAM NATIONAL PARK

Declared a national park in 1978, this area was earlier established as a sanctuary to protect the Nilgiri tahr (the only wild goat south of the Himalaya) of which it has the largest population (approximately 550 in 1988). The park covers 37 sq miles (97 sq km) of beautiful rolling grassy hills and forests in the valleys. It has been proposed that Eravikulam, together with the nearby **Chinnar sanctuary**, Kudakkadu and Pooyankutty forests, be made a national park of 196 sq miles (507 sq km). This together with Annamalai in Tamil Nadu and Peechi Vazhani-Chimony-Parambikulam sanctuaries in Kerala would form a contiguous protected area of 775 sq miles (2,007 sq km). It also has the highest peak in South India: Anamudi (8,853 feet/2,695 metres). The tahr are often seen near the bordering Rajamalai tea estate. Elephant, tiger, leopard, dhole (wild dog), Nilgiri langur, lion-tailed macaque and giant squirrel are found.

Best time to visit: November-April

Accommodation: Rest house at Rajamalai (separate arrangement needed for food)

Contact: DFO Munnar Division PO Devi Kolam, Kerala (Tel: 37).

Nearest town: Munnar (10 miles/16 km)

Rail & Air: Cochin (89 miles/143 km)

IDIKKI SANCTUARY

Established in 1976 with an area of 27 sq miles (70 sq km) above the Idikki arch dam. Sambar and elephant are usually seen and tiger, sloth bear and gaur occasionally.

Best time to visit: November-May

Accommodation: Inspection bungalows at Kulamaur and Vazhathope

Contact: Asst. Field Director, Idikki Sanctuary, Vazhathope, Idikki, Kerala.

Nearest town: Vazhathope (1.25 miles/169 km)

Rail & Air: Cochin (102 miles/164 km)

NEYYAR SANCTUARY

Established in 1958, it has an area of 49 sq miles (128 sq km) with the Neyyar reservoir covering slightly more than 3.5 sq miles (9 sq km). Boats are available to explore the narrow creeks, channels and islands. Most of the sanctuary is wet tropical evergreen forest although in higher areas the grasslands have tahr. Agasthyadoodam at 6,203 feet (189 metres) is the highest point. Rich bird and insect life. Lion-tailed macaque, Nilgiri langur, gaur, sloth bear and wild boar are seen. Occasional tiger sightings.

Best time to visit: Throughout the year

Accommodation: Inspection bungalow at Neyyar; 2 guest houses

Contact: Wildlife Warden, Forest Headquarters, Trivandrum, Kerala 695014 (Tel: 60674).

Nearest town: Kattakada (6 miles/10 km)

Rail & Air: Trivandrum (20 miles/32 km)

PARAMBIKULAM SANCTUARY

First established as a small sanctuary in 1962, the present area of 110 sq miles (285 sq km) was gazetted in 1973. A further extension to 156 sq miles (405 sq km) is proposed to include evergreen forest on the Nelliampathy Plateau up to the Sholayar River to the north and small area connecting the Annamalai Sanctuary in Tamil Nadu. The sanctuary stretches around the Parambikulam, Thunacadavu and Peruvaripallan reservoirs, each with a good population of crocodiles. Most of the area has dense deciduous forests and in one area old teak plantations can be found. Gaur viewing is good with the largest population is in Kerala. Sambar, chital, lion-tailed macaque and a few tigers and leopards are seen. Transport and boats available.

Best time to visit: February-April

Accommodation: Forest rest houses at Thunacadavu, Thelikkal and Elathode

Contact: DFO, TP Division, Thunacadavu Post, Via Pollachi (Tel: Pollachi 33)

Nearest town & Rail: Pollachi (30 miles/48 km)

Air: Coimbatore (62 miles/100 km)

PEECHI VAZHANI SANCTUARY

Established in 1958 over 48 sq miles (125 sq km) to protect the catchment areas of the Peechi and Vazhani dams. The mammal life is poor due to the area's proximity to habitation. Once the proposal to extend the connecting **Chimony Sanctuary** from 35 sq miles (90 sq km) to 50 sq miles (130 sq km) is enacted, the Peechi Vazhani-Chimony-Parambikulam sanctuaries will form a large unit of 254 sq miles (660 sq km) linked to the existing 324 sq mile (840 sq km) Annamalai Sanctuary in Tamil Nadu. Mostly moist deciduous forest with interesting forest birds.

Best time to visit: November-April

Accommodation: Rest house (4 beds) at Peechi

Contact: DFO, Ayyanthol, Trichur, Kerala (Tel: 23268)

Nearest town & Rail: Trichur (9.5 miles /15 km)

Air: Cochin (62 miles/100 km)

PEPPARA SANCTUARY

Established in 1983, this hilly area of mixed forest covering 20 sq miles (53 sq km) of the Western Ghats has fascinating birdlife. Elephant, sambar and lion-tailed macaque are seen and occasionally leopard.

Best time to visit: Throughout the year

Accommodation: Guest house with 4 beds; tourist complex at Ponmude (7.5 miles/11 km) (Tel: Vithura 30).

Contact: DFO, Trivandrum Forest Division, Trivandrum, Kerala 695014 (Tel: 60637).

Nearest town: Vithura (7 miles/10 km)

Rail & Air: Trivandrum (30 miles/48 km)

PERIYAR TIGER RESERVE & NATIONAL PARK

Established in 1934 as the Nellikkampetty Sanctuary, it was enlarged in 1950. It now extends over 299 sq miles (777 sq km) of which 135 sq miles (350 sq km) is National Park. The lake covers 10 sq miles (26 sq km) and is 20 miles (31 km) long. Most of the sanctuary is undulating. The elephant viewing is excellent, although few tuskers have escaped the poacher's gun. In 1983 there were 932 elephants in the sanctuary. Tiger sightings are rare. Woodland birds are abundant. Boats and dugouts are available.

Best time to visit: September-May (open all year)

Accommodation: Forest rest houses at Mankauala, Mullakudi and Thannikudy booked through the forest department.

At the park entrance and HQ at Thekkady tourist accommodation is available. Within the park there are three Kerala Tourism Department lodges (booked through KTDC, PB No 46, Behind Secretariat, Trivandrum 695001; Tel: 64705, 64261): Aranya Nivas Hotel (Tel: Kumily 23); Edapalayam Lake Palace (Tel: Kumily 24); Periyar House (Tel: Kumily 26) - only Indian food and dormitory accommodation.

Contact: The Field Director, Project Tiger – Periyar Tiger Reserve, Balarama Buildings, Erayil Kadavu, Kottayam, Kerala 686001 (Tel: Kottayam 8409).

Nearest town: Kumily (2.5 miles/4 km)

Rail: Kottayam (71 miles/114 km)

Air: Madurai (TN) (90 miles/145 km) or Cochin (118 miles/190 km)

SILENT VALLEY NATIONAL PARK

Established in 1984 after a national campaign to protect the peninsula's last substantial area of primary tropical forest. The 35 sq miles (90 sq km) of park holds a valuable reserve of rare plants and herbs. A neighbouring area of 87 sq miles (225 sq km) ranging from 980ft to 5,000ft (300m to 1554m) has been proposed as the Karimpuzha sanctuary. Elephant, lion-tailed macaque and tiger are among the animals seen.

Best time to visit: September-March

Accommodation: Rest house (4 beds)

Contact: DFO, Palghat, Kerala, 678009 (Tel: Palghat 8156)

Nearest town: Mannarghat (20 miles/32 km)

Rail: Palghat (47 miles/75 km)

Air: Coimbatore (TN) (96 miles/155 km)

THATTEKKAD BIRD SANCTUARY

Established in 1983 as Kerala's first bird sanctuary. Mostly moist deciduous forest on 9œ sq miles (25 sq km) of land between branches of the Periyar river. Many water and forest birds including rarities such as the Ceylon frogmouth and the rose-billed roller.

Also can be found are the lion-tailed macaque and flying squirrel.

Best time to visit: September-March

Accommodation: 1 forest bungalow

Contact: DFO, Malyathur Forest Division, Kodanad Post, via perumbavoor, Kerala.

Nearest town: Kothamangalam (12.5 miles/20 km)

Rail: Alwaye (31 miles/50 km)

Air: Cochin (44 miles/70 km)

WYNAD SANCTUARY

Established in 1973 although a game reserve since the 1920s. Borders Nagarahole and Bandipur in Karnataka and Mudumalai in Tamil Nadu. Area 132 sq miles (344 sq km). Rich birdlife in remarkable and varied forests. Elephant, chital, gaur, sambar and sloth bear are fairly common. Good roads.

Best time to visit: December-April

Accommodation: rest houses at Manantody and Sultan's Battery

Contact: DFO, Wynad, PO Manantody, Kerala (Tel: 33)

Nearest town: Sultan's Battery (0.5 miles/1 km)

Rail: Calicut (68 miles/110 km)

Air: Mysore or Bangalore (155 miles/250 km)

CULTURE PLUS

MUSEUMS & ART GALLERIES

If museum pieces and art are your interests, South India has a wealth of both to offer. There are well kept museums found in most major towns and fairly well maintained art galleries in the bigger cities. Most museums are closed on Mondays while the archaeological site museums are closed on Fridays. The following are recommended museums and art galleries in the South.

TAMIL NADU

Madras

Adyar Library – palm leaf and parchment Asian manuscripts.

Development Centre for Musical Instruments, Mylapore – old and new musical instruments.

Fort Museum, Fort St George – good collection of Exhibits of the East India Company era in Madras. An interesting collection of old prints and much memorabilia of Robert Clive.

Gandhi Illam, Rajaji Hall – Gandhian memorabilia.

Government Museum, Pantheon Road – superb gallery of bronzes, fine collection of weapons and Buddhist artefacts.

Science Museum and Planetarium, Kotturpuram (behind Leather Research Institute) – science explained with simple experiments and film shows on the stars.

Cholamandal Artists' Village, Injambakkam – an artists' co-operative exhibiting modern art and handicrafts.

College of Arts and Crafts, Poonamallee High Road – exhibition of students' work.

Crafts Council of India, Archbishop Mathias Avenue – exhibits handicrafts.

Lalit Kala Akademi, Greams Road – regular exhibitions of modern Indian art.

Kumararajah Muthiah School of Traditional Art and Crafts, Chettinad Palace – Thanjavur paintings and metal work.

Modern Art Gallery, Pantheon Road – Indian art collection over the last 100 years.

National Art Gallery, Pantheon Road – ancient Indian paintings and handicrafts.

Private art galleries include **Sarala** (Nungambakkam High Road), **Kala Yatra** (Spur Tank Road), **Mayur** (Ambassador Pallava), **Grindlay's** (at the Bank, Anna Salai), **The Gallery** and **Sakshi** (both Khadar Nawaz Khan Road) and the gallery in the Chola Sheraton.

Mamallapuram

Archaeological Survey's **Open-Air Museum** and School of Sculpture's Gallery.

Poompuhar

Art Gallery – the story of the epic *Silappathikaram* narrated in bas-relief.

Madurai

Gandhi Museum – Gandhian memorabilia.

Government Museum – exhibits of Tamil glory.

Meenakshi Temple Museum – sculpture and photographs.

Palace Museum – Tirumalai Nayak's contribution to Tamil Nadu.

Padmanabhapuram

Palace Museum – relics of Travancore rulers.

Thanjavur

Saraswathi Mahal – palm leaf and parchment manuscripts, art gallery.

Palace (Rajaraja) **Museum** – bronzes and sculpture.

Temple Museum – carvings and slides.

Tiruchchirappalli

Museum – sculpture and handicrafts.

Kodaikanal

Shennbaganur Museum – bio-museum and orchid nursery.

Udagamandalam (Ooty)

Botanical Gardens – fossils.

Thiruvakkarai

Geological Park – fossils.

Wellington, Coonoor

Regimental Museum (with permission).

PONDICHERRY

Botanical Gardens and Aquarium

Museum – sculpture, bronzes.

French Institute – maps.

KERALA

Trivandrum

Napier Museum – bronzes, Kerala lifestyles recreated.

Science and Technology Museum

Children's Museum

Sri Chitra Art Gallery – Ravi Varma and Roerich originals.

Cochin

Parishaath Tamburan Museum, Ernakulam – Cochin royalty heirlooms, oil paintings.

Hill Palace Museum, Tripunithura – arms and relics of royalty.

Museum of Kerala History and its Makers, Edappally – sound and light narration.

Trichur

Art Museum – ancient jewellery, sculpture and woodwork.

State Museum

Town Hall Chitralayam – gallery of Kerala mural paintings.

Calicut

Pazhassiraja Museum – archaeological finds, ancient murals and bronzes.

Krishna Menon Museum – Krishna Menon memorabilia.

Art Gallery – fine collection of Ravi Varmas.

KARNATAKA

Bangalore

Planetarium – daily shows.

Museum, Kasturba Park – sculpture, paintings.

Visvesvaraya Industrial & Technological Museum, Kasturba Road – science and its applications made easy.

Venkatappa Art Gallery, Kasturba Road – court painter K. Venkatappa's work is the main attraction.

Bijapur

Archaeological Museum – sculpture, Muslim relics.

Mysore

Folklore Museum, Mysore University – replicas.

Museum of Art and Archaeology, Mysore University – paintings, relics.

Rail Museum – relics of the Mysore royal family's railway.

Jaganmohan Palace Art Gallery – Ravi Varma paintings, regal furnishings and table services, sculpture and musical instruments.

Halebid

Archaeological Museum – sculpted stone images.

Hampi

Archaeological Museum – stone sculpture.

Srirangapatnam

Museum – relics of the age of Haider Ali and Tippu Sultan.

ANDHRA PRADESH

Hyderabad

Ajanta Pavilion, Public Gardens – copies of the Ajanta frescoes and other murals.

Archaeological Museum, Public Gardens – sculpture, paintings, arms.

Birla Museum, Prince Asman Ghad Palace – excavations from historical sites.

Birla Planetarium – daily shows.

Khazana Museum, near Golconda – stone sculpture.

Salar Jung Museum – a fabulous one-man collection ranging from the magnificent to the mundane. Tippu Sultan and Mughal relics.

Yelleshwaram Museum, Gun Foundry – art objects.

Nagarjunakonda

Archaeological Museum – island museum housing Buddhist relics and art.

Amravati

Archaeological Museum – Buddhist sculpture and other relics.

Vijayawada

Archaelogical Museum

Koloampuka

Archaeological Museum – relics of Chalukyan and Kakatiyan temple architecture.

Tirupati

Sri Venkateshwara University Museum

There is no music and dance festival in India as popular as the Madras "Season". That Season started 65 years ago, when the Madras Music Academy was founded and began organising annual conferences at which various aspects of classical Carnatic music and Bharata Natyam were the chief topics of discussion. The serious discussions were accompanied by day-long programmes comprising instrumental and vocal concerts and dance recitals, all in the purest classical mould.

That 3-week season from mid-December to early January still continues at the Academy; to be invited to perform at its concerts is the crowning glory of many artists' careers. Fans of classical South Indian music and dance come from all over India every year to attend these concerts. But nowadays these fans get much more than the Academy's offerings alone.

Several other societies which promote the arts have grown in Madras and now they all organise "Seasons" during the same period. Some of these societies are the Tamil Isai Sangam, Brahma Gana Sabha, Narada Gana Sabha, Krishna Gana Sabha and Mylapore Fine Arts Club.

One of the highlights of the Season is the annual dance-dramas of the Kalakshetra Institute, a training institution that nurtures the fine arts in traditional ways. Kalakshetra is where India's finest Bharata Natyam dancers train.

Later in January, there is the finest classical music feast in the South. It is held on the banks of the river Kaveri in a village called Tiruvaiyaru. The Thyagaraja Music Festival commemorates the greatest composer of Carnatic music and two other great composers who were from neighbouring villages. All the great instrumentalists and vocalists of Carnatic music come to this festival to pay homage to the "Trinity" by playing for them and singing in their memory.

Tiruvaiyaru, not far from Thanjavur, goes to sleep after this festival, but the societies and academies of Madras keep busy the rest of the year by offering their members concerts, dance recitals and even theatre and film shows to which the public are also welcome. Left-over tickets are available at the door; watch the newspapers for announcements. You can find some classical music recital or Bharata Natyam performance in Madras every evening right through the year, but during the Season just keeping up with the variety offered can be trying.

Kathakali – that ancient tradition of masked dance-drama – is Kerala's great contribution to the art forms of the South. Daily recitals can be witnessed in Cochin and Trivandrum. If all you want is a peep at this dance form, dropping in at the Durbar Hall Ground in Ernakulam (mainland Cochin) will satisfy your curiosity inexpensively; for full-length shows contact the hotel desks or tourism offices. Cheruthuruthi, 70 miles/110 km northwest of Cochin and near Trichur, is where Kerala's answer to Kalakshetra is to be found. Here, Kathakali, Mohini Attam and other Kerala dance and music forms are taught at the Kerala Kala Mandalam.

What the Music Academy's auditorium is to Madras, the Chowdiah Hall is to Bangalore and the Rabindra Bharathi Hall is to Hyderabad. While in Hyderabad you could scan the newspapers for announcements of ghazal concerts (Hindustani music). Mysore is quite similar to Madras with its sabhas fine arts, so keep a lookout for their varied programmes.

In Madurai, the Satguru Sangeetha Samajam stages regular dance and music recitals in its auditorium.

Most smaller towns have only occasional music recitals and classical dance performances, but the bigger hotels arrange regular items during dinner. If Carnatic music and the South Indian dance forms interest you, look them up in the four capitals.

In the rural areas there are several varieties of folk dances to be found, especially at festival time. Dance forms such as *Karagam* (in which pots are carried on the head), *Kavadi* (in which feathered arches are borne on the shoulders), *Poikkaal Kuthirai* (in which the dancers dress as mock horses) and *Kolattam* (a rhythmic dance in which sticks are clashed) are some of the more popular ones in the South.

Tribal dances in the Arakku Valley in northern Andhra Pradesh, *Balakkatu* at Coorgi weddings in western Karnataka and other ritual dances in Karnataka, like the *Dollu kunitha* (drum dance) and *Pata kunitha* (pole dance), are all enchanting dances. Karnataka and Kerala are also famous for "devil-dancing" by exorcists.

If you are unable to see this wide range of folk dances at temple festivals or other festive celebrations, you might still catch a glimpse of one of the occasional shows put up by the local tourist authority. In Madras, Sittrarangam, a tiny theatre-in-the-round that the local tourist authority has some interest in, occasionally stages folk dance and music performances, coming down from the lofty heights of classical dance-drama and avant garde Tamil theatre.

There is a sound-and-light show in English at the Tirumalai Nayak Palace in Madurai every evening.

THEATRE

Despite a long tradition of street theatre and peregrinating theatre groups, the theatre is not one of the South's cultural strong points today.

This is not to say that there is no theatre in the South. Almost every day, in the capital towns and in a few of the larger cities (watch the press for announcements), there are performances of low comedy and theatrical high tragedy in the local languages, usually by semi-professional groups or keen amateurs.

Kannada theatre in Bangalore and Mysore is, however, of a more serious variety and is the better for it. In Trivandrum and Cochin too there is fine Malayalam theatre. But fine theatre is rather rare in Tamil and Telugu, though the most active theatre is in Tamil Nadu.

English theatre is strictly amateur, local groups occasionally putting on plays for a couple of nights. West End and Broadway comedy or mystery is the favoured fare in the four capitals, but at least once a year, one of the groups in each city will attempt something more serious. The more professional Mumbei (Bombay) theatre groups occasionally visit the capitals to put on one of their productions – and that's likely to be slicker fare.

MOVIES

Madras is now more than the film capital of South India; it is virtually the film capital of India, considering that more than half the films made in India are in the city's well equipped studios. In fact, basing on output volume, the Indian film industry being the world's largest, Madras could well claim to be the film capital of the world.

As befitting Madras's role in the film industry, Tamil Nadu was the first region in the country – if not in the world – to introduce film stars into politics and have a matinee idol as Chief Minister. The film world still plays a major role in Tamil Nadu politics, with most of the political leadership having close ties with it. This example has been followed by Andhra Pradesh, and both Karnataka and Kerala have flirted with it.

The consequence of this is that there are more cinema theatres in the four southern states and Pondicherry than the rest of the country put together. Every town has several theatres, some of them the palaces of the 20th century. In rural areas, there are smaller permanent cinema theatres or thatched roofed sheds, and if those are not available the empty space reserved for the weekly *shandy* (the market fair, yet another cultural experience) is likely to be taken over by a travelling cinema.

The religious films, the mythologicals, the Robin Hood type action films are fewer now, and "social dramas" with songs, dance and fights thrown in to stretch the fare to 2½ hours – and musicals are the films most often made in the South. Cinema-goers used to Hollywood and European fare are unlikely to take to them, but a popular film of this genre is worth taking in, to enjoy the audience's involvement, especially if the hero is a superstar (few heroines achieve the same kind of popularity and fewer warrant fan clubs that provide cheering sections in the theatres).

There has, however, been a move to make more serious films, cinema removed somewhat from mere entertainment. In this field, the Malayalam film – from Kerala – has been particularly successful. In fact, even Malayalam potboilers are generally a class apart from the rest of South Indian film. The Kannada cinema of Karnataka occasionally produces some good serious fare that has received acclaim, but both Tamil and Telugu film-makers have not been successful with attempts that have tried to break away from the beaten track.

Consult hotel staff or tourist offices on what is the most successful and popular local film showing and what is the more serious local cinema being screened, and sample both.

English language films are generally Hollywood imports a few years old or Hong Kong-style *kung fu* films or cheap soft porn.

Theatres vary from the luxurious to the seedy, but most good theatres are air-conditioned. Shows are at fixed times – usually four timings a day are advertised in the newspapers. Tickets are priced in three or four classes, top of the market being balcony seats, priced around Rs. 8 each.

To watch film shooting on location is fun, but visiting the big studios, such as Vijaya Prasad, AVM – all in the Kodambakkam area of Madras – is an experience.

NIGHTLIFE

Prohibition is in force in Tamil Nadu but you wouldn't believe it. Obtaining a permit is no problem and, despite the limits imposed, you will have no major difficulty getting as much as you wish to drink. But the law does put a damper on public drinking. As a result, and except in the better hotels, clubs and a few restaurants, no drinks are served in public. (Foreign visitors can get liquor permits with their visas from Indian embassies and consulates abroad or from Government of India tourist offices in the country).

In the other states, bars – really taverns that specialise in the different variations of local arrack – are allowed to function, but they close early. Bangalore is the only southern city with a pub and bar culture like that in the West. The city's half a dozen pubs are cozy, friendly, and more like social clubs than public drinking places.

Some of the better hotels in the South have tried operating discos, but only Bangalore has succeeded in keeping a few going. Ballroom dancing, disco dancing or any other Western form of dancing is not every South Indian's favourite way to relax and most dances tend to be empty, though on occasion, in the privacy of a club where one is among friends, a dance can prove a success.

Nightclubs are non-existent, but a few of the sleazier restaurants in the southern capitals put on cabaret shows that are really strip shows of the crude variety. Some of these restaurants advertise their programmes in the local newspapers.

Gambling, except for betting at the racecourse, is forbidden. But most private social clubs permit members to gamble at the card table. The law thus makes the operation of casinos impossible. But it doesn't stop illegal gambling activities from flourishing.

SHOPPING

WHAT TO BUY

For centuries traders from East and West have sought the shore of Malabar and Coromandel in search of the riches of South India. In recent times, since Vasco da Gama, adventurers, merchants and conquerors from the West have come in search of its textiles, spices, ivory, jewellery and timber. There's little gold and diamonds in the South today, and elephants and peacocks cannot be exported, but that has not stopped the new South from being a shopper's paradise.

Handwoven textiles in cotton and silk are still the best buys in the South and there is also a wealth of handicrafts – out of wood, stone, metal and papier-mâché. But traditional gold jewellery and modern pearl jewellery, spices, tea and coffee, exotic musical instruments and perfumes are also some of the South's specialties.

It's safest to shop at government emporia and cooperative establishments, the large glossy shops and the bigger department stores. You won't be able to bargain in any of them and if they are government-run, service is likely to be tardy and language could pose barriers, but you can be sure of quality, your travellers' cheques will be accepted and most of these places will ship the goods to you – safely. This is not to say smaller, private establishments are not reliable; there are many that are, and in several of them – especially in the bazaar areas – you can haggle to your heart's content and pick up a bargain. But when shopping in such places for things like textiles, jewellery, handicrafts and spices it is always best to have at the back of your mind the thought "Buyer Beware!"

All four southern states have government-owned or sponsored handicrafts corporations as well as councils. These organisations have shops in their own state capitals and in the capitals of other states, as well as in some of the larger towns in the home state. All of them have a splendid variety of handicrafts made in the state each represents. LEPAKSHI is the Andhra Pradesh shop, KAIRALI is the Kerala shop, KAVERI is the Karnataka shop and POOMPUHAR is the Tamil Nadu shop. In addition to these handicrafts and handloom emporia, there are Khadi Gramodyog Bhavans and Khadi Kraft shops in all the southern state capitals. These outlets sell handicrafts and handlooms manufactured according to the manually-intensive philosophy Gandhi propounded for rural India to supplement its economy.

Besides these solid stand-bys there are a wealth of other shops in the state capitals – Madras and Bangalore particularly being shopping paradises – as well as in several of the larger towns. Some of the better shops and some of the best buys in each state are listed below.

SHOPPING AREAS

ANDHRA PRADESH

Hyderabad is the pearl capital of India, and pearl jewellery and silver filigree work are the best buys in the city. Hyderabad is also famed for its glass and lacquer bangles and the chunky silver jewellery of the Banjara Lambadi tribals. Venkatagiri and Pochampalli handloom saris, Dharmavaram silk fabrics, the famed Kalamkari "painted" cloths, and silken carpets from Warangal and Eluru are the best of the Andhra textile range. Gaily-painted Kondapalli wooden toys, Nirmal paintings (on wood) and inlaid bidriware are the best-known handicrafts of Andhra Pradesh and all of them are available in Hyderabad, no matter in which part of the state they are manufactured.

The pearl market is on Petherghati Road near the Charminar in Hyderabad. Nearby are also all the famed bangle shops. In this area too are numerous silversmiths and bidriware craftsmen.

Other good shopping areas are Abid's and Basheer Bagh in Hyderabad and M G Road in Secunderabad.

Besides the Lepakshi shops, **APCO Handloom House** is the best for saris from Andhra Pradesh, while **Co-optex** offers Tamil Nadu handlooms and Handloom House textiles from all the southern states. There are many privately-owned textile shops, but seek local advice for the best. A good rule of the thumb is that the bigger the shop, the more reliable it is likely to be.

Specialty shops are **Nirmal Industries** in Khairatabad for Nirmalware, and the **Handicrafts Sales Emporium** in Warangal for carpets and brassware.

KERALA

Shopping in Kerala is not quite as exciting as in the other southern states. Nevertheless, the state has its own specialised crafts. Coir products made from the retted fibre of the coconut husk are the state's specialty, but most coir products are meant for household furnishing. More in the handicraft line are rosewood (almost like ebony) carvings. Kerala spices and cashew nuts are other good buys.

Besides the Kairali shops, **SMSM Handicrafts Emporium** in Trivandrum, **Kerala Handloom and Handicrafts Emporium** in Cochin and **Surabhi** in Calicut are the best for handicrafts. These include the colourful Kathakali masks of wood and the jewellery that goes with them. All of them also have a range of handlooms, but among the specialised handloom shops are Handloom House and National Textiles in Cochin. The Coir Board and Spices Board also have show-rooms-cum-sales counters in all the major cities.

Good shopping areas in Kerala are the **Secretariat** and **Chalai Bazaar** areas in Trivandrum, the **M G Road** area in Ernakulam and the **Big Bazaar** and **Kallai Road** areas in Calicut. None of these, however, offer the variety to be found in Madras and Bangalore.

KARNATAKA

A shopper's paradise, Karnataka has much to offer the visitor from abroad. Silks – especially Mysore's own silks – hand-woven from the riches of its sericulture farms – and other handlooms, rosewood, and particularly, sandalwood carvings and household embellishments, brassware, perfumes and incense-sticks are only some of the rich variety that beckons a shopper in Bangalore or Mysore.

Brigade Road, M G Road and Kempe-gowda Road are the best shopping centres in Bangalore. The biggest and best sari and handloom sari showrooms are in Kempe-gowda Road, but Unity Building on J.C. Road and Public Utility Building on M G Road are shopping complexes with several good sari and handloom shops. Government-run establishments include **Handloom House**, the **Mysore Silk** showroom on M G Road and the **Karnataka Silk** industries showroom on Kempegowda Road.

Besides Kaveri – which has a large and splendid shop on M G Road – and the other handicrafts emporia belonging to the governments of neighbouring states, the privately run **Cottage Industries Emporium**, decidedly up-market, is recommended to those seeking the best in handicrafts. Still more expensive handicrafts – most of them with the antique label (make sure the antique you pick is exportable) – are to be found in **Natesan's Antiquarts** on M G Road.

Other shopping areas to explore are **Commercial Street** – for its wealth of inexpensive cotton readymades and its silversmithing – and **Avenue Road** for traditional jewellery, spices and incense-sticks.

Spencer's is the best department store in town and **Nilgiri** the largest supermarket; both are among the best in India.

Mysore offers almost as many shops selling silks and handlooms, but most of them are not as good as the Bangalore shops. For Mysore silks at less expensive prices, visit the **Government Silk Factory** on Manathody Road and the **KSIC Showroom** in the KR Circle shopping area. **Sayaji Rao Road** is another good shopping area.

Mysore is also famous for its sandalwood oil and soaps – another government factory makes these and sells them at discount prices to visitors – and its sandalwood handicrafts. Besides Kaveri, visit the **Chamarajendra Technical Institute** for these handicrafted curios and utilities. Remember, Mysore is the "incense-sticks capital" of India.

Outside the two major cities of Karnataka, there's good shopping in Bijapur in the north, around which a tourist circuit is fast-developing. The M G Road area here has several shops which offer local handlooms and silks of excellent quality, chunky gypsy jewellery made by the wandering Lambadi tribals and clay toys.

PONDICHERRY

This once-French town has its quota of good, locally-made handlooms – the linen especially – but papier-mâché icons are more interesting as curios.

The Aurobindo Ashram – the most famous institution in the town – encourages those who live and meditate there to participate in handicraft activity. The result is the Ashram shop which has much to offer visitors. This includes splendid hand-made paper in a wide range, perfumes, ceramics, clothes and some handicrafts. M G Road is the main shopping centre.

TAMIL NADU

Madras vies with Bangalore to be called the "shopping capital of the South". Besides its fabulous range of Kanchipuram silks and handloom cottons – both in much greater variety than even in Bangalore – and the usual southern range of handicrafts, Madras has much to offer by way of brassware, bronzeware and bell-metal work. Madras jewellery – whether traditional or modern – is exquisite. The city also offers a wide range of South Indian classical dance costumes and musical instruments.

Madras is the only major city in the South that, at the time of writing, does not have an "M G" – Mahatma Gandhi, of course – Road that doubles as Main Street. Here it's Mount Road, now called Anna Salai. Besides the delightful stretch in its lower reaches, other good shopping areas are Rattan Bazaar, in crowded Georgetown, Panagal Park in T'Nagar, Mylapore – around the temple – and Nungambakkam High Road, with its numerous new highrise blocks all boasting shopping complexes.

For silks and handlooms, besides the government-run Co-optex shops – their showroom in Pantheon Road claims to be the biggest silk showroom in India and it is certainly one of the few government establishments in the country where service is excellent – and the **Handloom Houses**, good buys in textiles are to be had at **Nalli's** and **Kumaran's** in Panagal Park and **Radha's** and **Sardha's** in Dhun Building, Mount Road. Radha's near the Mylapore temple is even better than its downtown establishment.

Handicrafts are best bought at the numerous government establishments. The metalwork and rock sculpture is particularly good at **Poompuhar** on Mount Road – but the **Victoria Technical Institute** – a volunteer organisation – runs the biggest and best handicrafts shop in town. The Cottage Industries Exposition in Nungambakkam is good, but expensive; **Cane and Bamboo** on C-in-C Road offers more attractive prices.

Madras is also famed for its leather goods; all the bigger hotels have shops specialising in leather items. But the best buys are in **Periamet** where the leather "kings" of India operate in unprepossessing surroundings.

Musical instruments, southern style, can be bought in the shops around the Mylapore Temple – where the dance costume shops are – at the **South India Music Emporium** on Broadway and in the **Pondy Bazaar**.

Spencer's – a much depleted operation nowadays – is still the best department store in town, though its century-old traditions of excellence and service are in need of revival. But it has to compete with the numerous modern shopping complexes, not only in the city centre but in the residential suburbs as well. **Nilgiris** is in a class by itself as a supermarket, but the government-run **Kamadhenu** tries hard.

Unlike in the other southern state, there's good shopping outside the capital too in Tamil Nadu.

The cooperative shops on M G Road in Kanchipuram are the best places in the South to buy the rich and colourful Kanchipuram silks – priced by weight of silk and gold thread embellishments – and the widest variety of cotton handlooms. Erode is excellent for handloom linen. Madurai too offers excellent textiles.

For handicrafts, shellcraft is excellent in Mamallapuram and Rameswaram, the former also offering rock sculpture and the latter palm work. In Mamallapuram, the shopping centre is by the Shore Temple, in Rameswaram it is Middle Street.

In Madurai, the streets around the temple abound with variety of goods. It's more limited in Trichy and Thanjavur. In the **Big Bazaar** area of Trichy you'll find the best cigars in India (Churchill's Trichinopoly cheroots), pith models and handlooms. In the neighbouring temple town of Srirangam, brassware is the specialty. And in Thanjavur, the famed Tanjore plate – copper of brasswork inlaid with silver and brass on copper – papier-mâché and bell-metal ikons, musical instruments and silk carpets are all good buys. The **Tamil Nadu Handicrafts Development Sales Emporium** on M G Road is the best place to search for these Thanjavur specialties.

Ooty too is good for shopping, especially for tea, spices and eucalyptus oil. **Bazaar Road** and the **Cooperative Super Market** are the best shopping spots here. Look out for the chunky Toda silver jewellery and the colourful ethnic shawls woven by these tribal communities.

SPORTS

Despite its poor record in international competition, most of India enjoys watching sports and large numbers participate in a variety of games. The South is particularly sports-conscious, and all sports draw large crowds.

Some of the biggest crowds in India are found at football matches in soccer-crazy Kerala. Athletics and volleyball are also popular in the same state. Cricket is the major crowd-puller in the other three southern states, especially in Madras and Bangalore, though football, hockey and volleyball are also favoured. Other popular games in the South are tennis, table tennis, basketball, swimming and chess.

Tamil Nadu – and especially Madras – is the tennis and chess capital of India, year after year producing some of the best players in Asia. Visitors can always get a game of tennis at any of the clubs in Madras or in the districts, in fact anywhere in the South, but the standards are likely to be higher in Madras. There's also always a chess game to be picked up in the Tal club in Madras on Kasturiranga Road.

Racing – with the largest stakes in India – is an 8-month activity in Bangalore and a 5-month winter sport in Madras. Hyderabad and Mysore offer racing from about July to October, and Ooty has meets in April and May. There is both totalisator betting as well as an active bookmakers' ring at all centres and the odds are often attractive. Racing draws large crowds, the competition is keen with some very good Indian breeds and jockeys seen in action and the betting is hectic. A day at the races may not be quite as enthralling an experience as a day at a cricket test match (international), but it can be fun – and both are part of the South Indian experience.

There are several golf clubs in the South with some good golf courses. Visitors are granted temporary membership and offered warm welcomes by the local members. Madras has two courses and the other southern capitals one each. There are also courses in Coimbatore and Cochin. But for golf with a difference, the finest courses are in the hill stations of Ooty, Kodaikanal and Wellington (Coonoor). On these links, visitors are likely to think they are playing in that home of golf, Scotland.

These hill stations, as well as the others in South India – Munnar, Ponnudi, Yercaud, Coonoor and Horsley Hills – also offer good fishing. But the trout and carp run best in Ooty and Munnar. Licences are necessary for fishing and the local tourist authority or the clubs will help you get them.

Shooting is now totally banned, so those in search of jungle adventure will be able only to shoot with a camera. All the southern states have some superb wildlife sanctuaries and spending time in them with still or movie cameras can be quite an exciting experience.

Ooty once used to ride to the hounds. But the Hunt is now dormant. However, there is still a Master of the Hunt and attempts are made from time to time to revive the sport. Your holiday might just coincide with one of the more successful revivals. Check with the Ooty Club for more details.

The Ooty Club is also where snooker was born – a fact commemorated on its walls. The club, like every other club in the South, continues the snooker and billiards tradition. But Bangalore is the only city where the public billiards parlour tradition survives.

Those who prefer the safety of a swimming pool to the uncertainty of the coasts of Coromandel and Malabar will find swimming pools in most large hotels as well as several public pools in the major cities. The hotel pools, however, are better maintained.

All the hill stations in the South – those already mentioned, as well as Kemmangudi, Madikeri, Kotagiri, Sultan's Battery and Nandi Hills – offer delightful trek. But there are several other lesser-known hill areas – like the Javadi and Elagiri Hills in Tamil Nadu, the Araku Valley in Andhra Pradesh, the Idukki region of Kerala (Silent Valley) and the Chikmagalur area of Karnataka that offer some interesting and little known treks.

PHOTOGRAPHY

Film is expensive in India and so are accessories such as flash bulbs, batteries, etc. They are, however, available in the larger cities. Reasonably priced and quite good processing facilities are also available. While Fujichrome and Ektachrome are available and E6 processing (of varying quality) is possible in most large towns, Kodachrome film and processing is no longer available in the country.

Protect your camera from heat, dust and humidity throughout your stay. Don't leave cameras on the back shelf of a car which can get extremely hot. Also make sure that exposed film does not go through baggage-scanners; some of the scanners are not photo-proof.

Photography is strictly prohibited at airports, sea ports and defence installations, and the authorities can also be quite sticky at some railway stations, bridges, etc. The Archaeological Department and the various state Museum Departments are also strict about photographing monuments and exhibits; tripods and artificial lights may not be used without prior permission (given only after a written application).

Photography is also prohibited in certain tribal areas (especially in those areas where clothing is scanty) as well as inside many temples, mosques and *gurudwaras*.

At many airports security officers often confiscate batteries or pencil cells from cameras, motor-drives, torches and other electronic items. It is safest to put the cells in your checked baggage.

LANGUAGE

In South India, Tamil is spoken in Tamil Nadu, Telugu in Andhra Pradesh, Kannada in Karnataka and Malayalam in Kerala and the Lakshadweep Islands. Hindi is understood to some extent in most urban areas, especially further north. Tamil is more understood in the four states than the other languages, especially in urban areas.

English is generally understood in South India in hotels, tourist offices, government offices and commercial establishments. This varies from the immaculate language of the Queen to a smattering that is an admixture with the local tongue but nevertheless understandable. You are likely to be more successful with French in Pondicherry and its three enclaves in the South.

Remember, even the best of spoken English in the South can be heavily accented and incomprehensible to foreign users of English. There is also much usage of local idiom in the English of the locals that makes things more difficult for the listener. Nevertheless, English will help most travellers get through South India – and enjoy it too.

FURTHER READING

Reading up on the South is not the easiest going; there's just not enough popular material on this part of the country, though quite a lot of scholarly work.

Nevertheless, here is a list of reading materials that travellers through the South might find useful.

A History of South India by Neelakanta Sastri (Oxford) is the fundamental work on the subject. It is scholarly, but well-written and eminently readable. *Outlines of South History* by M.N Venkata Ramanappa (Vikas) is an alternative, but nowhere in the same class.

In the more localised range are:

Hyderabad: A City in History by Raza Alikhan, a historical guide to the city; *Madras Discovered* by S Muthiah (AEW), another historical guide but one that's more gossipy and full of anecdotes; *Green, Green Kodaikanal* by the Kodai Club; M Panter-Downes' *Ooty Preserved* (1976) and G Woodcock's *Kerala: Portrait of the Malabar Coast* (1967), both rather outdated but delightful to read; Dervla Murphy's *On a Shoestring to Coorg: An Experience of South India*; the very expensive *Bangalore: City Beautiful* by T P Issar, and three other expensive books on Karnataka – by Dom Moraes (*Open Eyes*), the more solid Sharada Prasad (*Karnataka Impressions*) and that delightful story-teller, R K Narayan (*Emerald Route: Rediscovering Karnataka*).

The National Book Trust has published several books on South India, including rather drab but information-packed books about each state. Its *India: The Land and the People* series also includes such titles as *Temples in South India*. All these books are very inexpensively priced.

Also inexpensively priced are the TTK Guide Books on Madras, Mamallapuram, Madurai, Ooty, Bangalore, Mysore and Hyderabad and their environs – a series that is not particularly well-packed but is excellent on "What to See" information. Orient Longman's *Madras* and *Hyderabad* in their Disha Guides series are also inexpensive, spread their information further and offer rather detailed maps.

Among material published abroad are *Into India* by John Keay and *India in Luxury* by Louise Nicholson, the former to be read for pleasure, the latter for pleasure as well as for its perceptiveness and informativeness. There is also the more expensive *Splendours of the Raj* by Philip Davies and *Stones of Empire* by Jan Morries.

Shakuntala Jagannathan's *Hinduism*, Lakshmi Viswanathan's *Bharata Natyam*, C Sivaramamurthi's *South Indian Paintings* and K V Soundara Rajan's *Invitation to Indian Architecture* are easy to read – particularly the first two – but they are for those with specialty interests.

USEFUL ADDRESSES

TOURIST INFORMATION

The Government of India's Tourism Offices are located in the four southern state capitals and they have booths at the airports and the main railway stations as well. The Indian Tourism Development Corporation, which runs facilities in Madras, Madurai, Thanjavur, Tiruchchirappalli, Mamallapuram and Kanchipuram in Tamil Nadu, Kovalam and Trivandrum in Kerala, Bangalore, Mysore and Hassan in Karnataka, Hyderabad in Andhra Pradesh and in Pondicherry, also runs centres at these facilities to help tourists. Besides these information counters, the Department of Tourism of each state run counters in the various state capitals. The travellers' bungalows are managed by their respective Tourism Development Corporations.

Leading travel agents, like Thomas Cook, Travel Corporation of India, SITA, Mercury, Cox & Kings, Diners and PL Worldways, also have officers in the major cities of the South and their counters are always helpful to a foreign tourist, even if he or she is not travelling with them.

Each state's Tourist Development Corporation and the Indian Tourism Development Corporations's local branch in the state capital run a variety of sightseeing tours in luxury coaches taking in the city and places of interest in the state, as well as to important tourist centres in neighbouring states. These offices also provide coaches for groups, a variety of cars, guides and literature.

In every state capital there are several offices of headquarters of the local Chambers of Commerce or of the national Chambers of Commerce to provide businessmen with information. The Rotary, Round Table, Jaycees and Lions also have several busy chapters in each capital and major city and at least one chapter in each "A" class town.

University counselling offices, libraries and newspaper offices are also helpful in providing general information.

EMBASSIES & CONSULATES

There are no High Commissions or embassies in South India; all of them are in Delhi. But Pondicherry retains its French connections by hosting a Consul-General of France. Madras is the only other place in the South with consular services and hosts the following full-time consular offices:

Consulate General of the Federal Republic of Germany
22 Commander-in-Chief Road

Consul General of Japan
60 Spur Tank Road

Deputy High Commission of Malaysia
23 Khadar Nawaz Khan Road

Deputy High Commission of Sri Lanka
9D Nawab Habibullah Road
(off Anderson Road)

Deputy High Commission of the U K
24 Anderson Road

Consulate General of the U S S R
14 San Thome High Road

Consulate General of the U S A
220 Anna Salai

Full-time Trade Representatives' offices:

Czechoslovakia
31-A Haddows Road

Hungary
3/A Sivaganga Road
(off Sterling Road)

Romania
27 Khadar Nawaz Khan Road

Austria
114 Nungambakkam Road

HONORARY CONSULS

Belgium
1/E Spur Tank Road

Denmark
8 Cathedral Road

France
26 Cathedral Road

Greece
9 Harley's Road

Netherlands
738 Anna Salai

Norway
Parry House, 43 Moor Street

Philippines
SPIC Centre, 97 Anna Salai

Spain
8 Nimmon Road

Sweden
6 Cathedral Road

Turkey
202 Linghi Chetty Street

All honorary consuls usually refer matters to their embassies in Delhi. Anyone wanting to deal with any other country not represented in the list above will have to contact its embassy in New Delhi.

The four state capitals also have British Council offices and libraries, US and USSR information service centres, Max Muller Bhavans (Goethe Institutes) and Alliance Francaise centres. All these are only culturally active.

CREDITS

INDEX

U–V

W–Z